The
Wreck
of the *Belle*,
the Ruin
of La Salle

NUMBER EIGHTY-EIGHT

Centennial Series of the Association of Former Students,
Texas A&M University

The
Wreck
of the *Belle,*
the Ruin
of La Salle

Robert S. Weddle

TEXAS A&M UNIVERSITY PRESS • COLLEGE STATION

LIBRARY OF CONGRESS CATALOGING-IN-PUBLICATION DATA

Weddle, Robert S.
    The wreck of the Belle, the ruin of La Salle / Robert S. Weddle. — 1st ed.
        p.   cm. — (Centennial series of the Association of Former Students,
Texas A&M University ; no. 88)
    Includes bibliographical references and index.
    ISBN 1-58544-121-X (alk. paper)
    1. La Salle, Robert Cavelier, sieur de, 1643–1687.   2. La Belle (Frigate)
3. Explorers—North America—Biography.   4. Explorers—France—
Biography.   5. Mississippi River Valley—Discovery and exploration—
French.   6. Mexico, Gulf of—Discovery and exploration—French.
7. Shipwrecks—Texas—Matagorda Bay.   8. Matagorda Bay (Tex.)—
Antiquities.   9. France—Colonies—Texas—History—17th century.
I. Title.   II. Series.
F352.W4   2001
976.4'132—dc21   00-012164

In Loving Memory

NAN AVIS WILLIAMSON WEDDLE

January 27, 1919–August 13, 2000

Until her energies failed,
she read these pages as they were written.
At last I held her dying hand
and told her that the book was finished.

CONTENTS

ILLUSTRATIONS

FOREWORD

During the summer of 1995, archaeologists from the Texas Historical Commission discovered the wreck of *La Belle,* a small ship used by the French explorer Robert Cavelier de La Salle in attempting to colonize the Gulf of Mexico between Florida and Mexico. Realizing the great importance of the vessel and its contents, archaeologists planned and implemented an amazing recovery of the wreck. In 1996 a large steel structure, called a cofferdam, was built around the ship, and seawater was pumped out from the interior. This exposed La Salle's lost ship for the first time in more than three centuries. The relatively dry interior allowed the archaeological team to carefully excavate the ship's cargo over a six-month period and to dismantle and recover the remains of *La Belle.*

An amazing array of artifacts was found, numbering more than one million and representing a "kit" for building a French colony in a seventeenth-century New World. The artifacts are undergoing conservation at Texas A&M University to ensure their preservation and will be studied by teams of specialists to learn as much as possible about the French effort to settle the Texas Coast. The materials will also be displayed in museums around Texas and throughout the nation to tell the story of the French settlement in Texas.

While scholarly interest in France's attempt to colonize Texas has long existed, the discovery of *La Belle* has greatly increased attention among the general public about the Lone Star State's early French history. Extensive media attention to the recovery of *La Belle,* and now to the ongoing excavation by Texas Historical Commission archaeologists at La Salle's colony, Fort St. Louis, have whetted public interest and created a demand—and a responsibility—to provide more.

This volume is the first step in chronicling the La Salle expedition to Texas. Robert Weddle's detailed examination of La Salle describes his deeds and elucidates his motivations leading up to the expedition. Weddle uses firsthand archival documents, many written by La Salle and other members of the expedition, to expand our understanding of La Salle's true intentions in settling the Gulf Coast.

For the broader archaeological project, Weddle's volume provides the historical context for the French attempt to colonize the Texas Gulf Coast. This volume, then, serves as the historical background for others that are to follow on the archaeological excavations of *La Belle* and the Fort St. Louis colony. Future books will provide detailed descriptions of the artifacts left by the French colonists and will interpret these materials within this broad historical framework. Undoubtedly, when the new information is fully published, many new insights will be made into the La Salle expedition to Texas.

James E. Bruseth
Texas Historical Commission
November 13, 2000

ACKNOWLEDGMENTS

Life's greatest lessons often come from the most trying circumstances. Perhaps it is only from being severely encumbered that one appreciates the true worth of kind-hearted souls—friends and strangers—who stand ever poised for the rescue. Such thoughts come from contemplation of the task just finished: an undertaking that would have been impossible without the help of those whose names are recalled in the following paragraphs. To them I offer this work as a tribute, with the hope that it is a worthy one.

In a sense, my involvement in this project began more than twenty years ago when Barto Arnold—then state marine archeologist with the Texas Antiquities Committee—invited me aboard the *Anomaly* for a magnetometer survey of Pass Cavallo: the natural access of Matagorda Bay, where La Salle's ships entered—or died trying. Just back from a research trip to Spain (funded by the National Endowment for the Humanities), I had in hand a copy of Juan Enríquez Barroto's diary detailing the Spanish discovery of the wreck of the *Belle*.

There was, however, much yet to be learned about the *Belle* and the La Salle Texas expedition of which she was such a vital part. Discovery of the lost vessel by Texas Historical Commission (THC) archeologists in 1995 provided the incentive and brought forth the public interest requisite to sustained inquiry. I am indebted to the Texas Historical Commission; to Curtis Tunnell, then THC executive director, now retired; and James E. Bruseth, director of the THC Archeology Division, for providing the enabling stipend for this book; the opportunity to visit the *Belle* site while it was being excavated; and a significant quantity of research material and photographs.

Kathleen Gilmore, whose investigations into the La Salle Texas episode have often run parallel to my own, has been generous in sharing information, especially on Jean L'Archevêque and other expedition members.

Many other persons have provided important material, or assistance in locating books and documents. Foremost among these is Patricia R. Lemée, whose willingness to track down elusive facts and to share both her books and her own research files has been a boon to the project throughout. She and Al McGraw combined their efforts to make possible my visit to the site of La Salle's Texas settlement during THC's excavation, despite seemingly impossible circumstances at the time. Appreciated immensely are Al McGraw's sharing of maps and ideas.

The interlibrary loan of microfilmed translations of the Margry papers from the Burton Historical Collection, Detroit Public Library, was graciously arranged by Janet Whitson. Invaluable material from French archives was provided by John de Bry, Bernard Allaire, and Marcel Lussier, whose visit in my home to exchange material and ideas was a special treat.

Various other persons and agencies in Canada have been generous in their response to my inquiries. Included are individuals at the Toronto *Star* and Griffin Graphics—names not noted—who aided my tracking of the late Harrison John MacLean and the wrecked vessel he supposed to be the *Griffon*. Gilles Durocher of the Manuscript Division, Public Archives of Canada, Ottawa, granted permissions for the use of maps from the Minet journal and assisted in obtaining other permissions from France.

Donald E. Chipman not only located important works on La Salle's exploits but gave generously of his time to read the manuscript and offer valued suggestions. Barbara McCutcheon and staff of the Bonham Public Library obtained books and microfilm on interlibrary loan and made available their microfilm reader and printer. Assistance also was provided by H. G. Dulaney and Doretha Gay of the Sam Rayburn Library in Bonham; Daniel Spurr; Light T. Cummins; Kinga Perzynska (Catholic Archives of Texas); Leroy J. Politsch; Pauline Cusson; Mrs. William S. Doherty; Pierre Lebeau; Carl A. Brasseaux; and especially Roland Pantemuehl, who produced the maps.

Thanks are due Paul Newfield III, Roy Tallon, and Laura Watanabe for sharing with me their family connections to members of La Salle's company. Finally, it should be noted that much of this book has its basis in my previous ones; persons who contributed to them, therefore, have assisted this one also.

This work has provided an opportunity to reassess former conclusions, correct old errors of fact, and expand on tentative assertions. Those whose sharing has been a blessing, however, bear no responsibility for the outcome. To borrow a thought from the late President Harry S. Truman, "The buck stops here."

INTRODUCTION

Wild and untamed, the mighty river that sliced the continent and drained half the present-day continental United States excited the imaginations of adventurous seventeenth-century Europeans. Yet none had sailed upon it, save a band of lost Spaniards, defeated by the wilderness and seeking escape from its savagery; and even they, in their destitution and misery, were sparing in details of their odyssey.

As the century waned, the focus on the mysterious river called Meche Sebe (or some variant thereof) intensified until that historic moment in April, 1682, when the French explorer La Salle reached its mouth and claimed its valley for his king. But the discovery alone was not enough; lacking was the ability to put it into the proper context. The river itself, with tortuous meanders beneath a sunless sky, fading into a jagged maze of swamps and deltaic channels, had proved confusing enough. The technology for exact computation of longitude by celestial observation was a century in the future. A broken astrolabe (for determining latitude) and maps that did not fit the landscape added to the confusion; when La Salle emerged from one of the Mississippi's eastern passes into a salt-water lagoon, he saw it not as the Río del Espíritu Santo of ancient lore but as a different river in a different place.

On such an unproved hypothesis, backed by his monarch, La Salle launched from France a voyage to find his river mouth by sea. In the more than three hundred years since that undertaking, its story has been told in countless ways, from various perspectives leading to diverse conclusions. So much has been said, in fact, that a retelling of the tale scarcely seemed warranted. But all that changed on July 13, 1995, when archeologists of the Texas Historical Commission brought up from the depths of Matagorda Bay a 793-pound bronze cannon engraved with the arms of Louis XIV. Around this ornate piece of weaponry lay the crumbling hull of the French Royal Navy ship *La Belle* and over a million artifacts pertaining to La Salle's effort to plant within the Gulf of Mexico—that traditionally Spanish sea—a French colony that included women and children. The *Belle*, victim of storm-driven disaster, had been the colonists' last hope of seeing France again.

At once new questions arose. The moribund story of La Salle, his two hundred colonists, and their effort to establish the first European settlement on the Gulf coast between Pensacola Bay and the Río Pánuco in Mexico suddenly breathed new life. As history had provided the reasons for the archeological discovery, archeology now helped fill the blanks of history. With the emergence of new data, some old hypotheses and misconceptions have been disproved or brought to question; hence, a reframing of an old picture, for viewing in the light of new discovery.

My opinion of La Salle and his endeavors at the end of this study contrasts sharply with that held at the beginning. He who reads these lines with unjaundiced view quite likely will undergo a similar transition. One of the most striking aspects of La Salle's career is the often deliberate lack of candor that surrounded his endeavors. Nearly everyone who shared in his adventures and gave testimony thereof felt the need at some point to avoid the truth. Even the name of the French settlement on the Texas coast as it has come down to us (Fort-Saint-Louis) is an invention.

The web of deceit began with La Salle himself. As his failures mounted early in his career, so did his need to conceal certain facts from his creditors. The deception mounted rapidly when the Renaudot faction in Paris perceived the explorer's potential usefulness and began to polish his image with spurious accounts of his deeds. Deceitfulness spread among various members of the Gulf of Mexico expedition who, for one reason or another, had personal axes to grind—or guilt or inadequacy or failure to hide.

Accounts published in France followed the pattern. Apart from revisionists who found the original narratives (as of Henri de Tonti and Henri Joutel) too prolix or prosaic for the popular audience, there were writers with a religious thrust who sought to varnish over failure in priestly conduct by La Salle's clerics.

In the end, the Frenchmen who were captured and taken to Mexico related falsely events of La Salle's murder to conceal their own involvement or someone else's. They omitted from their depositions any facts that would betray the extent of France's designs on Spanish territory, for which they might be held culpable. La Salle's brother, Abbé Cavelier, the most impudent liar of them all, not only concealed his brother's death for personal gain but involved others in his deception. Included was the redoubtable Joutel, who, as a Cavelier loyalist, may stand guilty of omitting other details at the behest of La Salle or his mendacious brother.

The maze of falsehood is difficult to penetrate. My attempt to present a cogent narrative, with logical interpretation, has required careful study and thoughtful analysis. Yet it stands to reason that not all the myths have been perceived. La Salle's advocates are not likely to abandon him; it is not possible to undo at a stroke the accumulated mythology of three centuries, even if all of it were known. There have been other attempts, though largely piecemeal, to do so. Whatever may be said of this effort, it seems clear that the circumstances surrounding the wreck of the *Belle* and the tragic conclusion of the episode may now be seen as the natural culmination of La Salle's life and the way he lived it: a true reflection of the man himself.

No attempt is made here to survey the entire body of La Salle literature that has accrued since the end of this history-making episode; there would not be space for such in a single volume. Rather, the purpose has been to penetrate the shroud and present from the most reliable evidence a forthright narrative that will enable readers to draw their own conclusions.

I

THE PRICE OF GLORY

Chapter 1

Navío Quebrado

DERELICT AT SAN BERNARDO

A "broken ship," she lay on the bottom with a sharp list, her prow under water, her deck awash. Her masts, gnawed by shipworms, had fallen with all the rigging. The Spanish observers looking upon this sad relic—April 4, 1687—formed a mental picture of what the ship and her crew had gone through in the final moments. Out of control in a howling north wind, she had struck the bank stern first; her bow anchor, dragging, served only to turn the ship, so that the rudder and sternpost gouged into the bank and kept the poop deck above water.

The vessel—almost new when lost, the onlookers judged—had lain in her wilderness grave for more than a year. From the three fleurs-de-lis painted on her transom, they recognized that she was French: the object of their long quest. With navigational preciseness the Spanish pilot marked on his sketch map the position of the derelict and labeled it *Navío Quebrado* (literally "broken ship," or "shipwreck"). Beyond a doubt this unwelcome intruder in the Gulf of Mexico had come with the explorer they were seeking: Robert Cavelier de La Salle, the first Frenchman to breach this "Spanish Sea" with intentions of establishing a colony.[1]

The ship, in fact, was *La Belle,* oft described as La Salle's personal gift from his king, but actually a *barque longue,* or light frigate, of the Royal French Navy.

There were several puzzling aspects to the Spaniards' discovery. Obviously a six-gun vessel, she had on board only five four-pounder cannon.

An empty gun carriage rested on the peninsular beach bordering the lagoon, where other salvaged items had been taken. There were also emplacements for eight swivel guns, but only two such weapons, lacking chambers. The ship had but a single anchor, which obviously had failed as the ship scudded before the fatal norther; it still lay in twelve-foot water at the end of the cable that had kept the ship's bow pointing northward. Nor did the ship have a launch, a fact that led the observers to conclude that the crew had sailed away in the missing craft; unable to carry the cannon, they had taken only their manual arms. The Spaniards removed the two swivel guns and the five iron cannon to the holds of their own vessels to serve an immediate need for ballast, guessing that other guns had fallen into the water. They hauled in the single anchor and added it to their salvage, with booms, yards (still holding the topsail sheets), and masts that would also serve their own needs in the future.[2]

Had the observers been able to glimpse all that was stored below decks—now submerged in the hull of the derelict vessel—they would have found it stranger still. There lay the wherewithal for founding a French colony, including four bronze cannon bearing the arms of Louis XIV.[3] Not knowing, they completed their reconnaissance of the bay—but failed to enter the passage to the French colony itself—and sailed away from *Navío Quebrado* and the bay they had named San Bernardo.[4] The broken ship, settling quickly into her grave, was not to be seen again (except briefly by the native coastal tribes) for another three hundred years.

The Spanish mariners, veterans of the sea, well understood the hazards that in the flick of an eye could turn a seemingly secure and well-manned vessel into a death trap. Yet, preoccupied with the apparent threat to Spanish territory, they could not concern themselves with the failure and heartbreak that had seized the French vessel or the chaos that afflicted the colony itself. So the Spanish searchers sailed away, content for the moment with signs that the foreign threat had died aborning.

The Spaniards' complacency notwithstanding, the nightmare was far from over for the French men, women, and children who clung to their miserable existence at the feeble settlement a few miles inland. Those who had undertaken an eastward march with their leader still grappled with the aftermath of the grisly murders that rent their ranks. For all, the *Belle* had been their safety net, the colony's only shield against total isolation and despair. But the plan had gone badly awry. The first European effort to establish a Texas beachhead had fallen into chaos. Yet, the enterprise seemingly had been launched on solid footing.

La Belle was designed and built after La Salle returned to France from Canada late in 1683 to propose to the king a new voyage to plant a colony on the lower Mississippi River. As La Salle's plan unfolded, it called for a small ship *en fagot*—in unassembled pieces—to be carried on another vessel, erected on the American shore, and used to navigate the Mississippi. This, apparently, was the plan, even as Honoré Mallet, master carpenter and shipwright of international acclaim, completed the design. Under his supervision, three principal carpenters began in late March, 1684, to shape the pieces of the ship that was to be known as *La Belle:* Mallet's son Pierre, Jean Guichard, and Pierre Masson, all either rated as master carpenters (shipwrights) at the time or so designated later. The four carpenters, joined by four senior naval officers, comprised the *conseil de construction,* a committee mandated by the foreign minister Jean-Baptiste Colbert in 1671. Signatories to the construction papers, they were Jean Gabaret, *"le grand chef d'escadre"* and naval intendant at La Rochelle; François Colbert de Saint-Mars, naval squadron commander; and ship captains Alexandre-Adrien Chambon, Chevalier d'Arbouville, and Barthélemy d'Aralle, Chevalier de Perinnet. This body was charged with certifying the dimensions and architectural characteristics of every warship built in the Royal Navy yards. In late March, the work of shaping the pieces of the *Belle* began with the intention of placing them in bundles to be carried on the warship *Joly* and assembled after the ocean crossing. It soon became apparent, however, that the shipbuilding kit would not fit into the *Joly*'s hold.[5] The bark in bundles had to be assembled and manned.

Construction went on through May and part of June, 1684. On completion, *La Belle* had a certified capacity of 40 to 45 *tonneaux,* or tuns, designating the number of casks or barrels the ship could carry rather than tons displacement. Classified as a *barque longue,* or light frigate, she was launched in June and commissioned in the Royal Navy. She had a forty-five-foot keel, fifty-one-foot overall length, and a fourteen-foot beam. Fully rigged and loaded, she drew seven feet. The *Belle* was armed with six cannon (four-pounders) and carried a crew of twenty-seven, including her thirty-year-old captain, Daniel Moraud, and pilot, Elie (Hélie?) Richaud, ten years younger.[6] Both these officers would fall prematurely to what seemed like an evil spell that descended upon the ship. Thus, command fell to the dissolute second mate, Pierre Tessier, who failed repeatedly in his responsibility. Yet his fate, ultimately, was much less tragic than that of his shipmates—and far better than he deserved.

Upon completion, the *Belle* was turned over to La Salle after the king had commissioned him "to command in our name all the Frenchmen and Indians whom he will employ . . . in the newly subjugated territories from Fort-Saint-Louis on the Illinois River to Nouvelle-Biscaye."[7] Thus, he embarked on a multipronged enterprise, a colonizing venture with religious, commercial, and military objectives. Three other ships were fitted out for the voyage: the leased cargo vessels, *l'Aimable* (Captain Claude Aigron), 180 tuns, armed with ten guns and manned by a crew of twenty-two, and *Saint-François,* an unarmed ketch with a nine-man crew (Paul Giraud, or Girault, captain); and *Le Joly* (Captain Taneguy Le Gallois de Beaujeu), a thirty-four-gun warship of the Royal Navy, rated at 412 tuns burden with draft of fourteen feet and manned by a crew of seventy.[8] After a false start from La Rochelle on July 24, the four ships—forced back by a broken bowsprit on *Le Joly*—made good their departure from Rochefort on August 1, 1684. Of the four, only the *Belle* was to remain with the colony. *Le Joly,* having completed her mission of conducting La Salle and his colonists to their destination, would return to France for further assignment. The cargo ship *l'Aimable,* leased by La Salle, was to return to the islands, lade other freight for her owners' benefit, and return to France. The *Saint-François* was leased from François Duprat to carry provisions that could not be taken by the other ships. She would transfer her cargo at Saint-Domingue (Haiti) and return also. At least that was the plan.

Casualties began before the little fleet reached Saint-Domingue. During the fifty-eight-day voyage, illness spread throughout the ships; a soldier and a sailor (a sixty-five-year-old cannoneer on *La Belle*) died. A child was born on *l'Aimable,* with La Salle standing as godfather. The infant son of Lucien and Isabelle Talon, was named accordingly: Robert.[9]

In *Le Joly*'s rush to reach Petit Goâve on the Gulf of Gonâve, she left the other ships behind. *Saint-François,* after leaving Port-de-Paix on the north Haitian coast, sprang a leak and came to anchor. Two Spanish galleys sailed out from shore, attached a cable to the ketch, and towed her away.[10]

On November 25, after most of the ailing had recovered and intelligence had been gathered on the Gulf of Mexico from pilots of the local pirate fleet, La Salle's three remaining ships resumed their voyage. Almost before they were out of the Gulf of Gonâve three days later, *La Belle* had her first brush with disaster. Heavy swells driven by a stiff north wind sweeping through the Windward Passage dumped tons of water down her hatchways. As the storm arose, she lost steerage, took in her mainsail, and ran before the wind.[11]

Still greater trials lay ahead. Off Cuba's Cape San Antonio in mid-

December, the ships were beset by a nighttime squall and sudden wind shift that drove them upon their anchors. The *Belle* tangled rigging with the *Aimable,* splintering masts and yards. She lost a hundred fathoms of cable and one of her anchors.[12] It was a forewarning of the ship's ultimate disaster; lack of anchors would become crucial to the ship and the colony.

Thence, the little fleet set course north by northwest across the Gulf of Mexico, the "Spanish Sea," which the king of Spain considered his private domain. Among the pilots there was little idea of where that path would lead. La Salle had concluded that his river lay "at the far end of the bow in the Gulf"—the sector known today as the Texas coastal bend. Thus, they followed a track approximating 330° until they came within soundings on the evening of December 27.[13]

Approaching the shallow Louisiana shelf, only *La Belle* could get within view of the shore. From her masthead, land was sighted on January 1, 1685. The ships, at anchor, sent boats shoreward, but they found their way blocked by a sand barrier four feet high, shielding an impenetrable rush-filled marsh three hundred yards wide.[14] A few days later, *Le Joly* became separated from the other two ships. They were not reunited until January 20.

La Salle, aboard the *Aimable,* sailed westward, the *Belle* following. On Twelfth Day, January 6, he ordered the *Belle's* captain to hold close to shore to observe its features. The ship approached "a kind of bay," which appeared rather deep, with an island between its headlands. With the *Belle* becalmed next day, a launch crew went to explore the shoals that shielded the pass but found them obscured by fog. La Salle believed at the time that this was the mythical Espíritu Santo Bay; he was to reflect upon it later, regretting that he had not stopped here. In retrospect, he was certain that this was a link to his river.[15] He was wrong, of course; the body of water, which got its lasting name from a Spaniard a century later, was Galveston Bay.

One of the surviving pages of *La Belle's* log gives the latitude observed by Captain Moraud at noon on January 18: 27°30' north, indicating a point midway between Corpus Christi and Baffin Bays. The king's engineer, Jean-Baptiste Minet, and La Salle noted the same latitude a day later, when *Le Joly* rejoined *l'Aimable* and *La Belle* while the latter two ships, seeking fresh water, stood near "a river mouth"—evidently Aransas Pass.[16]

The pilot of the *Belle,* Elie Richaud, had believed all along that the voyage had progressed beyond La Salle's intended destination, but La Salle, as well as the other navigators, disagreed. Rather than take issue, Richaud kept a secret record until the southward-trending coast and diminishing latitude brought La Salle to the same view. La Salle, still believing he was near his river, at last decided to put the soldiers ashore to look for it, marching northeastward along the coast. The *Belle* was to stay close by in the offing, ready to give assistance if needed, but trouble with her ground tackle (anchors and related gear) prevented her from doing so. Minet, aboard the *Joly,* wrote on February 6: "We took an anchor to the *Belle,* which had lost her own. She had spent the night with a small anchor of 150 livres, not having any other. . . . Bad weather."[17] Anchor trouble stalked the *Belle.*

The ships found the soldiers stalled without a boat at Pass Cavallo, the Matagorda Bay entrance. Richaud sounded the channel, and La Salle decided that this was the branch of the Mississippi that he sought. Yet, with Richaud's soundings disputed, the *Belle* was the only ship that could enter. On February 18, 1685, she crossed the bar and dropped anchor near the head of the channel. While *Le Joly* rode at anchor offshore, the chartered *flûte* (storeship) *Aimable,* which carried most of the colony's supplies and provisions, sought to follow but drifted outside the channel markers and ran aground. La Salle had no choice but to salvage what he could from the wrecked ship and send the rest of his people ashore on Matagorda Island. About two hundred colonists and soldiers formed the bivouac of tents and makeshift shelters.[18] Some three weeks later, *Joly* set sail for France. Only the *Belle* remained. There would be no other vessel to take the colonists back to France, or to bring them sustenance from the far-off Caribbean islands.

In the months that followed, La Salle moved the colony to a more secure spot on Garcitas Creek, "two leagues" from the head of Lavaca Bay (an offshoot of Matagorda Bay). The *Belle,* remaining in Matagorda Bay, was able to sail only as far as the shallow passage between Indian and Sand Points, the Lavaca Bay entrance. In several trips, she transported effects of the colony to a supply depot on the west shore, just south of Indian Point. Thence, the goods were sent on by native canoes (dugouts) to the new settlement, which could be called a fort only by persons gifted of imagination. This "post erected in the Baye-Saint-Louis," as La Salle referred to it, was situated on the right bank, five miles above the mouth of Garcitas Creek—called Rivière aux Boeufs (River of Beeves) for the buffalo, or bison, that ranged its banks.[19]

The buffalo herds notwithstanding, food was scarce. The people, subjected to heavy work on short rations, scoured the fields for native fruits and herbs to sustain themselves. Many died from eating noxious plants. Especially heavy was the toll among the *Belle*'s sailors. While ferrying goods from the Grand Camp at the mouth of the bay to the supply depot at Indian Point—away from La Salle's watchful eye—they had more opportunity to partake of the poisonous fruits. As a result, Captain Moraud and several of his crewmen died. Others became ill, as La Salle says, "until there were scarcely two of them fit for duty." Shipworms gnawed into the vessel's hull, making it necessary to keep the bilge pumps running continually.[20]

With Moraud dead, the pilot Elie Richaud took command of the *Belle*. In early autumn La Salle made several short explorations, then decided to take the *Belle* and search out the bay shore for the supposed link to the Mississippi. Leaving Henri Joutel in charge of the post, La Salle himself would take fifty soldiers in small boats and row along the shoreline, while the ship, with enough substitute crewmen to make up the complement of twenty-seven, remained close by, sounding her way in the offing.

Toward the end of October La Salle had the ship reloaded with much of the goods that had been brought up on the vessel from Grand Camp: tools, utensils, arms, and provisions. "It was thought," he later explained, "that we could go up the Mississippi and carry out the rest of the enterprise."[21] Once the expected passage was found, he would choose a place on the main river channel to settle his colony permanently, unload the ship, and send her back to the post on the Baye-Saint-Louis for the rest of the goods and people. Thus, he would have his warm-water port on the Gulf of Mexico, connected by the Mississippi itself to his Fort-Saint-Louis on the Illinois River—as well as a base close to Mexico. But the geography was not as he supposed it to be, and his plans quickly went awry.

It was during this reloading operation (begun in September, as Joutel relates) that *La Belle* came close to meeting her end prematurely. Joutel and five companions in a native dugout canoe were taking La Salle's personal effects to the ship, which remained in the anchorage near the Lavaca Bay mouth. Descending the west shore, they sought a shortcut across open water—"an *anse* about a league and a half wide"—between Noble and Gallinipper Points. There they were caught by a strong northeasterly wind, driving giant swells that threatened to capsize their cumbersome craft and forced them into Chocolate Bay. Against a precipitous shore in a small cove, open on the weather side, they spent a miserable night in their boat, which was half filled with water, fearful for their own safety as well as that of the *Belle*. Next morning, they found themselves marooned by the ebb tide. The water had retreated the distance of a gunshot, leaving them fenced in by an exposed bed of oyster shell that cut their bare feet like razors.

During the day, the wind boxed the compass. It rained almost all night, but, when the breeze blew again off the Gulf, the tide came in and filled the cove. The canoemen, after a forty-hour delay, hastened on down the bay to the *Belle*'s customary anchorage. The ship was nowhere in sight. Fearful that she was lost, the men pressed on several leagues; still no ship. They turned about to return to La Salle's camp and give him the news.

As Joutel tells it, in confusing terms, La Salle then reconnoitered the left side of the bay while Joutel himself searched the right. La Salle, apparently, crossed to Sand Point and marched northeastward. Joutel, still on the west side of the bay, that evening reached the headland now known as Indian Point and made camp. The following day he arrived at the depot where the *Belle* had discharged the supplies brought from Grand Camp. At last they spied the ship, at anchor farther down the coast than her usual berth. With waves running high, the canoemen, unobserved, made camp for the night opposite the ship. Next morning, as they still hesitated to try to reach the vessel in their own unstable craft, a signal flag was hoisted on the *Belle* and a cannon fired. Three of the canoemen swam out to the ship and there found sieur de Moranget, who came ashore and described to Joutel the ship's narrow escape from the storm.

This young army lieutenant, Colin Crevel de Moranget—La Salle's nephew—revealed that the ship's officers had failed to follow La Salle's instructions, to let down a cannon with the single anchor that had been supplied by *Le Joly* after the *Belle* had lost all her own. When the storm arose, the ship dragged her anchor. Barely in time to avert a shipwreck, the cannon was put over the side and, after a time, the extra weight caught hold and held fast. The only casualties were the ship's launch, which was swept away in the storm, and the cannon, apparently not retrieved—the missing sixth gun noted by the Spanish search party. The *Belle*'s crew, without a boat to go ashore, was engaged in making a raft from yards and planks when the canoemen appeared. To remedy their plight, Joutel left them one of his canoes when he returned to the settlement.[22]

This close call might have sounded a warning for the men on the *Belle*: the single anchor would not hold in a high wind. Indeed, it should have been evident to the crew *and* to La Salle that in this bay, with its sudden squalls, the ship was in constant peril. Several times previously, La Salle had suffered incalculable loss of ships and cargo after he had abandoned them at a critical moment. The *Griffon*, lost on the Great Lakes in 1679, is the most notable example.[23] In that instance, the vessel carried the means of his economic survival. Now, the stakes were even higher. Yet, heedless, he had put on board the *Belle* almost all the colony's supply of dried meat (4,000 livres); 800 livres of lard, 800 livres of bacon, 3 livres of butter, 6 casks of wine, 4 of brandy, 3 of vinegar, with the salt, oil, and more than 10,000 pounds of bread or flour; all the crates of clothing, papers, utensils, linen, and plates and dishes belonging to La Salle, the six clerics, officers, and other privileged persons; also more than 2,000 livres of gold, all the trade goods, as well as arms, tools, and cannon, plus 40 hundredweight of powder and nearly 50 of lead, detonators, the forge, and "everything needed for his purpose," even to a litter of eight six-week-old pigs.[24]

To transport such items, Joutel made several additional journeys to the ship before La Salle left him in charge of the post and took his leave. With a cannon salute, La Salle and fifty men started for the ship the last day of October, 1685. His plan for exploring the bay shore in tandem with the *Belle*, however, never got off the ground.

Upon reaching the ship on November 2, he learned that hostile Indians were prowling the vicinity. Making camp near the bay, he took twenty of his fifty men to attack the natives' encampment, which consisted of four huts. While La Salle wrote of having routed the natives, Joutel reveals that the episode "amounted to no more than the capture of a woman and a young girl and another woman who was killed. . . ." The captured woman, having been wounded, tore away the dressing that La Salle had applied. Refusing to eat, she soon died.[25]

In the Indian encampment La Salle found a curious array of artifacts: "large pieces of Spanish point-lace, like that which the buccaneers brought from Veracruz, some gold buttons, a coconut chaplet with small tassels of gold embroidery, some medals of Spain's patron Saint James, a shoe, two Spanish swords, and some blue cloth bordered with lace."[26] The effect of this evidence on La Salle's future course remains in doubt. Was his next journey an attempt to reconnoiter the Spanish position?

Moranget, meanwhile, found the *Belle*'s shallop, lost in the recent storm, and took it from seven or eight Indians. But it was to be lost again, under even worse circumstances.

La Salle, returning to his camp near the ship, found a new disaster. Some of his men in the camp had choked to death after eating prickly pear tunas without removing the tiny thorns. He moved the camp "farther inland," away from this temptation, and sent orders to the pilot Richaud, whom he had placed in charge of the *Belle* upon Moraud's death. The new captain was to begin sounding for a channel by which the ship might enter Lavaca Bay and anchor nearer the settlement. La Salle assigned the mate Tessier to head a five-man boat crew to sound ahead of the ship, returning to the *Belle* each night for safety. Richaud—perhaps because of Tessier's record of shoddy performance—chose to conduct the sounding himself. Having advanced a considerable distance ahead of the vessel by nightfall, he and his men elected to spend the night on shore. La Salle, meanwhile, continued his own exploration around the bay and was out of touch with the ship for more than a month. When he came to look for the vessel at the end of December, he found the naked bodies of Richaud and his five companions, murdered in their sleep by Indians, their remains scattered by wolves and vultures around the smashed boat.[27]

After last rites, La Salle proceeded by boat along "a headland in the middle of the bay [Sand Point]" but found no fresh water on the sandy peninsula. He therefore determined on January 3, 1686, to explore by land, lest drinking salt water and consumption of noxious fruits cause the loss of more men. Again, he made arrangements for leaving the ship.[28]

La Salle's actions defy understanding. He gave command of the vessel to Tessier, the mate assigned by the naval commissary at Rochefort. The young nobleman, Marquis de La Sablonnière, an infantry lieutenant and a noted profligate whose debauchery at Saint-Domingue had left him with "a certain ailment that prevented him from walking," was to be the boatswain; sieur de Planterose, one of the volunteers, the commissary. The slain men, all skilled seamen, were replaced by rank-and-file members of La Salle's company. Among them was Abbé Chefdeville, a Sulpician priest who, like La Salle, Joutel, and Planterose, was from Rouen; he was deemed not hardy enough to march with La Salle. The ship also received six of La Salle's company with orders that they be put in irons—Guichard, La Jeunesse, (Pierre) Meunier, Turpin, Fontaine, and Ruiné—"for their thefts, desertions or plotting." Indeed, said La Salle, they merited a more severe punishment.[29] They were to get it, in an unexpected manner. Also put on board was the little Indian girl captured during the recent attack on the native village. She was baptized by Abbé Chefdeville, with Planterose standing as godfather: "the only one," says Joutel, "who enjoyed the blessings of Christianity through the sacrament of baptism." Some of the soldiers who had taken part in the Indian raid returned to the settlement.[30]

La Salle then had eleven casks of water boarded on *La Belle,* hoping to return before it was gone. Should the supply become exhausted, the ship's crew was to exercise extreme caution against surprise Indian attack when they went ashore to replenish it, keeping an armed guard posted.

There are different versions of the orders that La Salle gave Tessier before his departure. La Salle himself says the vessel was to proceed as far as possible inside the bay—apparently meaning Lavaca Bay, toward the settlement—and anchor to await the leader's return. Joutel, on the other hand, says the ship was to remain where she was until word came from La Salle. (The precise location when La Salle departed is not clear, but it evidently was on the upper side of Matagorda Bay northeast of Sand Point.) La Salle and twenty men stowed much of their gear on the ship and filled their packs with hatchets, knives, awls, glass beads, and vermilion for trading with the natives. They then boarded two native canoes and went, as Joutel says, "as far as they could go by water." They sank the craft near the edge of the bay, to be retrieved when they returned.[31]

It was now early January, probably the third or fourth. La Salle expected to be gone only ten days. By the time he returned to the anchorage, it was March 15. In the interim the *Belle* had suffered multiple disasters. La Salle's eight men—apparently all that survived of the twenty who had followed him—also suffered severely on the return trek. Their clothes in tatters, their ammunition exhausted, they had looked forward to relief upon reaching the ship, where they had left much of their equipment and provisions. The ship, however, was not to be found.

La Salle was beside himself, the more so when he learned that Pierre Duhaut, who had left the march eighteen days after their departure, also had failed to find the vessel.[32] He now realized the folly of having placed so much of the colony's necessities at risk, knowing, as he did, of the bay's occasional turbulence and the replacement crew's inadequacies as seamen. Without the ship, the colony was stranded on the wilderness shore, completely cut off from the outside world. La Salle's own grief was multiplied by the uncertainty of it all. Still haunted by the memory of the *Griffon* on the Great Lakes, he wondered: had the *Belle*'s crewmen, in an act of mutiny, conspired to make off with her? Or had they been caught in a squall and failed to make secure the vessel? If the former, surely Abbé Chefdeville and sieur de Planterose, his fellow townsmen whose loyalty was beyond question, would have dissuaded them. If the latter, why had they not anchored with a cannon, as had been done previously when the single anchor failed? If a norther had forced them to leave the bay, surely the prevailing southeast wind eventually would have enabled them to come in again—a far better alternative than risking a long voyage to the Caribbean islands without anchors or skilled seamen, at the same time "leaving to almost certain death those whose property and food they were carrying off." Such were the thoughts racing through his mind as he viewed the empty anchorage.[33] The answers to his questions were slow in coming, as was the tragic story of *La Belle*'s untimely end.

After a hasty search of the immediate area, La Salle left a number of his men to continue the quest while he returned to the settlement. On arriving March 24, as he tells it, he immediately sent them relief and additional men and later went back to search himself. Finding the others fifteen leagues away, he conducted them on a "careful examination of the coast," but found no trace of the *Belle*.[34] Joutel, asking for ten men and a boat, proposed going to "the other side of the bay" to try to learn what had happened to the *Belle,* but La Salle vetoed the idea because "we were at war with the Indians, who already had killed several of his men, and we should not run the risk of the same thing happening again."[35]

So convinced was the leader that the vessel had been spirited away in a conspiracy that he believed such a search would be futile. Indeed, his plight seemed hopeless. Everything he owned, says Joutel, was on the barque: goods, clothing, and papers. La Salle—evidently having reflected upon his folly during his prolonged absence—had planned to unload the vessel when he returned, overhaul it, and send it to the Caribbean islands with Moranget and Joutel. On the way, they were to follow the coast as far as the Baye-du-Saint-Esprit, seeking the mouth of the Mississippi. Such plans had been rendered unattainable. Shut off from both France and its island colonies, and lacking men capable of ascending the Mississippi in boats, he determined to proceed overland to New France, the nearest outpost of which was his Fort-Saint-Louis on the Illinois River. Ten days after writing this report (dated April 18, 1686), he left Joutel in charge of the post and set out with nineteen other men. He was to be robbed of his objective, it is said, by illness and desertion—reasons that have been disputed. He returned to the settlement in early autumn.

Scarcely three days after his departure on this journey, if Joutel's dates are correct, the fate of the *Belle* became known. About the first of May the fort was hailed from the creek. To Joutel, it seemed as though he were hearing a voice from the dead; as the boat came closer, he recognized six persons who had been aboard the *Belle:* Abbé Chefdeville, Sablonnière, Tessier, the servant girl from Saint-Jean-d'Angély, a "young lad"—doubtless Pierre Meunier—and an unidentified soldier. Joutel learned that the barque was stranded near the mouth of the bay and the rest of her company were dead.

Chefdeville recounted the series of tragic happenings since La Salle's departure. Several days afterward, Planterose had taken six men in the boat to seek fresh water on shore. After sunset, the boat was seen returning, fighting its way against a stiffening wind. As darkness fell, Chefdeville asked Tessier to hang a lantern at the masthead as a beacon. The mate, addled by drink, chose instead to rely on an ordinary candle that soon burned out. The boat never came. The next day was spent in anxious waiting. As darkness came again, the conclusion seemed inescapable: the boat had either been overcome by waves or cast back upon the shore, its crew perhaps slain by Indians. For those on board, says Joutel, "This loss plainly forecast their own, seeing that they had scarcely any water and had lost the five best men in the ship."[36]

For several days the ship stayed at the same place, feeling the lack of water more severely each day. The men slaughtered the eight pigs, which were to have been foundation stock at the colony's new location; otherwise, the animals would have died of thirst. Dehydration took its toll of the crew; several died. Tessier, the commander and the only naval officer on board, showed no inclination to act. He took possession of a large store of Spanish wine, which Abbé Cavelier had put aside for the mass, and each day drank his fill; never a day passed that he was not drunk. In danger of perishing, the crew at last weighed anchor, intending to enter Lavaca Bay and sail toward the settlement. It was a rash decision; there was not a skilled seaman among them, and all were weakened by thirst. When the north wind arose, they could not manage the rigging, and the vessel was carried across the bay. Approaching the strip of sand now known as Matagorda Peninsula, the enfeebled men managed to put out their single anchor, but it failed to hold. There was no thought of putting a cannon over, for the few men were too weak for the task. Dragging the bow anchor, *La Belle* plowed stern first into the bank a hundred yards off the peninsula. No notice is taken in Chefdeville's account, which comes to us through Joutel, of the man trapped in the forward hold, perhaps already dead of dehydration beforehand, possibly drowned when the ship's seams opened and water gushed in. He was to lie in his tomb, upon a coil of anchor rope, for 310 years before archeologists recovered his remains and he at last was repatriated to his native France. His name is supposed to be the one stamped on the pewter porringer that lay beside him: C. Barange. His leather shoes and remnants of his clothing suggest that he was a sailor of the French Royal Navy.

The wind moderated in the evening. The ship lay in relative calm as those on board pondered their plight. Without a boat, there was no way to maneuver the anchor to haul the ship off the bank. After daylight, Tessier fashioned a crude raft, and two men went to look for water on shore; but the timbers were poorly lashed, the wind came up again, and the raft fell apart. Both men drowned. Seemingly, misfortune of every kind, Joutel lamented, had been sent to plague the undertaking, the result of imprudence and bad management. Thus was demonstrated, he opined, "that the worst of mankind's vices is drunkenness."[37] In his view, the loss of the crewmen who had died previously was to be laid squarely at Tessier's feet.

With a new raft, the survivors gained the peninsula and found a source of fresh water. Setting up camp on the beach, they shuttled back and forth daily with the raft, taking from the ship the goods that remained accessible. Much, however—like the body of their shipmate in the hold—lay submerged and out of reach. Yet the salvage operation went on until a strong wind blew across the bay, stirring swells that drove the *Belle* deep into the sandbank. The entire deck, excepting only the stern castle, was awash. Comfortable in their camp on the beach as long as the food held out, the castaways shot ducks, caught fish, and gathered oysters, while avoiding the grim reality: eventually, they must find a way to escape their narrow prison. Tessier, never having contributed a great measure of leadership, manifested no change of spots; he had appropriated a cask of brandy, and, as long as it lasted, he was in no hurry to take up the challenge.

Actually, the means of escape were nowhere at hand. Even with a favorable wind, it seemed doubtful that the makeshift raft would hold together for a bay crossing. Seeking a land route, Chefdeville and some of the other castaways walked west along the peninsula to Pass Cavallo, more than six miles. From the point they could see the native camp on the opposite side, a reminder of the nighttime attack that had cost the lives of two men soon after the expedition's first landing.

An eastward trek along the neck of land posed a similar threat, aside from taking them far out of the way. To reach the settlement by that route, the castaways would have had to make a wide circuit of the entire bay complex, the shore of which was well populated with hostile natives. Trudging through marshy country on a journey that might have required months, they would have faced hazards greater than those of the stormy bay.

Chefdeville was keenly sensitive to their plight on the exposed beach: the ship lay in view of any passing vessel and within easy reach of the Indian village beyond Pass Cavallo. Considering the castaways' meager defenses, the abbé took care to gather and dry La Salle's papers, clothing, and other effects, and prayed for rescue. As if in answer, a canoe that had broken loose across the bay the previous fall turned up at the water's edge. The castaways, after three months with the wrecked vessel, departed for the settlement, unavoidably leaving the ship as a signpost for Spanish searchers.

After relating *La Belle*'s sad story to Joutel, Abbé Chefdeville asked the

Récollet friars to join him in singing a Sunday high mass, climaxed with the *Te Deum,* in thanks for their deliverance. (Wine for the Eucharist was rationed to Sundays only, because of the quantity lost with the *Belle.*) Wafers were made with a mold that Chefdeville had salvaged from the ship and the little remaining flour.[38]

The castaways, while bringing what they could carry in their heaven-sent boat, had left many things buried in the sand at their camp near the wrecked vessel. Lieutenant Barbier, with fifteen men and provisions for eight days, went in a boat to recover the cache, guided by Tessier and the unidentified soldier from the wreck. They found that natives had plundered the cache, taking some cloth, iron tools, and a swivel gun. Yet they were able to load their boat with sails and cordage, several fathoms of new sail cloth, and an almost empty wine cask. The five deck guns and four bronze cannon in the hold could not be salvaged with the means at hand. Back at the settlement, the cloth and sails were spread to dry in the sun; they were to fill a vital need later. When early the following year La Salle and seventeen men set out across Texas, hoping to reach his post on the Illinois River, they traded their way among countless Indian tribes with the merchandise salvaged from the ship: hatchets, hawk bells, vermilion, and glass beads. Their clothing having become threadbare from wilderness wear, they fashioned garments from *La Belle*'s sails.[39]

Thus, the *Belle*'s bits and pieces were scattered: to the doomed site of the settlement on Garcitas Creek; the Karankawa camps along the bay shore and on the coastal islands; to villages of countless tribes extending across Texas and Arkansas to the Mississippi; and across the Gulf of Mexico to the island fortress that guarded New Spain's principal port, San Juan de Ulúa. Among the traveling artifacts was one that might have revealed more than can ever be known of the *Belle*'s life and death: her logbook. It seems safe to assume that the book was carried back to the settlement by either Abbé Chefdeville or the pilot Tessier. Thence, La Salle may have taken it, among other important papers, on his final march toward New France. Following his death it possibly fell into the hands of his assassins. Or, it may have remained at the post on the Baye-Saint-Louis until the colony's fatal hour in the early days of 1689. In either event, it was torn apart by Indians, to whom the written word was only a curiosity, its pages scattered to the winds. At last, a four-page signature was carried by the Jumano Indian Juan Sabeata to faraway Chihuahua, near the mines of Santa Bárbara that La Salle had aspired to claim—had he, in his wildest of dreams, been able to march across northern Mexico. From the Chihuahua capital, El

FIGURE I

Resurrection. Remains of the French Royal Navy vessel La Belle, *exposed in her 300-year-old grave. Texas Historical Commission photo*

Parral, the four pages of the log went with the governor's report to Mexico City and thence to Spain. There, in the twentieth century, they were found in the Archive of the Indies in Seville, and, in facsimile, returned to Texas.[40] In their literal context, they tell but little; yet each scrap is another piece of the puzzle: one more clue to the beginnings of European settlement in Texas and America, joined to the other bits and pieces that have come from *La Belle*'s grave in Matagorda Bay.

The Spaniards of the Antonio Rivas–Pedro de Iriarte voyage were the last to avail themselves of the *Belle*'s contents before she settled into her grave. The five artillery pieces taken from her deck served to ballast the Spanish piraguas, shallow-draft vessels that bounced on choppy seas like Andalusian cork. The *Belle*'s main yard later supplanted a broken member on one of the Spanish vessels. Other timbers from the wrecked ship served the Spanish mariners for making oars and booms. They hauled away a smith's bellows, a cooper's plane, and leaves from French-language books on mathematics and artillery, some cable and cordage, and the fatal anchor that had twice failed.[41]

A year and a half later, the same two piraguas, *Nuestra Señora del Refugio* and *Nuestra Señora de la Esperanza,* visited the site again. The "Two Ladies," this time under the command of Rivas and Andrés de Pez, reached Matagorda Bay on September 11, 1688, and entered Pass Cavallo under tow because of a brisk northwest wind that followed a thunderstorm.[42] Next morning, after sailing to "the other coast" to fill the water casks from a *casimba* (hole dug in the sand) discovered on the previous voyage, the ships went in search of the French hulk. Wind and waves, however, had taken their toll; the derelict vessel was no longer visible. The only evidence of *La Belle*'s final resting place consisted of fragments—boards riddled by ship-worms, rusty bolts and wrenches, and cases of broken muskets—scattered along the beach where the French castaways, more than two years previously, had camped for three months. Rivas and Pez, with the pilot and diarist Pedro Fernández Carrasco, explored the bay's shoreline with the piraguas and small boats until September 19. If they entered Lavaca Bay at all, they missed the mouth of Garcitas Creek, the way to the French settlement, now in the final months of its miserable existence. Like the previous Spanish voyage, the mariners sailed away from Bahía de San Bernardo, oblivious to the tragedy being played out on the banks of the Rivière aux Boeufs, a few miles inland.[43]

As late as 1688 the inventory of "The King's Vessels in the Department of Rochefort" listed only one *barque longue,* the *Belle,* with the comment that "Monsieur de La Salle took her to [the Gulf of] Mexico, whence she has not returned."[44]

Ultimately, the drunken mate Tessier, whose negligence had played such a large part in the *Belle*'s disaster, gave the final word on the ship. Having returned to France with a handful of the Texas colony's survivors, he provided information for a marginal note on the inventory: "No crew is assigned to this vessel as her pilot says she no longer exists."[45]

Chapter 2

"Our Wise Commander"

ON THE PATH TO GLORY

Loss of the *Belle* spread a shroud of hopelessness over La Salle's dwindling Texas colony. The remedy immediately proposed by the leader seemed only a shot in the dark. Yet there was no other but to sit and wait for rescue that surely would never come. For a certainty, the shipwreck was pivotal for the colony, a major factor in its failure; but was it the *cause* of failure or the *result*? In fact, the turning was not from good to bad but from extremely bad to infinitely worse.

Even without the ship's devastating loss, the enterprise had any number of potentially terminal problems. The leader, unable to transcend the period's limited geographical knowledge, had landed the colony at an unknown destination, amid hostile natives with whom he could not communicate. The "tradesmen," whose recruitment in France had been entrusted to a contractor, were drawn from the scum of the English Channel ports and beggars at the church doors; they proved unworthy of their employment. In unfamiliar territory and ignorant of its hazards, half the colonists died within six months.[1] Nagging questions remain: Whence came the seeds of failure in this glorious undertaking, born of such a grandiloquent dream?

Look first to the man who had conceived the enterprise, the personality and motivation of sieur de La Salle himself: he who was to be described posthumously as "our wise commander, constant in adversity, intrepid, generous, engaging, dexterous, skillful, capable of everything."[2]

Robert Cavelier was born on November 21, 1683, in Rouen, the capital

FIGURE 2

*The Baptismal Record. In the Norman city of Rouen's Bibliothèque
Municipale, this baptismal record reveals that La Salle was christened simply
Robert Cavelier. He prefixed it later with "René." Photo by James E. Bruseth*

of old Normandy, probably on the rue de la Gross Horloge. The son of
Jean Cavelier the elder and his wife, Catherine Gest, he was christened next
day in Saint-Herbland Parish (the church was destroyed during World War
II) with Nicolas Gest and Marguerite Morice as godparents. The name
given him was simply Robert Cavelier, not René-Robert, a form that he
assumed as a young adult. He was the second of three sons, Jean (given his
father's name) being older, and Nicolas, younger. Nicolas, a lawyer, is said
to have died rather young. Madame Fauvel-Cavelier, mentioned as La Salle's
sister-in-law, evidently was Nicolas Cavelier's wife or widow. There was also
a sister (Christian name not found), who married Nicolas Crevel, a member of the King's Council and master of accounts in Rouen.[3]

Robert's uncle, like his father, was a wealthy merchant in Rouen. Henri
Cavelier was one of the Company of One Hundred Associates created in
the 1620s by the minister Cardinal Richelieu, with crown support, for the
development of Canada. Each member of the company—including government officials, merchants, nobles, and clergy—contributed three thousand livres as working capital. The company, as seigneur of lands claimed

by France in North America, held a monopoly on all trade except fishing.[4]

On the surface, it appears that Robert Cavelier de La Salle maintained close ties with his family. (The name La Salle, which Robert assumed, was that of a family estate near Rouen.) Yet little is known of his upbringing: virtually nothing of relationships within the family that might have shaped his character and personality. He seems always to have held to strict moral standards, which surely reflected those of his parents. Yet his later difficulty in personal dealings—his irrational response to criticism and offers of advice—hints at authoritarian parents or other oppressive influences. The treatment he afterward received in business dealings with his brother Jean, seven years his senior, suggests either an intense sibling rivalry or Jean's extremely jealous nature. The two rather strange personalities taken together seem to point toward a dysfunctional family.

Jean Cavelier, also born at Rouen, was baptized October 27, 1636, in Saint-Herbland Parish. He entered the Saint-Sulpice Seminary in 1658, was ordained a priest in 1662, and was sent to Canada in 1666. He arrived at Montreal on September 7 of that year, preceding his younger brother by less than a year. Jean Cavelier returned to France in November, 1679. He was still in France in 1684 when La Salle asked the Sulpician superior in Paris to provide priests for his expedition to establish a colony on the Mississippi River near the Gulf of Mexico. Abbé Cavelier was one of the three Sulpicians chosen.[5] La Salle also took two nephews: Colin Crevel de Moranget, his sister's boy who had been with him on his voyage down the Mississippi, and his brother Nicolas's son, young Colin Cavelier.

If, when a child is born, the path of its life could be foreseen, the birth in many instances would not be a joyous occasion. So it was with La Salle, who entered the world just half a year after Louis XIV, at the age of five, had become king of France. The lives of both Robert and Louis were to be historic; their paths would cross, but hardly could they have been more divergent. Yet La Salle, ennobled by "Louis le Grand, the Sun King," would carry the ruler's name to the far reaches of his American realm, and beyond.

La Salle's life, indeed, appears to have followed the course of the city and region of his birth. So steeped in history and tragedy was the place of his nativity that it seems only natural that his career should follow such a pattern. In the year 911 the Scandinavian Northmen (Normans), having settled at Rouen, claimed this section of northwestern France. The region took from these invaders its name (Normandy) and the character of its people—noted for intelligence, strength, and energy—and gave in return the French language and culture and the Christian religion.

From the Norman leader Rollo (Rolf the Granger) descended the line of dukes that included William the Conqueror: he who invaded England in 1066 and defeated the English King Harold in the famed Battle of Hastings.[6] Duke William of Normandy thus took the English throne; a Norman dynasty ruled England until 1154. Normandy was twice won by the English during the Hundred Years' War (1337–1453) but was finally restored to France in 1449.

It was during this series of conflicts, in 1431, that the illiterate peasant girl Joan of Arc, inspired by visions, led French troops against the invaders from across the English Channel. Betrayed by avaricious Frenchmen, she was captured by the English and burned at the stake in Rouen's market place. Tour Jeanne d'Arc, where this venerated heroine was imprisoned, still stands in Rouen, today a war-scarred but beautiful city on the River Seine.

It was this "veritable flower garden of Gothic architecture,"[7] with its historic and tragic past, that gave life to Robert Cavelier de La Salle and set him on the course of his own historic and tragic life. It seems a bit of irony that Rouen was the birthplace also of the playwright Pierre Corneille (1606–84), the father of French classical tragedy, with whom the Cavelier family may well have been acquainted. Corneille, in his writing, catered to the public taste of his day, which demanded heroic men and deeds and extraordinary adventures. His plots evolved around situations that called forth courageous energy and enterprise. The tragedian, had he outlived La Salle, might have found in his fellow townsman a natural subject for his plays.

La Salle was heir to the traits of the Vikings. Fixed in him were the lure of adventure, as well as a tradition of, and conditioning for, commerce. Such qualities were in tune with the times, and especially the place, of his nativity; French priorities were focused on colonial expansion with an emphasis on trade. Rouen in the late seventeenth century was one of the most populous and opulent cities of the realm. It was made up of thirty parishes, with as many as fifty convents. The port was jammed with cargo vessels bringing spices and furs from America and barges descending the Seine laded with lumber and Burgundy wines. A floating bridge that could be withdrawn to permit passage of the vessels, as well as ice floes, spanned the river; its arches, opened by an ingenious mechanism, raised and lowered with the tide's ebb and flow. The air was redolent with dried pelts and kelp dragged in from the sea by the far-ranging merchant ships.

For that period, Rouen offered a relatively comfortable milieu in which to be born. La Salle's father was a well-to-do textile merchant, secure in his dealings with the various churches that purchased from him their altar adornments of red and white damask, crimson taffeta, calico, and brocade. Jean Cavelier *père* stood in high favor with the local ecclesiastical authority; he was elected master of the Brotherhood of Notre-Dame when Robert was nine years old.

Not everyone enjoyed such comfort and prestige. As the crown passed from Louis XIII to his child successor, the French army won a decisive victory over Spanish forces in the Battle of Rocroi on May 19, 1643. This triumph yielded the promise of a final solution to the Thirty Years' War. Yet the war continued until 1648, only to be followed by the *Fronde* ("slingshot"), so named for the stone-throwing mob that assaulted the royal residence in Paris. This civil war, lasting from 1648 to 1653, was the outgrowth of opposition by the *Parlement* of Paris to the tyrannical measures of the prime minister, Cardinal Jules Mazarin. Armed bands laid waste to the countryside. At the same time, epidemics ravaged the population. In 1651 alone, more than 17,000 persons are said to have died in Rouen. Yet, it seems that the Cavelier family suffered relatively little; in fact, less than their young king. With Cardinal Mazarin temporarily banished, Louis, his mother, and their small following lived in humiliation and destitution at Saint-Germain, where food was short and the bedding threadbare, and the growing Louis's clothes fit all too snugly.[8]

Robert Cavelier, meanwhile, enrolled in the Collège de Jésuites de Rouen, known today as the Lycée Corneille, for the playwright. Virtually nothing has come forth of Robert's time at the Jesuit school. Like his fellow students, he surely studied Latin, mathematics, and geography. Having completed this curriculum, he left Rouen for Paris to become a novice in the Society of Jesus. It was October 15, 1658, just before his fifteenth birthday.

La Salle's time with the Jesuits was crucial to the shaping of his career; it was a period of self-discovery, the beginning of a drama to be played out in the course of his life. For two years he endured the discipline of Père Mouret: a studious and impressionable pupil but never a submissive one. In vigorous good health, he tended to be haughty, headstrong, overbearing, impetuous, and quick-tempered. So said his mentors. He also had a great desire to dominate, to subdue, and to master—qualities that presaged his behavior in later life—a far cry from the subservience required of novices in the order. Yet, though "tormented by ardent passions," he managed by dint of a daily struggle against his natural temperament to curb his impatience. He beseeched the patron saint of the order, Saint-Ignatius—it is said—to strengthen him in his religious vocation. When he took his vows

FIGURE 3

*The Youthful La Salle. Pierre Margry used this
portrait as the frontispiece of volume one of his
six-volume* Découvertes et établissements *because,
he said, it was the most accurate image
of the explorer he was able to find.*

in October, 1660, he altered his baptismal name to include that of the order's
founder. Thus he became Robert-Ignace Cavelier, but the new appendage
was no more permanent than his affiliation with the Jesuits.[9]

That year was significant also for the French king. Louis XIV in 1660
married María Teresa (Marie-Thérèse) of Austria, daughter of King Philip
IV of Spain. The union, contrived by the minister Mazarin, was deemed a
master stroke of diplomacy.

Having taken his vows, "le Frère Cavelier," as he was then known, left Paris for two years as a student at the Collège de La Flèche. While not particularly dedicated to his studies, he nevertheless demonstrated considerable aptitude for the physical sciences. He went forth in 1662 to teach philosophy at Alençon but returned to La Flèche a year later to study mathematics for a year. Yet his inner conflict raged on, the monastic walls closing in upon him. Increasingly, it was becoming obvious that the young man was suited for neither the priesthood nor the classroom; he required a wider, less restricted field. His rector at La Flèche, with marked insight, recognized that Frère Cavelier possessed talent but lacked judgment and discretion. Thereafter, Robert-Ignace seems to have had little success in curbing his obstinate tendencies, for the same criticism surfaced again.

Leaving La Flèche a second time, Robert did one-year teaching stints at Tours and Blois. By then he was twenty-three years of age and in the throes of severe discontent, which he occasionally expressed without reticence. In March, 1666, he petitioned the Jesuit superior-general in Rome, Father Jean-Paul Oliva, for assignment to a foreign mission field. The father superior, possibly recognizing that his charge was more interested in adventure than in saving souls, demurred: Le Frère Cavelier was still young, and the request was ill-timed; while awaiting the appropriate time, Robert-Ignace should strive to prepare himself better for the assignment he desired.[10]

Robert saw this reply as a message without hope. Yet, resuming his theological studies at La Flèche, he sought, with little success, to follow the superior-general's advice. In a second letter, he proposed pursuing his theological studies in Portugal as a means of preparing himself for foreign missions. Again, the reverend father-general saw little reason to the request. Robert-Ignace should content himself to remain in his province, complete his studies, and serve out his probation. It was a prescription young Cavelier could not accept. On January 10, 1667, he wrote again to the superior-general, this time asking to be relieved of his vows. The request came as no surprise to the superior. He, too, had seen that the young neophyte was temperamentally ill-suited for the religious life. With his approval, the request sailed through ecclesiastical channels without resistance. On March 27, 1667, Robert, absolved of his vows, left La Flèche "to reenter the world." He was not, however, completely free of the Jesuits. Discipline in the Society of Jesus in this period has been likened to that of the military; La Salle's defection, to desertion: "In Jesuit eyes, Cavelier would always be a renegade."[11] In the years ahead, he would be haunted by the bitterness that lay between him and his erstwhile mentors. Suspicion and mistrust were to mark his future dealings with the order, as factional conflict arose on this and other fronts.

La Salle's withdrawal from the Society of Jesus seemed to typify his mode. Throughout his life he had to soothe his itching foot and slake his thirst for adventure while seeking fulfillment of his visions of greatness and glory. He often pursued these dreams impetuously. Always impatient with discipline—or advice, even—he was prone to taking giant steps without full consideration of the consequences or adequate preparation for the unexpected. There are many examples, but the greatest is surely his final voyage. Not even his iron will, his superhuman effort, and his great courage could overcome the obstacles that rose in his path.[12]

La Salle, in essence, was a product of his region and its history, as well as his immediate environment. While endowed with the adventurous spirit and courage of the Vikings, he had acquired knowledge and skills from his Jesuit schooling. Yet, surely, at the roots of his strange temperament lay family influences that cannot be documented. Certainly, in the final act of his life's drama, his relationship with certain family members contributed vitally to his undoing.

For whatever reasons, he found himself at age twenty-three cut off from all means of support. Upon entering the Society of Jesus, he had taken the requisite poverty vow, renouncing all claim to his inheritance. His father, Jean Cavelier *père,* had died the previous year; he was buried on January 12, 1666, in the parish of Notre Dame de la Ronde in Rouen. The will could not now be undone. Thus, by severing his connection with the order, Robert (no longer Robert-Ignace), placed himself at the mercy of his siblings.[13] From their father's estate they granted him an allowance of 400 livres per year. It was far too little to enable him to pursue his great dream of empire that evidently had blossomed while he chafed within the confines of the Jesuit cloister and classroom. His siblings, on hearing his plan, made a further concession: they allowed him to draw the full amount that they had set aside for his annuity, although it appears that his brother Jean actually "held the purse strings."[14] If they expected this gesture to enable Robert to make the big strike, while giving them a stake in it, there was grave miscalculation. It was not to be their last contribution to his chimera chase; the recompense would be far different from the expected.

Following Robert's return to Rouen, there was scarcely time for boredom to set in. With his destination already determined and with cash in hand, he soon "sailed for New France, in search of glory."[15]

The word *new*, as in "New France," "New England," and "New Spain," often suggested fresh opportunity to the minds of footloose adventurers. Indeed, many emigrants satisfied their desire for riches in the American colonies; most did not. If La Salle expected to escape the problems of his homeland—the political intrigue, the corruption that often plagued both church and state, and the international and internecine conflicts—he was sadly mistaken. With striking fidelity, the difficulties then afflicting Louis XIV's France transferred themselves to Canada.

The reign of "Louis le Grand," since his ascension at age five, had not run a smooth course. Cardinal Mazarin, a near-genius at international diplomacy, was less adept at domestic relations and less than scrupulous in the handling of public funds. He had built a personal fortune principally through the sale of government posts and perquisites. It was a method of graft that La Salle himself was to encounter when he was extorted by François Bellinzani, intendant under Mazarin and director of commerce under Mazarin's successor, Jean-Baptiste Colbert.[16]

Then there was the brazen grafter Nicolas Fouquet, whom Mazarin had made finance minister. Fouquet built Château de Vaux, possibly the grandest in all France, with embezzled funds, then invited the king and his court to a housewarming. Such arrogance led to the miscreant official's arrest and imprisonment. With Château de Vaux as the first model, the Sun King drafted Fouquet's cadre of artisans to build his palace at Versailles.[17]

Colbert, who was Mazarin's handpicked successor, accorded high priority to France's economic solvency. Trade with the colonies and with other countries gave rise to huge government-controlled corporations; new factories hummed, producing luxury goods for export. Yet, "war was the natural condition of nations; during the whole seventeenth century, there were only seven years of peace in Europe." The expanding trade often was choked off by quarrels and armed conflict. As the France of Louis XIV ascended toward political, military, and commercial supremacy in Europe, furs from Canada were a significant stimulus to the economy. For that trade, which "obliged completely different cultures to meet and come to terms," the French, the English, and the Dutch competed, and Frenchmen vied fiercely with each other. In Canada, three religious orders—Jesuits, Sulpicians, and Récollets—struggled for dominance in the winning of Indian souls and territorial rights. This contest for the lands whence came the furs and where lived the American natives who trapped them, it has been said (in notable understatement), shaped events in North America for a hundred years.[18]

The fact that La Salle's brother Jean was already in Canada may have influenced his entry upon the stage of this history-making operation. He scarcely had time to discover "the narrow and uneventful life of a bourgeois in Rouen" before embarking for America.[19] It was still springtime, 1667. By late summer he was at the ragged frontier village of Ville-Marie, the forerunner of Montreal.

La Salle already had crossed the line in his relationship with the Jesuits. He now confirmed it by his association with the Sulpicians. The Society of Jesus, he alleged, aspired not only to religious domination in New France but also to monopoly of the fur trade. In 1663, the Order of Saint-Sulpice had acquired the island of Montreal, formed by the deltaic confluence of the Ottawa River with the Saint Lawrence. From this base they hoped to extend themselves throughout New France. Thus, the Sulpicians became a stumbling block to Jesuit ambitions. La Salle, in effect, made himself a partisan in this rivalry by accepting a concession from the Order of Saint-Sulpice. Naturally suspicious, he began to see—justifiably or not—Jesuit connivance in many of his reverses.

The primitive Montreal was, as Parkman says, "perhaps the most dangerous place in Canada." A recent peace treaty had done little to ease tensions; the dreaded Iroquois, resentful at the terms, still threatened. A venture into field or forest exposed one to their vengeance. Even so, the time was auspicious for the young adventurer La Salle. The Sulpicians, eager for settlers in the outlying areas to shield their island and extend their influence, granted land on easy terms. Whether or not La Salle had come to Canada "with objects distinctly in view," he eagerly grasped the opportunity offered: a large tract above the rapids a few miles up the Saint Lawrence River from Montreal, where Lachine stands today. It was a location well suited for the fur trade, yet dangerously exposed to attack.[20]

There at the place at first called Saint-Sulpice, La Salle's strides in building a settlement enhanced his self-confidence as a colonizer. A village of crude dwellings, each with its own garden plot, took shape within a protective palisade. The enclosure was surrounded by larger tracts (sixty arpents per settler) from which La Salle collected rent, and the colonizer's own personal domain of larger proportions. These were solid gains; yet they could not suppress his obsessive vision.

His study of Indian languages stemmed from simple practicality, for the mood of the Iroquois was still uncertain. When a band of Seneca—one of the Iroquoian Five Nations—settled in for the winter, claiming ancestral rights, La Salle made no protest. Instead, he took advantage of the opportunity to hear their account of a distant river, which, they told him, flowed westward. This river, according to Dollier de Casson, was called Ohio by the Iroquois, Mississippi by the Algonquians. (At this stage the French thought the two names represented but a single river.) La Salle immediately envisioned a link to the South Sea and the China he had dreamed of while cloistered with the Jesuits.[21]

Always a challenge to present-day understanding of that period is its prevailing ignorance of the North American interior. To comprehend La Salle's concept—widely shared in that time and place—that this river might provide a passage to the Pacific Ocean and China, one must realize that no European since Hernando de Soto had seen the Mississippi, and none had seen the mouth of the Ohio. The Mississippi River's western branch, the Missouri, which rises in southwestern Montana, had never been glimpsed by white men.

La Salle, his imagination inflamed, hastened down the Saint Lawrence to Quebec, where he found Governor Daniel Rémy de Courcelle and his intendant, Jean-Baptiste Talon, ready to send him on a journey at his own expense. The young seigneur of Saint-Sulpice, characteristically, charged ahead. Sacrificing his two-year gain, he sold his seigneury to outfit his expedition. Most of the property went back to the Sulpicians, but the last parcel was purchased by two established Montreal merchants, Jacques Le Ber and Charles Le Moyne. Le Ber was La Salle's distant cousin, being the son of Robert Le Ber and his wife, Collette Cavelier, of Pitre in the bishopric of Rouen. Le Ber had married Le Moyne's sister Jeanne. The Le Moynes' sons, Pierre Le Moyne d'Iberville and Jean-Baptiste de Bienville, in the distant future, would take up La Salle's failed enterprise—an ironic twist, in view of the enmity that arose between the explorer and their father— and form the link between the Gulf Coast and Canada.[22]

With four canoes laded with provisions and trade goods and fourteen hired companions, all paid for with proceeds of the sale, La Salle was ready to plunge into the wilderness: an all-or-nothing gamble. This was to be his life's pattern: to sacrifice the sure thing for a chimera, to mortgage his very being, as it were, for a chance at the big prize beyond the distant horizon— akin to what poker players call drawing to an inside straight. The motivation for such a life pattern would seem to involve more than simple greed, but there have been those who thought otherwise.[23]

At Courcelle's urging, La Salle's expedition was joined to that of a Sulpician group from the seminary at Montreal. Led by Abbé François Dollier de Casson, it included Abbé René Brehan de Galinée, a noted astronomer to whom we owe the account of the expedition; seven hired men;

and three canoes. It was a symbiotic arrangement that surely rankled La Salle, "who was unfit for any enterprise of which he was not the undisputed chief." The combined force of twenty-four men with seven canoes departed from Saint-Sulpice (Lachine) on July 6, 1669. It was duly reported to the minister Colbert in France that "Messieurs de La Salle and Dollier . . . have left the country with the purpose of going to reconnoiter a passage that they think will give us communication with Japan and China."[24]

This journey stands among the most enigmatic of all La Salle's exploits. The explorer's movements are shrouded in mystery and controversy; yet, whether truth or fiction, they exemplify the explorer's secretive nature, for he neither confirmed nor denied the claims made in his behalf by others. In their obscurity, they correspond to La Salle's journey westward from his Texas colony in the early months of 1686, during which time the barque *Belle* was lost. His interpreters, in both instances, still argue over the course of his travels and his motivation; the written record yields only partial and confusing answers.

Before the 1669 journey was over, La Salle was to stare death in the face and have his mettle tested in various ways. If he lacked wilderness seasoning, he would get it in some measure, watching as the Seneca Iroquois tortured and cannibalized a captive, apprehensive that he and his companions might shortly suffer a similar fate.

After spending a month at a Seneca village on Lake Ontario's south shore—where La Salle's claim of fluency in the native language proved woefully inadequate—the explorers paused at a native habitation (Tinawatawa) near the lake's western end. Here La Salle received the present of a Shawnee prisoner. (Some have said it was Nika, who would be his servant to the end and who was to die for his devotion to La Salle, but Nika's affiliation with the explorer remains obscure.) The Shawnee offered to guide the Frenchmen to the Ohio. La Salle brightened at the prospect, but a chance encounter with Adrien Jolliet, brother of the more famous Louis Jolliet, altered plans. Jolliet induced the Sulpicians to accompany him to the Potawatomi on Lake Superior. La Salle, one version has it, was bent on reaching the Ohio; claiming that a recent fever had rendered him unfit to continue, he parted from the Sulpicians, who went forth to a noteworthy but unfulfilling adventure of their own. The Sulpicians, by all accounts, were as glad to be free of him as he of them. Galinée, whose narrative Frances Gaither refers to as "acrimonious," had cast aspersions at the young man when his facility with the Iroquois language fell short, as well at his apparent fragility that caused him to excuse himself from their company.[25]

La Salle, however, did not immediately return to Montreal; he was now free to follow his own course. Where that course led and with what results are still debated, for he was not seen again in Saint-Sulpice or Montreal until the following summer (1670). Yet the preponderance of opinion holds that he made no significant discoveries.

Thenceforth to the end of his life, La Salle's career is shrouded in deceit and obfuscation. His claims often rest on falsified documents written by others to serve their own ends. Reports known to have come from the explorer's own hand frequently conflict with other "reliable" sources. A completely accurate, fully knowledgeable assessment, therefore, is virtually impossible.

Soon after the Sulpicians had departed, it is claimed, most of La Salle's men deserted. Some of them are said to have returned to Saint-Sulpice, which then was given its lasting name, Lachine, in mockery of La Salle's dream of finding a passage to China.[26] Undaunted, so the story goes, La Salle pressed on with the few remaining men and his native guide to discover the *"grande rivière d'Ohio"* and follow it "to a place where it falls from great height into vast marshes, to 37° latitude, after having been expanded by another very large river from the north." Thus, it has sometimes been assumed that he reached the falls at Louisville.[27]

La Salle himself has oft been judged the author of this document, which, like many of those published by Pierre Margry, appears without date or attribution. The author, however, has been identified as Claude Bernou, one of two Sulpician abbés who, to serve their own ends, sought to shape La Salle's image and direct his course. In so doing, they muddled the record so that the truth in this and many other instances may never be known. The other abbé was Bernou's friend Eusèbe Renaudot, author of the second document that claims for La Salle discoveries that he never made. Of the explorer's connection to these clerics, Jean Delanglez says, "Even while La Salle feared and berated imaginary enemies, he cast his lot with two theory-spinning abbés who meant him no good. They concocted a madcap enterprise, they assigned him the role of a pawn, . . . they got him moved into a desperate position, they abandoned him to his fate."[28]

There is scarcely room to doubt that the two abbés took over the management of La Salle's career and sought to maneuver him to their own ends. They put into La Salle's mouth words that he himself could not have spoken in truth; they deceived the king for their own purposes. It would be naive to believe that the explorer did not countenance the deception. While allowing himself to become the abbés' puppet, he became his creditors' pawn. Beyond a doubt, Renaudot and Bernou, with blind disregard, contributed to the ultimate disaster. Whatever else they were guilty of, they shrouded La Salle's exploits in falsehoods, leaving his interpreters to follow a trail of deceit in an often futile effort to sort out the truth. La Salle, perhaps blindly, joined in their deception; more likely, he did so willingly, for their scheme appealed to his ambition and his delusions of grandeur.

The purported Ohio discovery in the winter of 1669–70 almost certainly never occurred. E. B. Osler, calling it "extremely doubtful" that La Salle explored any new territory, believes it fairly certain that he traveled "a path that would establish him as a favored trader among the 'western' nations of the Iroquois." After disposing of the furs from the Seneca, he went among the Ottawa and was in Quebec the following summer (1670) when Governor Courcelle sought to smooth over a rupture between the Ottawa and the Iroquois. He was still there on August 18, when the intendant Talon returned from a visit to France with new instructions that modified, for the moment, the court's ambivalence concerning exploration. With the way cleared, Talon quickly ordered two expeditions: he sent Simon-François Daumont, sieur de Saint-Lusson, to the northwest to look for the copper mines that Adrien Jolliet had failed to find and a water route to the South Sea (Pacific Ocean); and he commissioned La Salle to explore southwest and south, seeking an all-season route to the sea that would preempt water access to the interior by the English, the Spaniards, and the Dutch. Those chosen for these assignments, Talon said, were "men of resolution" who promised to penetrate farther than Frenchmen ever had before. La Salle, he reported, "has plenty of enthusiasm for these enterprises."[29]

The extent to which La Salle carried out his orders remains a mystery. Talon still had not heard from him more than a year later. The intendant reported to the king on November 2, 1671, that Saint-Lusson was back after traversing more than five hundred leagues, but "La Salle has not yet returned from his journey to the south coast." Yet La Salle had made a brief appearance in Montreal—without contacting Talon—the previous August 6, when he received on credit from an official of the Sulpician seminary merchandise valued at 450 livres.[30] Had La Salle slipped quietly back to the settlement without notifying Talon, possibly to outfit himself for resuming his exploration on a new tack? Or simply for a trading expedition?

La Salle himself has left nothing to clear the mystery. As to whether he got anywhere near the Mississippi, or the Ohio, the only documentary evidence is the highly questionable *mémoire* based on his 1678 interviews in France with "a friend of Abbé Gallinée"—Abbé Eusèbe Renaudot.

Renaudot, editor of the *Gazette de France,* belonged to the Jansenist faction within the Roman Catholic Church. His anti-Jesuit sentiments strongly influenced his use of tongue and pen. He, like Abbé Bernou, was affiliated with an anti-Jesuit fraternal group called the Confrérie des Beaux Enfants ("Brotherhood of Good Children"), whose ideas and objectives were opposed by its Jesuit counterpart, the Confrérie des Beaux Amis ("Brotherhood of Good Friends").[31]

The first part of Renaudot's memorial deals at length with the jealousies and hostile competitiveness that marked relations of the various factions and religious orders in Canada with each other—seemingly a reflection of La Salle's complaints and his attempts at self-justification. The second part, in no uncertain terms, claims for La Salle the discovery of the Mississippi prior to the 1673 journey of Louis Jolliet and Father Jacques Marquette. Did La Salle himself make such a claim? Or did he stand silently by while the abbé polished his image with falsehoods?

In 1671, the document states, La Salle (having found his way through the Mackinac Straits) coasted Lake Michigan southward past Green Bay to the Chicago portage; proceeding thence to the Illinois River, he reached the Mississippi and followed it from latitude 39° to 36°. Thus, it is claimed, he confirmed his previous conclusion that the river emptied into the Gulf of Mexico and not the Pacific Ocean and vowed some day to follow it to its mouth.[32]

La Salle's silence on this purported discovery and the apparent bias of the author of the "Histoire" caused Francis Parkman, and others, to reject it. More recently, Conrad Heidenreich, a Canadian scholar, has proclaimed that "there is no evidence that [La Salle] undertook any explorations until after 1678."[33]

The opposing theory reflects that La Salle was never one to vaunt his accomplishments; in view of his grand vision, he could have considered it only a partial discovery, which, if revealed at the time, might have provoked his competitors to redouble their efforts to thwart his objective. They surely would have managed to discredit him, usurp the discovery, and reap its rewards. As for his secrecy, La Salle had every reason to hold his cards close to his vest. Yet, if this was his strategy, it had its hazards.

Further word of the great river to the west came in 1672 from Indians visiting Father Marquette's Ottawa mission of Saint-Esprit. Talon, with fresh instructions from Colbert that top priority should be attached to discovery of the South Sea, cast about for the right person to lead the quest. La Salle, as far as Talon could see, had defaulted on his previous assignment.

Having had no report on anything La Salle had done, the intendant had lost patience with him. Talon, eager to find the all-season route to the sea before ending his term, chose Louis Jolliet to seek the river, which he believed, in accord with the age-old hypothesis, might empty into the Pacific, thus providing a route to China and Japan. The new governor, Louis de Buade, Comte de Frontenac,[34] just arriving from France, confirmed the choice of the departing intendant.

Jolliet, joined by Father Marquette and five other Frenchmen, left the Ottawa mission about the first of June, 1673, "to enter country where no European had ever put the feet." They reached the Mississippi by way of a portage from the Fox River to the Wisconsin and descended to latitude $33°40'N$. Thus, they established to their satisfaction that the river flowed south to the Gulf of Mexico, not west to the Vermilion Sea or east to Virginia.[35] Returning via the Illinois River, they visited the Kaskaskia village near Starved Rock. Jolliet viewed the Illinois Valley as a desirable place to form a settlement. The explorers also brought back information that the Missouri River might well provide the way to the Vermilion Sea. This crucial report, however, ran afoul of Colbert's ambivalent, if not self-contradictory, stance concerning exploration. He approved of far-ranging discoveries, of lands that the French could never settle, only if such lands were of economic importance and were being threatened by a foreign rival.[36] The minister, however, held one reservation: he still longed for access to the southern seas as an alternative to the freeze-prone Saint Lawrence River.

Any attempt by La Salle to assert a prior claim to a Mississippi discovery at this point—even if there were grounds for such—would have had a hollow ring; he had to keep his own counsel. Afterward, La Salle's supporters spun a web of trumped-up rhetoric to convey the idea that, if Jolliet and Marquette had reached the Mississippi, they had not found its mouth or proved the way to the Gulf of Mexico. La Salle himself would do so. He would be the one to develop the Mississippi Valley fur trade and open a warm-water port to serve it; he would bridge the continent with French commerce and shut off the westward expansion of the English and the Dutch and hold back the Spaniards on the south. Yet ambiguity of purpose—attributable to a lack of funds and confused focus—was still to frustrate his plan for several years.

The question of whether La Salle actually discovered the Mississippi ahead of Jolliet and Marquette lingers, in part because of what has become known as the Ellington Stone. This curious limestone tablet bearing the date 1671 was found in the early part of the twentieth century by Samuel N.

FIGURE 4

Historical Mystery. The Ellington Stone, found on the Ed Cook farm near Quincy, Illinois, early in the twentieth century. The date poses a mystery. Photo by Leroy J. Politsch

Cook (1844–1931) on his farm in Illinois's Ellington Township. It had been washed up by a spring freshet on a southern branch of Cedar Creek, a few miles northeast of Quincy, Illinois, a great distance inside the Cook farm's boundaries. Now in the possession of the Quincy Museum, the stone has been an abiding interest of Leroy Politsch of Quincy since 1956.

Through the years, Politsch has consulted countless experts and collected a variety of opinions, including some that would brand the stone an

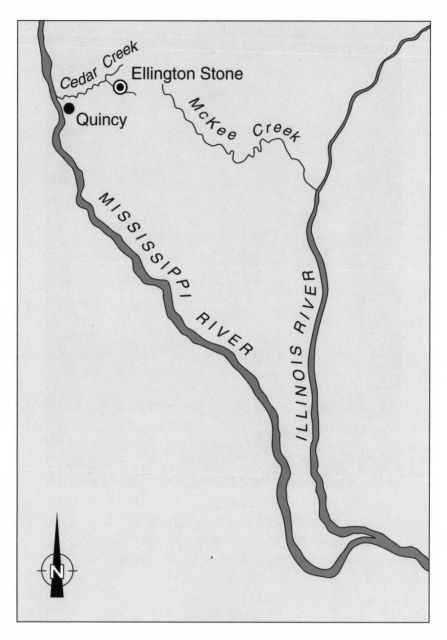

FIGURE 5

Shortcut to the Mississippi? The Ellington Stone was washed up
by a flood on Cedar Creek. The stone, with its 1671 date, suggests
that some canoe-borne Frenchman—perhaps La Salle?—
portaged between Cedar and McKee Creeks en route to or from
the Mississippi prior to the Jolliet-Marquette expedition of 1673.

outright fake. The location and circumstances of the find, however, seemed to Politsch to be incongruous with a hoax. The stone bears only the date of 1671, beneath an inclining cross with "IHS" (used as a Christian symbol and monogram for "Jesus") arched above it; without a name, there would have been no motive for faking it. Politsch proceeded to the question of who might have been in the Illinois Valley as early as 1671, two years ahead of the Jolliet-Marquette expedition. The only logical answer seemed to be La Salle, whose whereabouts during the "mystery years" of 1668–72 have been established only by conjecture. With support from several eminent historians—and staunch disagreement from others—Politsch has kept fresh in mind the advice of the Franciscan scholar Father Francis Borgia Steck, a noted Marquette authority: La Salle should not be ruled out.

But why, Politsch pursues, would La Salle (or anyone) have been in this particular place? The answer, he believes, lies in the local topography; specifically, the juxtaposition of the head of Cedar Creek, which flows into Quincy Bay on the Mississippi, and that of McKee Creek, joining the Illinois River opposite the present town of Naples, Illinois. The two streams, with deeper channels and more constant flow in earlier times, would have provided, with a portage, a shorter canoe route between the Mississippi and the Illinois. The portage, Politsch believes, would have been well known to La Salle's Indian guides.[37]

Whether or not La Salle traveled this way in 1671, planted the stone, and kept it to himself is a matter for historians to argue about. It cannot be ruled out completely until evidence turns up to establish his whereabouts at the time.[38] It would be consistent with his character, always marked by suspicion and mistrust, even in dealings with his closest associates. His paranoia manifested itself repeatedly throughout his career—in the Great Lakes Region, the Illinois Valley, and in the Texas colony—as he sought to navigate the Great Lakes with sail, develop his chain of trading posts to the west, and open the way to the Gulf of Mexico by way of the Mississippi River.

Chapter 3

"A Step from Madness"

THE WRECK OF SHIPS AND DREAMS

The wreck of the *Belle* on the Texas coast in 1686 tells much about La Salle's character. Considered in the light of three previous ship losses—especially that of the *Griffon,* which he built to ply the Great Lakes—the *Belle*'s disaster speaks even more eloquently of the man's true nature. La Salle was well focused on the wide spectrum. He contemplated in broad sweep the path of his intended exploration and its far-reaching objectives. Yet, when forced to deal with the small components and fix immediate priorities, he fell apart in confusion. The *Griffon* and the *Belle* serve as examples. Both carried cargoes that he could ill afford to lose. Yet, under multiple pressures, he forsook them at a critical moment. In one instance, his financial solvency was at stake; in the other, his very existence and that of his colonists.

The wreck of the *Griffon,* a key element in La Salle's design, drastically changed both the plan and the result of his Mississippi enterprise; it altered both his life's course and his accomplishments. The loss of the *Belle* and the misplaced colony of which she was a part marked the ultimate, tragic failure of his aims and ordained his fate.

With the realization that the Mississippi River flowed into the Gulf of Mexico and not the Pacific Ocean, La Salle plotted his strategy: first a way into the Upper Great Lakes and a string of outposts across the Illinois country; then warm-water access to the Gulf as an alternative to the Saint Lawrence River, historically the only outlet to the sea for shipping furs and other produce of New France. Aside from being ice-bound in winter, the Saint Lawrence above Montreal had a series of rapids that forbade travel with any craft but canoes. On the descent, these flimsy vessels ran the rapids at high risk; on the ascent, they had to be portaged around swift water, a time-consuming, backbreaking task. A year-round port on the Gulf promised great advantage to whoever controlled it. But first the intervening territory had to be explored.

La Salle's obsession with probing the unknown gave him a decided advantage over his more sedentary rivals. In time, however, this fixation became his heaviest liability, as his thirst for discovery overruled rational and practical judgment. His seemingly quixotic objectives at first caused him to be ridiculed as a dreamer or a madman. As his vision gelled into a cohesive plan and the pieces began to fall into place, detractors viewed him more seriously. Ridicule was transformed into vicious slander and deliberate obstruction. And, as the debts incurred to support his enterprise piled up, he was constantly hounded by his creditors.

From the beginning, La Salle had been a player in the vicious factionalism that characterized seventeenth-century Canada and especially the fur trade. Religious, political, and economic interests were pitted against each other, vying for the native peltries. La Salle, manifesting both vigor and determination, was viewed as a threat by all. With malicious diatribes and false rumors, they sought to destroy him. Thus, his men were moved to desert; his creditors to seize his assets; his brother to undercut his objectives; the French crown to question his sanity.

La Salle, however, was not to be denied. He found a powerful ally in the new governor-general of Canada, Comte de Frontenac, and opportunity opened. The two men, though from different stations, had much in common; their needs and abilities meshed. As a result of this relationship, La Salle came into possession of an outpost at Cataraqui on the north shore of Lake Ontario (present-day Kingston, Ontario).

Fort Frontenac, as it was called, ostensibly was designed to hold back the Iroquois while thwarting Dutch and English trade with natives on the Upper Great Lakes. In more forthright terms, it gave Frontenac control of the fur trade on the Upper Lakes. It may be, as Heidenreich says, that Frontenac, knowing that he could not get away with operating an illegal fur trade himself, cast about for someone to do it for him. The ultimate choice fell to La Salle.[1]

The trade monopoly, assigned first to Charles Bazire and Jacques Le Ber, failed to produce the revenue to retire the debts incurred for construction of the post. La Salle, perceiving the advantages of the location, offered to assume the governor-general's obligation and maintain the post at his own expense if the court could be persuaded to grant him the fort and adjacent lands in seigneury. With Frontenac's letters that would give him entry to the Royal Court, he sailed in the fall of 1674 for France. After being presented to the court by Louis-Armand de Bourbon, Prince de Conti, and paying a bribe to a corrupt official, La Salle returned to Canada with a patent of untitled nobility and the grant he had sought. He was to govern the post and settlement, subject to the governor-general's orders.[2] He brought with him from France the man to whom he would eventually assign the post command: François Daupin de La Forest.

The terms of the grant, which La Salle himself had proposed, might well have been more than he could fulfill. Friends and family, hoping for a share of the returns, helped make it possible.[3] He met his obligations to the crown, rebuilt the fort in stone, and maintained its soldiery. La Salle was positioned to make a fortune, but two factors blocked his way. One was his own nature: he "was not a mere merchant, and no commercial profit could content his ambition."[4] Additionally, he and the monopolistic trading partnership he had formed in liaison with the governor-general constituted a trip wire to others' aspirations. Men like Jacques Le Ber and Charles Le Moyne, once his friends, became his bitter enemies. They were joined by virtually all the traders of the colony who were excluded from what they perceived as Frontenac's attempt to monopolize the fur trade. It had become apparent to these commercial rivals that La Salle, with the governor-general's backing, intended to control the Ohio and Mississippi valleys; that not only was he a man of insatiable ambition but also that he seemed to be afflicted with a touch of madness. They had no intention of standing idly by while this free-ranging lunatic brought to ruin their own golden dreams.

La Salle's plan conflicted, too, with the Jesuits' objective of religious domination over the region without the corrupting influence of fur traders and *coureurs de bois*. The Society of Jesus has been accused of various intrigues aimed at curbing La Salle, even to causing war with the Iroquois and maligning him to the crown. Frontenac himself, in a lengthy missive to the minister, charged the "Ecclesiastics"—read "Jesuits"—with responsibility for nearly all the internal troubles of New France; that they "aimed to create an absolute domain for themselves," having intended from the very first "to make themselves powerful by their riches and influence."[5]

Unquestionably, La Salle's enemies went to extreme lengths to destroy him. Yet La Salle himself, in many ways, was his own worst enemy. So utterly vicious were the attacks against him that almost any tender heart would be inclined to accord him sympathy. So bold and courageous were his ex-

FIGURE 6

Son of the Sun King. The crest of Louis de Bourbon, Comte de Vermandois, is found on each of the three bronze cannon recovered from the wreck of the Belle. *Born in 1667 to Louis XIV and Louise de La Vallière, the child was given the title of grand admiral of France when he was barely sixteen months old and held it until his death in 1683 at age sixteen. The Prince de Conti married Vermandois's sister, Marie-Anne. Texas Historical Commission photo* ploits that any adventurous spirit must find cause to admire him. And yet accusations of cold disregard for his followers' welfare and the wild impracticality of his schemes justify a harsher judgment. It is difficult to determine which takes precedence: his enemies' allegations of his aberration or his own proof thereof. Indeed, the methods employed by his foes were enough to cause an ordinary man to lose his sanity. But no ordinary man could have persevered in the face of so many obstacles. Thus, it becomes difficult to distinguish cause from effect.

La Salle's followers were often pushed to the brink by his exacting demands and were apt to be overdue for their pay. They were easy prey to rumors planted by his rivals: that all his enterprises had failed; that he had deserted them or had died and they would never see him again; that the dreaded Iroquois were about to go to war; or that he was leading them into other trials and dangers too horrible to imagine. It was enough to drive the leader to distraction, his followers to defection—or even assassination, which, for La Salle, was an ever-present threat.

The first attempt on La Salle's life came during the rebuilding of Fort Frontenac. A man called Joly-Coeur, one of his domestic servants, tried to poison him by putting hemlock and verdigris in his salad. La Salle, as a result, became gravely ill, "vomiting almost continuously for forty or fifty days." Only a strong constitution saved him. Yet, instead of putting the culprit to death as he might have, La Salle accorded him leniency, the writer claims, to demonstrate his evenhandedness to the real perpetrators.[6] Other such attempts by La Salle's disenchanted followers awaited their turn.

Subsequent developments make La Salle's first two years as governor of Fort Frontenac seem like his halcyon days. Aside from completing the stone compound, with nine cannon mounted on the parapets, his garrison of eighty soldiers and laborers had constructed soldiers' barracks, officers' quarters, and a guardhouse. There were refinements including a mill, a blacksmith shop, and a bakery, as well as a community of French families to whom La Salle had granted farms; also the residence of the two Récollet friars—Luc Buisset and Louis Hennepin, who had come with him from France in 1675—and a chapel. A hundred Iroquois families, settled nearby, were under the religious tutelage of the friars. For commercial purposes, La Salle had built four barques, from twenty-five to forty *tonneaux* each. The local natives had assisted in construction of the settlement and were learning to cultivate the land in the French manner. "Feudal lord of the forests . . . , commander of the garrison, founder of the mission, and patron of the church, [La Salle] reigned the autocrat of his little empire."[7]

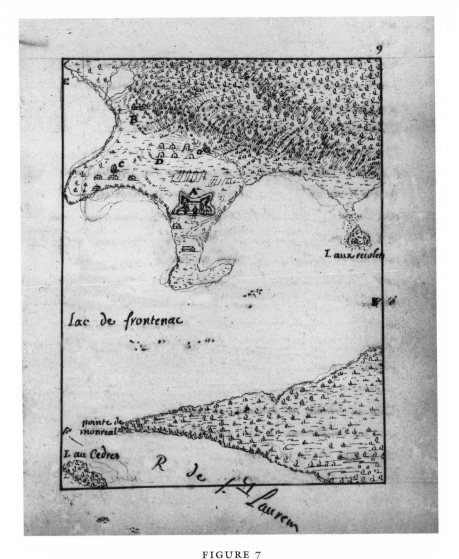

FIGURE 7

Fort Frontenac Environs. This map illustrates Jean-Baptiste Minet's
"Voyage Made from Canada Going Inland": (A) Fort Frontenac;
(B) the Récollets; (C) French dwellings; (D) Iroquois villages; (E) shore of
Lake Frontenac (Lake Ontario); (F) head of the Saint Lawrence River;
and (G) spring. Courtesy Public Archives of Canada

Still, it was not so much for commercial gain that the young Norman had thrown himself into the settlement but as the major step toward his grander design. Furtherance of the plan demanded that he again voyage to France. Leaving La Forest in charge at Fort Frontenac, he sailed in November, 1677, for La Rochelle.

Nothing illustrates the depravity that La Salle encountered in both France and Canada more than his trials at the court of Louis XIV. His coming had been heralded by a Jesuit priest fresh from Canada, Father Ragueneau, whose purpose was to convince the minister Colbert that La Salle was crazy. The previous year Colbert had refused Louis Jolliet permission to establish a post on the Mississippi and was not eager in any event to consider another such proposal, much less from a lunatic. The Jesuit father's testimony was the clincher; the minister refused to see La Salle. La Salle, however, had learned the ropes on his 1675 visit. On that occasion he had smoothed the way by paying off a corrupt official. Extorted by the commerce director, François Bellinzani, La Salle gave him a promissory note of 8,000 livres and agreed to make regular payments.

Now faced with certain failure, La Salle found Bellinzani still playing his old game. The venal functionary, recognizing La Salle's desperation, was ready to pave the way again for a price. Through Bellinzani's bribed intervention, La Salle gained access to Colbert and presented his memorial.[8]

The document cites his discoveries and his achievements as governor of Fort Frontenac. He extolled the advantages of the fertile plains and temperate climate south and west of the Great Lakes in contrast to the barren and inhospitable forests of Canada. The four vessels that he had built at Fort Frontenac to ply Lake Ontario and adjacent rivers, La Salle offered, could be used to establish a new colony in that region. The record, indeed, seemed to speak for itself, demonstrating his ability to carry out what he proposed: to build a post on Lake Erie above Niagara Falls and another on Lake Michigan. La Salle, of course, intended much more. Louis XIV's patent gave him the latitude he needed.

Dated at Saint-Germain-en-Laye on May 12, 1678, the patent is as notable for what it did not say as for what it said. It conceded La Salle the right to discover (at his own expense) "the western parts of New France"; to establish forts wherever he deemed necessary; and to reap the commercial benefits. Nothing was said about establishing colonies; the Sun King traditionally had opposed siphoning off Canada's populace to settle new regions beyond his controlling reach. Yet, in a twist of syntax, he opened the door to that very thing: "Our heart desires nothing more than the *ex-*

ploration of this country, *in which it appears that a road may be found for entering Mexico.*"[9]

Thus, with the Sun King's imperial heart scarcely concealed, La Salle's plan gained a new dimension. This rhetorical turn pointed it for the first time toward the western Gulf of Mexico, the Texas coast, and the disaster waiting there. Did Louis le Grand and Colbert know what they were doing?

There was no specific verbiage about discovering the Mississippi. Nor was there mention of building a vessel on the Lake Erie side of the Niagara escarpment, in itself a bold stroke that would carry sail navigation beyond Lake Ontario to the Upper Great Lakes. No such vision coursed the mind of King Louis or his minister, in whose geographical ignorance lay the key to La Salle's license. The means to the discovery so authorized was left to La Salle himself, whose bold vision had long danced in his head. The crown allowed him five years to explore the country and build forts to protect it, at locations of his own choosing. His preparations had already begun.

Having taken lodging on rue de la Truanderie in Paris, La Salle went first to his cousin, François Plet, *marchand bourgeois,* on rue Saint-Martin. Between March 23 and June 10, 1678, La Salle took delivery from Plet—on credit at forty percent interest—of merchandise valued at 11,483 livres. The note, which would accrue to 16,076 livres, would be due at the end of 1679.[10] Plet surely recognized the high risks involved, as well as the great potential for gain if the plan succeeded.

Among La Salle's purchases before leaving France were sails, rigging, and fittings for the building of not one vessel but two. The first would be built on the Lake Erie side of Niagara Falls, to communicate—by way of a route he probably had not traveled previously—with the mouth of the Saint Joseph River at the lower end of Lake Michigan. The second vessel, after a long portage of its components, would be constructed on the Illinois River for use in descending the Mississippi.

To carry out such an enterprise, La Salle needed more help than Plet had to offer. From various other investors, in both France and Canada, he obtained advances of some 65,000 livres. By far his most liberal backers were members of his own family, who later claimed to have advanced their kinsman 500,000 livres from 1678 to 1683.[11]

La Salle, though encouraged by his success at fund-raising, found that he was not yet through with Bellinzani, whose greedy hands still held La Salle's commission and the documents requisite to his sailing. The corrupt official—well schooled in dirty tricks by the late Cardinal Mazarin—held another trump card. La Salle had committed himself to staggering debts;

failure to carry out his enterprise would mean certain ruin. Bellinzani demanded payment of 4,000 livres in cash before releasing La Salle's commission. Before granting clearance for sailing, the extortionist squeezed again; he required a contract whereby La Salle would pay him 6,000 livres annually for six years, as though he were a partner in the enterprise. Default of the payment could have dire consequences for the explorer. His burden of debt increased again. On sailing, La Salle left Plet in charge of his affairs in France. Bellinzani, recognizing Plet's vulnerability in his dual role as investor in La Salle's enterprise and also his business agent, struck once more. With threats to cripple La Salle's venture, he extorted 2,000 livres from Plet. First and last, Bellinzani lined his pockets with 14,000 livres from La Salle and his agent.[12]

La Salle, his patent and the needed financing in hand, turned his attention to recruiting. The Prince de Conti, who had presented him at court in 1675, introduced him to Henri de Tonti, age twenty-nine, who was destined to play a major role in La Salle's endeavors. Tonti, the son of Italian immigrants, had just returned from French naval service. Having participated in numerous sea battles, he was minus his right hand, which had been blown away by a grenade; he had substituted an iron hook. Among La Salle's company also was another young man destined to accompany him down the Mississippi and to sail on his voyage to the Gulf. This was Nicolas de La Salle (no relation to the explorer), the son of a naval clerk. At La Rochelle the sieur de La Salle was joined by another trusted aide, La Motte de Lussière. In the company were thirty others, including shipwrights and carpenters. La Salle's strategy depended on their skills.[13] Yet this uninitiated band had scant inkling of what was to be demanded of them.

During his stay in France, La Salle developed a relationship with the two Sulpician abbots who, for better or worse, were to exert an influence over his affairs: Eusèbe Renaudot and Claude Bernou. It was Renaudot, editor of the *Gazette de France,* who composed the account of La Salle's first eleven years in Canada attributed to "a friend of Abbé Gallinée," based, he said, on "ten or twelve conferences" with his subject. La Salle also made an arrangement with Bernou to serve as his agent after outlining for the cleric his plan and "his glorious expectations." Bernou offered his assistance, and an agreement was reached on his emolument, which the explorer never paid. Yet La Salle filled the abbot's curious mind with details of his explorations. Bernou in turn composed the memorials that La Salle presented to the king.[14]

FIGURE 8

*Explorer in Bronze. Robert Cavelier de La Salle as pictured on a medallion in
Rouen's Bibliothèque Municipale. Photo by James E. Bruseth*

Before leaving France, La Salle, mindful of the attempt to poison him at Fort Frontenac, took care to provide himself with an antidote, should another such incident occur. Murder by poison in the France of that day was a more common occurrence than anyone liked to admit. Paris, in fact, was in the throes of the infamous poison scandals in which a cadre of "witches" (fortune-tellers) and their clients were rounded up and imprisoned, a few condemned to burn. The investigation eventually touched royalty. Trumped-up accusations against the king's mistress, Madame de Montespan, caused the monarch to stop the procedure and order 147 suspects held, without benefit of trial, in solitary confinement and incommunicado for life.[15] The efficacy of antidotes to the poisons of that day is much in question, but La Salle's life appears to have been spared by his caution.

The explorer and the band chosen to carry out his scheme sailed from La Rochelle on the ship *Saint-Honoré* on July 14, 1678. In the fleet were thirty-two other vessels bound for Newfoundland and Canada. After a two-month crossing, the new arrivals left La Salle and Tonti at Quebec and battled their way up the Saint Lawrence rapids to Fort Frontenac. On November 18 La Motte, Father Louis Hennepin, and sixteen men boarded one of the post's small barques and set sail across Lake Ontario. From the mouth of the Niagara River, they spent six weeks hauling tools and supplies around the falls to the Lake Erie side.

After La Salle recovered at Quebec from a five-week illness contracted during the crossing, he and Tonti brought additional workmen, the ship rigging, and supplies. They crossed Lake Ontario in a twenty-six-tun barque to approach the mouth of the Niagara River early in December. Contrary winds prevented a landing, but the two men managed to get ashore nine leagues down the coast. Thence, they walked to a Seneca village, where La Salle sought the natives' acquiescence to the building of the ship and a fort at the river mouth. While Tonti remained at the warehouse La Motte had erected on the lower river, La Salle ascended the escarpment to look for a suitable shipbuilding site above Niagara Falls. During the night the barque that had brought them wrecked on the coast through the pilot's neglect. The man was skillful enough, La Salle conceded, but he and his crew of seven foolishly left the vessel at anchor and went to sleep on shore. When the wind arose during the night, they were unable to go aboard. The barque dragged anchor and crashed on a rock.[16]

This was the first of four shipwrecks that afflicted La Salle's efforts. He was aboard none of the vessels at the time; therefore, he was able to cast the blame on others. "It is not for want of method and foresight that I have suffered these disasters," he wrote, "but from the disloyalty of my men, or mishaps at sea, which the wisest cannot avoid."[17] Each successive wreck was more costly than the previous one, until at last came the devastating loss of *La Belle.* (She, too, dragged her anchor). In the present instance, the barque carried the rigging for the vessel to be built above the falls. The anchors and cables were saved, but needed supplies and equipment were lost. La Salle calculated the cost apart from the ship at 5,000 or 6,000 livres. Ten or twelve men spent the entire winter at the grueling task of transporting the salvage up the steep incline to the shipbuilding site on the Lake Erie side of the falls and in scouring the countryside for provisions to feed his workmen.

Nevertheless, the shipbuilding camp was set up on Cayuga Creek, on the New York side of the Niagara River. The enterprise went forth under the ominous gaze of the Iroquois, who caused no serious difficulty but nevertheless were none too happy with the project. It was only a matter of luck at this point that La Salle had the services of the solid and resolute Tonti, who was not inclined to exceed his authority or give unwelcome advice. The leader alleged that La Motte, in whom he had placed his trust, "had been won over by my enemies . . . and had treated me very badly." Almost blind from an eye infection, La Motte soon returned to France.[18] But not even Tonti—he of the iron hand and steel courage—could spare his leader from the consequences of his own folly.

Under Tonti's supervision with Moïse Hillaret as chief carpenter, a sailing vessel that might have passed for a sister ship of *La Belle* took shape on the Cayuga bank during the early months of 1679. This was the *Griffon,* so named for the mythical creature with the body of a lion and the head and wings of an eagle, borrowed from Governor Frontenac's escutcheon to grace the ship's transom. Close to the *Belle* in size, the *Griffon* had a 45-foot keel and other similar dimensions: a 14-or 15-foot beam and 7-foot draft.[19]

It was a remarkable feat with immense portent, seemingly at odds with La Salle's record of frustration in so many other undertakings. Thus were the contrasts of this enigmatic character of such prophetic vision and enormous human failings. History has not fully recognized his achievement in the conquest of the great barrier to navigation of the western lakes. The outflow of those four inland seas pours from Lake Erie into the Niagara River, spilling over the 167-foot precipice of Niagara Falls into Lake Ontario. In Lake Ontario is gathered the drainage of 300,000 square miles, nearly all of it to reach the sea through the Saint Lawrence River over three great rapids, a volume of some 246,000 cubic feet per second. Besides the Saint Lawrence cataracts, the difference in the level of Lakes Ontario and Erie had to be overcome. In La Salle's day that required a backbreaking portage up the steep ridge and around the falls; in the present day, it is done with a manmade channel, locks, and dams.[20]

This bypass was achieved by the Canadian government in 1933, when it channeled around the Niagara River and its falls with the 28-mile Welland Canal, comprising eight locks. Completion of the joint United States–Canada Saint Lawrence Seaway project in 1959 opened the way for ocean-going freighters entering the Gulf of Saint Lawrence to reach Duluth, Minnesota, by way of a 2,400-mile navigational system.

The first step to that engineering feat was La Salle's. His accomplishment in 1679 transcended the mere building of the first sailing ship to ply the Upper Lakes; it heralded the coming of the seaway itself—rivaling, even, his Mississippi River voyage in its far-reaching consequences.[21]

La Salle himself could not be present for the launching in early spring, 1679, of this first sailing ship of the western fur trade. After seeing Fort Conti's block houses begun for a new fort at the mouth of the Niagara River in Lake Ontario—named Fort Conti for the prince who had assisted him in France—he set out in February across the ice for Fort Frontenac. It was late July before he returned, bringing three Récollet friars to carry the gospel to the western tribes. Among them was Père Zénobe Membré, who would follow him down the Mississippi and across the Gulf of Mexico to end his days on the hostile Texas shore.[22]

They found the little ship already anchored in the river above the falls, ready to begin the ascent into Lake Erie. La Salle's late coming, however, had seriously upset the sailing schedule; the seasons would change before the *Griffon* could complete her round-trip. Furthermore, the news that La Salle had received was not good. It was well understood among the competing interests that the Niagara held the key to the inland fur trade, and La Salle was about to spring the lock. His rivals intensified their efforts to spoil his plans. They spread the word to all who would listen: La Salle had overstepped himself with a harebrained scheme ordained to failure; the wild schemer himself was sure to fall among its ruins.

In fairness, La Salle had sought to head off the crisis before leaving Quebec. He had instructed his agent to pay his brother almost 15,000 livres to be apportioned among his creditors, including Abbé Cavelier himself. The explorer later sent instructions for the agent to surrender to his brother all his peltries for the same purpose. The abbé, however, betrayed his trust, appropriating the entire proceeds to satisfy his own claim. La Salle learned of the pending litigation aimed at seizing his assets when he returned to

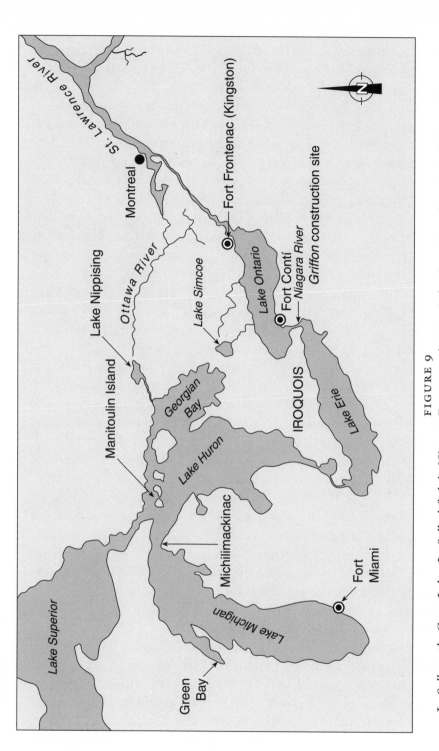

FIGURE 9

La Salle on the Great Lakes. La Salle defied the Niagara Escarpment between Lakes Ontario and Erie by building the Griffon above the falls and sailing her to Green Bay (route indicated by dotted line). Headquartered at Fort Frontenac, he built Fort Conti on the Niagara, Fort Miami on the Saint-Joseph River, and Forts Crèvecoeur and Saint-Louis on the Illinois.

Niagara, but there could be no turning back. He pinned all his hopes on the little *Griffon* and the cargo of furs she would bring back from Green Bay to pay off his creditors and silence his critics. With singing of the *Te Deum* and the firing of cannon, the little barque made sail on August 7, 1679, and set course west by south on Lake Erie, where sails had never been seen before. While the *Griffon* proceeded through the lakes, La Salle's lien-holding creditors pursued him through the court in Montreal. Before he returned the next year, his brother's treachery would have had its full effect.[23]

La Salle is said by his supporters to have traveled this way by canoe on his questionable journey of 1671: via the Detroit River, Lake Saint Clair, and the Saint Clair River into Lake Huron; thence north across the mouth of Georgian Bay to a sighting of the Manitoulin Islands; west past the mouth of the Saint Mary's River flowing out of Lake Superior; through the Straits of Mackinac into Lake Michigan; and on south to Green Bay.

It was not an easy course. Strong headwinds and the current gushing through the Detroit Strait checked progress. First a calm, then a gale so strong it caused the masts to be laid down, marred the passage up Lake Huron. The surly pilot called Luc—the one responsible for wrecking the little vessel near Niagara, a profane man who accorded respect to neither man nor deity—was even more contrary than the weather. La Salle had every reason not to trust him. His judgment had been formed while the *Griffon* was being taken up the swift Niagara River into Lake Erie: "I observed so much ill-will and so little care on the part of my pilot while making this maneuver that I did not think I should put him in charge of the vessel on its first voyage. . . . I therefore decided to take charge of it myself to avoid abandoning the lives of my men, and all the equipment vital to my enterprise, to the treachery of a man whom I suspected."[24] It was sound reasoning, too quickly put aside.

Well before leaving Niagara, La Salle had sent his traders to the Illinois country to obtain furs for loading the *Griffon*. At Michilimackinac, on the Mackinac Straits connecting Lakes Huron and Michigan, he found several of his agents. These men had turned back or stopped short of their destination because of rumors that La Salle's enterprise was doomed to failure and the *Griffon* would never arrive. Some of their companions had deserted, claiming 3,000 livres' worth of goods as back pay. Two of these, André Hénault and Rousel (*dit* La Rouselière) were soon arrested. They were given a second chance, Hénault to become a worthy ally, Rousel only to cause further trouble. Another, Gabriel Barbier, called Minime, later admitting that he had been "debauched," also made amends. Of Barbier, prominent in La Salle's Texas colony, much will be said later.[25]

The desertions caused La Salle to make a sudden and unfortunate change of plans. He had intended putting Tonti in charge of the Illinois expedition, while he himself returned to Niagara with the *Griffon*. Confronted by the desertions and thievery, he sent Tonti after the culprits, hoping that he could rejoin the ship at Green Bay.

When the ship reached Green Bay, some of La Salle's traders were waiting with a large quantity of furs, gathered illegally from territory forbidden to him. The pelts were to be the means of holding off his creditors, who at that moment were winning a court judgment that would allow them to seize his mortgaged property. It is reasonable to suppose that La Salle intended sailing the *Griffon* on south to the Saint Joseph River mouth with the rigging for the vessel to be built on the Illinois River. Thence, Tonti would see it transported overland to its destination while La Salle returned to Niagara with the *Griffon*. Tonti, however, failed to appear, and matters spun rapidly out of control. La Salle felt compelled to make hasty decisions, which proved disastrous.

The furs here loaded on the *Griffon* would have to be sent back with all haste to absolve his debts and circumvent the impending financial disaster. It was now September, and the time of equinoctial storms was at hand. The ship would have to begin her return voyage through the lakes without delay. Yet the Illinois expedition would have to go forward. La Salle, under such pressures, acted in desperation, ignoring the advice of everyone. In a huge gamble, so typical of the mixed priorities that so often plunged him into disaster, he entrusted the ship to the pilot Luc, who had already proved himself insubordinate and lacking in judgment. As Hennepin observed, La Salle "never took anyone's advice."[26] It was an observation that would be made by others, again and again.

The *Griffon* sailed on September 18 with orders to leave the rigging for the future barque at Michilimackinac—which was not done—proceed to Niagara with the furs, and return to Michilimackinac forthwith. Back at the straits, she was to reload the gear for the new vessel and pick up a waiting guide to take her to the mouth of the Saint Joseph River, on the canoe route to the Illinois valley. La Salle himself, meanwhile, would lead his men to the Illinois.

With fourteen men in four heavily laden canoes, he embarked from Green Bay. Besides the arms and trade goods, these craft carried tools with which to begin the building of the new ship intended for descending the Mississippi. Having conquered the barrier to upper-lake navigation by building the *Griffon,* the intrepid (if foolhardy) explorer now would conquer the great river to the west. Between squalls that several times put the canoes in jeopardy, the voyagers paddled south, hugging the Wisconsin shore, then east around the southern end of Lake Michigan to the mouth of the Saint Joseph at present-day Saint Joseph, Michigan. While waiting for Tonti, La Salle put his near-starving men to work sounding and marking the harbor channel and building Fort Miami. Here, according to the plan, the *Griffon* would make port; she would discharge her trade goods and lade prime furs destined for European markets via the Niagara portage, Lake Ontario, and the Saint Lawrence rapids. Thus passed the month of November, during which time, says Hennepin, "we ate nothing but bear meat that our hunter killed."[27] Tonti and his men at last arrived but not the *Griffon,* by now a matter of grave concern. As ice threatened to close the river, thirty men in eight canoes began the voyage for the Illinois. Among them were the artisans and laborers who had built the *Griffon* and who, at their destination, would set to work on the second ship.

It was in mid-December, 1679, as La Salle's party portaged over snowy plains between the Saint Joseph River and the Kankakee, that one of the men raised his gun to shoot the leader in the back. The would-be assassin was Nicolas Duplessis, a soldier from Fort Frontenac. A comrade observed the man's intention and somehow thwarted the act. Neither La Salle nor Tonti was aware of it at the time. Scarcely two weeks later, after the Frenchmen had reached an Illinois village on January 4, 1680, several men deserted, and another attempt was made on La Salle's life by putting poison into the stew. The antidote brought from France in 1678 saved him.[28]

Understandably, the men were edgy, considering the toil and hardships forced upon them. Their disloyalty and enmity directed at La Salle, however, cannot be written off entirely to the ordinary rigors of the march or to the crude woodsmen's baseness. Whether La Salle's rivals in the fur trade were directly involved in the assassination attempts is an open question. Those jealous souls, however, were an unscrupulous lot, accustomed to playing rough. They sought with telling effect to undermine La Salle's plans any way they could. Even so, as with the wreck of the *Belle,* La Salle's own character and behavior must be considered. Not only did he call for superhuman endurance and inhuman suffering, but he also expected undying loyalty from men who were apt to be long overdue for their pay.

Those who knowingly had committed themselves to suffer the leader's stern manner and undertake his grueling and dangerous treks were themselves desperate men. Illiterate *coureurs de bois* for the most part, they were accustomed to the hard life. They acknowledged no discipline but their own lusts. The craftsmen recently brought from France, on the other hand, had little inkling of what their assignment demanded and lacked wilderness conditioning. Unaccustomed to the suffering and dangers implicit in all of La Salle's marches, they surely fell victim to culture shock. Members of both groups, seldom having been accorded a paycheck or even a kind word from La Salle, were easy targets for the vicious rumors constantly fed them by his rivals. Some sought a solution to their suffering in desertion. In others, the pressures provoked a desire to kill.

The two distinct types that were most inclined to fail their leader are counterbalanced by loyal followers like Tonti and Henri Joutel—even Barbier who, after his one indiscretion, remained as staunch an ally as La Salle could ask for. Yet the steadfastness of these men seems to bespeak their own character more than their leader's. La Salle was obsessive, and his fanaticism obscured human consideration. With three attempts on his life having already been made, one more was due before the final, fatal episode in the Texas wilds.

The explorers, having navigated the Saint Joseph out of Michigan into Indiana, portaged to the Kankakee and descended the latter stream to its confluence with the Illinois River. Near present-day Utica, Illinois, about January 1, 1680, they passed a large Illinois Indian village, deserted because it was the time of the winter hunt. Farther downriver, at the present site of Peoria, stood a lively village of eighty lodges.

The Illinois were friendly at first, though not pleased with the Frenchmen's plans to build a fort and a "great wooden canoe" with which to sail down the Mississippi. La Salle, with considerable savoir faire, at first impressed himself upon the native chiefs. Yet he could not counteract the various contrary influences: his hosts' warnings—understood and repeated by some of the *coureurs de bois* who had lived long among the Indians—of terrible dangers to be encountered along the Mississippi; the Miami messengers who, having been stirred up by La Salle's enemies, brought accusations that the explorer was in league with the Iroquois; or the contagion of desertion. On January 6, Feast of the Kings, or Epiphany, he awoke to find half a dozen men missing. These were the workmen he had ordered to make sleds for transporting merchandise from the French camp to the Illinois village: Martin Chartier; Nicolas Duplessis, the would-be assassin; Jacques Monjault; Jean Rousel (*dit* La Rouselière), who had deserted previously; one Bribault; and Jean Le Croix.[29]

Nevertheless, the building of Fort Crèvecoeur and the barque intended for use in descending the Mississippi went forward.[30] The effort was overshadowed by growing anxiety for the *Griffon,* which was supposed to be bringing to Fort Miami gear and rigging for the new ship. On February 28, 1680, La Salle sent Father Hennepin with Michel Accault and Antoine Arguelle, *dit* Le Picard du Gay, to ascend the Mississippi to the Sioux. On March 2, 1680, La Salle himself left Fort Crèvecoeur in Tonti's charge and set out on foot through the half-frozen slush of approaching spring; he must either find the *Griffon* or continue to Fort Frontenac to seek the equipment needed for the new ship from another source.

This grueling and hazardous trek through the wintry North finds a strange parallel in the tropics: Hernán Cortés's anxious march from Mexico to Honduras in 1524 to confront Cristóbal de Olid's disloyalty.[31] The common ground of these widely disparate episodes, apart from the desperation with which they were undertaken and the great suffering involved, lies in the disastrous consequences for the leaders. For Cortés, beset by mutiny and shipwreck, the Honduras march came close to costing him the Conquest; for La Salle, plagued by multiple enemies and the volatile Iroquois, there followed a series of happenings that put to naught his labors toward winning the Mississippi waterway. After his departure from Fort Crèvecoeur, the Illinois valley enterprise rapidly fell apart.

La Salle, finding canoes useless in the icy river, soon left them for snowshoes. After a brief stop at the Illinois village where Fathers Membré and Gabriel de La Ribourde were seeking conversions, he pushed off into the wilderness with his Shawnee hunter Nika and four Frenchmen: Jacques de Bourdon, sieur d'Autray; André Hénault; La Violette; and "Collin."[32] On reaching Lake Michigan, he encountered Nicolas Laurent, *dit* La Chapelle, and Noël Le Blanc, whom he had sent from Fort Miami to meet the *Griffon* at Michilimackinac. They had learned nothing of the ship. La Salle sent them now to Fort Crèvecoeur with orders for Tonti to fortify Starved Rock, above present-day Peoria, which he had seen in passing. Le Blanc, however, carried a message of a different sort—one calculated to wreak havoc with La Salle's enterprise and cause further desertions.

While Tonti was away at the native village, Le Blanc spread his lies and half-truths among the men of Fort Crèvecoeur: that La Salle, on receiving the news that his creditors had seized Fort Frontenac, had declared that he was ruined and would never return to Fort Crèvecoeur. This blatant falsehood was calculated to enflame those who were due back pay. It took effect on François Sauvin (called La Roze) and Hillaret, carpenters working at building the barque, who had not received full pay for more than two years; also Jean Le Meilleur, *dit* La Forge, the nailmaker. These three joined with Le Blanc to collect what was due them by plundering the warehouse. In a stolen canoe they made off with bundles of beaver and otter skins and buffalo robes, two muskets with powder and ball, and various trade goods.[33] The wave of desertions went on until nearly all the men were gone. The different groups joined at Fort Miami, which they plundered and burned, then proceeded to Michilimackinac to pillage the warehouse.

La Salle and his five companions, having learned nothing of the *Griffon* at Fort Miami, trudged on toward Niagara. After a thousand miles of tortured travel, they reached Fort Conti on April 21, 1680, and there received grim news: the *Griffon,* carrying the means to assuage his creditors, had never arrived. There was more bad news: the ship *Saint-Pierre,* bringing from France 22,000 livres' worth of La Salle's goods and thirty men he had engaged, had wrecked at the mouth of the Saint Lawrence with a loss of sixteen lives; the intendant, Jacques Duchesneau, La Salle's dedicated enemy, had detained some of the thirty men, while others, told by the intendant that La Salle was dead, had returned to France.

The explorer was beset at every turn. At this juncture he learned of the outcome of the litigation against him in Montreal and his brother's part in it. The judgment granted his creditors in September, 1679, authorized them to seize and sell La Salle's goods. Jean Cavelier, however, appealed the Montreal judgment to the Sovereign Council of Quebec, pushing for a quick settlement as his ship was about to sail for France. On October 23, 1679, Abbé Cavelier, proving La Salle's debt to him and his family of more than 29,000 livres, was awarded some 23,000 livres, to be satisfied by the sale of La Salle's furs in the Montreal and Quebec warehouses. He ignored La Salle's instructions to apportion proceeds from his furs among his other creditors. The council ruled only that any amount in excess of Cavelier's judgment might be distributed among the various claimants, but the furs proved to be worth less than the abbé's award. Prior to the final hearing, the other creditors appealed to Cavelier: La Salle's enterprise in the west would be hamstrung if he were deprived of credit in Montreal and Quebec. Cavelier held fast to his determination to get his money before sailing for France, regardless of the disastrous outcome for his brother or anyone else.[34] Greed dominated his behavior. That he would go to any length to satisfy his selfish desires would be manifest also in his mendacity a decade later when the lives of the Texas colonists were at stake.

During the next year, 1680, while La Salle began work in the Illinois country against overwhelming odds, the aggrieved creditors petitioned the Sovereign Council for the right to seize his remaining assets. Other misfortunes, meanwhile, magnified the burden of his brother's treachery. Several of the explorer's canoes, laden with valuable cargo, had been lost in the Saint Lawrence rapids. As news of his reverses were certain to reach his partners and creditors in France, he sought to square himself with detailed reports. His letters, written in snatches and stretching to unfathomable length, became a litany of defensiveness and self-justification. There seems to have been a subliminal message in his letter to Thouret:

> . . . I do not know how you will take the treachery my brother has worked against me, but surely it will disgust you. Should the confidence you have placed in me be destroyed, I will have no one but him to blame. I assure you that what I am about to tell you is nothing more than the work of those who wish to destroy me, and that I have acted only in good faith, such as always governs my conduct. You may judge that of my brother by the papers I have from him. He has always been so strange toward me, because of the little love he has for me, that I had everything to gain when he left, since he did nothing during his stay here but cross all my plans and disrupt my efforts, which I had to change every little while to suit his whim.[35]

The tone of the letter hints at disillusionment, as well as disappointment, in an older brother whom he had looked up to and perhaps sought to emulate. Jean Cavelier's betrayal of La Salle's trust was a severe blow to the explorer, of the kind that might well have cast a pall over all their future dealings. Yet, if that was the case, the record does not reveal it.

In this unhappy summer of 1680, La Salle received news of the desertions from Fort Crèvecoeur and the plunder of his stores at three locations. These developments raised his anxiety for Tonti and his companions. Doubtful that they could hold the post without succor, he sought credit again in Montreal. Though seemingly devoid of means, he was able to obtain the supplies he needed. In July, as he prepared to return to the Illinois, he received word that the deserters had reached Lake Ontario and had vowed to kill him if he were found. With half a dozen men in two canoes, he embarked to intercept them. One group of deserters, following the south shore of Lake Ontario, escaped to New Holland (New York), but La Salle and his men succeeded in capturing the occupants of two canoes with the goods they had stolen. Among them were Le Blanc and his dupes, Hillaret and La Roze. Then came another canoe with four deserters who refused the order to surrender. When they took up their guns to resist, La Salle's men opened fire, killing two, including Bois d'Ardenne, whom La Salle had brought from France to serve as his secretary. The others were imprisoned at Fort Frontenac.[36] Thus, La Salle foiled the fourth attempt on his life but would have to face Duchesneau's charge of murder as a result.

Such an affair also raised questions among La Salle's partners and backers, to whom he recounted his losses and sought to absolve himself for his followers' weak loyalties and the deadly confrontation. The questions directed to him apparently included the reasons for the high incidence of desertions to which he attributed part of his failure to turn a profit. The man behind the defections, Martin Chartier, he explained, had never been in his employ. Those who had been led by Chartier to desert had known him but fifteen days, during which time he had struck one—"only one"— for blaspheming. On the other hand, those remaining had been with him from the beginning; their loyalty had not wavered in six years. The chief carpenter, Hillaret, he said, had returned to his employ and regretted every day that he had been led astray by bad advice. It was the same with two others who had returned to duty, Gabriel Barbier (called Minime) and André Hénault. These two testified to the role of the Jesuits in helping them conceal the goods they had stolen and in thwarting pursuit.[37]

The defectors and would-be murderers dealt with, La Salle fixed his sights on returning to the Illinois. On August 10, 1680, he embarked on Lake Ontario with twenty-five men, including La Forest,[38] a surgeon, soldiers, carpenters, joiners, masons, and common laborers. They carried all the items needed for completing the ship begun at Fort Crèvecoeur.

Instead of the Niagara portage to Lake Erie, the travelers paddled westward to the mouth of the Humber River, which enters Lake Ontario from the north, near present-day Toronto. After ascending that stream, they portaged to Lake Simcoe and thence cruised down the Severn River into Georgian Bay and Lake Huron. It was at a native village called Teioiagon that La Salle found Barbier and one Grandmaison, who had absconded the previous year from Michilimackinac under the influence of rampant reports of La Salle's failure and death. While Grandmaison took flight, Barbier readily admitted that he had been "debauched" and asked to be taken back into La Salle's service. He surrendered the goods he had taken, and the request was granted.[39]

Barbier confirmed what La Salle had already taken as a virtual certainty: the *Griffon* was indeed lost with the pilot Luc and the other five crewmen. With the ship in a sheltered anchorage near Mackinac Straits, Barbier had learned, the pilot was warned by natives of an approaching storm. The *Griffon,* heedless of the warning, sailed forth into Lake Huron. When last seen, she was battling mountainous groundswells, making toward the Manitoulin Islands with reduced sail. The following spring there were found along the coast a pair of torn and tar-splotched breeches, a hatch cover, some bits of cordage, and bundles of rotten beaver skins. The conclusion was inescapable—the *Griffon* had perished among the Manitoulins. Even so, La Salle readily believed a story told him later by a young "Pana," age sixteen or seventeen, who had been given him as a slave on the Mississippi: "that he has seen the pilot of the barque that was lost in the lake of the Islinois and one of the sailors, whom he described to me with such specific details that I cannot doubt it. [They] were captured with their four comrades in the Mississipi River while ascending to the Nadouessiou in bark canoes. The other four were killed and eaten. The pilot escaped by using one of the grenades that they had hidden in the canoe. . . . These scoundrels must have undertaken a plan, advised by my enemies, to sink the bark and go by the Mississipi to join du Luth [Du Lhut]."[40]

Such a tale notwithstanding, the precise fate of the *Griffon* remains a mystery. Through the years, there have been eleven claimed findings of the wreckage.[41] Small wonder that the 1954 disclosure of old boat timbers in Georgian Bay, including a keel that seemed to match the *Griffon*'s in length, failed to create much of a stir. Small wonder also that Harrison John MacLean, who championed the find as La Salle's vessel, failed in twenty years to bring about either the wreck's scientific investigation or support for its preservation. MacLean, then a young reporter-photographer for the now defunct Toronto *Telegram,* learned in 1952 of the wreck, which had been known to the Vail family of Tobermory, Ontario, for three generations. In 1974 he published a book in which he noted that nothing had been done toward recognizing or preserving it. The timbers lay in a cove of Russell Island, north of Tobermory at the tip of Bruce Peninsula. After extensive research, MacLean proclaimed in the *Telegram* of August 16, 1955, that the *Griffon* was believed found. In his continuing investigation, he relied heavily on the opinions of Rowley W. Murphy, noted marine artist, and C. H. J. Snider, whom he referred to as "the dean of Canada's nautical historians."[42]

Snider and Murphy visited the site with MacLean and Orrie Vail, whose father and grandfather had known of the wreck and kept it a closely guarded secret for years, while removing parts of it from time to time. They concluded that the wreck was compatible with all available information on the *Griffon,* affirming their identification in published articles. Murphy extended the lines of the actual remains to offer a sheer plan of the *Griffon,* drawn to scale. He also did a black-and-white drawing based on Father Hennepin's depiction of the ship under construction, conceptualizing the vessel under sail.[43]

That, however, was not to be the last word. The wreck had been badly abused, both by time and the elements and its "protectors." In 1978, when the site was finally excavated by the Fathom Five National Marine Park staff, a graduate student at Texas A&M University, Paul Hundley, began a minute investigation, the basis for his master's thesis. By then MacLean, Murphy, and Snider were all dead. Hundley's aim was to determine once and for all whether the wreckage was that of the *Griffon.* He concluded that the superstructure projected by Murphy from the actual remains had never existed; whereas the vessel's ascribed length and beam were approximately correct for the *Griffon* and compatible with Hennepin's account of the construction, the maximum draft was 3 feet 5 inches rather than 7 feet. Failing to find evidence of decking, Hundley concluded that the timbers in what Murphy renamed Griffon Cove (now in Fathom Five Park) were those of an open vessel. The hull lines he was able to develop suggested a variation of the Mackinaw boat, a type in popular use on the Great Lakes in the mid-1800s.[44]

Thus, *La Belle,* built at La Rochelle a few years later, remains, at this writing, the oldest French shipwreck in North American waters to be discovered and thoroughly investigated. Both wrecks, the *Griffon* and the *Belle,* say much about La Salle, his methods, and the reasons for his failures. The Russell Island wreck and the *Belle,* in contrast, speak volumes about the role of nautical archeology in preserving records of the past. Had the remains in Griffon Cove proved to be the *Griffon,* most of the information it might have provided would have been destroyed.

The news received from Barbier came as no great surprise to La Salle. As he went on his way toward Michilimackinac, his thoughts were on Tonti who, at best, remained in a precarious position at Fort Crèvecoeur. Leaving La Forest to come later, he paddled south on Lake Michigan to the ruined Fort Miami on Saint Joseph Bay. Thence he followed the established route, making the portage from the upper Saint Joseph to the Kankakee and thence to the Illinois River. There was a pleasant interlude during which the men, finding the plains aswarm with buffalo and other game, partook of a hunt to lay in a supply of meat to relieve the hunger of Tonti and his companions. Then came the scene of devastation and horror where once had stood the great Illinois town. In its place they saw an ashen landscape, whereon the only life was wolf packs and swarms of vultures, feasting on human corpses. Charred lodge poles, each with a human head spiked upon it, stood like ghostly sentinels, witnesses to the work of the Iroquois.

Among the death heads—separated from corpses that had been disinterred or cast down from their scaffolds—La Salle searched for one that might have been French. He took heart at not finding it. Seeing no indication of an actual battle, he "supposed that on hearing of the approach of the Iroquois, the old men and other noncombatants had fled and that the young warriors had remained behind to cover their flight, and afterwards followed, taking the French with them. . . ." The Iroquois, having found no living victims, he concluded, "vented their fury on the corpses in the graveyard."[45]

Descending the river, La Salle's Frenchmen observed that the Iroquois had pursued the Illinois Indians on the opposite bank. Their victims were women and children; the bodies of several Illinois women were still bound to torture stakes. Reaching Fort Crèvecoeur, the Frenchmen viewed the destruction the deserters had wrought on their own work. On the board side of what was to have been the ship to descend the Mississippi, someone had scrawled, "Nous sommes touts Sauvages. [We are all savages.] Ce 15 a[oust] 1680."[46] The framework of the ship still lay on the stocks, but the Iroquois, having learned the usefulness of iron, had pulled the nails and spikes. Still no sign of Tonti. La Salle's small band went down the Illinois to its mouth. There, at its confluence with the Mississippi, La Salle wrote a message to Tonti and secured it to a tree. Possibly understanding their leader's despondency on viewing the great water, his companions offered to go with him to the sea. But the time was not right. It was early December, and ice was forming on the river. La Salle had left three men guarding his stores at the Illinois village. And, above all, he must continue his search for Tonti.

Anyone but a person obsessed surely would have acknowledged defeat. "An obsession as intense as his," one interpreter has written, "was only a step from madness. . . ."[47] If adversity brings on insanity, La Salle surely stood at the edge.

Chapter 4

Seeds of Confusion

THE RIVER OF MYSTERY

At the close of 1680, La Salle counted a series of setbacks that might have driven any sane person to distraction. If not at the brink of madness, he surely succumbed to his paranoid tendencies. His letters refer so often to "my enemies" that a diagnosis of paranoia seems inescapable. His persecution was not imaginary. While suffering from his own bad judgment, La Salle was afflicted by the enmity of his commercial rivals, the venality of his creditors, and the jealousy of both the Jesuit fathers and the Sulpicians. These forces, in combination with his phenomenal run of bad luck, had succeeded in putting his most valiant efforts to naught. Not only would he have to make a new beginning, but he would have to come to terms, in one way or another, with the renewed hostility of the Iroquois: their intimidation of the Illinois and Mississippi valley tribes could not be allowed to continue if his dream of opening the great river to navigation was to succeed.

While La Salle was making his way back to Fort Crèvecoeur in the fall of 1680, Tonti, having been caught in the middle of the Iroquois-Illinois war, was withdrawing toward Green Bay. With him at the start were Fathers Membré and La Ribourde, François de Boisrondet, and Étienne Renault. They wandered through the wilderness, often lost and near starvation. Scarcely able to stand, they finally reached the Potawatomi at Green Bay—all but Father La Ribourde. The old missionary had been slain by Kickapoos when he went off alone to pray. The others, having walked barefoot on snow and ice, used his cloak to make shoes for themselves.

Boisrondet became lost and was given up for dead but used extraordinary ingenuity to survive. Without musketballs or gun flint, he made balls by melting his tin cup and fired his piece with a coal to kill turkeys.[1]

In mid-June, 1681, Tonti's small band was reunited with La Salle at Michilimackinac. La Salle had spent the winter at Fort Miami on the Saint Joseph, where, as Parkman says, "he might have brooded on the redoubled ruin that had befallen him. But . . . he had no thought but to grapple with adversity, and out of the fragments of his ruin to build up the fabric of success."[2] In the long term, however, success would be elusive. That which bore the gloss of triumph would tarnish into failure.

For the present, though, the need was clear: to weld the native groups opposed to the Iroquois into a defensive alliance for holding the aggressors in check. The move was vital to his aim of exploring the Mississippi and controlling the Mississippi valley fur trade by means of a warm-water port on the Gulf of Mexico. It would also serve to thwart his own enemies, who he claimed had agitated the Iroquois to obstruct his efforts. By the time he rejoined Tonti and Father Membré at Michilimackinac in June, 1681, he had convinced the various Illinois tribes—the Foxes, the Miami, and the Shawnee—to join the alliance.

La Salle was at his best in such an undertaking. Not since Cortés had the New World seen such skill employed to sway the natives. He proceeded "with his usual vigor, joined to an address which, when dealing with Indians, never failed him."[3] "Never" is a strong word; in the grim future, there would be exceptions.

From Michilimackinac La Salle returned to Fort Frontenac with Membré, Tonti, and his whole company, a thousand miles by bark canoe. He would have to assuage his creditors and consolidate his resources to build anew. The pressures on him mounted when he learned that the intendant Jacques Duchesneau had written to Colbert the previous autumn with allegations against him. Under pretext of making discoveries, claimed the intendant, La Salle himself had traded or sent others to trade among the Ottawa in violation of his royal restrictions. The king, in turn, complained to Frontenac that he had seen little evidence of La Salle's progress toward discovering the western country; he should be warned that issuing licenses for trading among the natives exceeded the intent of his patent. In the face of all his encumbrances, Membré opined, "Anyone but [La Salle] would have abandoned the enterprise; but . . . by a firmness of mind and an almost unequaled constancy, I saw him more resolute than ever to continue his work and to carry out his discovery."[4]

Strong resolution, indeed, was required. La Salle already had sacrificed most of the benefits of any discovery he might make to his financial backers, some of whom were little better than loan sharks. Even his cousin François Plet, of whom La Salle always spoke with the highest regard, employed a shrewdness that the explorer, in his preoccupation, seemed scarcely to grasp. Plet's willing support in 1678 had come at the price of forty percent interest.[5] In 1680, with La Salle in arrears, Plet had voyaged to Canada expressly to seek payment. Arriving at Fort Frontenac in September, he found that La Salle had left the previous month "to continue his discoveries in the Illinois country and on the southern coast." He found the post in deplorable condition, lacking both supplies and trade goods; for want of proper management, it was in a downward spiral. François de La Forest, the commandant, was absent, having returned with La Salle to the Illinois country to assist him in forming the native alliance. The interests of all La Salle's other creditors also were suffering. If the natives failed to find the goods they needed at Fort Frontenac, Plet deposed to Duchesneau, they would take their pelts to the English or the Dutch, to the detriment of the French colony and interests of the crown. As a remedy, he asked authority to build a barque to service Fort Frontenac's trade around Lake Ontario and to stock the post with merchandise. Profits from the enterprise should be applied to what La Salle owed him. All the furs that came to Fort Frontenac would be delivered to Plet's agent in Montreal and credited to La Salle's account. Duchesneau, who never passed up an opportunity to hamstring La Salle, approved the plan on October 31, 1680, while La Salle was on his way back to Fort Crèvecoeur.[6]

La Salle had to confront this development when he returned to Fort Frontenac and Montreal in the summer of 1681. Plet was still in Canada but decided not to remain after hearing La Salle's plan to lease the post to La Forest for the coming year. It was Plet or his agent who again made it possible for La Salle to renew his plan of exploring the Mississippi to the Gulf of Mexico. Yet, if Plet's actions at this point seemed beneficent, there was more to consider. The Paris merchant meant to be paid. La Salle, to guarantee Plet's continued financial support, found it necessary to make this "cousin who had befriended him" the beneficiary of his will:

> . . . In view of the great dangers and continuous perils where the voyages that I make will take me, and wishing to recognize the great obligation that I have to M. François Plet, my cousin, for the signal service that he has rendered me, and because it is with his assistance that

I have preserved Fort Frontenac against the efforts that have been made to ruin me, I give, yield, and transfer to the said sieur Plet, in case of [my] death, the seigneury, proprietorship of Fort Frontenac and [its] lands and dependencies; all my rights to the land of the Miamis, Illinois and others of the south coast, with the Miamis' settlement in the state that it may be at the time of my death; that of Niagara, and all others that I may have made, with all the barques, *bateaux,* shallops, furnishings and real estate, rights privileges, rents, lands, buildings and other things of my appurtenance. . . .[7]

Plet, however, was not willing to wait for La Salle's death for repayment of his loans. Fort Frontenac's business affairs, with La Forest in full charge, did not go to his liking. With La Salle not having returned from his exploration, in July, 1682, Plet took further action to assure himself the proceeds of the post's fur trade. Through Lucien Boutteville, who held his power of attorney, he again petitioned Duchesneau and again found the intendant a willing accomplice.

Boutteville alleged that the amount owed Plet, with construction of the barque and stocking of the post with trade goods, had risen to almost 50,000 livres. This aid notwithstanding, he claimed, La Forest was circumventing the previous order by doing business with another supplier, to whom he was taking all the furs received at the post. In consequence, Duchesneau strengthened his initial decree by ordering that no merchant or anyone else should supply trade goods to Fort Frontenac. Income accrued by La Forest or anyone who might succeed him in command was to be sequestered until Plet's claim had been satisfied.[8]

To that end, Duchesneau assigned to the post a clerk, who was to see that the prohibition against trading beyond the Lake Ontario environs was abided by. Plet's agent in Montreal was to receive all the furs that passed through Fort Frontenac. After his claim was paid, it was suggested, the post's trading barque should be given over to La Salle's other creditors, the trade applied to their benefit.[9]

The significance of this affair goes well beyond the deprivation of either La Salle's future credit or his present income. In reality, it portended the explorer's loss of all potential monetary benefit from his enterprises. His future successes, however grand, were pledged to pay for his past failures. Even a post controlling the mouth of the Mississippi would have been but the means of satisfying his creditors, who held him firmly in their grip. In fairness, it was they who had risked their capital to make his ventures possible; but it was La Salle who had gambled life and limb — and sanity — to become their pawn. Still, he plunged doggedly ahead.

He had long since given up his plan of building a barque to descend the Mississippi. With the clock ticking on the five years the king had allowed him to fulfill the terms of his concession, he would have to make the voyage in bark canoes. As he wrestled with his past-due obligations, he saw his hopes dim for an early start: "We had determined to make the voyage to the sea this fall, but the trip to Montreal has delayed me so much that I don't know whether we can. I realize also that it would not allow me to send to M. Plet all that I have promised him." His concern for dealing fairly with Plet endured, despite the fact that Plet had not always dealt fairly with him. He complained that his cousin had sent him "some wretched friese," calling it Iroquois cloth, "which it does not resemble in the least." The cheap material had to be used for making overcoats or hoods for the want of something better.[10] Presumably, it was Plet's agent in Montreal who had outfitted him once again — and sold him defective equipment. Included were a faulty astrolabe and a flimsy compass that played a large part in putting askew his geographical perceptions.

The season was late, but La Salle had nevertheless started toward the Illinois country, intending to begin his descent of the Mississippi at the earliest possible time. He wrote during a fifteen-day stop while his effects were being portaged from the Huber River to Lake Simco. After following this shorter route to Lake Huron, his entourage continued through Mackinac Strait into Lake Michigan and southward to Fort Miami. He arrived at the latter place on December 16, 1681, to complete preparations for proceeding to the Mississippi. From the "thirty good Frenchmen" and more than a hundred natives from New England tribes, he chose his companions for the journey. Twenty-three Frenchmen made the cut. There were eighteen Mohegan ("Loups") and Abnaki Indian men, who insisted on taking ten of their women as cooks, three of them with infants or small children: a total of fifty-four persons. (The number would be increased along the way by a few Indian slaves acquired at the Quapaw and Taensa villages.) Among the Frenchmen were men whom La Salle felt he could count on in every situation. Besides Tonti (brigade captain) and the chaplain Membré, the Frenchmen included François de Boisrondet; Jacques de Bourdon, sieur d'Autray; Jacques de La Métairie, the notary; Jean Michel, surgeon; and two men who had once defected but since had given proof of their constancy: André Hénault and Gabriel Barbier. There was also Colin Crevel de Moranget, the explorer's nephew, and Nicolas de La

Salle, who was no relation but who was to contribute an account of the expedition.[11]

While La Salle waited for the last of his men to arrive, Tonti took one group, including Membré, and went ahead. Instead of ascending the Saint Joseph River, they crossed the southern end of Lake Michigan to the mouth of the Chicago River. La Salle and the others, following the same route, joined them on January 4, according to Membré; January 14, by Tonti's account.[12]

Finding the Chicago frozen, Tonti had made sleds to transport the six canoes to the Illinois River before La Salle arrived. This strange procession along the frozen rivers was to spark the imagination of artist George Catlin in the 1840s. For sixty leagues the men dragged the sleds down the frozen Illinois past the deserted native villages to Fort Crèvecoeur.[13] The post was also deserted and would remain so. The small ship begun there almost two years previously still lay on its stocks, unfinished. Just as La Salle had given up his idea of building a barque for exploring the Mississippi, he would have to postpone building an entrepôt on the Illinois.

Below Fort Crèvecoeur, the ice had yielded and the Illinois was navigable. The Indians, having broken up their canoes on Lake Michigan to avoid pulling them, occasioned a layover while they built new ones. On February 6, the entourage reached the Mississippi, which La Salle had named *le fleuve* Colbert. The larger river still carried ice floes that endangered the bark canoes. Not until the thirteenth were the voyagers able to proceed.[14]

If "standard" interpretations are correct, the confluence of the Illinois River with the Mississippi marked La Salle's farthest previous penetration in this direction. Thus, it was at the very outset of his "new discovery" that he was launched on a confused course that ultimately would rob his enterprise of success. His only compass broke. "During the whole voyage," says Minet, apparently quoting directly from one of his firsthand sources, "we oriented ourselves with the sun." But often no sun was to be seen, for it was frequently hidden by clouds or fog. Furthermore, the latitudes obtained with the seven-inch astrolabe that La Salle had obtained in Montreal were grossly in error throughout the journey. From his sun shot at the mouth of the Illinois, he computed 37°N, about two degrees short.[15]

The Illinois entered the Mississippi, or Colbert, from the west. Leaving this confluence on February 13, the Frenchmen followed the larger stream on an east-southeast course until, after six leagues, it received the mud-laden torrent of the Missouri. From that point the river inclined southwest, then southeast, relatively meander-free until just before it was joined by the Ohio. Thenceforth, it ran a serpentine course that would have been confusing, even with a clear sky and an accurate compass.

With no provisions but Indian corn, the explorers advanced slowly, hunting and fishing for food. One day after leaving the Illinois, they passed on the east bank, near present-day Saint Louis, the village of the Tamaroa, an Illinois tribe. Its occupants were away hunting. The voyagers left a friendly sign.

From Tamaroa, it was forty leagues to the Ohio, the river that La Salle once had believed would lead him to the Pacific Ocean and the Orient. His alleged exploration of 1669 notwithstanding, he now seemed confused as to its identity. Membré called it the Oüabache. Nicolas de La Salle thought it "the Rivière de Saint-Louis or Ouabache, also called the Chucagoua." Tonti noted that to the Iroquois it was the "Oyo."[16]

La Salle had brought forth the name Chucagua (Chucagoa, Chucagoua) from Pierre Richelet's French translation of Garcilaso de la Vega. Richelet's work, a condensation of Vega's account of the Hernando de Soto expedition, 1539–43, was first published in 1670. The name Chucagua is attributed to Vega's informant Juan Coles. Vega himself identifies it as Soto's *río grande,* or the Mississippi. La Salle, in contemplating the Chucagua and Vega's descriptions of it, ultimately concluded that his *fleuve* Colbert was entirely different from Soto's river.[17]

After passing the Ohio, the voyagers found the river full of twists and turns. Wind and rain, with clouds obscuring the sun, contributed to their disorientation as they found the stream divided by three islands formed by cut-off meanders.

Pressed by hunger, the voyagers paused near the Chickasaw Bluffs for a hunt. The gunsmith Pierre Prudhomme became lost. Barbier, out looking for him, encountered two natives and employed a ruse to capture them. As they started to flee, he laid his gun on the ground and made a peace sign. When the Chickasaw came near, he drew a pistol from behind his back. Although La Salle later set the Indians free, one chose to remain with the Frenchmen.[18]

While searching for the gunsmith and hunting for food, La Salle had an entrenchment made. He gave it the name Fort Prudhomme, for the man who by now was believed either captured or killed by the natives. The expedition was preparing to leave without him when Prudhomme, near starvation, came floating down the river on a raft of driftwood.

On March 18 the explorers continued their descent in thick fog until they heard drums and war whoops in the distance. The young Chickasaw informed them that the sounds came from the Acancea (Arkansas). This, the first and largest of four Arkansas villages, that of the Kappa or Quapaw, was near the turning point of Jolliet and Marquette on their exploration of 1673.

The Frenchmen withdrew to a small island near the left bank and, within an hour, threw up a redoubt against a possible attack. The tension resolved itself when, with the help of an Illinois slave, the natives were assured that the visitors were friendly. The Frenchmen remained three days among this hospitable people, with feasting and elaborate ceremony. Gifts were exchanged, and La Salle received two slaves, a young Mozopelea and a Chickasaw woman, whose subsequent fate is not revealed.[19]

Here, on March 14, 1682, with the notary Jacques de La Métairie recording the proceedings, La Salle took possession of "the country of Louisiana and all its lands, provinces, peoples, nations, mines, ports, harbors, seas," the Ohio and Mississippi Rivers and all their tributaries, and the intervening land as far as the River of Palms (the Soto La Marina River of Mexico). Through the Illinois interpreter, La Salle explained to the Quapaw that they were now subjects of, and under the protection of, the "prince of the world," Louis XIV, who had sent him. A column bearing a cross and the arms of France was erected, with an inscription proclaiming the reign of Louis le Grand. Father Membré chanted the *Exaudit te Dominus,* followed by shouts of "Vive le Roi!" and the firing of three volleys.[20] The ceremony held later near the Mississippi's multiple mouths is often deemed the more important. Yet the act of March 13–14, 1682, among the Arkansas represents the first French claim to this wide territorial expanse. Based on consummate geographical ignorance, it spanned what was to become known as the Louisiana Territory, as well as northern Mexico and Spanish-claimed Texas.

With two guides from the Quapaw, the Frenchmen proceeded past the second Arkansas village, then the third, at the mouth of the Arkansas River. (The fourth lay five leagues up the Arkansas.) Coming to the Yazoo delta, where several branches of the Yazoo River entered the Mississippi, the explorers perceived the latter as being divided by islands into three channels. Beyond this maze, they passed up the village of the Tunica because they were enemies of the Arkansas. Thence, the Mississippi wound about so much that in more than thirty miles, there was little forward progress.[21]

As the canoes descended the river to the sea, a combination of factors contributed to La Salle's confusion. Gross error still marked his efforts to obtain the latitude with the faulty astrolabe. He failed to perceive the inaccuracy. When on March 20 he computed a latitude of 31°N near the Taensa villages—more than a degree short—he began to realize that something was amiss. There was no sign of the Bahía del Espíritu Santo, which, according to his maps, he should have encountered a degree farther north. This, says Tonti, "caused him to believe that we were on the Abscondido [Escondido] River, which was later found to be correct." The stream course, La Salle believed, had carried his canoes beyond the mountain range shown on numerous maps dating from the previous century.[22]

In his growing confusion, La Salle found no clue to set him straight. The explorers visited among the Natchez and Koroa Indians on March 26 and 27 and shortly camped at the mouth of the Red River. They then drifted southward in heavy rain, on flood waters pouring out of the Red. Beneath leaden skies, the Mississippi still pursued its convoluted course, its tortuous meanders causing disorientation in the leader as well as his followers. Nicolas de La Salle and Barbier, afterward recounting the voyage to Minet, recalled a strange phenomenon: "[They] told me [says Minet] that in descending the river they almost always saw the sun set in front of them."[23] Yet their general course was south or southeast.

But then the clouds lifted, the river straightened, and their sense of direction was restored. The country began to change. The voyagers entered the water-logged deltaic marsh, with only the tops of reeds and grass visible above the flooded plain. Only the natural levees formed by river-borne alluvium separated the stream from these seemingly endless lagoons. For sleeping at night, the men made piles of cane on the sodden levee.

The mornings were shrouded in fog that floated in from northeast. La Salle believed the mist came from the mythical Bahía del Espíritu Santo. Having failed to find this bay where the maps placed it, he judged it to lie in the direction whence the fog came. The stream for many miles flowed east, then southeast, and finally east again.[24] Hence La Salle's conclusion that the river he was following, which he called the *fleuve* Colbert, was entirely distinct from the Río del Espíritu Santo, Chucagua, or Soto's *río grande*.

Having frightened away some Indian fishermen on their right, the canoemen espied a native village on the left, where there was considerable activity. Approaching, they saw that the crowds were not of people but of vultures and other scavengers, feasting on the corpses of men, women, and children of the Tangipahoa, on blood-soaked ground among the broken ruins of their huts and canoes. The next day the Frenchmen took two kinds of meat from a native canoe whose occupants they had frightened away. Part of it was identified as caiman (alligator). After tasting the other, they concluded that it was human flesh.[25]

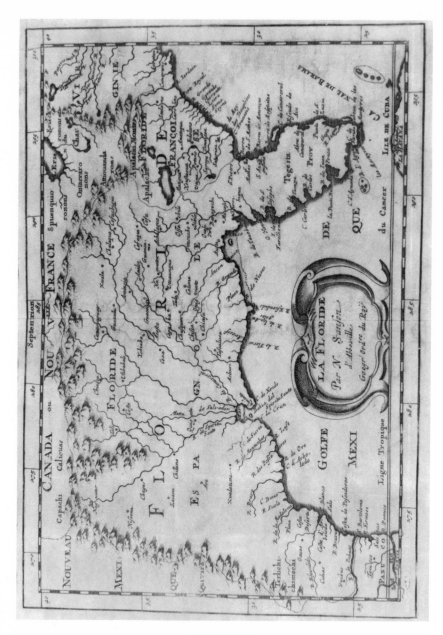

FIGURE 10

Before the Discovery. Nicolas de Sanson's map La Floride *gives his concept of the Río del Espíritu Santo (Mississippi River). Three other major streams are shown entering the Gulf of Mexico through the Bahía del Espíritu Santo, with the rivers called Magdalena and Escondido entering the Gulf from the west. Courtesy Special Collections Division, The University of Texas at Arlington Libraries*

On April 6, 1682, the canoemen found the river dividing into three channels. La Salle himself later declared that all the river's mouths are to the east-southeast and not to the south: an observation crucial to an understanding of his perception.[26] Unable to conceptualize the delta, he envisioned a continuous land mass to the west as well as the south, with his river issuing out of it to the east. A less hasty reconnaissance would have revealed his error, but there was not time for thorough exploration: food was running out.

The three channels were explored in scarcely more than two days. On April 7, La Salle, descending the right-hand branch with six canoemen, found it confined by natural levees of mud extending "six leagues" into the sea. Tonti, probing the channel on the left, found that it ended seven leagues from the forks in an alligator-infested "lake or sea." Tonti describes the water as fresh, Membré as brackish at first, turning to "pure salt" after two leagues.[27]

Between the three channels, it was written later in one of La Salle's memorials to the minister Seignelay, were bays three to four leagues by five or six. At flood tide, they were five or six feet deep, but they were drained at the ebb; the men walked about the mud flat shooting marsh birds. By the time of this writing, however, La Salle's reports were being either composed or edited by Abbé Renaudot or one of his employees, with the Renaudot faction's own objectives in mind. In this as in other instances, the truth was slanted accordingly. All the passes, it was said, were "fine, deep, and capable of admitting large vessels"—certainly a questionable description in view of the driftwood and mud lumps that choked the mouth a few years later.[28] The character of the passes, greatly altered since La Salle's day, has always been subject to change from season to season, especially with floods.

La Salle's concept of the river mouth, as it can be understood from the tampered documents, would not have made it easy to recognize later from the sea, even if he had looked in the right place. At certain seasons he might have seen similar features in other estuaries along the Gulf shore, which were remarkable for their sameness; at this same river mouth at a different time, he might have failed to recognize any landmark.

Withdrawing to a spot of dry land on the right bank three leagues above the forks, La Salle conducted the ceremony by which he claimed for the Sun King "possession of this country of Louisiana." His declaration embraced "the seas, harbors, ports, bays, adjacent straits, and all the nations, peoples, provinces, cities, towns, villages, mines, minerals, fisheries, streams, and rivers" from the Mississippi's source to the Gulf of Mexico and all the rivers that emptied into it, as far as the River of Palms. A cross and a copper plaque made from a kettle and engraved with appropriate Latin wording and three fleurs-de-lis were mounted on a column hewn from a tree trunk. A lead plaque engraved with the arms of Louis XIV was buried at the foot. The *Te Deum* was sung, a salute was fired, and all the men shouted in chorus, "Vive le Roi!"[29] It was the first formal territorial claim yet made on the Gulf coast by Europeans other than Spaniards.

Want of provisions hastened the journey back upriver, begun on April 10. The voyagers camped on the second evening at the ruined Tangipahoa village and learned from neighboring Quinipissa that it had been victimized by the Houma and the Chickasaw. They were then attacked before daybreak by the Quinipissa. Crevel de Moranget, as sentinel, alerted the camp when he heard the breaking of reeds on the Indians' approach. The Frenchmen killed at least two of them and cut off their heads. "We lifted their scalps and we mounted the heads on some posts, the faces turned in the direction of their villages [Minet records]. The Loups opened the two bodies, which they found fat and appetizing. . . . They took out the hearts to dry to show that they had killed some men." The incident very nearly brought the wrath of the Koroa down upon the voyagers.[30]

Pausing again at the Taensa villages, "sixty leagues" from the Gulf, La Salle chose the intended site of his future colony. The voyagers feasted on dog with the Quapaw. Proceeding thence upriver, the leader contracted a strange malady, described as "mortal." He sent for the surgeon, Jean Michel, to bleed him. Delirious much of the time, La Salle remained ill at Fort Prudhomme (Chickasaw Bluffs) in the care of Michel and Father Membré while Tonti went ahead with five men to Michilimackinac. The explorer, ill for forty days, remained enfeebled and with impaired concentration for four months. In mid-June he proceeded upriver with the rest of the men.[31] He rejoined Tonti at Michilimackinac the following September.

The nature of this illness, though the subject of much conjecture, cannot be precisely known. There had been previous illnesses of similar duration; most notably, upon his return to Canada from France in 1678.

As for the present instance—occurring at age thirty-eight—a stroke, malaria, and manic depression (bipolar disorder) have all been suggested, any one of which could have produced delirium. The symptoms were to recur several times during the remainder of La Salle's life. Any of the suggested afflictions might follow such a pattern, though the odds are against his having so many strokes without a fatal one. His affliction seemed to reappear under challenging circumstances when uncertainty and doubt took hold of him. Throughout his career, La Salle vacillated, emotionally, from the peaks to the valleys. Thenceforth it would be more so. Were his illnesses the cause of his altered behavior or the result? Had some change occurred within the man that transformed him? Or were his periodic illnesses a natural outgrowth of manic-depressive tendencies, which, though latent at times, had been present all along?

In any case, each instance was severely enervating, requiring weeks for recovery. It was in this debilitated state that La Salle began his effort to sort his thoughts concerning his Mississippi discovery and to reconcile his observations with established concepts. The record of his confused cerebration is the aforementioned "Chucagua fragment," a letter in La Salle's own hand but without beginning or ending, hence without date.

Whether the fragment represents a true reflection of the explorer's mental processes following his discovery has been the subject of vigorous debate. That La Salle actually is the author scarcely seems open to question. Yet obfuscation arises from knowledge of the role played by the two conniving abbots, Bernou and Renaudot, in writing La Salle's memorials and diverting him onto a course that fit their own designs. The date and the circumstances under which this piece was written, if known, would certainly have a bearing on how it should be regarded. Without that information, we are left with a dilemma: Was La Salle influenced by Bernou to proclaim his river "near Mexico"—or did his identification of the Mississippi with the Escondido spark the plan in Bernou's mind?[32]

There are, however, ample reasons for believing that La Salle was genuinely confused. On the fringes of geographical knowledge, he had no prior accounts to aid his understanding. The Soto chronicles served only to compound his confusion. It is reasonable to believe that he expected the river to bear some resemblance to the maps at his disposal. His exploration revealed nothing that fit the map portrayal. Mapmakers of the period, seldom hesitant to hypothesize, based their river courses on ill-founded tradition or pulled them from thin air.

Whatever maps La Salle consulted, as Wood has noted, had these features in common: the northern Gulf coast running east-west at about 30° north latitude, with no indication of the Mississippi delta; the legendary Espíritu Santo Bay, extending inland a full degree, with the shoreline west of the bay inclining southwest; and the Río Escondido entering the Gulf from the west or northwest between 28° and 29°.[33]

There was, in fact, no map representation of the Mississippi delta yet in existence; there would be none for another fifteen years. La Salle found a river course entirely different from any of the maps. He surely was puzzled by the absence of the legendary Espíritu Santo Bay. Some of the reasons he gives for believing that he had followed a different river, apart from the Chucagua mentioned by Vega, are cogent; others, less so. He claims to have found no Indian groups by the names that Soto's followers had given them, and the natives along the Colbert now were far less numerous; his river, though "subject to continuous floods," was not as wide as the Spaniards had described it, being "hardly larger than the Loire where it falls into the sea." In two Indian villages along the river, he claims to have found a Spanish coat of mail, some muskets, and daggers; the natives told of having seen "bearded men like us" who lived to the southwest. "If all the maps are not worthless," he concluded, "the mouth of the *fleuve* Colbert is near Mexico." Its mouths, by La Salle's observation, were east-southeast and not south like all the other rivers on the south coast of Florida. The only exception was the one the maps called Escondido. Hence, "this Escondido is assuredly the Mississippi."[34]

The Río Escondido ("Hidden River") that attracted La Salle's attention first appeared on an unsigned Spanish map dated 1527. Most probably, it was the work of Diego Ribero, who the previous year had begun working on the Spaniards' master chart of discoveries in Seville. The Escondido, situated in the Texas coastal bend about where the Nueces is today, continued to appear on maps of several nations at least until the latter part of the seventeenth century.[35]

The explorer's identification of his river with the Escondido was music to the ears of Abbé Bernou, who was to write the "official report" of the Mississippi discovery. (Indeed, if La Salle's confusion were less plausible, one might be tempted to believe that the abbé had planted the whole idea.) Bernou had long dreamed of a French conquest of Mexico. He had aspirations of becoming a bishop, and his best chance lay in the acquisition of a new overseas territory that would necessitate creation of a new diocese. His hopes were raised that La Salle might be the one to provide it.[36]

Had La Salle owned the capability of computing longitude from celestial observation, he would have been able to distinguish between the Mississippi and the Escondido. There was simply no way for him to determine at what point on the east-west coast he had arrived. Essentially, longitude could be determined in this period only by guesswork or by ground tracking.[37] The Mississippi's convoluted course rendered both methods impossible. Before leaving Fort Frontenac the previous year, La Salle had written that the Mississippi was 500 leagues or 24° of longitude from Quebec, but even that was five degrees off.[38] The means of calculating east-west distance by celestial observation was almost a century in the future. La Salle, therefore, could compare only the features he had observed with those appearing on available maps.

Ultimately, imprecise latitude computations—with the seven-inch astrolabe that gave nothing but erroneous readings, according to Minet—played an equally important role. From a sighting of the pole star three leagues above the forks, La Salle placed the latitude at the river mouth in "about" 27°—at least two degrees or sixty nautical miles too far south.[39] Uncertain himself, he discussed the location only in vague terms.

The observations recorded in the Tonti and Membré accounts attest the confusion over the discrepancies. Each states that the Baye-du-Saint-Esprit (Espíritu Santo Bay) lay northeast of the river mouth. Tonti testifies that La Salle "believed that he was eighty leagues from the Santa Barbara mountains [in the present Mexican state of Chihuahua]. He kept to himself the latitude of the mouth." Membré confirms that La Salle "kept to himself the exact point [but] we have learned that the river falls into the Gulf of Mexico between 27° and 28° north, and, as is thought, at the point where maps lay down the Rio Escondido."[40] The trail of deceit goes on. Was it contrived by La Salle or by the Renaudot-Bernou *confrérie*? At some later date, the latitude of La Salle's river mouth was altered to approximate that of the Río Escondido: 28°20' N.[41]

La Salle's discovery of the Mississippi led him directly to the Texas coastal bend, not by navigational error but simply by a geographical misconception that spelled opportunity for his manipulators. He had succeeded in descending the Mississippi to its mouth. In understanding it, he had failed miserably. "Subsequent generations of interpreters," as Wood notes, have "managed to compound the confusion."[42] At the roots of the confusion were the scheming abbés, Bernou and Renaudot.

Legion are those who have written with a regional orientation or actual bias; while stressing La Salle's exploration (or commercial operation) around the Great Lakes or in the Illinois and Mississippi basins, they have given short shrift to the Gulf expedition and the Texas colony. Even among those directly concerned with this latter episode, much confusion surrounds the reasons for La Salle's failure to find the Mississippi's mouth from the Gulf. The relevance of the Chucagua fragment to that question has been elusive. Parkman apparently never knew it existed, but in that he is not alone. Compilers and editors of documents have written their introductions without being able to assess the reasons for La Salle's geographical confusion.

The source of bewilderment for others has been a constricted focus, wherein concern for proving a minor ancillary point obscured consideration of the broader question. Apart from those who have surveyed La Salle's career without getting seriously involved with the Gulf of Mexico expedition, two outstanding examples come to mind.

In 1910 J. F. Steward translated the Chucagoa fragment from what the Jesuit scholar Jean Delanglez calls "the defective Margry text" and included it in his "La Salle a Victim of His Error in Longitude." His focus on the longitude question, however, clouded his perception of the document's real significance. In 1940 Delanglez himself wrote of the fragment: ". . . in it he [La Salle] merely comments on the narrative of the De Soto expedition as written by Garcilaso de la Vega, comparing what he himself had seen with the fanciful description by the Inca of what purported to be the Mississippi."[43]

Five years later, Delanglez was more perceptive concerning the fragment and its importance: "Besides explicitly identifying the Mississippi with the Rio Escondido the [cited] passage helps to explain his [La Salle's] fundamental misconception of the geography of the Gulf, a misconception which was to have such fatal consequences a few years later." Delanglez's singular purpose, however, was to prove that the Río del Espíritu Santo shown on maps since 1519 was not the same as the Mississippi: ". . . no one in either America or Europe made this identification." In that he errs.[44]

As Wood has proclaimed, "An elaborate but flawed representation of [La Salle] and his colonizing plan has gradually taken hold over the years. . . . From the start, intrigue and uncertainty affected the record of [his] expeditions."[45] The effort to set the record straight has gained new impetus from the "window to the past" presented by the discovery of La Salle's lost ship *La Belle*.

2

A NEW DIRECTION

Chapter 5

The Pawn Game

IN THE HANDS OF THE SCHEMERS

While La Salle recuperated at Fort Prudhomme, Tonti proceeded from the Mississippi to Fort Miami and Michilimackinac. A little more than a week after Tonti's departure, La Salle, though still seriously ill, started up the river again with the rest of his company, a journey recounted briefly by Nicolas de La Salle and elaborated upon in his interviews with Minet. They reached the Tamaroa in fifteen days, the mouth of the Illinois River in two more, and the ruined site of Fort Crèvecoeur in another thirteen. Both the fort and the little ship begun there for descending the Mississippi lay in ashes, burned by natives since last seen. After leaving eight Frenchmen at Crèvecoeur, the explorers arrived at the Illinois village on July 15 and found it abandoned. Thence, La Salle went by land to the Miamis and from there to join Tonti at Michilimackinac in September.[1]

When his health permitted, La Salle intended going to France to report on his discovery to the Royal Court. He forthwith sent Tonti back to the Illinois portage to build a fort for the security of the Shawnee he had settled near the Miami. His recovery, however, was slow, and events conspired to thwart the plan.[2]

La Salle, meanwhile, confronted the challenge of understanding and articulating his discovery while attempting to plot a future course. In the latter task, he faced new complications. Frontenac, who as governor-general of New France had favored La Salle's enterprises, had been recalled. In his place the king sent Joseph-Antoine Le Febvre de La Barre, who, supposedly to correct Frontenac's abuses, allied himself with the opposing clique. He focused his avarice on La Salle and his trade monopolies. There was also a new intendant, Jacques de Meulles, to succeed Duchesneau. Each of the new officials came with royal orders that had to do with La Salle's discoveries and whether they were of value. Thus, new problems compounded old ones.

In early October, after Tonti's departure from Michilimackinac, La Salle devoted himself to correspondence. Uncertain of La Barre's stance, he wrote to him with candor, if not naivete, to inform him of his patent from the king, the success of his discovery, and the illness that had detained him. Having heard that La Barre planned to remove La Forest from command at Fort Frontenac, La Salle asked that his appointee be allowed to remain until the following June; he himself would return then and name a successor to the governor's liking. Otherwise, he feared the post would be in danger from the Iroquois. Also fearing an Iroquois move against the fort at the Illinois portage, which he had sent Tonti to rebuild, he asked the governor to provide arms and ammunition to withstand an attack.[3]

The letter triggered La Barre's hasty reaction. Already determined to turn La Salle's every word and deed against him, the new governor saw his opportunity in the Iroquois problem. Heedless that La Salle had been a stabilizing influence in relations with the Five Nations—always volatile at best—La Barre would blame him for all their aggressions and suspicious moves. But his first ploy, suggested by the king himself, was to disavow La Salle's discovery.

The royal instructions to both La Barre and Meulles had expressed doubt that explorations toward the Mississippi and the Sioux were of value: better that the colonists devote themselves to cultivating the land than seeking new sources of peltries. The monarch's time-honored ambivalence toward exploration had surfaced again; even though La Salle should be allowed to carry out his Mississippi reconnaissance, he wrote, La Barre was to grant no more licenses for such expeditions. Meulles, in the meantime, would determine whether La Salle's discovery was of value and report his findings to La Barre.[4]

If the new governor had not come with his mind made up, he lost no time in forming a judgment. He had learned through Tonti, he wrote to Colbert in November, that La Salle had discovered the mouth of the Mississippi. La Salle himself, being ill, had not reported. But, wrote La Barre, "I don't make much of this discovery, until better informed, because it is surely the River Spiritu Santo, in the Gulf of Mexico, at 21 degrees latitude." Instead of making discoveries, he declared, the colony would be better served to apply its energies to "preventing the English from ruining our commerce and on subduing the Iroquois." The governor wrote hurriedly to Colbert two days later to catch the ships already making sail for France: Father Membré had arrived with dispatches to inform the minister on La Salle's voyage. Although Membré surely had brought La Salle's October 5 letter to La Barre, the governor complained that he himself had been given no clue to the contents of the report to Colbert. The explorer's secrecy, which, it was noted, others also disdained, filled La Barre with resentment. This, he wrote, "obliges me to . . . inform you of the concern I have over the sieur de La Salle's conduct." Instead of coming to Quebec, the explorer had reacted to a rumored Iroquois offensive by going back to the Miamis, there to make a stand with twenty-five men at his fort. La Barre postulated an all-out Iroquois war would result from La Salle's "imprudence." La Salle's exploration, shrouded in falsehoods, he pursued, had little value, while the man carried out his private schemes that he chose not to reveal.[5]

La Salle, indeed, had delayed his voyage to France, partly out of concern for the restlessness of the Iroquois but also because of his enfeebled condition. He felt the urgency of consolidating his alliances with the Illinois tribes and their neighbors with a new fort on the Illinois River as a focal point; thus the Iroquois could be held in check. Before starting on his journey, he composed a letter to "a friend," which Membré carried to Quebec and thence to France on the same ship that took La Barre's scurrilous missives. Also on board was the retiring governor Frontenac, who took the *procès verbal* of the Mississippi voyage to Colbert. The "friend" to whom La Salle wrote undoubtedly was Abbé Claude Bernou, his "agent" since shortly after their first meeting in 1678. This mystifying letter, supposedly reflecting La Salle's candid view of his discovery and his future plans, raises many questions, in view of the strange mix of ideas being tossed about. Were these La Salle's own thoughts or those of Bernou, who was putting forth similar notions on behalf of the renegade former governor of Spanish New Mexico calling himself the Count of Peñalosa?[6]

Tonti, meanwhile, had begun laying the groundwork toward La Salle's objectives. Arriving at the Illinois portage, he found the Shawnees had gone hunting, the Miamis ready to take flight before the rumored Iroquois incursion, and the Frenchmen already "dispersed." With the few men he had, he proceeded to the Illinois River. Thinking La Salle had gone to France,

Tonti was surprised when his commander arrived at his encampment on December 30, 1682. "During the winter," Tonti relates, "we built Fort-Saint-Louis upon an inaccessible rocky height [Starved Rock], and M. de La Salle brought the Chaouanons [Shawnee] there." Then came the Miamis and the Illinois. The following March (1683) Tonti journeyed "a hundred leagues" across the prairies, forming various other tribal groups into an alliance to withstand the Iroquois.[7]

The fort completed, La Salle left Tonti in command and departed on August 23 to go to France, accompanied by two Shawnees, Nicolas de La Salle, Barbier, and the man called L'Espérance. Early in the journey, they met Chevalier Louis-Henri de Baugis, a lieutenant in La Barre's guard, with several men in canoes. Baugis carried the governor's summons for La Salle to come to Quebec and report on his discovery. Baugis also had La Barre's authority, flimsy as it was, to assume command of Fort-Saint-Louis of the Illinois and seize the goods there. La Salle gave Baugis a letter to Tonti, charging the commandant to receive him with good graces and to live with him "on the best of terms"—a matter that Tonti found most trying.[8]

A man called Vital, who had come with Baugis, returned to Quebec with La Salle. Says Minet, "[Vital] lent [La Salle] 200 pistoles after he had recounted all the discovery" and what he planned to do in France. Apparently Vital failed to get as much information as he desired, for La Barre sent him to France in the same fleet as La Salle to keep tab on developments.[9]

La Barre, besides his move on the Illinois post, sent Aubert de La Chesnaye and Jacques Le Ber to seize Fort Frontenac. La Forest, who commanded there, returned to France rather than serve the new regime. In May, 1684, La Barre ordered Tonti to leave Fort-Saint-Louis and come to Quebec. By that time, however, La Salle had arrived in France and played a trump card of his own.

La Salle, it has been said, "was more or less hustled out of Canada by the governor."[10] If so, it was a foolish move on the governor's part, for La Salle's first concern on reaching France was to lobby the court for a reversal of La Barre's usurpation. The explorer and his companions sailed from Quebec in mid-November, 1683, aboard the *Saint-Honoré*. On the same voyage, "in all probability," Delanglez claims, was Pierre Le Moyne d'Iberville, the future founder of the Louisiana colony, who carried La Barre's dispatches; Pierre Esprit de Radisson, famous voyageur and discoverer, noted also for his confused loyalties; and Jean-Baptiste-Louis Franquelin, the vaunted hydrographer and mapmaker.[11]

Franquelin, having been in Canada for twelve years, had lived in obscurity and virtual poverty until he came to La Barre's attention. La Barre recommended him to the Marquis de Seignelay, Colbert's son who, upon his father's death in September, 1683, had succeeded him as minister. At the request of the governor and the intendant, Franquelin voyaged to France at his own expense to take to the Royal Court some of his maps and plans "that had been asked for."[12] La Barre must have cringed on learning that Franquelin was officially assigned as La Salle's draftsman to prepare a map of the explorer's journeys, though pleased when the arrangement failed to work out.

The resulting map, now known only in facsimile, reflected La Salle's idea that the Mississippi flowed into the Gulf at its northwest corner, while the Bahía del Espíritu Santo retained the position it had occupied since the earliest discovery. Minet's 1685 sketch map of "Louisiana"—drawn to show La Salle's concept rather than his own—had a similar distortion. Until the end of the century, mapmakers continued to place the Mississippi too far west. This was La Salle's miscalculation that would take his forthcoming Gulf voyage to the wrong destination and its tragic end.

La Salle, arriving at La Rochelle in December or January,[13] was filled with uncertainty as to how best to gain advantage from his Mississippi discovery. His credit already worn thin, he had little idea of how to rebuild his base; hardly a thought on the kind of approach that might win either support from the king or a new following among private investors. From the start, he encountered circumstances that were scarcely anticipated. Peñalosa's proposals for leading an invasion of Spain's colonial possessions, gestating since 1678, had gained new life since Spain's declaration of war on France the previous October. The Spanish renegade, after arriving in France about 1673, boasted of having explored from New Mexico the ill-defined native provinces of Quivira and Teguayo. In 1678—encouraged and directed by Abbé Claude Bernou—he sought to interest Louis XIV in conquering those regions, but the Sun King declared the timing inappropriate.[14]

That Peñalosa's scheming was fostered by Bernou is well established. Significantly, the Peñalosa memorials that bear Bernou's stamp began in 1678, which also marked the inception of La Salle's involvement with the "Renaudot coterie" with which Bernou was aligned. The common interests that linked Bernou and Abbé Eusèbe Renaudot included strong anti-Jesuit sentiments and a fascination with geography. Bernou, however, was spurred by a driving ambition; his interest in geography was closely allied with his desire to become a bishop.[15]

From their first acquaintanceship with La Salle, the two abbés recognized his potential value to them. Renaudot, seeing that the explorer's image needed polishing, contributed a remarkable bit of press-agentry to that end. Writing anonymously as "a friend of [the late] Father Gallinée," with whom La Salle had begun his 1669 exploration, he attributed to the explorer–fur trader feats of exploration that have since been branded as false. Renaudot's document, purportedly an account of La Salle's first eleven years in Canada, claimed as its basis a series of interviews with the explorer in June, 1678, in the presence of "other knowledgeable persons."[16] These, undoubtedly, were other members of the anti-Jesuit Brotherhood of Good Children, including Bernou. Thus began the relationship that was to have far-reaching consequences for La Salle.

With La Salle again in France and fumbling about for the means to launch another new venture, Bernou reviewed for Renaudot his own role as the explorer's agent: "When, five or six years ago, [La Salle] proposed his schemes . . . , I offered my humble assistance, [and] he accepted." An indefinite arrangement was made as to Bernou's fee, which La Salle never paid. Yet the cleric wrote the detailed chronicle of La Salle's explorations from 1679 to 1681 ("Relation des descouvertes"), a sort of background report to Colbert while the court awaited news of the Mississippi River expedition. Then, early in 1683, Bernou compiled the "official report" of the Mississippi exploration. Even without remuneration, the abbé claimed, "I have always encouraged [La Salle] and done all in my power to help him."[17]

When La Salle returned to France late in 1683 without a clear-cut strategy for following up his Mississippi discovery, Bernou again stood ready to "help." The means for reaching the great river through the Gulf of Mexico, for a time, remained elusive. La Salle wished at least to keep open the option of returning via Canada and the Illinois to establish a post on the lower Mississippi; indeed, the idea of approaching the river through the Gulf of Mexico may not have occurred to him. Even later, his repeated equivocation on the matter seemed to be born of his uncertainty as well as a desire for secrecy. The two abbés, perceiving La Salle's lack of focus, moved into the breach.

Upon arriving in La Rochelle, La Salle wrote immediately to Renaudot in Paris. The letter, unfortunately, is not at hand, but it seems clear that Renaudot promptly communicated its contents to Bernou in Rome, where the latter had gone in April, 1683, as a diplomatic agent for the Portuguese government. Bernou in turn suggested to the abbé in Paris, by letter dated January 1, 1684, that La Salle join his efforts with Peñalosa's, as the Spanish count could inform him on Mexican geography. Later the same month, Bernou wrote again to Renaudot, advising against La Salle's returning to the Mississippi by way of Canada; if the explorer would be willing to go through the Gulf of Mexico, he would find assistance in Paris.[18] The Peñalosa scheme, he seemed to be saying, was already brewing, and La Salle would win favor with the Royal Court by offering his assistance, rather than advancing a wholly new plan.

Bernou's aims stand out clearly in his letters to Renaudot. Having accepted Peñalosa's scheme for a Mexican conquest by which he might become a bishop, he hoped to improve the odds by joining La Salle with Peñalosa. His "help" went out to both. Of Peñalosa, he wrote, "It was I who suggested to him the great scheme, which he had not thought of; I drew it up and amended it in consultation with M. de Pouancey, M. [Jean-Paul Tarin] de Cussy, and others, who approved it and thought it certain to succeed." It has been said that Bernou, "for all his shrewdness . . . , had been hoodwinked by Peñalosa." In reality, it was a trade-out; each played upon the other's objectives to advance his own.[19] In La Salle's case, it was Bernou who dangled the carrot; like a confidence man who beguiles his mark with promises of easy wealth, he seduced his victim with an appeal to his ambition. La Salle, taking the bait, plunged in over his head, involving himself in a complex scheme for which he was wholly unsuited.

Only after hearing La Salle's plan concerning the Mississippi in 1678, in all likelihood, had Bernou started Peñalosa on his curious track. The Spanish turncoat's convoluted description of New Spain made the abbé's own objective of conquering Mexico seem plausible.

In January, 1682—*before* La Salle had started down the Mississippi—the court was offered a proposal in Peñalosa's name that resembled what La Salle would propose afterward. It took note of the fact that no European nation occupied that part of "La Florida." With *flibustiers* from Saint-Domingue the renegade would establish at the mouth of the Río Bravo a base for the conquest of Nueva Vizcaya. At the appropriate time he would lead these freebooters across northern Mexico to seize the Spanish gold, silver, lead, and copper mines by rallying to his aid the Indians, mixed bloods, and Creoles, who were eager to "throw off the Spanish yoke."

There are interesting parallels between Peñalosa's proposal, offered just as La Salle was poised to embark on the Mississippi, and La Salle's the following October. The similarity, however, lies only in the suggestion of an offensive against New Spain, a thought that was original with neither. No more novel was their specific target: the mines of Nueva Vizcaya, which the French had long looked upon with cupidity. If the two men were linked in any way, the common thread was Abbé Bernou—the "friend" to whom La Salle had written from Michilimackinac in October, 1682, more than a year before he returned to France. This letter, as far as the record goes, marks the genesis of La Salle's evolving plan for exploiting his discovery. To Bernou, it was a clear sign that the explorer could be bent to his purposes.

> The useful character of this enterprise [La Salle had written] is shown . . . by the convenience of the harbours formed by the mouths of the river, in proximity to the Spaniards and near to where their fleets pass, where it would be easy to maintain a strong colony on account of the fertility . . . of the soil, and the abundance of provisions. There is all the necessary material for building whole fleets, except iron, which has not yet been found. The mouth of the river is easy to defend, and therefore the entrance to the whole country . . . ; and an army could not go by land without great difficulty, on account of the depth [density] of the reeds. . . . Thus with a small force we can protect all the riches which are to be expected from the fertile lands bordering this river and seven or eight rivers of the same size which fall into it, five of which come from New Biscay and New Mexico, where the Spaniards have found so many mines. From there we could harass New Spain and even destroy it entirely, merely by arming the Indians, whom we could also easily discipline . . ., and they very naturally hate the Spaniards because they make them slaves.[20]

This latter statement, Henry Folmer declares, was purely La Salle's invention; the Indians of the Mississippi had no reason to hate the Spaniards, for they had never even seen any: "Thus began a series of lies . . . and fantasies which were ultimately to lead to La Salle's ruin and violent death and that of most of his companions."[21]

Was the similarity of La Salle's ideas to the Bernou-Peñalosa scheme a mere coincidence? Had Bernou influenced La Salle's goals and the concept of his river—as set forth in the Chucagua fragment—even before he set out on the Mississippi expedition? The lack of a date on the fragment renders difficult any hard-and-fast answer. On the other hand, the paper in La Salle's own handwriting seems almost certainly to reflect the tortured workings of an overburdened mind. In view of the information at his disposal, the reasons he gives for concluding that his river could not be the one Hernando de Soto had discovered seem quite logical: map portrayals of the Río del Espíritu Santo, or Soto's *río grande,* bore no resemblance to the river La Salle himself had descended; the Río Escondido did. Although the document was found among Bernou's papers, when and how it got there are not of record. Its tenor, suggesting La Salle's first-blush effort to understand his discovery, seems to indicate an earlier date than the October, 1682, letter. It probably went to France on the same ship, and La Salle's agent, Bernou, was the likely recipient. Bernou, having initiated Peñalosa's "great scheme," greeted La Salle's identification of his river as the Escondido with enthusiasm. Compiling the "official report" of the expedition early in 1683, he wrote: "[The Mississippi] empties into the Gulf of Mexico beyond the bay of the Holy Spirit, between the 27th and the 28th degree of latitude, and at the place where some maps put the Rio de la Madalena, and others the Rio Bravo; it is about 30 leagues from the Rio Bravo, about 60 from the Rio de Palmas, and about 90 to 100 from the Rio Panero [Pánuco], where lies the nearest settlement of Spaniards on the coast."[22]

For this report, Bernou drew on letters and reports of Father Membré, Henri de Tonti, and La Salle himself. La Salle, in the fragment, had freely admitted to brainstorming: "I have made this digression without thinking about it." His conclusion that the river he had descended was the Río Escondido, entering the Gulf at its western end, has been greeted in certain quarters with skepticism. Whereas there is scarcely a shadow of a doubt that he wrote his true thoughts, Bernou stood ready to make capital of it, true or not. He wrote two more memorials, which were submitted to the minister Seignelay in Peñalosa's name. Whatever the abbé's role in the affair, he justified himself by claiming that it was all for La Salle's benefit: "This union of the two schemes cannot fail to be of service to M. de La Salle," by increasing the minister's interest, by giving him [La Salle] access to Peñalosa's information, and by making it possible for him to become the leader of both enterprises.[23]

There were aspects of Peñalosa's scheme that appealed to La Salle, even though the explorer came to regard the Spanish imposter as a thorn-in-side. His immediate objective was to win royal favor. He had no interest in sharing the glory (as Abbé Renaudot well knew), and he saw no benefit in the renegade's geographical assertions in which he could already see outstanding flaws.[24]

Within little more than a month after La Salle's return to France, Bernou contributed a two-part proposal that spelled out projects for both the French explorer and the renegade Spaniard. Geared to the renewed state of warfare with Spain, the *première proposition* sought to give Peñalosa a stake in La Salle's enterprise. It called for an invasion at the mouth of the Río Pánuco instead of the Río Bravo, which Bernou had finally managed to identify with the Mississippi. After capturing the Pánuco settlement, Peñalosa would proceed with a thousand pirates from Saint-Domingue, led by the notorious pirate Michel Grammont, to seize the entire province of Nueva Vizcaya and its mines.[25]

To this memorial a "second proposal" was appended, offering an alternate, or complementary, approach to invading New Biscay (Nueva Vizcaya): by ascending "the river called by the Spaniards the Río Bravo, which, fortunately, turns out to be the same as the one the Indians call the Mississippi." La Salle, it is noted, had "just completed exploration of this river to the sea and has recently arrived in Paris to give an account of it. . . ." This document contains some features similar to the memorials that La Salle himself—guided by Renaudot—would present in the Royal Court. But it reflects Bernou's ideas—and especially his rhetoric. (La Salle had never identified his river as the Río Bravo.) The purpose of this "second proposal" is spelled out in midpassage: "These two different methods of conquering New Biscay can be employed without any great expenditure; one of them might be chosen or both at the same time, so as to attack the Spaniards in this province from two different quarters." The two ships asked for in the first proposal would suffice for both, one going to the Pánuco, the other to the mouth of the "new river," sixty leagues away.[26]

La Salle, meanwhile, struggling with his own memorials, leaned heavily on Abbé Renaudot, to whom he had written soon after arriving at La Rochelle. Uncertain of his reception at court, he sought, without success, backers for his project among merchants at La Rochelle and Rochefort. He then took the coach to Paris and, after a hasty visit to Rouen, installed himself in his old quarters on the rue de la Truanderie, having found no more interest in those two cities than in the seaports.[27] His only hope lay in obtaining royal support. The key proved to be Abbé Renaudot, who helped him shape his memorials to appeal to the king and his minister and steered him through the intricacies of court protocol.

Even after La Salle fell into step with the Bernou-Renaudot scheme, he continued to harbor reservations. He was familiar with the way through Canada, difficult though it might be. The Gulf of Mexico was unknown to him. He still equivocated, therefore, hesitant to commit himself firmly to either. Not even his ship captain—not even his own mother—knew until the last minute which way he intended to go.

La Salle offered a spate of memorials to the Marquis de Seignelay, Colbert's son, on whose shoulders his late father's burden had fallen heavily. Two of the undated documents sought restoration of the explorer's rights in New France, without which the option of returning to Canada would be nullified. The petition was promptly granted. Two other memorials recount his discovery and propose returning through the Gulf to the Mississippi, thence to undertake the conquest of Nueva Vizcaya. There is, as Frances Gaither has noted, "nothing to show when or by what process [La Salle's memorials] took the form in which they were finally recorded."[28]

That La Salle relied upon Renaudot's guidance in shaping his appeal is certain; just how much of the verbiage was La Salle's and how much Renaudot's is questionable. In third person, the proposal was made to establish a port and a fortified settlement on the lower Mississippi, as the late minister Colbert had desired. The place La Salle had chosen lay "sixty leagues" up the river, above the flooded marshes of the delta. Near the Taensa villages on a Mississippi River ox-bow known presently as Lake Saint Joseph (Louisiana), the settlement would be secure from attack by either land or river. From the various native groups he had gathered in the Illinois country, it was claimed, an army of fifteen thousand could be formed for attacking Nueva Vizcaya. This province "was very rich in silver mines," which would benefit the French more than the Spaniards because of "the proximity of the river" for convenient transport. In this remote region "150 leagues in length and 50 in breadth," and 150 leagues from Mexico City, the memorial postulated, there were no more than four hundred native Spaniards, and they incapable of defending themselves.

If the war with Spain continued, La Salle offered, he would leave France with two hundred men and take fifty *flibustiers* from Saint-Domingue. Four thousand warriors from Fort-Saint-Louis-des-Illinois would be directed to descend the Mississippi to the French settlement. The native horde could be assembled the following winter, the conquest completed in the spring of 1685. Nueva Vizcaya, it was represented, could be reached by ascending the Red River (called the Seignelay) and crossing a forest "fifty leagues" wide. (Remember, he visualized the Mississippi not as being where it actually is but in the position of the Nueces River of Texas, shown on various maps as Río Escondido, with the Red River as its tributary).

With his army divided into three contingents, the attack would be made overland, through mountain passes of which the Spaniards had no knowledge: a far better plan, he believed, than attacking via the Río Pánuco, which had settlements along its banks that would slow progress and cost the invaders the advantage of surprise. Thus, the author—whether La Salle or Renaudot—reveals his familiarity with Peñalosa's schemes before the memorial was given final form. While never mentioning Peñalosa by name, the writer replied obliquely to some points of the Spaniard's scheme: La Salle would, for example, take only a limited number of the Saint-Domingue pirates. Yet the buccaneer fleet might be of service by attacking the New Spain coastal settlements prior to the launching of his campaign, thereby diverting Spanish troops and leaving the inland towns defenseless.

To counter any lingering skepticism by the minister or the king, the explorer proclaimed the benefits to be derived: taking the gospel to the natives; enhancement of the king's glory by conquest while seizing the Spanish mines; and controlling the great navigable river and the riches along its banks. For confirmation of his claims regarding the Mississippi discovery, he referred the minister to Father Membré's report and the three other persons who had accompanied him on the expedition and were now in Paris—Barbier, Nicolas de La Salle, and the man called L'Espérance. And there was also La Barre's agent Vital, who had come to France to follow La Salle's movements "and has confirmed the truth of the discovery."[29]

It was a plan, like many of La Salle's previous ones, based too much on brainstorming and too little on sound reasoning and certain knowledge. The explorer's reliance on hypothetical map portrayals of unknown regions, in combination with his own misunderstanding of what he had observed, lay at the roots of his confusion and his susceptibility to manipulation. He fell prey to the muddle of Bernou and Renaudot's "expert" opinions; Peñalosa's pretensions and false portrayal of Mexico and its peoples; and his own geographical misconceptions and driving ambition. Furthermore, La Salle either purposely dissembled or yielded to undue influence by the two abbés—especially on his proposals to employ in his proposed conquest a considerable number of pirates and four thousand Indians. The pirates, as he surely knew, would escape his control; the maintenance of such a large native force—he must have recognized—was wholly impractical.

Abbé Renaudot, by virtue of his relationship with the king's secretary, François de Callières, and others in the court, arranged for La Salle to present the memorials to Seignelay. Shortly afterward, Callières set up a meeting of the explorer and Peñalosa. Bernou, while pleased that the two had met, expressed disappointment at La Salle's reaction. That the explorer found the Spaniard rather ostentatious came as no surprise, for he himself felt the same way. Writing to Renaudot, Bernou defended Peñalosa on other counts: "I give more credence to what he says . . . , having never found him false in anything he claims to have seen, except for some exaggeration of detail. . . . So I believe that M. de La Salle will do well to treat with the Count," both to please the minister Seignelay and to obtain information that would enable him—should the Spaniard die—"to carry out *our* plans." He would counsel La Salle, therefore, to humor and praise the man and use every means to gain his confidence. "This union of the two schemes cannot fail to be of service to M. de La Salle. . . ."[30]

In so writing, however, the abbé who aspired to a bishopric left no doubt as to whose plans he expected La Salle and Peñalosa to carry out. La Salle, however, was amenable to Bernou's scheme of joining his plan with the renegade Spaniard only as far as it suited his own purposes. Esprit Cabart de Villermont, a king's councilor, tried unsuccessfully to set up a second meeting of the two. Bernou read the news in letters from both Villermont and Peñalosa. He concluded therefrom that the councilor had "no great influence" on La Salle, "and the Spaniard understands him [La Salle?] as you and I do."[31]

Even though parts of the Peñalosa scheme obviously were incorporated into La Salle's, Renaudot had steered La Salle's proposals to the minister without a hint of combining the two. Bernou, responding to the news in late March, approved, while urging that Peñalosa's plan not be allowed to languish. If the Spaniard could proceed to Saint-Domingue to join Governor (Jean-Paul) Tarin de Cussy before year's end, he might still carry out his plan in the 1685 spring: "Nothing but good would come of it; our friend's [La Salle's] affairs would go all the better."[32]

There is no discernable time line for the movement of La Salle's memorials through court channels. Evidently presented by early February, they received more prompt attention than had generally been allowed. If Renaudot himself was kept informed of the court's timely action, it is not reflected in Bernou's letters. On March 23, 1684, Seignelay informed the munitioner Dumont at Rochefort that the king had granted La Salle the thirty-four-gun naval frigate *Joly,* commanded by Captain Pingault, "for going to Canada with 200 men." Of that number, 100 would be raised at royal expense, with La Salle himself to bear the cost of the rest. The port official was to proceed forthwith to outfitting the ship, which, in view of the number of workmen and soldiers engaged in the enterprise, would require no more than 70 sailors. Attached to the letter was a list of munitions and supplies to be provided.[33]

Bernou and Renaudot, meanwhile, carried on their correspondence, seemingly unaware of all that had transpired. Renaudot's response to

Bernou's insistence that a part in the enterprise still be reserved for Peñalosa provoked further comment by the abbé in Rome. With obvious reference to the Spaniard, Bernou wrote: "You tell me that I am making an idol of a certain gentlemen. . . . I know his faults, but he has his merits." He had never "found any important error" in Peñalosa's claims and was puzzled at Renaudot's reference to "gross errors in geography that our friend [La Salle] has discovered." Bernou did not rely solely on Peñalosa, for he was aware of his "endless exaggerations."[34]

Bernou was cheered by the news that La Salle had taken his two memorials to Versailles, though disappointed that Renaudot had not sent him copies. Having maneuvered the two schemes and brought them together— however fruitlessly—the abbé in Rome now was applying mortar to another stone in his well-structured design: to influence a map portrayal of North America that made plausible La Salle's geographical concepts, as amended by Bernou. To this end he was compiling a summary of La Salle's explorations to be incorporated on the Venetian cartographer Coronelli's map and globe. La Salle had written to Bernou in March, promising to send his map and narrative of the 1682 exploration. Renaudot advised Bernou that the explorer did not have time for such. The abbé in Rome then suggested, presumably tongue in cheek, that La Salle be shut up in his room till the task was finished. It would not be necessary for him to write a narrative but merely to amplify and correct, with notes, the one Bernou himself had written. "As for the map, it is absolutely necessary that he not go away without leaving you one, drawn on a large scale, for the [Coronelli] globes." It need show only the discoveries from Fort Frontenac to the mouth of the Mississippi. The success of Bernou's effort is attested by Coronelli's famous globe and his map of North America, showing the Mississippi entering the Gulf of Mexico near the Rio Grande. Both were completed in 1688.[35] But by then the abbé's dream had crumbled, along with La Salle's.

Renaudot evidently failed to share fully his friend's enthusiasm for Peñalosa. Having drawn the line on combining the Spaniard's scheme with La Salle's, the abbé in Paris must have intimated that some of his friend's advice to La Salle was inappropriate. What did it matter, as long as La Salle resumed his exploration, one way or another? It mattered very much indeed, Bernou replied: "As it is *my diocese,* I know that he may have many dangers to face on his voyage." He would continue his advice, as Renaudot would see from "the attached letter [to La Salle]."[36] In his own mind, the scheming cleric already was laying claim to his bishopric, to be conquered by either La Salle or Peñalosa or by their combined efforts. He can scarcely

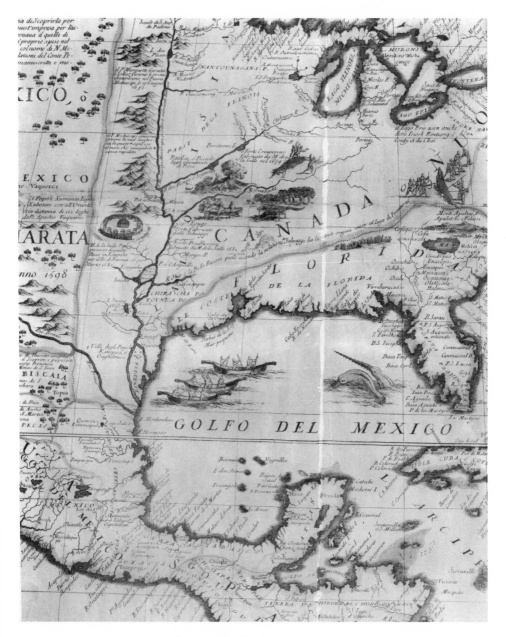

FIGURE 11

How La Salle Changed the Map. Father Vincenzo Coronelli—completing this map in 1688 with the help of Abbé Claude Bernou and the information Bernou extracted from La Salle—has the Mississippi entering the Gulf near the Río Bravo, with the Bahía del Espíritu Santo far to the northeast. Detail Courtesy Special Collections Division, The University of Texas at Arlington Libraries be blamed for the outcome of La Salle's venture, but he showed himself remarkably insensitive to its potential for disaster.

Although Peñalosa failed to pass muster with La Salle, the Marquis de Seignelay regarded his scheme with enthusiasm. Early in March he informed Tarin de Cussy, about to embark for Saint-Domingue, of the king's decision to proceed with "an enterprise against the Spaniards settled on the coast of New Biscay." As soon as Cussy reached the Haitian coast, the king wished him to gather all the *flibustiers* ("freebooters" or "pirates") ported there "to prepare them for setting out next October or November" and to outfit them "for the journey and the enterprise that they must carry out, details of which I defer explaining until His Majesty sends from this place the forces to join the *flibustiers*." Cussy's diligence in the matter, and its success, the minister promised, would be rewarded with "a very important post . . . , which I shall obtain for you." The reference here to attacking "the coast of New Biscay" with pirates supported by French troops may be taken to mean that Peñalosa's scheme—or La Salle's—was about to be implemented.[37]

Royal backing for La Salle's new voyage to America having been approved by March 23, preparations moved rapidly forward. In view of the assignment of a ship for the voyage, the king must have granted his commission at the same time. Louis XIV thereby empowered the explorer "to command in our name all the Frenchmen and Indians that he will employ in carrying out our orders; . . . to command under our authority in the territory newly subjected to our domination in North America, from Fort Saint-Louis on the Illinois River to Nouvelle-Biscaye, . . . to establish governors and commanders, to maintain commerce" and to enjoy the benefits thereof.[38]

The same day, the court responded to La Salle's list of things needed (which he had submitted with one of his memorials) for the projected six-month voyage, the colony, and the proposed military campaign.[39] The two documents yield indications of the expedition's multiple objectives: armed conquest, colonization, religious conversion, and trade. La Salle asked for "600 muskets for arming 400 savages besides the 1,600 already armed and for the 200 Frenchmen."[40] The king reduced the number of muskets to 400. Other munitions requested were passed without comment: 30,000 livres of musket balls; 300 swords (espées) and sabers; a hundred pairs of pistols; twelve cannon "for the two fortresses," eight of iron, firing balls of ten to twelve pounds (livres), and four bronze four-pounders, with 200 balls for each and powder in proportion. The specifications, however, were subject to change.[41]

FIGURE 12

Silent Guns. The eight iron cannon carried across the ocean on the storeship
Aimable, *placed at the corners of the French settlement on Garcitas Creek,*
buried by Spaniards in 1689, and recovered by the Texas Historical
Commission in 1996. Texas Historical Commission photo

In addition to this ordnance, there were to be 300 to 400 grenades;
twenty-five partisans and the same number of halberds; six small petards—
a hard-to-define explosive device—100 pairs of pistols; 20,000 pounds of
powder for muskets and 100,000 of hunting powder. In his requisition,
La Salle had specified that four to five pounds of powder be given each
Indian—those taking part in the conquest of Nueva Vizcaya—with the
remainder left at the forts or used by the French "during the expedition
[to Nueva Vizcaya]."[42]

Besides a warship of the *Joly*'s proportions, La Salle had asked for a barque
of forty tuns, fully constructed and rigged, or in bundles *(en fagot),* with
the necessary rigging, to be carried on another vessel. His reasons are not

entirely clear. Was he still thinking of taking all or part of his expedition to Canada, to assemble the ship on Lake Erie above Niagara Falls (as the *Griffon* had been), thence to reach the Mississippi by way of the Ohio? There is reason to think so.

No such ship was immediately available. Four *barques longues* (sometimes called light frigates or corvettes) ported at Rochefort the previous January had been sent to protect French shipping along the Spanish coast against pirate or corsair attack. A ship would have to be built for La Salle. The explorer's idea for a ship *en fagot* that could be assembled at the destination, wherever that might be, was duly considered. In fact, the *munitionnaire* Dumont, on receipt of the royal order dated March 23, turned the project over to master carpenter (shipwright) Honoré Mallet and work was promptly begun to fashion the pieces from timbers salvaged from old vessels. It was soon perceived, however, that the timbers for a forty- to fifty-tun barque would not fit in the *Joly's* hold. On April 3 the *munitionnaire*-general wrote to advise the king, proposing what seemed like an easy solution to the problem: supplant *Le Joly* with the *flûte Le Dromadaire,* recently arrived from the Baltic with a cargo of masts for the shipyard. By the time Dumont received the king's reply of April 14, rejecting the idea, Mallet's crew had a barque in bundles near completion. The monarch, informing Dumont that he had just appointed Taneguy Le Gallois de Beaujeu to replace Pingault as captain of *Le Joly,* did not wish to make a substitution: "Concerning the barque in bundles, since it cannot be carried on that ship, His Majesty favors outfitting a dispatch vessel [*traversier*] or a good barque," to be laded with all that could not be carried on the *Joly.*[43]

Dumont, while waiting for the king's decision on the *Dromadaire,* had come up with another idea, which he transmitted to the Marquis de Seignelay under date of April 9: why not assemble the barque in bundles — as yet without a name — and offer it to La Salle? The officers, masters, and royal pilots at the Port of Rochefort, headed by the port captain, Heurtin, subscribed unanimously to written testimony on the matter: a barque of forty to fifty tuns, made seaworthy and in good trim, could easily make the crossing from the coast of France to that of Canada in the summer season.[44] Before the end of the month the crews were back at work and the keel was laid for the vessel that was to become *La Belle.* The work went on through May and into June. The hull at last finished, woodcarver and painter applied their embellishments. On the ship's transom were painted three white fleurs-de-lis on a blue field, the mark of a vessel of the King Louis XIV's Royal French Navy. Completed to masts, yards, halyards, sails, and ballast, she was christened *La Belle,* floated in the bay, and laded with the tools, provisions, and weaponry destined for the Gulf of Mexico. Even with the *Belle* burdened to capacity, needed supplies remained on the docks and in the warehouses. The *Joly's* decks were so crowded that there was scarcely room for working the guns.[45]

Besides instruments of war (already mentioned), the goods granted La Salle included the wherewithal for building a settlement: 400 pounds of wrought iron, including crowbars and angle iron; 600 livres of bar iron, 2,000 of iron rod, and 600 of steel; a forge with all its appurtenances; tools for carpenters, joiners, ploughwrights, armorers, masons, and ropemakers; hatchets, shovels, mattocks, pickaxes, and spades; two surgeon's cases and medicines; two sets of church furnishings and the necessary religious ornaments.

As preparations went forward, skepticism lingered among those knowledgeable of the affair. The Sulpician superior, Abbé Tronson, trying to judge the discovery objectively, had found tinges of doubt among his informants in Paris. La Salle had made a great discovery, he wrote in mid-March. Some viewed it as possibly damaging to Canada, while others saw it only as useless. Still keeping a watchful eye, he wrote in early April to Abbé Belmont in Canada: "Louisiana has had no great popularity here. That is not the case with the discovery of M. de La Salle. Although some doubt the truth of what he says, he has been listened to. Time will tell. . . ."[46] And two days later to Abbé Dollier de Casson, with whom La Salle had begun his first journey in 1669: "I have heard with pleasure the report that M. de La Salle gave us of his discovery. It was a good voyage, which intelligent persons believe very considerable, if things are as he represents them. The king has listened to him, received him well, and is satisfied. His affair is still very secret, and there are few who do not believe it called off."[47]

Shortly after learning that La Salle had received his commission, Tronson wrote again to Abbé Belmont:

> I am very well informed by M. de La Salle concerning his discovery, of which he has given me a very good map. What the two men who accompanied him [Barbier and L'Espérance] have told you does not agree with what he himself has told me, for he claims to have entered the Gulf of Mexico not at the baye du Saint-Esprit but in latitude 27° and on the meridian of Pánuco at the far end of the Gulf and far from that bay.
>
> The Marquis de Seignelay has heard him out. The king has received him well; and, if his enterprise succeeds, though many doubt that it can, he probably will recoup his losses.[48]

Beaujeu, as the *Joly's* captain, would be in full charge of all matters concerning the ship and navigation, while conducting her to La Salle's chosen destination. His Majesty's intention was "that he should do all that the said sieur de La Salle desires." Beaujeu should furnish all the assistance that La Salle might ask, excepting only that which might endanger the ship.[49]

La Salle and Beaujeu met for the first time in Paris, probably in conference with Seignelay the latter part of April. Before leaving Paris, they dined in the home of Morel, a clerk of the Royal Court. The same day they paid a visit to another man to whom La Salle was to refer later in an interesting but obscure manner. Beaujeu relayed the explorer's comments in a letter to Cabart de Villermont.

At the time, the explorer had just informed Beaujeu that the pilot for the forthcoming voyage would need to be familiar with the Saint Lawrence River, as well as the coast of Saint-Domingue and the Gulf of Mexico. (Was he still thinking of sending part of his force to the Mississippi via Canada?) "Upon that," Beaujeu related, "he told me that we were but the vanguard of the man whom we went to see the morning we dined with M. Morel, and that he would follow us next year with a large force."[50]

Interpreters have generally identified the gentleman in question as Peñalosa. Actually, the reference is to Maréchal d'Estrées. The Marquis de Seignelay, La Salle advised Beaujeu, had wished this expedition to go "this year," and the matter was almost settled when "he [the minister] had put it off until the next year upon his [the marshal's] asking for the remainder of this year [to prepare] and that an experienced man go to reconnoiter the place."[51]

Ten days later Beaujeu reported to Villermont, "Tomorrow I shall go and dine with the Maréchal. There is no more talk of [a second] expedition here." La Salle, however, had been told authoritatively "that there certainly would be one, and that ours would be involved with it. They still go on raising soldiers in all directions, and M. le Mareschal intends to leave Sunday for Brest. M. Minet, our engineer, tells me that last Sunday M. de La Salle told the Maréchal that he knew that he would very soon follow him; and the Maréchal told him that he knew it also, and was very glad. We are informed by a ship that has arrived from the islands that M. de Blenac and M. Bégon have gone to the coast of Saint-Domingue to muster the men who are fit for service."[52]

Plans, however, were changing faster than they could be communicated. Beaujeu informed Villermont of the latest development some days later, after taking the latter's message to the field marshal's house. "We spoke of sieur de La Salle," the captain related, and he repeated what La Salle had told him concerning plans for the marshal to join him the following year. "M. le Mareschal assured me that there was nothing to it, that surely the Court had put M. de La Salle on a false trail. I could get him to say nothing more."[53]

When La Salle embarked, there was no hint that he would be reinforced by Peñalosa, Maréchal d'Estrées, or anyone else. Peñalosa faded quietly away. Talk of an early peace, in any case, would have stalled any royal intentions of sending the Spaniard later, to pursue the "great scheme" that Bernou had put into his head. Furthermore, Peñalosa was sixty-three years old by this time; he may well have decided—Bernou's conniving notwithstanding—that he was past the time of life for going to such lengths to avenge his old grievance. He died in Paris, probably of natural causes, in 1687, also the year of La Salle's death in a faraway land.

The realization that there were to be no follow-up expeditions, no reinforcements from any source, brought upon the explorer an overwhelming sense of foreboding. Yet the wild scheme that he and Peñalosa had espoused, with Abbé Bernou's encouragement, "was universally considered plausible." Dollier de Casson, thirteen years previously, had believed that the Ohio-Mississippi (considered one river) might disembogue near the Spanish mines. The idea had lingered until, six years ago, Colbert had intimated to La Salle that a port on the Gulf of Mexico would furnish a base for harassing the Spaniards. Colbert's son, Marquis de Seignelay, having succeeded him as minister, authorized La Salle to explore the lands through which might be found a way to Mexico. No one doubted that La Salle's river lay near New Biscay or and that the Spanish mining province could be handily reached by way of a Mississippi tributary, the Rivière Seignelay (Red River). The geographers, "far from attacking the hypothesis," welcomed it as a new concept to be portrayed on their maps.[54] The plausibility of such a march passed without question over the heads of everyone.

Chapter 6

Storm Flags

FORECAST OF FAILURE

Rancor and mistrust; charge and countercharge; calumny and innuendo. Such was the ambience attending preparations for the 1684 voyage to the Gulf of Mexico. The enmity that had dogged La Salle in Canada had followed him across the Atlantic; he still saw the workings of his enemies in every setback. In this new act of the drama, only the *dramatis personae* had changed. The vaunted discoverer quickly came to be regarded in France as he had been by his adversaries in the overseas colony: a visionary whose sanity was open to question. As in Canada, where he had been the willing instrument of the governor-general Comte de Frontenac, those whose interests he served stood by him—for a time. They included the Abbés Bernou and Renaudot and the king and his foreign minister, Seignelay. Ultimately, these good graces, too, would fade.

Clearly, La Salle was out of his element in trying to organize an expedition of such a scope. He lacked both knowledge and skills for outfitting an overseas voyage with multiple objectives and a colony in an unknown land, completely out of reach of the nearest outpost of civilization. Thus, as he went about his business in Paris, Rouen, and La Rochelle, his problems multiplied.

La Salle's partisans, of that time and this, have been wont to assign a disproportionate share of the blame for his failure to Captain Beaujeu. Yet the king's choice of the sea commander was not inappropriate. The monarch's mistake lay in his refusal to heed Beaujeu's warnings.

The division of authority between La Salle and Beaujeu seems quite forthright. Although it pleased neither, a more reasonable La Salle could have made it work. Beaujeu, apart from his gloomy prophecy of the expedition's failure, stands guilty of an indiscretion that aggravated the friction arising from La Salle's unreasonableness. A breach of trust by Beaujeu's confidant and friend at court—Cabart de Villermont—compounded his faux pas and thus complicated his relationship with La Salle.[1] Other loose tongues and gossip-prone functionaries exacerbated the already tense situation. La Salle's abrasiveness alone was sufficient cause for trouble; with the stimulus of what he deemed undue meddling in his affairs, he became during the months before sailing an irritant to virtually everyone with whom he had dealings.

Countless problems pressed upon both commanders as they went about preparations for the voyage. Beaujeu's task was one for which he was well qualified by thirty years' service in the Royal Navy. Yet distracting personal problems pressed upon him from many angles: about to sail to an unknown part of the New World, he confronted the life-threatening illness of his wife; the uncertain future of a puerile son who provided little comfort for his parents; the likelihood that during his absence he would be passed over for pensioning and forfeit the compensation due him for "the affair at Algiers." In that episode, he had been taken captive by the Spaniards, assigned blame and imprisoned after his repatriation, and dismissed from service. Held in the Saint-Nicolas Tower at La Rochelle from August 1, 1675, to May 2, 1676, he was reinstated in January, 1677.[2]

Appointed captain of *Le Joly* in place of Captain Pingault on April 14, 1684, Beaujeu arrived at Rochefort to take command on May 19. He found his ship careened, the commissary-general Dumont temporarily in charge of the fitting out. When the intendant, Pierre Arnoul, arrived next day, he was "greatly astonished" that La Salle had not yet appeared; he was anxious for a meeting with the explorer and the captain to make sure that both of them understood the minister's plan for the expedition.[3]

La Salle finally arrived at Rochefort via La Rochelle on May 26. Beaujeu took him on a tour of the warehouse and the *Joly*, which the explorer thought rather small. The king had allowed him only one other ship, the barque *Belle*, now being built in the Royal Navy yard at Rochefort, not far from the laid-up *Joly*. The goods that La Salle wished to load on *Le Joly* vis-à-vis the ship's designed capacity occasioned repeated arguments between the explorer and the captain. La Salle reported to Seignelay by letter of May 30. The minister's reply was brief and to the point: "I am astounded that you have been so long in going to Rochefort. It is most important that you get yourself in shape to leave promptly to do the things I have charged you with." Instead of the usual rations for sailors, the minister advised, flour and brandy should be taken to conserve space, "for the King will send no more than the two ships [*Le Joly* and *La Belle*]. . . . As for the men needed for the enterprise, it is up to you to act as speedily as possible to raise the necessary complement. Above all, you must get ready to sail without delay." Recruiting of military personnel for the enterprise had already been put in motion by Beaujeu's junior officers and cadets; upon his arrival at Rochefort, they were "scouring the country to raise 400 men for this expedition, but they found only the leavings of the infantry and the cavalry." More than 3,200 men had been raised in "this and bordering provinces" for service on land during the current conflict.[4]

La Salle's insistence that more goods be put on the *Joly* than she could reasonably carry met Beaujeu's adamant resistance. At last the explorer was forced to lease from Jean Mallet of La Rochelle the storeship *Aimable*. Even the additional vessel proved insufficient, and Arnoul provided the ketch *Saint-François* to carry the overflow as far as Saint-Domingue.[5]

A variety of unresolved problems had kept La Salle over long in Paris; hence his tardy arrival at the seaport. There were, for example, the matters of regaining rights to his two forts that had been seized by the Canada governor-general La Barre. He petitioned for the return to New France of La Forest, who was still in France, to gather the men "who have been withdrawn from his service by the authorities" and take them back to the Illinois country. Besides restoration of his property in Canada, La Salle sought from the court recompense for alleged damages at the hands of La Barre's men. As a result, La Barre found himself rebuked by the king, who wrote on April 10, 1684: "I hear that you have taken possession of Fort Frontenac, the property of the sieur de La Salle, driven away his men, suffered his land to run to waste, and even told the Iroquois that they might seize him as an enemy of the colony." If this were true, he added, the governor-general would have to make restitution and return both men and property to La Forest.[6]

La Forest, however, awaited a financial settlement with La Salle and was in no great hurry to leave France. A week before sailing for the Gulf of Mexico, La Salle consented for his lieutenant to recover, "preferentially," 5,200 livres that he had lent the explorer from his salary while serving in New France.[7]

To obtain this concession, La Forest had to await his turn behind François Plet. Plet made on May 5, before the king's councilors and notaries of Paris, a reckoning of all the goods he had sent to La Salle and La Forest at Fort

Frontenac. To this Plet added sums that he had paid to others on La Salle's account. The grand total came to 30,534 livres. La Salle was credited 12,777 livres for bills of exchange and furs given as payment to Plet, leaving a balance of 17,575 still owed; and

> as a deduction therefrom he binds himself to give and pay in acquittance and discharge of the said Sieur Plet the following, to wit: the sum of 3,198 livres to the sieur Pierre le Carpentier, merchant at Rouen; 2,000 livres to the widow of the sieur Le Bailly; 1617 livres to the sieur [Jean] Cavelier, priest, and 2,000 livres to Madame Cavelier, widow [La Salle's mother] for which sums the said sieur de La Salle promises to bring valid receipts to the sieur Plet forthwith; and the sum of 8,844 livres, being the balance of the sum in which the said sieur de La Salle has been found to be indebted, he shall be bound to give, deliver and pay to the said sieur Plet . . . for which payment he assigns all his property, presently owned and to be acquired, and in particular, Fort Frontenac and its appurtenances.[8]

This agreement reaffirmed that whatever rewards La Salle might have derived from his venture would accrue not to his own benefit but to his creditors. The instrument, executed at La Salle's Paris house on the rue de la Truanderie, did not absolve him of the judgment in Plet's favor, for 25,881 livres, granted at Montreal in 1680. Altogether, his indebtedness to Plet amounted to 34,835 livres, a sum he had no means of paying without canceling the voyage for which he was pledged to the king. They therefore came to an agreement whereby La Salle would postpone the initial installment until the end of 1685. He would pay interest of fifteen percent until then and ten percent thereafter "until the actual full payment."[9]

La Salle, of course, would never return to France to pay his debts. Not even Plet's cat-like agility could recover all that was due him, even though he knew how to take advantage of his opportunities. The occasion that first presented itself came as the result of the indiscretions of François Bellinzani, the extortionist whose safety net had vanished at Colbert's death. Bellinzani, it will be recalled, had extorted considerable sums from La Salle in both 1675 and 1678 before releasing the commissions granted the explorer by the king. The corrupt official also cut himself in for a paper partnership in La Salle's enterprises and put the squeeze on Plet as well. Bellinzani's misappropriation of funds from the royal treasury at last had come to the king's attention. He was removed from office and placed under arrest. While commissioners appointed by King Louis investigated his case, sieur Morel, with whom La Salle and Beaujeu had recently dined, took over his court duties.

La Salle, setting forth his claim to the commissioners, sought relief from making payments to Bellinzani that were "founded on an imaginary partnership," clearly shown to be false, a mere pretense to cloak his graft. Confronted by La Salle at his trial, the accused "was not able to specify when, or by whom, he had supplied the funds for the pretended partnership." La Salle petitioned for restoration of the 14,000 livres that Bellinzani had extorted and nullification of the spurious partnership agreement, "which was received by a bribed notary in sieur Bellinzani's room." Plet also confronted the accused, to whom he had paid 2,000 livres upon Bellinzani's threat to cause harm to La Salle (and hence to Plet's financial interests). He gave a deposition substantiating Bellinzani's malfeasance.[10]

Either during or shortly after his trial in 1684, Bellinzani died in prison, leaving his widow, Louise Chauvreau, and their son, François, bereft of inheritance. The Cour des Aides promptly attached the late Bellinzani's real property, and the *procureur-général* sought to sell it at auction. Included were four houses and two building sites in the Paris suburb of Saint-Germain. Enter La Salle's lawyer, with his power of attorney and, coincidentally, the same authority from Plet. On May 8, 1685, François Chastillon, attorney-at-law, went before the court registry on behalf of both Plet and La Salle to oppose the sale. For La Salle, Chastillon sought priority over all other claims for return of the money (with interest) that Bellinzani had extorted from him. At the same time, he asked that any settlement awarded La Salle "from the houses and hereditaments situated at Saint-Cloud" that had been seized from the widow and son be applied to La Salle's debt to Plet.[11]

Undoubtedly, the Bellinzani affair was a distraction for La Salle, delaying his appearance at La Rochelle and Rochefort. His first meeting with Beaujeu at Rochefort on May 26, 1684, occasioned an outburst that portended their subsequent stormy relationship. When Beaujeu gave him the papers that had to do with the forthcoming voyage, La Salle observed among them a memo that he himself had written to the minister Seignelay. He became so angry, Beaujeu declared, "that he could scarcely contain himself." La Salle later apologized and, Beaujeu says, "we parted good friends." Beaujeu, however, complicated this and other sensitive matters with his own indiscretion: he wrote regularly to Cabart de Villermont—a friend of both La Salle and Abbé Renaudot—of his dealings with the explorer. He also complained on at least three occasions to Seignelay. In this initial set-to, the captain noted La Salle's suspicious nature with the comment, "This distrust does not please me."[12] And a great deal more. Although he asked Villermont to keep his letters in confidence, his friend failed to do so, with unpleasant consequences.

For reasons not apparent, the captain manifested an excessive concern over La Salle's confrontation with Alphonse de Tonti, younger brother of Henri de Tonti who served La Salle in Canada and the Illinois country. It may be that Beaujeu and Villermont had influenced the explorer to sign on young Tonti and obtain for him a royal commission as commander of one of the two infantry companies to embark on *Le Joly*. At the same time, the passionate and profligate young nobleman Marquis de La Sablonnière received a lieutenant's commission to serve in Tonti's company. Sieur d'Autray (Jacques de Bourdon), Barbier, and La Salle's nephew Crevel de Moranget, who had been with him on the Mississippi River journey, accepted similar orders to serve in the company of an old army regular, sieur de Valigny.[13]

Concerning Alphonse de Tonti, La Salle soon changed his mind, for it became apparent that two such abrasive personalities could not live harmoniously in close confines. Difficulty arose over La Salle's having promised payment of wages due Henri de Tonti, still in Canada, to his family. It may have all been a misunderstanding over where and when the money was to be paid. Yet, when young Tonti's expectations were not promptly met, he made improper remarks about the leader—though exactly what is not found—in the presence of La Forest, Barbier, and the mapmaker Franquelin. He told La Salle himself that if he were deceiving him, he would be deceiving the king also, and "a thousand other things," Beaujeu acknowledged, "that were hard to put up with." La Salle, troubled enough with his own affairs without the constant annoyance of someone of Tonti's disposition, refused to take him on the voyage. Still, the matter was batted back and forth in the correspondence between Beaujeu and Villermont. In mid-June La Salle relented to Beaujeu's intercession and agreed to reinstate Tonti. Yet, when the ship captain sought to speak to him further, to offer justification for Tonti, La Salle rebuffed him: "The matter is settled and there is no need to speak of it again. . . . It remains for M. de Tonti to conduct himself toward me and all his comrades so that you, Monsieur de Beaujeu, who have made yourself responsible for his behavior, may incur no reproach. He will see from the esteem in which I hold his brother that he has only to discharge his duties well to become one of my friends. He may come, therefore, when he likes. . . ."

Again La Salle changed his mind. The matter was not settled till near the end of June, with sailing time less than a month away. La Salle, Beaujeu wrote, "told me that the statements he [Tonti] had made had come back to him from so many sources that he could not take him without injury to himself." The ship captain afterward heard from Tonti that La Salle had wanted to confront him with Barbier, Franquelin, and others who claimed to have heard his inappropriate remarks. Tonti refused. La Forest, meanwhile, had changed his story and—at least according to Beaujeu—claimed never to have heard Tonti speak disrespectfully of the leader.[14]

Trouble also arose between La Salle and his official mapmaker, Franquelin. The explorer conveyed to Franquelin his data to be drafted into a map reflecting his discoveries. Franquelin's map, sent to Seignelay, soon was given a wider distribution than La Salle desired. Franquelin, he believed, had betrayed him by leaking information on his destination.[15]

Indeed, the vaunted explorer clashed with almost everyone with whom he came in contact. Early in June, the young engineer Jean-Baptiste Minet, under the king's orders to serve La Salle, arrived. There can be little doubt that Minet, age twenty-three, was brash and full of himself. Like Alphonse de Tonti, who was two years older, he came up short on discretion. It is a fair certainty also that La Salle, as Beaujeu often alleged, was suspicious and distrustful to excess. Minet from the first identified more with Beaujeu than with La Salle, enough in itself to raise La Salle's suspicions. He reported to Beaujeu from time to time on what La Salle had said or done and incurred further suspicion by going frequently to see the intendant.[16]

La Salle constantly had difficulty with the outfitters in the port towns. He had frequent quarrels with the munitioner's deputy, Parassis, and complained to the intendant that the man was paid by his enemies to ruin his enterprise. When La Salle made mistakes in his requisition, he alleged that a certain royal official had confused his affairs purposely out of resentment at having been bypassed in the review process. Nor was he on the best of terms with his own men. La Forest, who remained with La Salle until he sailed, complained publicly of having to return to garrison duty at Fort Frontenac. Valigny, the infantry captain provided by Morel, appeared—Beaujeu judged—to be dissatisfied; Minet quickly became disenchanted and began writing a journal, which he was to keep throughout the voyage. And, Beaujeu confessed, things were not exactly going to suit him either. He blamed La Salle, whom he had come to believe lacked confidence in his own enterprise and was already making plans to cast the blame on others, should he fail. As for La Salle himself, he provided justification for such a judgment by hurling accusations in every direction.[17]

The burden of organizing the expedition weighed heavily on the explorer, who now was cast in the additional roles of military commander and colonizer; all this while attending to business affairs, a task that he found all the more nettlesome because he was little suited for it. He was further handicapped by having to deal with people in a civilized society, to which he had become unaccustomed during his years in the North American wilderness.

Beaujeu's letters provide a chronicle of preparations for the expedition, albeit from his own point of view. From La Salle, we have next to nothing. Allowing for Beaujeu's misconceptions here and there, his record seems fairly accurate: La Salle was running true to form, in his secretiveness, his paranoia, and his generally abrasive conduct. The captain's flawed judgment in reporting everything to Villermont is another matter.

Beaujeu felt a growing discomfort at the manifestation of La Salle's strange personality and erratic behavior. As a seaman he understood the urgency of the season; yet the man he was charged with delivering to an uncertain destination, by a course of unknown hazards, seemed to offer nothing but delays. On May 29, he met with La Salle and the intendant Arnoul and drew up a schedule for reaching the "far end [*fond*] of the Gulf of Mexico."[18] It would not be possible to leave before July, the captain advised; two months would be required to reach Saint-Domingue, where a week's watering stop would be required. After a September departure, it would take another month to reach the far end of the Gulf, by sailing to windward (south) of Cuba to avoid the currents off the Bahamas (the Gulf Stream). It would be well into October before La Salle's river was found, and *Le Joly* would have to winter there to avoid being wrecked by the Gulf's ferocious northers. Leaving the Mississippi in late February, the ship would not return to France before May. La Salle agreed to this plan in Arnoul's presence. But there was another problem: extra provisions for the ship's complement would be required for such a lengthy voyage and, with all that La Salle wanted to put on the ship, there was simply not enough space in the hold. Beaujeu seemed to have borrowed a page from the explorer's book: it was La Salle's fault for not having informed him beforehand. "You have ordered me," he wrote to the minister, "to facilitate this enterprise in every way." He would do so as best he could; "but I hope you will permit me to claim great credit for doing so, for I am most reluctant to put myself under sieur de La Salle's orders." The man had never been to war except against Indians, and he had no military rank, whereas Beaujeu himself had served on land and sea for thirty years. "I beg you, Monseigneur, at least to let me share the command. . . ."[19]

His was a sentiment to be expected from a military man well schooled in his profession. Quite naturally, he did not want to be subordinated in a quasi-military operation to one who lacked military training. La Salle gave proof of his inadequacies for organizing such an expedition at every turn. When he and La Forest came over from La Rochelle a few days later, Beaujeu found further cause for uneasiness. Having been led to believe that the destination was "the far end of the Gulf of Mexico," he was shaken by La Salle's sudden announcement that he had changed his plans and would go in a different direction. At next report, La Salle seemed in a hurry to sail, because of the many people he had to feed while they waited at dockside, as well as the advancing season. At last, Beaujeu reported, the explorer had determined to go by way of Canada, as not enough time remained to reach the Gulf before winter storms set in. Beaujeu agreed, but that was not the end of it. La Salle, noting that the captain as yet had no pilot, wanted to know why. Beaujeu replied that when the explorer informed him of the destination, he would choose a pilot who had knowledge of the route. La Salle answered that the pilot must know, besides the Saint Lawrence River, the coast of Saint-Domingue and the Gulf of Mexico, as he might go there from Canada.[20] Such vacillation, whether a reflection of La Salle's uncertainty or a deliberate attempt to confuse, was to be a constant source of difficulty between the two leaders, but by no means the only one.

Beaujeu's letters to Villermont and Seignelay indicate his awareness that he had been given a difficult assignment, his feeling that he was well qualified for it, and his expectation of reward. In fairness, he sought to assist La Salle, even though the explorer made it difficult. He wrote in his June 5 letter:

Seeing that the sieur de La Salle was handicapped by his lack of knowledge of business matters, I offered him my services as his agent, urging him to depend on me, who would do everything he has to do here [at Rochefort]; that he give me a list of what he needs from the commissary and the arsenal, and he would have only to go to La Rochelle and take care of his own business; I would do the rest and give him a good accounting. He told me that he was much obliged to me, but I do not know whether he will accept my offer, for he is still possessed by his customary suspicion, which would drive anyone but a Norman mad.[21]

It was not an easy time for the ship captain. Madame de Beaujeu's illness worsened. With unrelenting fever and convulsions for fourteen days, she lay "at death's door." While the Rochefort naval physician "treated her with skill and attentiveness, even to passing days and nights at her bedside," a priest came to hear her confession. At last the fever broke. She owed her life, "under God," to the physician.[22]

Le Joly's fitting out, meanwhile, had to go forward. On June 15, the sails were fitted up to the yard. La Salle had confided that he now wished to go to the Gulf of Mexico, as there was still time before equinoctial storms set in. Beaujeu discerned La Salle's effort to hide his insecurity; he actually did not know which course to take. The explorer continued to be nettlesome in other matters. He and Parassis constantly abused one another; the munitioner's brother-in-law baited the explorer by claiming certain knowledge that the expedition would never sail and that everything being put on *Le Joly* would have to be taken off. La Salle composed written protests to Arnoul and advised Beaujeu "hourly" that he planned to complain to Seignelay and that the outfitters had surely taken money from his enemies to wreck his enterprise. The captain must have brightened at the prospect of La Salle's going to Paris soon to arrange for extra provisions for his soldiers in passage; he would be rid of him for a time.[23]

On June 20 Captain Beaujeu brought his ship out of the Port of Rochefort and took her down the Rivière Charente as far as Île-Duy. With the *Joly* anchored at Vergeroux to wait for flood tide, La Salle "came to me and said in a haughty voice, sounding very much the general, that I must put on my ship his hundred men and provisions for three months more. I told him it was impossible. . . . He would not listen to reason." La Salle became angry, and words were exchanged. "Then he complained," the captain wrote to Villermont, "that I was writing and telling you everything." (The truth of that must have stung Beaujeu a bit.) They argued further over arrangements for the mess for La Salle's officers. At last La Salle stalked away to complain to Dugué (giving, according to Beaujeu, a false account of the confrontation, which caused him to abandon his belief that the explorer was an honest man). The captain believed that he had done everything possible to assist La Salle and that the latter had repaid him with ill will: "I have made him a thousand offers of assistance, even to standing as surety for him at La Rochelle for the money he was seeking and had not been able to find." He urged Villermont to disabuse Abbé Renaudot and Morel about the man and assure them that he is not what they think him to be, "and he will certainly deceive them."[24] Beaujeu thus provided a basis for Villermont's future action, which the captain surely regretted later.

By June 21 the *Joly* was ready to proceed down the Charente and thence to the Chef-de-bois roadstead of La Rochelle. Actual sailing awaited La Salle's pleasure. Beaujeu, having had no answer to his May 30 letter to Seignelay, wrote again to the minister, renewing his complaints and adding a host of new ones: La Salle's refusal to communicate his plans, his mercurial behavior, his unreasonable distrust and secrecy. Whatever the minister wished, he would do, but he asked for clear-cut orders, so that La Salle could have no complaint against him, should the explorer fall short in his accomplishments. (The distrust with which the commanders regarded each other had brought forth extraordinary precautions by each one to protect himself against incrimination in the future.) Beaujeu enumerated the vague points in his original orders, specifically asking that he himself be authorized to command the soldiers until he deemed it safe to disembark them at the destination.[25]

Beaujeu realized his miscalculation when, shortly after posting his letter, he received Seignelay's answer to his of May 30. The minister was unshakable, as well as somewhat dense; he failed to understand Beaujeu's need to employ soldiers to man the rigging on the crowded ship and to have them under his orders in case of enemy attack at sea or at the landing site. The sieur de La Salle was to have control of "all that is to be done on this voyage"; Beaujeu should not concern himself with happenings on shore, for he was never to leave his ship. The captain might enhance his merit in His Majesty's eyes by applying himself to making it all work smoothly and controlling his rancor.[26]

The Marquis de Seignelay at this time was wrestling with a plethora of details related not only to launching La Salle's voyage but also to fitting out the ships destined for Canada. It was on this same day that he wrote, with some irritation, to La Salle, urging him to hasten the recruiting of his men and to make ready to sail without delay.[27]

The intendant Arnoul also received a letter bearing the same date, with instructions for provisioning La Salle's soldiers and passengers and specifying who aboard *Le Joly* should dine in the captain's mess. Less than a week later Arnoul was reminded that "His Majesty awaits with impatience news of the ship's departure. It is important that she make sail quickly. [The king] finds that the orders he gave on this subject have not been carried out with dispatch, especially regarding the raising of soldiers. They write to him that they are scarcely more than children, or men little suited for service." And, above all, the *Joly* should sail as soon as possible. And again on June 30: "His Majesty learned with sorrow that the soldiers raised for the sieur de

La Salle were so ill-suited and scarcely in condition to serve. [Arnoul] must take care that those destined for Canada are not the same, as they must be employed in difficult service requiring vigorous, hardy men. It is feared that His Majesty's service may be greatly prejudiced by the poor choices that have been made."[28] In such a vein the minister continued to write to Arnoul until the ships sailed.

Beaujeu's letter and Seignelay's, meanwhile, had crossed in the mail. When the minister received the captain's of June 21, he took it as a reply to his of June 17 and was upset at Beaujeu's failure to comprehend his message. He delivered a more stinging rebuke under date of June 30, as evidenced by Beaujeu's reply. Though taken aback by the minister's censure, the captain stood his ground. He had, he maintained, never created any obstacle for La Salle but had merely tried to show how impossible it was to carry out his wishes. The man had so crowded the *Joly*'s decks with crates and boxes that it would be next to impossible to work the guns or the capstan; and so on, through his list of complaints, hoping that the minister "will see that it is not I who causes problems, but he who creates them for himself." Seeing that La Salle was in difficulty and short of cash, Beaujeu had lent him a hundred pistoles: evidence, he claimed, that he was not hindering the enterprise. To get a true picture of La Salle's disposition the minister might consult others who had worked for him in outfitting the voyage, such as Arnoul and his assistants. Then he could judge the future from the past. Beaujeu professed anger that the esteemed minister had been "pledged to a matter, the success of which is most uncertain." Even La Salle was beginning to doubt that it could be carried out; yet if it were at all practicable, it would succeed, "or I will perish in the effort." La Salle had presented the captain with "a long declaration," asking him to sign it, that the explorer might be exonerated of future difficulties. When Beaujeu objected to one paragraph, Arnoul drew up a substitute, and the captain signed. The intendant, Beaujeu wrote, had asked him to give the minister his opinion of the soldiers embarked on the *Joly:* "I swear to you, Monseigneur, that, for new recruits, I have never seen better troops." True, there were some young men, but they were strong and would acclimate more readily than older ones.[29] Thus, La Salle's attempts to blame the poor quality of his men for his present and future difficulties is disputed. Yet their future performance, as reported by both La Salle and Henri Joutel, was to reflect error in Beaujeu's appraisal.

The minister's remarks to Arnoul concerning this and other matters reveals that La Salle, as well as Beaujeu, was writing complaining letters to the court. A letter to Arnoul under date of July 5, with reference to the afore-mentioned memorial, serves as an example: "His Majesty awaits with impatience some news of the departure of the ship *Le Joly,* fearing that its delay will cost the season for going to the ship's destination. Although he has made the sieur de Beaujeu understand his intentions concerning the difficulties that he has created on the subject of [La Salle's command role], he agrees that he [Arnoul] should intervene to end their accusations against each other, and he should send a copy of the memorial that he had them sign."[30]

Further unpleasantness arose between La Salle and Beaujeu as a result of the captain's correspondence with Villermont. La Salle showed the captain a letter he had received from Abbé Renaudot. Even though Beaujeu had asked Villermont to disabuse Renaudot and Morel about La Salle, he claimed to have instructed the king's councilor to burn his letters. Villermont may well have felt that the best way to carry out the first request was to ignore the latter. Thus, the captain's comments were made known to the abbé. Renaudot, in turn, felt no compunction about informing La Salle: Beaujeu was writing to the king's councilor of everything that was going on at the seaport and conveying his speculations concerning the voyage. The captain vented his wrath at Villermont (and Renaudot) in a letter that ran to more than 2,500 words. He would be pleased, he advised Villermont, if he would inform the abbé (with whom Beaujeu was not personally acquainted) that he should not involve him in his conversation. Renaudot, he said, might exalt La Salle and place him in the ranks of Cortés, Pizarro, and the Almagros; "but he should not speak of me as an obstacle to his hero." He believed that La Salle, "irascible as you know him to be, intends to use this to ruin me."[31]

On receipt of the captain's letter, Villermont hastened to keep intact his friendship with Renaudot, who, after all, had a public voice in the *Gazette de France.* Regretful of the misunderstanding, the councilor wrote, he hoped that he had not failed in the duties of his friendship with La Salle that began in 1678. Yet, if La Salle had withdrawn his friendship without cause, "upon slight inferences and groundless suspicions," it was not his [Villermont's] fault. Renaudot responded that he saw no reason for La Salle to be angry with Villermont, and he himself would not take up La Salle's grievance. The abbé gave assurance that he continued to hold the councilor in great esteem and friendship, which nothing would ever change.[32]

Beaujeu, his pique notwithstanding, still kept Villermont informed of goings-on at the seaport. *Le Joly*'s officers had carried out the king's order to recruit soldiers for the enterprise, but La Salle had given no end of trouble over the matter. "The argument over this," the captain wrote, "has made La Salle a bit ridiculous at Rochefort. There are very few who do not believe him demented. . . . Some who have known him twenty years say he is inclined to be a dreamer. One St.-Michel, who knew him in Canada and has crossed swords with him, speaks none too well of his courage. He does not get along as well here as in Paris."[33]

Beaujeu, nevertheless, pledged to continue to hold La Salle in high esteem until he saw that his enterprise had failed. Despite his struggle with himself to reflect a reasonable and objective attitude toward La Salle, the captain had come to be viewed as indulging in the same kind of blame throwing of which he had accused the explorer.

Time for sailing was only a fortnight away when Captain Beaujeu reported, on July 10, to both Villermont and Seignelay. The *Joly*, now at La Rochelle, had been ready to sail seven or eight days ago. While waiting for La Salle to complete his arrangements, the captain had been "enjoying myself with my friends." La Salle had always been invited to join the festivity but never would: "I do all I can to gain his friendship." La Salle, however, viewed the friendly overtures as "suspicious"—a habitual attitude that had always prevented him from responding to Beaujeu's benevolent gestures and stood in the way of his developing amicable relationships with anyone. He had made known also his suspicions of Madame de Beaujeu's devotion to the Jesuits, who, he said, governed her. La Salle was still "making a mystery of his project," but Beaujeu learned that, when he first came from America and was trying to find backers, "he spoke of it to everyone." It was still a mystery to the captain. He knew only that they would depart La Rochelle's roadstead with ten or twelve ships, which *Le Joly* was to convoy beyond the capes. Then, with four ships—the *Joly*, the storeship *Aimable,* a ketch *(Saint-François)*, and "a barque called *La Belle*"—they would pursue their own course, which he believed would be southwest.[34]

Beaujeu assuredly gave the minister and the king information concerning La Salle that they did not want to hear; he sought also to get his message to the court by means of his letters to the king's councilor Cabart de Villermont. Any assessment of his writings and how they reflect the captain's character and motives depends on one's perspective. Viewed through one pair of glasses, they may be seen as the petulant whining of a perpetual complainer, driven by jealousy and an overweening pride. Such a view, in essence, was Francis Parkman's.[35] Yet, seen through a different lens, it may be judged that Beaujeu had just cause for complaint, and for warning the minister of the portent for disaster implicit in La Salle's limitations of personality and ability. That he reaped rebuke for his efforts is not surprising, for complaining—although a most human quality—is seldom pleasing to hear. The refusal by minister and king to take him seriously was, for the men and women who made up the expedition, a death sentence.

The king, seeing nothing more in Beaujeu's words—or La Salle's—than a personality clash, was unsympathetic. Only at the end, as the monarch looked forward to being free of the two leaders' harangues, did he solicit an unbiased report from the intendant. If it was motivated by any slight suspicion that he had made a tremendous mistake, it came too late. The monarch wrote on the very day the ships sailed:

> The delay of *Le Joly*'s sailing could also postpone and jeopardize the success of the sieur de La Salle's enterprise. His Majesty must tell him [Arnoul] that this is almost always the case at Rochefort: that what should be dispatched in three weeks is sometimes delayed for three months. It is intolerable that His Majesty's service should be conducted in such a manner.
>
> His Majesty has seen the memorial that [Arnoul] has drawn up concerning the dispute between the sieur de La Salle and the sieur de Beaujeu. He approves of everything contained in this memorial, although it may not provide for all the disputes that have arisen between these two officers.
>
> Sieur de Beaujeu wrote that sieur de La Salle seemed very uncertain of the success of his enterprise, and, although what he has made known in that regard is truly the effect of their animosity, His Majesty will be pleased to be informed of the sieur Arnoul's opinion on the subject. He should make known all that he learns by way of La Rochelle that concerns the sieur de La Salle's sailing. His Majesty has no doubt that he may now be making sail, and it would be a great misfortune should he still be in La Rochelle's roadstead.[36]

Indeed, as these words were written, the wind filled the sails of the four ships and bore them out into the Bay of Biscay. The king's urgency testifies that the expedition was intended not merely as one of colonization but also of conquest. His anxiety arose from a fear that the war might end, and he would be deprived of his imperial objectives. But "great misfortune" often comes in unexpected packages.

Chapter 7

The Parting Gun

A FAREWELL TO FRANCE

During June and July, 1684, participants in La Salle's venture gathered at La Rochelle in preparation for the voyage. Among the first to arrive was Jean-Baptiste Minet, king's engineer assigned by His Majesty to oversee fortifications at La Salle's destination. Minet, age twenty-three, reached the port town on June 2 or 3. At La Salle's urging, he obtained a salary advance to invest in the enterprise and influenced his friends to do the same, but the more he saw of its leader, the more he doubted. Assigned to the *Joly*, he had a seven-week wait before departure, while would-be colonists and *engagés,* or hired men, dribbled in. Long after the Royal Navy vessel was ready to sail, La Salle still had not completed his business. In the interim, Minet made the acquaintance of Gabriel Barbier, a lieutenant in La Salle's soldiery, and Nicolas de La Salle of the ship's company. From these two who had journeyed with La Salle down the Mississippi he was to take down an account of the 1682 canoe voyage that he believed to be free of the contradictions and bias afflicting other accounts. The young engineer also kept his own journal of the *Joly*'s round-trip to the Gulf of Mexico, which, had it fallen into the wrong hands, would have been destroyed as some others were.[1]

Barbier was one of five officers in charge of the one hundred soldiers sailing on the *Joly*. Sieur de Valigny, who had replaced Alphonse de Tonti, was the senior captain; Bihorel, second captain. Lieutenants besides Barbier were Colin Crevel de Moranget (La Salle's nephew) and the profligate young nobleman Marquis de Sablonnière. As for the soldiers themselves, recruited in late May or early June by the *Joly*'s officers, only a few can be identified by name. Of their quality and condition, La Salle complained to the minister, thereby bringing reproach upon both Captain Beaujeu and the Rochefort intendant Arnoul. The soldiers, on the outbound voyage, supplemented Beaujeu's crew of seventy, which he declared insufficient for defending the thirty-four-gun warship, or even for working the rigging. In battle-readiness, the vessel was designed to carry two hundred men. Aside from being dissatisfied with the ship's quality, the captain foresaw that, after landing the soldiers, he would have to return her to France with a skeleton crew.[2]

Also embarked on the *Joly* were all or most of the eight volunteers: Joutel, Le Gros, Thibault, La Villeperdrix, Gayen, Marle, Hurié, and Planterose. La Salle's personal attendants included the surgeon Liotot; the Shawnee Nika; a Huguenot secretary whose name is not known; and two servants, Dumesnil and Saget. One of the latter two may have been the man called L'Espérance, who is described as La Salle's servant and who is known to have embarked on the *Joly*. He had journeyed with La Salle down the Mississippi and, like Nicolas and Barbier, returned with him to France. And, as with Nicolas and Barbier, the river adventure was much in his conversation. He found an eager listener in a peasant lad named Denis Thomas, who was to find his place in history in an unexpected manner.[3]

Names of only a few of the *Joly*'s seventy-man regular crew are known. Those who can be connected to Captain Beaujeu's company, besides Nicolas de La Salle, are Chevalier d'Hére, lieutenant; Ensign Du Hamel; chief pilot, François Guitron; Christophe Gabaret, second pilot; sieur de Juif, ship's surgeon; Duval, scrivener; and Pimont, clerk *(commis)*.

La Salle himself, like several of those who were closest to him, would sail on the *Joly* only as far as Saint-Domingue (present Haiti). With him on the first leg of the journey was the younger of two nephews, Colin Cavelier, whose age is variously given but who was little more than a child. Also, there were five of the six clerics, Récollet Franciscans and Sulpicians, charged with carrying out the expedition's religious aims. La Salle had applied to the appropriate religious authorities to supply the desired number of missionaries. At the start, there were three Sulpicians and four Récollets. At La Salle's request Father Zénobe Membré, who had shared in the explorer's travels in Canada and on the Mississippi, was designated superior of the Franciscans. His companions at first were Fathers Maxime Le Clercq and Denis Morguet from the Récollet province of Saint-Antoine in Artois, northern France, and Father Anastase Douay, from Quesnoy in Hainault. Father Morguet, however, withdrew because of illness when the ships returned to port after their abortive initial departure.[4]

By some strange circumstance, La Salle's brother showed up with the Sulpician group. It seems reasonable that La Salle would have been surprised and dismayed at this turn of events, for Abbé Cavelier had caused him nothing but trouble in the past. Yet it is claimed that the explorer had "effected a reconciliation with his brother" and "invited him to come along. . . ."[5] In late May the archbishop of Rouen assigned two priests of Saint-Sulpice to go "to those regions of New France in which there is no bishop or apostolic vicar, as laborers for the Gospel, empowered to preach the Gospel, to baptize, perform divine service, hear confessions . . . and administer the sacraments." They were the Abbés Cavelier and François Chefdeville of Rouen, La Salle's cousin.[6] There actually were two Chefdevilles on the expedition, probably the sons of the Rouen merchant François Chefdeville. The younger brother succumbed to an illness during the layover at Saint-Domingue. All the priests began the voyage on the *Joly* except one. Either Father Le Clercq or Father Douay sailed on the *Aimable*.[7]

Having continually pressured Beaujeu to load more of his goods on *Le Joly* than the ship could reasonably accommodate, La Salle at last took steps to obtain additional vessels. He evidently appealed to Seignelay in his letter of May 30, 1684 (not extant), to which the minister replied unequivocally on June 17: the king would furnish no more than two ships. La Salle by that time had acted on his own, accepting the offer of La Rochelle merchant and shipowner Jean Massiot the younger to lease him the armed cargo ship *Aimable*. On June 5 the explorer signed an agreement with Massiot by which he would take on the voyage the 180-tun *flûte* (storeship) for 1,550 livres per month.

Before the royal notaries at La Rochelle appeared in person the honorable Jean Massiot *le jeune*, merchant of this city, sole owner of the good and suitably watertight ship named *l'Aimable* of one hundred eighty tuns burthen or thereabouts, captain [Claude] Aigron; provisioned, fully rigged, and seaworthy, with enough food, bread, wine, lard and other needs for the nourishment of the captain and the 22-man crew for the entire voyage . . . and armed with ten cannon and small arms. The aforementioned sieur Massiot has leased his ship voluntarily to Monsieur Cavelier de La Salle, governor for His Majesty of the territory of Louisiana . . . who will load within its roadsteads the cargo of merchandise for the voyage to North America, and then send it back to the island of Martinique, there to be discharged.

The agreement further guaranteed the monthly lease payment for at least four months, with two months paid in advance, beginning when the ship set sail from her home port. Should La Salle need the ship to send to France merchandise obtained in the Indian trade, the agreement would extend to her return to La Rochelle, the same monthly rate to apply up to six months. Massiot was to provide all the food and wages for the crew for the entire voyage. Damages or breakdowns occurring during the voyage would be "supported between both parties, according to the ways and customs of the sea."[8]

The ship's twenty-two-man crew list was drawn on July 2, from the thirty-five-year-old Captain Aigron and the pilot Zacherie Mengaud, age fifty, of Oléron, down to two lads of twelve years. On July 3 Massiot signed the cargo register for *l'Aimable*. The list of items that La Salle had placed on board included eight cannon and their cannonballs; eight thousand pounds of powder; thirty casks *(tonneaux)* of wine; 150 quintals of bread; fifty barrels of beef and lard; various types of cloth and clothing; axes and other tools; and four hundred *fusils* (rifled muskets).[9]

The *Aimable*'s passenger list can be partially gleaned from a variety of sources. Besides the crew, there were "seven cadets and 40 hired workers," according to Minet; one of the Récollet priests (probably Douay) and "thirty other persons, officers and volunteers," according to Joutel. The Talon family accounted for seven, including the mother and two young daughters. The other women and girls destined for the Texas settlement numbered six, for a total of nine. Besides Madame Talon, whose husband was a soldier, there was only one other married woman. She is presumed to have been Madame Bréman, wife of a soldier, who had a young son.

Lucien and Isabelle Talon, and their three sons, and two daughters had come from Canada two months previously, specifically to join the La Salle expedition. Lucien Talon *pére,* a native of the bishopric of Beauvais, Picardie (north of Paris), had migrated to Canada in 1666 at age twenty-two. He worked two years as a servant for Jean de Bourdon, the first *procureur-général* of Quebec and father of Jacques de Bourdon (sieur d'Autray), who probably was about Lucien's age. By 1671, Talon had settled at Neuville, across the Saint Lawrence River from Quebec. That same year he married Isabelle Planteau, native of Saint-Méry Parish in Paris, with Jacques Lussier as a witness to the Quebec ceremony. In the next ten years five children were born.[10] As an *habitant* of Neuville, Lucien the elder farmed a small tract of land, struggling against the inhospitable environment to support his growing family. When Jacques de Bourdon, sieur d'Autray, returned from the voyage down the Mississippi with La Salle, he recounted the adventure to his father's former servant in terms that held forth the promise of a grand opportunity. On that basis the fateful decision was made: the Talon family would cross the ocean twice to seek its fortune in a warmer clime with limitless natural resources and pleasant surroundings. When Lucien, Isabelle, and their already sizable family arrived at La Rochelle in the spring of 1684, Isabelle was pregnant with their sixth child. There was just time enough for a hurried trip to Paris for a final visit with friends and relatives before boarding the *Aimable* to cross the ocean once more.

Among the other young women and girls standing by to embark was a servant girl from Saint-Jean-d'Angély, seventy-three kilometers by road from La Rochelle, where she had been employed. Whether she was acquainted with Jacques Labaussair, a twenty-two-year-old baker from the same town, who probably sailed on the same ship, is not of record. (Labaussair comes back into our narrative later.) Another of the young women claimed to be a cousin of the Curé de Saint-Eustache. Although the girls surely joined the enterprise in hope of finding husbands, only one of them was to marry; thus she gained her identity as Madame Barbier, the first European woman of record to bear a child in the territory that was to become Texas. One lass, described as *une jeune fille de Paris,* chose to be called "Mademoiselle Paris," perhaps, it was thought, to conceal her true identity; her low station was to cost her the chance of marriage.[11]

On the same ship was a youth who is noteworthy for two reasons: the deposition that he made a few years later in Mexico City and his life after the destruction of the French colony. He was Pierre Meunier, son of Louis Meunier, sieur de Preville, of Paris. Probably no more than fifteen at the start of the voyage, he claimed to have come to La Rochelle from Paris "as companion of Monsieur de Salas [La Salle], with whom he embarked on an *urca* [hooker] called *la Ymable.*" A witness to the first round of murders in the East Texas wilds, he told in his deposition far less than he knew.[12]

Probably passengers on *l'Aimable* also were the merchant brothers Duhaut, Pierre and Dominique. Pierre is described by Minet as a sergeant soon after the Texas landing. The brothers had a small fortune in merchandise for trade in Saint-Domingue or with the American natives, laded on the *Aimable,* and perhaps the *Belle* also, with expectations of substantial profit. Their disappointment turned to smoldering bitterness, then burst forth in the white heat of hate and rampant brutality. Joining them at Petit Goâve was a young lad, not quite twelve, named Jean L'Archevêque, who had come to the islands from his native Bayonne with his merchant parents. A lackey of Pierre Duhaut, with whom he claimed kinship, he was to be drawn into Duhaut's misdeeds.

Whereas Minet ascribes a total of eight merchants, the names of only three others are known: Merlin, Burel, and Massiot. The relationship of the latter with the *Aimable*'s owner, if any, is not known. Villiers has concluded that all but the Duhaut brothers either remained in Saint-Domingue or returned from the Texas coast with the *Joly*.[13]

Probably the most numerous group sailing on the *Aimable* were the *engagés,* the hired men contracted on La Salle's behalf by Jean Massiot the younger. Minet places at forty-four the number of "hired men or servants." Between June 7 and July 6 Massiot made contracts at La Rochelle before the notaries Rivière and Soullard with thirty-seven men who claimed various trades and professions. With the exception of the two surgeons, Étienne Liotot (who as surgeon-major sailed on the *Joly* with La Salle) and Louis Ruiné, none of these has been known previously.[14]

They came from scattered provinces of France, from Provence in the southeast to Upper Normandy in the northwest. In age they ranged from eighteen to forty, excepting only Jacques Jean of Moeze, Saintonge, the oldest volunteer at age sixty. Contract terms were two and three years. Trades represented singly include baker, edge-tool maker, furrier and glover (Pietro Pauollo di Bonardi, an Italian from Turin), ship's pilot, cannoneer (a German from Brandenburg), blacksmith, shoemaker, and gardener. Two were classed as laborers, one a farm worker. There were the two surgeons, as well as two coopers, two flour millers, and two masons. Eight were carpenters or shipwrights (ship's carpenters), including one master carpenter. Most numerous were the eleven sailors, none of them linked to any of the ship crews.[15]

La Salle was to rate these and other tradesmen who signed on as a sorry lot, drawn from the scum of the channel ports and beggars at the church doors: "untaught in any craft, intractable to any discipline." As another interpreter with a pro–La Salle bias has put it: "Inexperienced, ill-adapted to the task, ill-recruited, rendered hostile to de la Salle during the crossing by the intrigues of Beaujeu, d'Aigron, and Minet, most of these men were bound to become sick, mutinous, and trouble makers."[16]

One who was to turn troublemaker was the surgeon Liotot, who made this contract with La Salle:

Before the Royal notary at La Rochelle appeared in person Estienne Liotot, surgeon major, of Provence, about thirty years of age, who by these presents voluntarily commits himself to the sieur Cavelier de La Salle, governor for the King in the country of Louisiana, agreeing to serve him or his representatives in his profession of surgeon major in all reasonable things that he will be commanded to do during two consecutive years to commence at the moment he sets foot on shore in the said country and end on the same day [two years later]. During that time he will be fed, lodged, bedded, and paid for his passage, going and coming, should he wish to return to France immediately upon the end of the time. To achieve the foregoing, the said Liotot promises to board at the first command of the sieur de La Salle on the ship that he designates.

Liotot was to be paid quarterly at the rate of 250 livres per year, either in Louisiana or La Rochelle, at his option. He acknowledged receipt of 62 livres 10 soles as payment in advance for the first quarter.[17] Little else is known of Liotot: only that whatever humanitarian impulse caused him to become a surgeon ultimately gave way to unbridled hatred and vengeance-driven butchery.

Even with the *Aimable,* La Salle still needed more cargo space. Almost immediately, he contracted with François Duprat of La Rochelle, owner of the ketch *Saint-François,* for the use of this vessel on "the voyage to the islands." By Minet's account, the intendant (Arnoul) paid half the charter fee to carry the provisions that could not be taken on the *Aimable.* The cargo manifest, drawn July 8, lists twenty tonneaux of wine, four hogsheads of flour, a dozen of lard, forty of brandy, and a dozen *fusils.* The *Saint-François* had made a voyage to Saint-Domingue the previous February, freighted with wine, brandy, and various other merchandise. Upon her return to La Rochelle, she was given an entirely new nine-man crew, consisting of Paul Giraud (or Girault) of Auvert as captain and eight others, ranging in age from eighteen to thirty-two. The *Saint-François* was not intended to continue beyond Saint-Domingue. Joutel suggests at one point that her cargo was to be sold in the islands as a means of defraying expenses. After the ketch was captured by Spanish privateers, he claimed that she carried "the greater part of our provisions . . . but also nearly all our cooking pots."[18] Whether her cargo was to be transferred to one of the other ships (replacing provisions consumed on the first stage of the voyage) or sold in Saint-Domingue, the intent was for her to return from the island colony to France.

Unfortunately, neither the *Belle*'s crew list nor her cargo manifest has turned up. Daniel Moraud was the captain, Elie Richaud the pilot. They and most of the original crew were to be replaced long before the ship's final disaster. Only the dissolute mate Pierre Tessier survived to the end. Built from April to June, 1684, in the Royal Navy yard at Rochefort, the *Belle* was armed with six iron deck guns and eight swivel guns and commissioned in the French Royal Navy. It now appears certain that four bronze cannon were placed in her hold and remained there until she was wrecked on Matagorda Peninsula early in 1686, to be recovered three centuries later. These guns, which fired a four-pound ball, do not appear on the *Aimable's* cargo manifest; they are not to be confused with four twelve-pounders mentioned by La Salle as being intended for his fortress and lost with that ship, which, incidentally, cannot be accounted for. The record of the bronze cannon, traced by John de Bry, reveals that they were cast at the Rochefort naval foundry by master founder Jean La Tâche, prior to July, 1679, the month of Tâche's death. They originally were part of the armament of the forty-two-gun, five hundred–tun naval vessel *Faucon,* built at Rochefort in 1673–74.[19]

The expurgated version of Joutel—better to call it a synopsis with which undue liberties were taken—attributes to the expedition historian this account of the journey to the seaport: "Our Rendezvous was appointed at Rochel, where we were to imbark. Messieurs Cavelier, the one Brother, the other Nephew [young Colin Cavelier] to Monsieur de la Sale, Messieurs Chedeville, Planterose, Thibault, Ory, some others and I, repair'd thither in July 1684." (While other members of the Rouen group embarked on the *Joly,* Thibault sailed on the *Belle.*) A third Sulpician priest from Rouen, Abbé d'Esmanville (or Damonville), had been waiting at the seaport for more than a fortnight. The extract of his journal begins: "We arrived at La Rochelle on the 14th of June, 1684. On the 16th of July the parting gun was fired and we went on board. We set sail on the 21st."[20]

The latter two dates represent the fleet's early attempts to get underway, only to be frustrated by contrary winds; the ships did not make good their departure until July 24. Beaujeu, on July 10, had expressed the hope of sailing next day, but the fresh west-southwest wind prevented it. A letter addressed to Cabart de Villermont dated July 22 explains: "M. de Beaujeu set sail several times to depart, but the wind has gone west and he has always been compelled to come in again." The writer, Machaut-Rougemont at Rochefort, a friend and fellow officer of Captain Beaujeu, believed that the ships had finally put to sea "two days ago [July 20]," on a south-southeast wind.[21] It was only another false start.

FIGURE 13

Bronze Cannon from the Belle. *Three of the four bronze cannon provided for defense of La Salle's settlements were salvaged from the* Belle's *wreckage by Texas Historical Commission archeologists. The fourth was missing. The first gun recovered is shown here after conservation. Texas Historical Commission photo*

Villermont's correspondent seems to typify the partisanship that attended the voyage and its preparations and the meddling in the affair by persons on the sidelines. "One could not be more absurd," he wrote, "than the sieur de La Salle was before he embarked, with regard to all his pretensions to the command. He put forth no less than sixty clauses, which our intendant adjusted the best he could. It is a bad start for the voyage. I am very sorry for poor Beaujeu, who has to deal with a man of such a sullen disposition."[22]

Machaut-Rougemont had assumed Beaujeu's former role as Villermont's chief informant. To Villermont he offered his opinion on the dismal prospects facing the voyage. Most recently, La Salle had declared his destination to be the Gulf of Mexico, but the winter northers would surely force him to lie over in the Windward Islands. On the other hand, if he went to Canada, he would be compelled to travel overland to reach Mexico and carry out "his fine schemes." Far from being a clever man, "as *they* have tried to represent him," La Salle seemed not even to know how to reckon the seasons. Machaut-Rougemont believed many of the explorer's claims to be fictional; his description of the Gulf of Mexico based on insufficient data; his report of a great river entering the Gulf either mistaken or an outright fabrication: "We have enough information . . . to know that there is no such important river." Even though La Salle had taken the latitude, the longitude must also be known to prove that he had not entered a great salt lake rather than the sea. (How he proposed to obtain the longitude at this early date is not revealed.) "Furthermore, we have been in those regions enough to know that ships cannot sail in the gulf without danger from the shoals."[23] The busybodies continued to work in tandem with La Salle's ill temper to frustrate his "fine schemes." Their ignorance was no barrier to their representations.

All seemed in readiness for sailing on the sixteenth, when Abbé d'Esmanville and the others went on board and the parting gun was fired, but a favorable wind still was lacking. On the eighteenth, La Salle wrote a farewell letter to his mother:

> Madame and most honored mother,
>
> At last, having waited a long time for the favorable wind, and having had many difficulties to overcome, we are leaving with four ships and nearly four hundred men. Everyone is well, including little Colin and my [other] nephew. We all have high hopes of a favorable outcome. We are not going by way of Canada but through the Gulf of Mexico. We fervently wish that the result of this voyage may contribute to your repose and comfort. Assuredly, I shall spare no effort [to that end]. I beg you to preserve yourself for the love of us.[24]

La Salle, it appears, had at first spoken to his mother of returning to the Mississippi by way of Canada and had not bothered to correct the impression after his destination became fixed. To the ordinary mind, with any concept of the geography, the very idea of proceeding up the Saint Lawrence River to plant a colony on the Mississippi is preposterous. Yet, for La Salle, it was the known versus the unknown. The outcome could hardly have been worse had he chosen differently.

After the several attempts to depart, a favorable wind at last filled the sails on July 24 and carried the ships from the Chef-de-bois roadstead to the open sea. The "parting gun" marked the hoisting of sail, the time for all the passengers and crew to be on board and all others to go ashore. It seemed also to have been a signal for a number of the voyagers to take up their pens to keep journals or take notes from which to write letters or memoirs.

FIGURE 14

Port of Embarkation. La Salle's small fleet sailed from the port of La Rochelle on July 24, 1684. Although little changed in general appearance, the port today is largely used by pleasure craft. Photo by John de Bry

Most notable among the scribes is Henri Joutel of Rouen. More than La Salle's fellow townsman, Joutel belonged to a family that had long been associated with the Caveliers. Being six or seven years younger than La Salle, Joutel may have had very little previous contact with the leader himself but was well acquainted with other members of the family. His father had been a gardener for La Salle's uncle, Henri Cavelier. Joutel had enlisted in the army at age seventeen, about the time La Salle first sailed for Canada. He had returned to Rouen only recently when he heard of the expedition La Salle was planning and, at about the age of thirty-four, offered his services as a volunteer.[25]

Joutel's loyalty to La Salle and Abbé Cavelier, though strained at times, remained intact till the end. Even though his journal occasionally expresses criticism of his commander's actions or judgments, he can be considered only as a La Salle partisan, especially in the leader's controversy with Captain Beaujeu. Furthermore, military discipline was instilled in him; he obeyed his commander and respected his authority. Joutel is unrivaled as the expedition's historian; his is the only account to chronicle the episode from the departure from France until the return of the surviving remnant. If La Salle had ever had a confidant, it would have been Joutel. Yet Joutel's account has its limitations; he could not be knowledgeable of all La Salle's activities. Nor does he in every instance present an accurate, fair, and complete picture. The reportage of other writers or deponents in some instances parallels Joutel's; yet some of the relations deal with journeys or episodes not witnessed by or fully known to him. Unfortunately, the other accounts are often less truthful and not as well informed as Joutel's; in fact, several of those who gave information about the expedition afterward found reason for lying about one aspect of it or another, and some accounts were fabricated or embellished in France.

Although Joutel's narrative remains the most comprehensive and reliable of the entire voyage, there are others that help to round out the picture. A case in point is Minet's journal, which covered the *Joly*'s entire voyage to and from Matagorda Bay. From La Rochelle to Saint-Domingue, Minet and Joutel, being on the same ship, provide different perspectives on the same events. From the latter place, Joutel, with La Salle, traveled on *l'Aimable;* the journals relate the goings-on on different ships for the rest of the voyage to the Texas coast, important especially after the ships become separated.

Minet and Joutel were but two of several of the *Joly*'s passengers who chronicled all or part of the voyage to Texas. One of the more lucid and straight-forward narratives as far as Saint-Domingue is an anonymous letter written at Petit Goâve, obviously by a knowledgeable and articulate person, such as one of the priests. Aside from the fact that this writer was a passenger on the *Joly* and the evidence that he was La Salle's ally in his continuing squabble with Beaujeu, the only clue is that he had a brother on the expedition. Although the brother was ill at Petit Goâve, he apparently had recovered by the date of the letter. Several circumstances point to Père Maxime Le Clercq as the writer. A volunteer with the same surname appears later—possibly the brother referred to in the letter. In the colony, Father Le Clercq exercised his literary bent by keeping a journal of happenings in the Texas settlement, in which he made comments critical of La Salle. If Le Clercq was the author of the anonymous letter from Petit Goâve, however, he did not sail on the *Aimable,* as Father Habig supposed, but on the *Joly*.[26]

Abbé d'Esmanville kept a journal of the entire outbound voyage. From the published extract, it appears to be significant chiefly for what he reveals of La Salle's military objectives that caused him to return to France. La Salle's brother, Abbé Cavelier, wrote not only of the entire voyage but of several inland journeys. Much of what he wrote is seen only as a flagrant disservice to historical truth.

It should be noted that three of the five writers reveal themselves to be La Salle partisans. The exceptions are Minet and Abbé d'Esmanville, both of whom returned to France with *Le Joly*. There was, in fact, a sixth journal kept on board the *Joly* of the voyage to Saint-Domingue, by Father Membré. The private document, which related the arguments between Beaujeu and La Salle, was discovered and destroyed, as Father Le Clercq's would be.[27]

The ships had been loaded and ready to sail at least since July 10. The holds were packed with provisions to sustain the soldiers and colonists for nine months, instead of the six originally planned: tools for building a fort and settlement; goods for bartering with the American natives; cannon and cannonballs for the projected fort, and cases of small arms for the hundred soldiers and their Indian allies to come from Illinois, the intended conquerors of Nueva Vizcaya. On deck were coops of chickens and pens of goats and swine, anathema to Beaujeu, who saw in them an encumbrance to the management of the ship in heavy weather or manning the guns in case of attack. Always hard put to determine La Salle's next move, he was due for one more surprise.

With at least two hundred men already on board the *Joly*, La Salle, on the day of sailing, brought thirty-six more. The captain, without forewarning, had not arranged for water for the extra people. The space between decks was taken up by the stores, so that the soldiers and sailors had to make the entire voyage on the upper deck, alternately exposed to scorching sun and chilling rain. Despite Beaujeu's warning, La Salle refused to send some of these late-comers to the other vessels. The *Joly*, therefore, put to sea with "almost 240 men," and the unhealthy arrangement gave rise to rampant illness. If La Salle's claim in the letter to his mother is correct, that the four ships carried nearly 400 persons, then his company numbered almost 300 at the start. The crews of the three ships that were not to remain with the abortive colony totaled approximately 100. There is no reliable accounting of the extent to which the would-be colonists were diminished by death, desertion, and defection; hence no accurate number can be assigned to the colony on the Texas coast. In all likelihood, close to 200 persons were to go ashore at Matagorda Bay and share the miseries of the misplaced French settlement.[28]

After days of sweltering in the July heat in crowded quarters below or exposure on the open deck, those on board at last felt the stir of a refreshing breeze as, again, the parting gun sounded and sails were hoisted. The four ships sailed from the Chef-de-bois roadstead with twenty other vessels bound for Canada and the Caribbean islands. Aboard one of the ships for Canada was La Forest, carrying orders for supporting La Salle's military operation.[29] The *Joly* was assigned as the command vessel until the fleet was beyond Cape Finistèrre, the last of the Spanish promontories known to harbor English, Spanish, and Dutch pirates euphemistically calling themselves privateers. From that point the other vessels would go their own way. The plan was frustrated, however, by an accident aboard the *Joly*. At eight o'clock on the morning of July 27, almost forty-six leagues from La Rochelle, her bowsprit broke in the middle. The anonymous writer attributes the mishap to rough weather, a matter disputed by Joutel and Abbé Cavelier (who says the wind was "very moderate and we were under full sail"), and, by inference, La Salle. "Some of us," Joutel comments, "thought that this did not happen by accident." That thought, according to the abbé, occasioned some uneasiness: "A report had been circulated on the ship, even before we sailed, that we should not get very far, and that a *lettre de cachet* ["royal order"] would come to La Rochelle that would prevent continuation of the voyage."[30]

The other twenty ships pursued their own course unescorted, their sails soon lost to view. The *Joly* furled her own canvas and cut away the rigging from the broken mast. Considering the alternatives, the officers' council thought first of proceeding to Lisbon for the needed repairs but ultimately decided to return to Rochefort for greater security and faster service. With the other three vessels trailing, the *Joly* reversed course. On July 30 all four ships dropped anchor between the mouth of the Rivière Charante and Île-d'Aix and sent a shallop to notify the intendant. The promptness with which the new mast was fitted, Joutel wrote, "banished all our suspicions." Even La Salle, writing to the marine minister from Rochefort, had praise for intendant Arnoul's diligence in getting the ship ready to sail again. There was no hint of suspicion that the *Joly*'s broken bowsprit had been purposely caused; in fact, he puts forth a more charitable attitude toward Beaujeu, whose past testiness—La Salle now believed—had been provoked by persons with a grievance. Since the two of them had been alone together, all had gone well. Harmony among his own men boded well for the success of his enterprise.[31]

The contents of this letter given in summary tell much about the mission on which the French crown was sending La Salle and how the explorer himself intended to carry it out. The missive reflects La Salle's original expectations that La Forest would descend the Mississippi with native reinforcements from the Illinois River post. He feared that Governor La Barre in New France would use the Iroquois war as an excuse to forestall La Forest's journey. Yet, if he failed to rendezvous with La Forest, he himself would go—while the fort he had been ordered to build on the lower Mississippi was under construction—to meet the expected Indian troops from Fort-Saint-Louis (Illinois). Thus, in five or six months, the minister would have news of his departure for "la Biscaye."[32]

Beaujeu wrote the minister in a different vein. While acknowledging that the *Joly*'s damage had been repaired in good order, he asseverated that the mishap occasioned no real delay, "for we must wait either here or at Saint-Domingue for the September equinox to pass." The captain, however, had other business in mind. Playing an old theme, he reminded Seignelay that he would not be at court that winter to apply for his pension. He noted that most officers quit the sea in winter to go to court to solicit favors; it was a common saying in the navy that if one expected to obtain the king's largesse he must be present. "Hence . . . so many officers, when winter comes, pester you for their leaves under pretense of family affairs or their health but nevertheless appear at Versailles well and hearty." Even were he not one of the navy's senior captains, with thirty years' service, his present undertaking would deserve the consideration he asked: "I am going to an unknown country to seek something almost as hard to find as the philosopher's stone, late in the season . . . and with a troubled man."[33]

While the new bowsprit was being fitted and La Salle and Beaujeu were contemplating their reports to the minister, Minet was having his own problems. Feeling ill, he went ashore with Barbier on the island of Aix. There he "let blood with a broken stone, like the savages," and immediately felt fine.[34]

In scarcely more than twenty-four hours after the return to Rochefort, the new timber was in place and the ships were ready to sail again. In the evening of August 1, the parting gun sounded once more, the sails caught the breeze, and they glided through the strait at the lower end of Île-d'Aix to the open sea.

Behind remained a host of La Salle's former well-wishers whom he had managed to alienate. Even the Abbés Bernou and Renaudot, who had written his memorials and strongly influenced the crown in the explorer's favor, now equivocated their support. He had offended Renaudot by his apparent ingratitude, which seemed evident from his failure to communicate with him. Bernou, in receipt of Renaudot's complaint, replied that he "would never have believed that [La Salle] could have remained so long at La Rochelle, returning to port three times, without writing you a single letter, and worse, without returning the originals [maps?] that you had lent him." More than once Bernou had observed that La Salle's consideration for his friends endured only in their presence. The abbé in Rome had written to "M. de Clairambault *le fils*" in hope of obtaining for La Salle "plenary indulgence." The disagreement with Alphonse de Tonti had cost the explorer the friendship of Cabart de Villermont, who had openly declared against La Salle and was attempting to turn Cartigny and Morel (chief clerk of the admiralty) against him. Yet, Bernou continues, "I think it is necessary to endeavor to preserve his credit with his benefactors and patrons and, until we receive news of him, to pray for the success of his voyage." At the next opportunity, he must be taken to task for his inconsiderate behavior and urged to mend his ways.[35]

In short, the two abbés now saw that their having made La Salle the cat's paw of their private schemes had the potential to discredit not only La Salle but also themselves. Still, the Marquis de Seignelay clung doggedly to his position, refusing to believe that La Salle had failed long after he had evidence that it was so.

Chapter 8

Voyage of Destiny

THE HIDDEN RIVER

The favorable wind held, bearing the four ships from the Chef-de-bois road-stead out into the Bay of Biscay a second time. On August 8 they doubled Cape Finistèrre, the westernmost Spanish promontory, without encountering the "Ostend privateers."[1] All went very well between the two leaders on the *Joly* until the little fleet came into the latitude of Madeira, in 32°N, twenty-one days out of Rochefort. At that point Captain Beaujeu sent his lieutenant, Chevalier d'Hère, to ask La Salle to make port for water and fresh provisions. La Salle rejected the idea, claiming that there was need for neither, that eight or ten days would be lost by the stopover, the expedition's secrecy compromised. Beaujeu was not pleased, nor were his officers. A passenger named Paget, "bourgeois from La Rochelle," took up the matter so insistently that La Salle angrily ordered him to silence. When the explorer complained to Beaujeu, the captain replied that La Salle must know that Paget was one of his own men. La Salle withdrew to his quarters in a huff.[2]

Thus, the tension between the two was rekindled. "Thereafter," says the anonymous writer, "M. de Beaujeu, could scarcely conceal his annoyance" and vowed not to put into any port until they reached Petit Goâve. The captain and La Salle continually raised new points of dispute. "M. de La Salle has not passed a week without being attacked . . . and has been constantly on the defensive."[3]

The ships came into the northeast tradewinds on the twenty-fourth and a week later took a battering from a two-day storm. With a stern wind, the *Saint-François* lost steerage, fell behind, and was out of sight of the other vessels for twelve days. In the latitude of Hispaniola (comprising Spanish Santo Domingo, the present-day Dominican Republic, and French Saint-Domingue, or present Haiti) on September 11, a calm enabled Abbé d'Esmanville to board the *Belle* (from the *Joly*) and administer the sacraments to a sixty-five-year-old gunner who died two days later. With return of the wind, the lagging ketch hove into view.

At the Tropic of Cancer, tension was renewed when La Salle forbade the traditional "baptism" of those on board who had never before crossed the line. Joutel allows that the sailors, expecting to receive prizes from those wishing to avoid the keelhauling, "would have gladly killed us all." There were disputes also on the *Aimable*. La Salle sent Joutel to arbitrate.[4]

After Sombrère Island was sighted on the sixteenth, gale-force winds scattered the fleet. The *Joly* sailed alone. With more than fifty sick men on board, including La Salle and both his surgeon and the ship's, it was agreed in council to crowd on sail for Port-de-Paix, the nearest French port. Yet, when the time came, Beaujeu sailed north of Île-de-Tortue, thus bypassing Port-de-Paix during the night and proceeding into the Gulf of Gonâve. Some of La Salle's adherents viewed it as retaliation for La Salle's refusal to allow a stop at Madeira.[5]

At five in the evening of September 27, *Le Joly* dropped anchor in twenty fathoms before Petit Goâve, on Haiti's southern peninsula, fifty-eight days out of Rochefort. She sailed farther into the bay next morning. Several persons noted that the voyage could have been made in half the time, had the other ships been able to keep pace. "M. de La Salle," Captain Beaujeu wrote, "had chartered such wretched vessels . . . that we had to sail with our two lower sails furled and our two topsails upon their caps [*sur son ton*] to wait for them." Thanks to the skillful care of the *Joly*'s surgeon, sieur Juif, the captain reported, only two men—a soldier and a sailor—had died, out of more than fifty who were ill, and they only after both Juif and La Salle's surgeon (Étienne Liotot) were stricken and unable to attend them.[6]

It was reckoned as an unusually good passage, "although it was distressing and irksome because of the bad food and the scantiness of fresh provisions; but all that would have meant nothing if there could have been peace on the ship."[7]

The other three ships, having fallen behind during the storm, lagged the *Joly* by several days. *La Belle,* on Sunday, October 1, having doubled Cape Saint-Nicolas to enter the Gulf of Gonâve, sailed south along the coast of

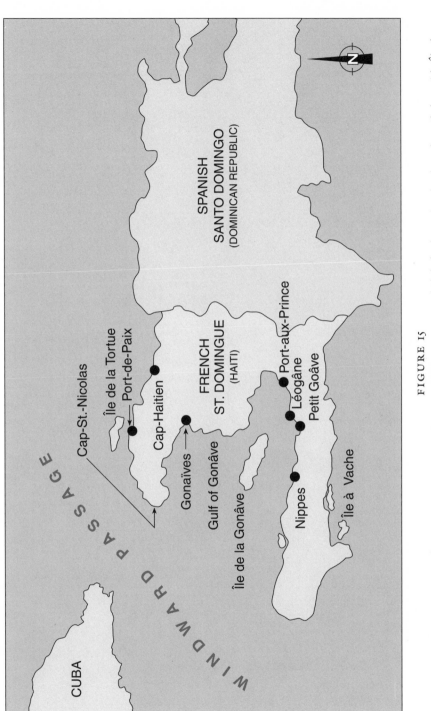

FIGURE 15

Eventful Way Station. La Salle's stopover at French Saint-Domingue portended difficulties ahead. The Joly sailed outside Île de Tortue to bypass the intended landing at Port-de-Paix. The Belle was left to find her own way; the Saint-François, to fall victim to Spanish pirates. Desertion, disease, and death compounded the voyagers' woes.

Saint-Domingue. The pilot, Elie Richaud, wrote in the ship's log for Sunday and Monday, October 1 and 2:

> . . . The wind from the east, we set sail from the Arcahay Islands at 6 in the morning and ran along the coast of Gonaïve until noon, when the wind calmed. It remained calm from noon till 2 in the afternoon, then came around to the west and freshened. We set a southerly course until 10 that evening, when we were struck by a strong storm. We were obliged to lie to until 6 in the morning, when the wind shifted to northerly and we set course for Petit Goâve until 10 that morning, Monday, the second of the same month. We anchored there in 20 fathoms, mud shoal.
>
> On arriving, we saluted Monsieur de Beaujeu with five cannon shots, and he gave us three. He arrived five days ago. And there was also Captain Durand and Captain Aigron and a ship from Nantes and also a *flibustier* vessel in the roadstead. As soon as we had anchored, Captain Morraud and Monsieur Thibaud [Thibault] went aboard the flagship.[8]

The *Aimable* had come in the same day, a little ahead of the *Belle*. But where was the *Saint-François*? True, she was a poor sailer, especially in a storm or contrary wind. Yet her failure to appear raised immediate fears, for Spanish sea raiders ranged the island coasts constantly, seeking a likely prize.

Such occurrences notwithstanding, the various observers' fascination during the voyage focuses on the conflict between the two leaders; thus, historians have been wont to accord the dissension more notice than it deserves. La Salle's brother, Abbé Jean Cavelier, wrote of the Rochefort–to–Saint-Domingue journey: "Nothing happened worthy of note except some difficulties between M. de La Salle and some other persons. . . ." He goes on to recite the various affronts to himself as well as to La Salle, with Beaujeu as his principal target.[9]

One noteworthy event during the crossing that none of the writers mentions is the birth aboard the *Aimable* of Lucien and Isabelle Talon's sixth child, a boy. The infant was given La Salle's name, Robert, and, according to Villiers, was La Salle's godson. The birth, however, is known only from a controversy that arose later over who should claim the ennoblement offered by the king to the first born of a French colony. The birth date does not appear.[10]

Father Membré, the Récollet superior, meanwhile, had "written down all that took place on board the *Joly,* which is to say, all the disputes that arose between M. de Beaujeu and M. de La Salle . . . nearly as they had happened." Early in the sojourn at Petit Goâve, his writings were removed from his chest by "someone," says Joutel, "who took them to M. de Beaujeu." The captain flew into a rage. Membré's biographer suggests that the "someone" who took the journal and caused it to be destroyed was Joutel himself. If there is foundation for such a charge, it raises questions concerning Joutel's motives. It is noted that he later commandeered Father Maxime Le Clercq's diary that was critical of La Salle and had it destroyed also.[11] Did he feel that he himself owned exclusive license to keep a journal? Was he bent on safeguarding his own role as the expedition's historian? His repeated criticism of Chrétien Le Clercq's work, including the journal attributed to Father Douay, may reflect jealousy as well as a desire to set the record straight.[12] Yet he lets pass unchallenged Abbé Cavelier's fabrications and distortions, made for the cleric's own sinister motives.

Had Joutel known of Minet's writings, he surely would have cringed at the young engineer's scathing comments:

> Monsieur de La Salle always had five or six spies on the bridge. One could not say a word that was not wrongly interpreted. . . . I said not a word and tried to calm his mind, which would become sour over nothing. . . . He said that I was a spy on his actions, that they had sent me with him to see everything he was doing, that it was his enemies who had given me to the Marquis de Seignelay to go with him, etc. I had already had time [before sailing] to take his measure, but I succeeded in understanding the mind of this man who, with all the qualities of the country where he was born, had mixed among the savages, and had a great esteem of himself.[13]

In the days following the Mémbre incident, concern for the *Saint-François* mounted. The apprehension was justified with the arrival on October 18 of the king's appointed representatives in the islands. The ketch, they related, had sailed from Port-de-Paix a fortnight previously and shortly was captured by two Spanish *piraguas,* each carrying sixty men. The seizure was but one of many incursions the Spaniards of Santo Domingo (present-day Dominican Republic) made on their unwelcome neighbors. In their nimble galleys, carrying both oars and sail, they concealed themselves in rocky inlets until sighting likely prey.[14]

It was a most inauspicious turn for La Salle. Ill when he arrived at Petit Goâve, he was greeted with the news that the island officials—the Marquis de Saint-Laurent, the king's lieutenant-general for the Caribbean islands; Tarin de Cussy, the new governor of Île-de-Tortue; Franquenet, lieutenant of Saint-Domingue; and the intendant, Michel de Bégon—were awaiting him at Port-de-Paix. His vexation mounted over Beaujeu's having broken the agreement to stop there. After the *Te Deum* was sung in gratitude for the safe passage, La Salle rallied enough to go ashore for fresh provisions for the sick and arrange for moving them from the stifling heat of the ship to a small island apart from the town. He wrote to Cussy asking that the officials at Port-de-Paix come to Petit Goâve to assist in arrangements for the remainder of his voyage.

Then La Salle himself became critically ill. His fever was slight, Minet says, yet "he had great attacks of delirium." In his frenzy the explorer seemed to be having an attack of conscience, believing "that all those he saw were coming to prosecute him, saying that he had betrayed the Marquis de Seignelay."[15] When his condition improved, La Salle went about preparations for the rest of the voyage. At this stage he made himself beholden to two men of his company who would exact a severe penalty later. The surgeon Liotot nursed him back to health. Without cash or credit, he turned to the brothers Duhaut, who sold some of their trade goods to lend him money to buy provisions. La Salle was to pay dearly for such favors.

His illness lingered. When the island officials arrived the evening of October 20, he was too ill to pay his respects; he sent Valigny in his stead. The news they brought of the seizure of the *Saint François* was kept from him until one of the Duhaut brothers revealed it, plunging him again into feverish delirium.

These first few weeks at Petit Goâve were a bad time for Beaujeu also. He found himself blamed by Bégon for the loss of the ketch, which might not have occurred, had he stopped at Port-de-Paix as agreed upon. But the worst of it was La Salle's incapacity. Neither the captain's authority nor his knowledge extended to the explorer's affairs, which La Salle had taken great pains not to reveal. Almost a month after their arrival, the captain wrote in perplexity to the Marquis de Seignelay. But for La Salle's illness, he explained, "I should not report to you on our voyage, being responsible for nothing but the navigation." The surgeons had given a gloomy prognosis for La Salle: a long illness, his "violent fever" dangerous to the mind as well as the body. His mental state is reflected by a message Beaujeu received through Valigny: "I should hand over his soldiers and return to France from Saint-Domingue, as he had no further need of me." It was an insane idea, for La Salle had no means of transporting either his men or their sustenance without the *Joly*. After Beaujeu asked for the order in writing, he heard of it no more. A few days after La Salle was stricken, the Abbés Cavelier and d'Esmanville had come on board the *Joly* and asked the captain to take charge of his affairs. "I declined," Beaujeu reported, "on grounds that M. de La Salle would not approve." The explorer had made it quite clear that he wanted no one meddling in his concerns. When the captain pressed the two clerics for details of La Salle's business matters, they could tell him nothing. Abbé Cavelier doubted that his brother kept any account; he had been unable to obtain such information, despite having asked for it repeatedly. Only Le Gros knew La Salle's business, and apparently he was not talking. Beaujeu, concluding that there was little method to La Salle's operation, referred the two clerics to the intendant. He himself would do nothing without the advice and consent of island officials.[16]

Certain problems, nonetheless, demanded immediate action. Because of the unexpected length of the voyage, the stores put on board at La Rochelle had dwindled beyond expectations. Beaujeu, working with Joutel and Le Gros, sent provisions to the *Aimable* and the *Belle*. Ovens were built, and the baker brought by La Salle, Jacques Labaussair from Saint-Jean-d'Angély, plied his trade to make biscuit to feed the soldiers and the volunteers during the rest of the voyage. Sadly, Labaussair would not always apply himself to such honorable pursuits.

Petit Goâve at this time was little more than a pirate haven, a cesspool of debauchery. The soldiers and sailors, finding temptations stronger than themselves, consorted with evil men and virtueless women. Among the freebooters, they glimpsed the gold of a recent strike and heard exaggerated tales of the wealth and adventure offered by buccaneering. The sea rovers, noting a map feature called Costa Desierta on the northern Gulf coast, painted a grim picture of a barren and desolate wasteland, at great variance with La Salle's description. Several men succumbed to the *flibustiers'* blandishments, much to their later sorrow. Joutel was to lament that the expedition had not sailed again immediately, after obtaining fresh provisions and allowing the sick time to renew their strength. It was a wretched place: the air and the fruits were bad, and there were women worse than either.[17] Among the latter, whose livelihood derived from separating the pirates from their loot, some of the men contracted maladies that remained with them the rest of their lives.

La Salle and Beaujeu likewise found themselves dependent on the sea rovers, for neither had knowledge of the Gulf of Mexico and its navigation; its winds and currents were a mystery. Because of La Salle's secrecy, the naval commander had been unable to inform himself on such matters before leaving France. Whatever information they could glean from the pirates was vital. Of all the freebooters who had sailed the Gulf, however, none claimed extensive knowledge of La Salle's river. Their report was gloomy: northers blew from October to January, often so strong as to carry a ship across the Gulf to the shoals of Yucatán. In other seasons, the south wind was just as hazardous. Ships nearing the northern coast were apt to be driven upon the lee shore, where shoals extended well out to sea, swamps a great distance inland; the country was populated by wild savages whose sustenance consisted largely of roots.[18]

Beaujeu encountered a *flibustier* captain named Le Sage, who in his youth had sailed with a Dutch crew looking for the Mississippi. They had found the river but were unable to enter because of the shoals at its mouth. The Dutch ship, Le Sage claimed, had anchored in the Baye-du-Saint-Esprit (Espíritu Santo Bay), which had four fathoms at the entrance—a likely description of Mobile Bay.[19]

A pirate captain named Du Chesne had more recent information. After pillaging Tampico eighteen months previously (March, 1683), he and his crew believed that they had seen the Mississippi. Du Chesne described a hazardous coast, flanked by shoals extending ten leagues into the offing with the bottom rising a foot per league toward the shore. The coast, being flat, he said, was inundated when the great river overflowed—certainly a description that fit the Mississippi and its delta. The buccaneer chief lent Beaujeu a hand-drawn Spanish track chart of the Gulf, which indicated that it was not navigable from September till March because of the frequent northers. He described the Baye-du-Saint-Esprit, where, Beaujeu says, "we intend to go first," as having only two fathoms over the bar— half the depth ascribed by Le Sage. Du Chesne warned also of the Spanish Armada de Barlovento ("Windward Fleet"), which patrolled the Gulf and Caribbean Sea with Mediterranean-type galleys and six warships armed with from thirty to sixty guns each. Such warnings did not frighten him, Beaujeu declared: "Whatever may happen, I will bring you news of the Mississippi or perish in the attempt"—a promise he could not keep. He was at a loss to understand La Salle's reasons for bringing women and hired men in the place of soldiers to a country of Spaniards and wild Indians. Should La Salle's illness prove fatal, the captain would adopt different measures for carrying out the mission.[20] That was a prospect which, to the misfortune of the voyagers, would not come to pass.

The sickness, which Beaujeu attributed to the lack of fresh provisions, overcrowding on the ships, and the tropical heat, raged on. Several men died, including the younger Chefdeville from Rouen, La Salle's cousin and, according to Joutel, "a priest like his brother." Abbé Cavelier places the number of fatalities at "seven or eight," adding that "six or seven" deserted. Some justified their defection by claiming to have been tricked or forced to join the expedition. Among those who hastened to leave was Denis Thomas, who testified later that he boarded a ship expecting to be returned to France, only to learn too late that it was a pirate vessel. Thus, Thomas and half a dozen others enticed by the buccaneers set their lives on a course as tragic as that of the company they left. Also among those who quit the expedition was the troop commandant Valigny; La Salle's secretary; the Huguenot Paget, who had protested La Salle's decision not to stop at Madeira; a merchant named Merlin; and several others. Three "boys" whom La Salle had taken on in Paris and La Rochelle as "secretaries" bought up their contracts with money. To stem the outflow, La Salle ordered his men back aboard the ships.[21]

The attrition at Saint-Domingue, by Marc de Villiers's estimate, amounted to some thirty men. To make up the loss, La Salle sought recruits on the island and thereby took on the dregs of humanity. Among this riffraff were a German pirate named Hiems (James), and Jean L'Archevêque, who were to involve themselves in La Salle's murder. By Villiers's questionable calculation, the net loss amounted to about twenty; a few others chose later to return to France from Texas with the *Joly*.[22]

By the time the rampant illness at last overtook Captain Beaujeu, La Salle was recovering. He was able to consult with Bégon, Cussy, and Saint-Laurent, whom he found most cooperative. They arranged for corn to replace the flour lost with the *Saint-François,* as well as for wine and other provisions. With their influence, La Salle's bill of exchange was accepted in payment. Cussy proposed sending a ship laden with provisions to the mouth of the Mississippi the following spring, and recognition signals were arranged. (With hostilities having ceased in the interim, the ship never sailed.) To assist the voyagers, Bégon offered La Salle a barque that had been taken by the local buccaneers as a prize. The offer was declined, as La Salle feared the vessel would not be suitable for the Gulf's choppy waters because of its low freeboard. The little ship, had he accepted it, might well have proved the salvation of his colony. So might one of the Petit Goâve pirate captains, who proposed joining the expedition with his well-armed ship and sizable crew. La Salle refused that offer also, on grounds that he had no authority from the king to take a company of buccaneers.[23]

Minet says La Salle asked the intendant to buy the barque for him, then changed his mind after it was bought, leaving Bégon stuck with it. Whereas Joutel writes that the officials were about the business of appointing magistrates and military officers for the French colony's various settlements, Minet claims that they had come to arm the buccaneers for attacking Spanish Santo Domingo. He declares that "we would have been in the party," had not Michel de Grammont's twenty-five–vessel pirate fleet departed unannounced.[24]

Captain Beaujeu remained unwell when, on November 7, La Salle went with Saint-Laurent and Bégon to the *Joly* for a conference with the expedition's pilots and captains. They were joined by a pirate navigator who had sailed many times in the Gulf of Mexico. With his help they charted the course to be followed from Saint-Domingue westward: along Cuba's south shore to Cape San Antonio, three hundred leagues from Petit Goâve, to wait in the lee of the cape for a favorable wind. Should a storm from the north arise after they entered the Gulf, they would fall back to the cape for protection.[25]

After the visitors departed next day for the neighboring town of Léogâne, preparations for sailing began in earnest. La Salle chose to proceed on the *Aimable* rather than the *Joly,* a matter for which various motives have been ascribed. He himself says that he acted out of concern for the safety of the ship that carried the bulk of supplies and provisions. In an extremely polite and beneficent tone, he wrote Beaujeu of his decision, saying that his presence would inspire confidence among the soldiers and sailors in case of attack. At the same time he soothed a sore spot by exonerating Beaujeu for the loss of the *Saint-François;* it was her captain, he declared, who was at fault. If Beaujeu agreed, they would sail round the clock to take advantage of the favorable wind. He designated meeting places, should the vessels become scattered: "I ask you still, should the winds separate us before Cap Saint-Antoine, to wait for us at the Isle of Pines and, beyond, at the Baye-du-Saint-Esprit; after that, in 28° 20', where I declare to you is the mouth of the river I intend to enter, quite at the far end of the Gulf's bend."[26] The latitude that La Salle gives here differs somewhat from the 27° reported in the *procès verbal* drawn near the mouth of the Mississippi in 1682. Having concluded that his river actually was the Río Escondido, he had adjusted the latitude to conform with his maps. His intended destination was the "Hidden River," concealed behind barrier islands of shell sand in the Texas Coastal Bend.[27]

On the *Aimable,* La Salle's company included his brother the abbé; Joutel and several other volunteers; and two of the three Récollet fathers: Anastase Douay, who probably had been on the storeship all along, and Zénobe Membré, whose welcome Beaujeu had withdrawn after finding himself criticized in the priest's journal. La Salle also took his surgeon, Étienne Liotot— leaving the *Belle*'s surgeon to attend those still ailing on the naval vessel—and his nephew Moranget. Left on the *Joly* were Father Maxime Le Clercq and Abbés d'Esmanville and Chefdeville, as well as La Salle's younger nephew, Colin Cavelier. Villiers claims, without citing his source, that La Salle had the Talon family and the other women embark on the *Joly*.[28]

To the munificence expressed in La Salle's letter, Beaujeu responded in kind, heaping praise upon the explorer's passionate regard for the king's service. The *Aimable,* he readily agreed, would carry the lantern, by which the *Joly* and the *Belle* would steer at night. In daylight, the ships would endeavor to stay within sight of each other; should they become separated, they would meet at the designated rendezvous. In case of attack, Beaujeu wrote, La Salle should sail on with the *Belle:* "I will keep the enemy occupied, for you were not sent to fight. With such a poor vessel, you would find it difficult to defend yourself."[29]

On such a harmonious note, the three ships weighed anchor after midnight on November 25, 1684, and made sail out into the Gulf of Gonâve. Yet, scarcely hidden beneath the surface, the evils of jealousy and mistrust still lurked.

The *Belle*'s log for that day indicates the slow start, due to alternating calm and contrary winds. Weighing anchor at two in the morning, the barque made frequent course changes because of the shifting wind until noon the following day, when a favorable easterly breeze arose. By the twenty-eighth, the ships had advanced no farther than Petit Trou de Nippes, eight leagues from the starting place. Here was one last chance to obtain items not available at Petit Goâve. La Salle and several men went ashore to buy hens, while the *Joly,* having taken on board a cow and some young pigs, sent her shallop to get water for the animals.[30] This meager French settlement was the expedition's last contact with other Europeans before sailing off into unknown waters.

As the ships raised sail and steered northwest into the freshening wind and heavy swells of the Windward Passage, the *Belle* fell behind. The *Aimable* furled sails to wait for her. Afterward it was learned that she had been in danger of swamping, as she lost steerage and shipped water while taking in her mainsail and running before the storm. With the lessening wind, the ships spread sails to cross the passage toward Cuba. Minet, on the *Joly,* took note of the difficulty the warship was having in following the storeship: "The *Aimable,* as usual, stayed behind. We were constantly forced to heave to and wait for her. It is to be noted that from the time we left France, we always navigated with only the two topsails, yet most of the time tacking because never had a flute been so bad. It was always necessary to wait for her."[31]

Losing Cuba behind a cloud bank, the voyagers came within sight of Little Cayman, then ran west by northwest to come back toward Cuba. The *Joly* hove to at midnight December 3 near the rock-studded Isle of Pines and next day ran along the palm-lined shore in search of an anchorage. She dropped anchor in a suitable cove at noon on the fifth, sixteen fathoms, sand bottom, near the island's western end: probably behind Punta Francés in the Ensenada de Siguaneu. The *Belle* came to anchor three hours later, but it was midnight before the *Aimable* arrived.[32]

During the next three days, the men refreshed themselves on the uninhabited and waterless island. Game that was killed—crocodiles, feral pigs of Spanish stock, and a rat-like animal as big as a rabbit (or a cat), with reddish fur—varied the steady diet of corn served them on the ships. Two men wandered off into the woods and became lost but found their way back to the shore after Joutel's search party had kept a night-long vigil on the island.[33]

Everyone back aboard, the ships weighed anchor and hoisted sail on a northerly wind at eight in the morning of December 8. Toward evening the following day, they were becalmed within sight of Cape Corrientes and then set back several leagues by a strong west wind. They doubled the cape on the eleventh and reached the point of Cape San Antonio a day later, only to find the wind against them for entering the Gulf of Mexico. The *Belle,* sent to take soundings, found anchorage in fifteen fathoms. The ships weighed anchor on the thirteenth and sailed northwest, but, after a day's sail, a north wind forced them back to the lee of the cape. On shore, Minet relates, a sun shot taken with Captain Beaujeu's eighteen-inch quadrant gave latitude 21°50'N, approximately correct according to modern navigational charts.[34]

Still anchored at the cape on the seventeenth, the *Joly* and the *Belle* were driven upon their anchors by a sudden wind gust an hour after midnight; the *Belle* struck the *Aimable*'s bowsprit, breaking the other ship's main yard and her own mizzenmast and topsail yard. Before the fouled rigging was untangled, the *Belle* had lost an anchor and a hundred fathoms of anchor rope.[35] The loss was to prove critical, for the failure of her ground tackle was to prove the *Belle*'s undoing.

The accident notwithstanding, the ships were able to make sail by 10 o'clock next morning, tacking north-northwest into the enclosed sea to which the Spanish king claimed exclusive rights. "The Gulf of Mexico," as Marcel Moraud has noted, "in reality was then a closed sea into which foreign ships ventured at their own risk . . . of capture or destruction." Ever since French pirates had first sacked Campeche in 1561, Spain had battled foreign intruders in this "Spanish Sea" with fierce determination. The Gulf of Mexico and the Caribbean Sea, which Spain claimed by right of discovery, reinforced by papal decree, had been considered a war zone until the early seventeenth century, even when there was peace in Europe. Even after this policy was set aside, Spain's Gulf Coast settlements suffered continual harassment. Especially during the latter half of the seventeenth century, the coastal towns were afflicted by pirates as well as privateers licensed by Spain's European rivals. Multinational sea rovers—renegades who acknowledged no allegiance but their own lust and greed—struck repeatedly where the Armada de Barlovento was not: most often against exposed and long-suffering Campeche but also at Tampico, Alvarado, Villahermosa, and even Veracruz. Their fate if captured was likely to be death by the garrote or imprisonment in San Juan de Ulúa's dungeons for terms that only death could end.[36]

The Spanish policy that denied other nations freedom of navigation and commerce in the Gulf of Mexico had long been anathema to Louis XIV. Recurring incidents resulted from Spain's territorial jealousy and Louis's aggressive effort to break down the barrier. In 1672, the French envoy in Spain dispatched news to France that Spanish forces had seized a French ship in Gulf waters and sent the crew as prisoners to Seville. The Marquis de Villars had ascertained that the ship at the time of its capture had been engaged harmlessly, without designs on Campeche as the Spaniards alleged. In response, Colbert instructed the envoy to warn Spain against renewing "this sort of war," for if all French ships traversing the Gulf were subject to seizure, so would all Spanish ships in waters surrounding the French Caribbean islands. In short, France would resurrect "the old policy of war in America and peace in Europe." A six-vessel French squadron already in the Indies would be unleashed to counter Spain's offensive moves. Still, the matter was not resolved. Following the 1679 seizure of a small French frigate by the Armada de Barlovento, Louis dispatched to the Gulf the Comte d'Estrées, lieutenant-general of French naval forces, to find the Spanish Windward Fleet and force return of the ship. In 1682, he ordered squadron chief Jean Gabaret, who had commanded a vessel in Estrées's fleet, to arm at Rochefort the *Faucon,* the *Perle,* and the *Tempeste* for a voyage to the Gulf. Gabaret was to make the French presence known to the Spanish colonies and reinforce French demands for open navigation.[37]

The importance that the Sun King attached to the matter had much to do with his espousal of La Salle's enterprise, as with the caution with which La Salle's small fleet now entered the Gulf of Mexico. No relaxing of the Spanish guard had resulted from the effort thus far. To the Spaniards of New Spain, any foreign ship sailing Gulf waters was still subject to seizure. Fresh in the minds of the Spanish colonials as La Salle's ships set sail across the Spanish Sea were the 1683 rape of Veracruz and pirate assaults on Tampico in both 1683 and 1684. The Armada de Barlovento, therefore, had reason to be on guard against foreign intruders, and the French voyagers had ample cause to fear the armada.[38]

No one aboard the three ships knew that the war between France and Spain had ended two weeks after their departure from Rochefort. Had they been caught in their violation of Spanish policy, however, it probably would have made little difference to the Spaniards. Either officially or unofficially, the war in the Gulf went on.

Before leaving Saint-Domingue, La Salle had informed Beaujeu that his river was in 28°20′, at the far end of the Gulf's bend. His intention was to make landfall somewhat east of that point and reconnoiter the intervening coast. Thus, he expected to find the mythical bay called Espíritu Santo before arriving at the mouth of his Rivière Colbert, or Mississippi, which he believed to be the same as the Río Escondido. Upon leaving Cape San Antonio, he reminded Beaujeu: "If the northers persist, I ask you to await us at the Baye-du-Saint-Esprit, if you go there, until the end of January, and at the Mississippi until the end of February. . . ."[39]

Crossing the Gulf in good weather, the ships varied their headings according to the shifting wind. The smooth sea permitted almost daily sightings of the sun or Polaris to obtain the latitude. Successive positions determined by the *Aimable*'s pilot Zacharie Mengaud and noted by Joutel indicate that the course made good during the crossing was about 330°.[40]

On the *Joly,* the longitude west from Paris was calculated from a lunar eclipse at 5:20 in the evening of December 21. With the time of the occurrence in Paris known, the time difference was computed at six hours and seven minutes, which converted to 91°45′ of longitude—not completely accurate because a timepiece that would maintain its accuracy at sea was still in the future. The latitude, derived from the altitude of the pole star at the time of the eclipse, was 25°16′.[41]

Coming within soundings at forty fathoms on the evening of the twenty-seventh, the *Belle* sailed ahead, heaving the sounding lead. She ran up a flag at thirty-two fathoms to signal the diminishing depth, and the ships anchored at midnight in seventeen fathoms. Thence, they groped their way along the Louisiana coast, taking continuous soundings by day and anchoring at night. In daylight, the *Belle* led the *Aimable* by half an hour's sailing time. On the twenty-eighth, noon latitude 28°37', the *Belle* again hoisted her signal flag when she came into five fathoms without sighting land. Some sailors on the storeship were able to see the shore from aloft, but those on the *Joly*, holding to deeper water, were not aware of it. Course was changed on the twenty-ninth from north-northwest to west-northwest, then to west. That night, fires appeared to the north-northwest.

The ships were now well west of the Mississippi delta, but the pilots still believed that the current had carried them eastward and that Espíritu Santo Bay lay fifty leagues farther west. In any case, the Río Escondido, which La Salle had chosen as his destination, lay in that direction. The shore having been sighted from the *Aimable*'s masthead with the ship in five fathoms suggests a location southwest of Grand Isle, near the eastern point of Timbalier Bay. From there westward past Galveston Bay, the continental shelf widens, the ten-fathom curve lying as far as ten leagues (about thirty miles) from the mainland, the depth toward the shore diminishing scarcely more than a fathom per league. This shoal water forced the ships to alter course to the west as the coastline angled northwest.

When land was next sighted, on January 1, 1685, the voyagers had cleared Trinity and Tiger Shoals, the guards that allowed few seamen to observe the western Louisiana shore for years to come. At midmorning the sky cleared, the *Belle* hoisted her signal flag, and sailors on the *Aimable* went aloft and sighted land "four leagues" away.

The shore inclined southwest, indicating a location near present-day Sabine Pass. Captain Beaujeu sent his shallop with Chevalier d'Hère and Minet to take La Salle ashore, the *Belle* following. The water was so shallow that not even the boat could get closer to land than 150 fathoms (300 yards). Wading, the men reached a sandbar four feet high, enclosing a mud flat with no vegetation but dwarfed rushes as far as they could see. Treading into this morass, Minet sank into the mud. Joutel, following in the *Aimable*'s shallop, noted only some big logs that had washed out of the river: probably cypress, from which the Sabine River takes its name.

On January 2, the ships lost sight of each other in heavy fog. Signals were misunderstood and, while the *Joly* groped through the haze near the anchorage looking for the other ships, the *Aimable* and the *Belle* pursued their westerly course, expecting the *Joly* to follow. A simple misunderstanding, compounded by the persistent fog, the incident gave rise first to anxiety, then to suspicion and anger. The ships did not reunite until January 19.

The *Belle,* keeping as close to shore as she dared on January 6, found Galveston Bay in latitude 29°23'. The island within its mouth caused La Salle to believe it to be the legendary Espíritu Santo Bay, a considerable distance northeast of his river's mouth. He was perplexed, however, by the barrier sandbanks, features he had not found on any of the maps.

The ships becalmed on the thirteenth, men sent ashore for water encountered Indians: the expedition's first contact with Karankawans. The boatmen persuaded nine of them to board the shallops and go to the ship. After giving them tobacco and clothes to cover their wet and shivering bodies, La Salle tried to get information about his river, but neither he nor Nika could communicate with them. La Salle gave each a knife and some strings of beads and sent them ashore in the shallops near the end of the day.[42] With a freshening wind, the ships weighed anchor at seven in the evening, bearing southward and constantly heaving the sounding lead as the coast bent southwest.

Deer and bison frolicked on the beach as the *Aimable* and the *Belle* lay becalmed again next day near the mouth of the Brazos River. La Salle believed the wildlife an indication that his river was near. Sailing south-southwest along Matagorda Peninsula on January 16, the ships came within view of a "point of land jutting out into the sea," with breakers warning of shoal water. They stood to the offing to double the point and sailed past Matagorda Bay. A noon sun shot placed them in 28°20', the latitude at which La Salle expected to find the Río Escondido: the "Hidden River," shown on various maps since 1527. The diminishing latitude and the southward trend of the coast marked the beginning of "the Gulf's bend," where he had told Beaujeu that he would find his river.

The voyagers paused at "a small river"—today's Cedar Bayou, separating Matagorda and San José Islands—in a fruitless search for water. It was here that the English sailor or German pirate called James or Hiems, whom La Salle had engaged at Petit Goâve, became lost. Had he not been found, La Salle's followers would have been spared his villainy in the final act of the drama.

From Cedar Bayou the ships sailed ahead to double a headland before turning back to Cedar Bayou to try again to find water. Differing accounts and imprecise latitudes, as well as a strong shore current that caused a south-westerly drift, make it difficult to mark the exact turning point. At noon on January 17, Captain Moraud of the *Belle* observed 27°30', the pilot Elie Richaud, who kept the log, 27°45', both south of Aransas Pass.[43]

This natural channel opened into Corpus Christi Bay, which receives the "Hidden River" named long ago by some anonymous Spaniard. La Salle, realizing that he was well past the latitude at which his maps showed the Río Escondido, was perplexed. Where he had expected to find the mighty discharge of the Mississippi, or Rivière Colbert, issuing from natural jetties extending far into the sea, there was only a narrow pass between sandy isles. The current, instead of flowing east or southeast, coursed southwest or south along the coast.

On Friday, January 19—the ships anchored a league from Cedar Bayou— the two shallops, laden with water casks and fifteen men between them, cast off in a foggy predawn. Up in the morning, as daylight came and the fog lifted, the lookouts on the *Aimable* espied sails. Because the French ships stood in Spanish waters and were coming from the southwest, by Joutel's mistaken reckoning, small arms were broken out and crews scrambled to man the big guns. A cannonshot signaled the men on shore to return.[44]

Minet, meanwhile, kept track of the *Joly*'s progress as she fumbled her way along the foggy coast, trying to locate the other two ships or find the rendezvous at Espíritu Santo Bay. The *Aimable* had last answered her cannonshot on January 3, but, says the young engineer, "We kept firing," thinking perhaps the ships had passed one another in the fog. "Our food began to run short. We were 18 at [the captain's] table, two priests, two Récollets, some officers, some cadets, and one hundred soldiers who are all ill, not counting the crew of the *Joly*, who are 80 persons more."[45] On the twelfth the pilots observed latitude 29°18', placing them near the west end of Galveston Island, where the *Aimable* and the *Belle* had been five days previously. The *Joly*'s pilots believed themselves at the Matas de Salvador, a name that first appeared on maps about 1525 and kept its place just east of the mythical Espíritu Santo Bay for two hundred years.[46]

On the fifteenth, Minet noted, "All the crew is nourished with corn and is in good health. The soldiers have eaten all their food and drunk all their brandy. They live at present on corn and water at the expense of the *Joly*'s crew." On the sixteenth, while a water detail from the *Aimable* and the *Belle* was going ashore at Cedar Bayou, the *Joly* anchored off Matagorda Peninsula. The shallop was lowered to take men ashore, but they found the water too shallow even for the boat a hundred yards in the offing. Several men waded in and crossed the narrow strip of barrier sand to glimpse "another

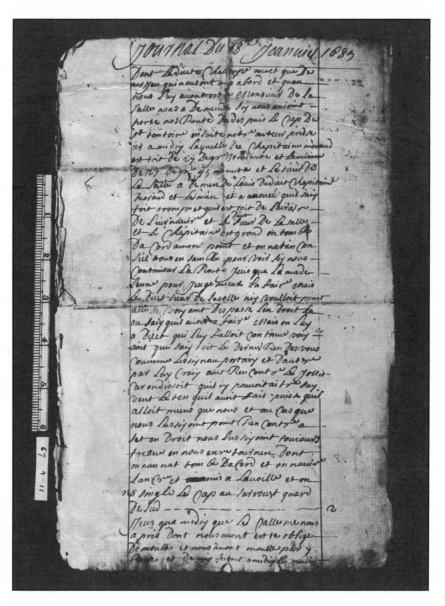

FIGURE 16

Log of the Belle. *January 18, 1685, in Texas Coastal Bend.*
Courtesy Barker Texas History Center

sea whose opposite shores they could not see." This was oyster-filled Matagorda Bay. That evening they anchored near Pass Cavallo, thinking "that it was the entrance to the Baye-du-St.-Esprit because we could see an island at its mouth, but . . . it was full of reefs and jetties that were thrown up far out to sea." The observed latitude, 28°02', however, altered this con-clusion. "Everybody," says Minet, "wanted to go back to look for it in lati-tude 30°," believing La Salle would be found waiting there. Beaujeu opposed the idea, "saying that M. de La Salle had wanted to leave us and had gone to search for the river, and that it was necessary to continue, that we might find him."[47]

Minet noted the passing of latitude 28°20' without finding the jetties said to mark the mouth of La Salle's river. The engineer studied his copy of the map that La Salle had given the king, which showed the river at 25°50'. The *Joly* would continue to that latitude to seek the other ships and the river mouth: "If we do not find [the river mouth], assuredly it empties into these lakes [behind the barrier islands]."[48]

Early in the morning of January 19 the *Joly* weighed anchor and hoisted sail on a north-northeast wind, course west-southwest. At 8:30, two ships appeared on the distant horizon, and, believing they were Spanish, "we put ourselves under arms." Shortly a cannonshot was heard from one of the other vessels. The ships, with weapons primed, stood ready to do battle with each other before they realized that the *Joly* at last had overtaken the *Aimable* and the *Belle*. Half an hour later the *Joly* anchored near the other ships in latitude 27°30', according to Minet—at least half a degree too far south. Minet observed that Captain Beaujeu had been correct in believing that La Salle, instead of going to the rendezvous that he himself had speci-fied, would proceed without the warship to seek his river.[49]

La Salle—seeming much embarrassed, according to Abbé d'Esmanville— made excuses and sought to cast the blame on the *Joly*. The Sulpician ab-bot, keeping his feelings in check, gives a dispassionate view. After he and Chevalier d'Hère had gone to see the leader on the *Aimable,* La Salle re-turned with them to the *Joly* to discuss their future course with Captain Beaujeu: whether to continue the search for his river mouth by sea or to put some of his men ashore. After dinner La Salle agreed to furnish provi-sions for his soldiers on the *Joly,* "that they might go back together and look for his river." The agreement, however, was only tentative. Next day (January 20), d'Esmanville sought him out on shore, where he had gone to compute the latitude from the sun, "to ask him his final determination. He told me that he was resolved to take the soldiers and go against the

Spaniards in Nouvelle-Biscaye [Nueva Vizcaya]; that he was not concerned with finding a [. . . harbor] as he was in the country to which the King had sent him." The abbé, La Salle charged, must keep his plans secret except from his brother (Abbé Cavelier).[50]

The priest, taken by surprise, replied that the Sulpician superior, Abbé Tronson, had sent him to make war on demons, not Christians. He then returned to the king's vessel with La Salle's message that he wanted his soldiers landed where they were. On the twenty-third, Beaujeu again sent d'Esmanville to ask La Salle for a letter relieving him of the troops.

The letter, written the same day, was dated from "the mouth of one of the branches of the *fleuve* Colbert, *rivière* Mississippi." Their present location, La Salle wrote, was closer to where His Majesty had ordered him to go than the other mouths of the Mississippi. He would reconnoiter the harbors after establishing his colony; finding the main channel would be a simple matter. Asking that the troops be sent ashore, he declared Beaujeu free of any further responsibility, "since you have brought us safely to the land where His Majesty has sent me. The rest of the journey can be made by land."[51]

La Salle's true intention, and the King's, is here emphasized clearly. This "western branch" was indeed closer than the actual Mississippi to the destination for which His Majesty had sent him: the real objective was the mining region of northwestern Mexico.

3

THE LOST COLONY

Chapter 9

Unhappy Landing

SHIPWRECK AND SAVAGERY

The future course was not so easily decided, even in the leader's impetuous mind. Having gone ashore to seek a clue to his location, he found a maze of sloughs and marshes in a harsh and scarcely habitable plain. Fatigue and anxiety seized him. His frustration grew as the weather turned sour. D'Esmanville, bearing La Salle's order for Captain Beaujeu to land the soldiers, had no sooner made it back aboard the *Joly* than mountainous swells rolled in from the Gulf, so that none of the troops could disembark.[1] It took eight days to get them all ashore. In the meantime, La Salle had cause for serious reflection.

The ships were taking a pounding in the open sea. The wind blew first from northeast, bringing a hard freeze, then turned to south-southeast, threatening to send the ships upon the lee shore. Giant breakers and high tides swamped the bivouac on the beach, washing over the grass-thatched lean-tos thrown up for the soldiers' shelter. As the sea surge flooded the island storm passes, La Salle, with forty men, found himself marooned without provisions; the soldiers became unruly. The mountainous waves forbade the sending of help from the ships.[2]

The landing of the soldiers was effected in stages, as the weather permitted, from January 23 to January 30. Scarcely had the last ones reached the shore when the renewed southeasterly blow forced them to mount the highest dunes to escape the flooding. The ships were hard-pressed to hold their ground. An anchor cable snapped on the *Aimable*. Fortunately, her other anchors held, but her stem was broken; she afterward had a notice-able list, the result of a cargo shift or of water leaking into her hold. At the same time, the *Belle,* having already lost one anchor at Cape San Antonio, lost another; it seemed a miracle that she held off the beach. The incident gave clear warning of the *Belle*'s vulnerability; she was in constant danger from inadequate ground tackle, bad seamanship, or both.[3]

Free of the soldiers, Beaujeu sent word to La Salle that he could not endanger his ship by remaining in the exposed anchorage. The plight of the vessels, the difficult landing, or the inhospitable coast also caused La Salle to alter plans. D'Esmanville learned that he had put on hold his march on Nueva Vizcaya; he must first find the Mississippi's main channel and ascend it to Fort-Saint-Louis of the Illinois.[4]

"On the first of February," Minet says, "M. de La Salle told us that the principal mouth of the river was forty leagues northeast of this place. He was going to send his soldiers and cadets (volunteers) by land, following the seashore, and he himself would embark on the *Aimable*."[5] The destina-tion he indicated was shoal-ringed Galveston Bay, which the *Aimable* and the *Belle* had passed on January 6, believing it to be the legendary Bay of Espíritu Santo. La Salle now expected to find that one of the Mississippi's distributaries observed in 1682 emptied into that bay.[6] The stream he envi-sioned, however, was the Atchafalaya River, flowing out of the Mississippi on the right an estimated sixty leagues above its mouth.

After a brief respite, the wind turned back to the southeast, again rais-ing concern for the ships' safety. Beaujeu's sailors dredged up the *Aimable*'s lost anchor but found it broken. The *Belle* had lost a third anchor, for on February 6, Minet—still aboard the *Joly*—noted, "We took an anchor to the *Belle,* which had . . . lost all her own. She had spent the night with a small anchor of 150 livres, not having any other."[7]

All this occurred against the backdrop of an argument about provisions for the soldiers, which had begun the day after the ships were reunited. Whereas Beaujeu demanded two months' rations, La Salle offered enough for only two weeks. Both Minet and Joutel claim—without consideration of La Salle's plan to march on Nueva Vizcaya—that this disagreement pre-cipitated La Salle's decision to have his troops put ashore. Clearly, D'Esmanville had a different perspective.[8]

For whatever reason, the exchange of letters between Beaujeu and La Salle retained an argumentative, if not petulant, tone. La Salle's defensive-ness reflected an anxiety doubtless born of his dawning realization that he had blundered. Minet ran afoul of the leader's ill disposition by pointing out the hazards the soldiers would face in marching up the coast; he suggested that the wiser course would be to send provisions to the *Joly,* return the soldiers to the ship, and keep all the ships and men together while seeking La Salle's river. Never one to take advice, La Salle responded in temper: he knew what he was doing and would carry forward his strategy. He himself would proceed to his chosen destination with the *Aimable.* As for Beaujeu, he had already been told that he could take his leave and return to France. And Minet might go with him if he wished; La Salle himself—so he claimed—could do all that the king had sent the young engineer to do.[9]

Although Minet's writings reflect a critical attitude toward La Salle almost from the beginning, he was to write differently later, under different circumstances: "Up to that time," he was to claim, "I had been his friend, and had scrupulously carried out the Marquis de Seignelay's orders to obey him." Having gone to La Salle in friendship, Minet could not face the leader's ridicule. Rebuffed in person, he went back aboard the *Joly* and "wrote him as reasonable and polite a letter as I could," begging him "to consider calmly what I represented to him. . . . It was then that he stormed at me and sent me a letter full of invectives."[10]

La Salle's response to Minet is not found. He did refer to the matter a few days later in a letter to Beaujeu, who evidently had broached the subject. "I will accept what you write to me, as I am committed to do it," he wrote, "and if I have only you to deal with, I expect the result will be satisfying to both of us; but in truth, I do not recognize in M. Minet any quality that justifies his writing to me, as he has done, like a servant. . . ." But that affair, he added, was between himself and Minet.[11]

Minet, had La Salle only listened, offered sound advice: between the channel now known as Cedar Bayou and Galveston Bay there would be many passes to the interior lagoons that could not be crossed; fresh water on the barrier sand reefs was scarce or nonexistent; the marshes, the scarcity of food, the Indians, and the weather all posed obstacles. La Salle's intemperate response brought from the young engineer a conclusion that echoes Father Hennepin's a few years earlier: La Salle "never took anyone's advice." As Minet put it, "No one tells him anything. I saw a man who had made a mockery of the court and was making a mockery of us. . . . This is a man who has lost his mind."[12]

Heedless of Minet's warning, the soldiers, volunteers, and hired men— including one who had gone blind—began their march on February 3 or 4, guided by four young Normans, by Minet's account; according to Joutel, in the charge of himself and Crevel de Moranget. Joutel marched at their head; Moranget brought up the rear. The number is given variously from "only about a hundred" to "120 or 130." Each man carried provisions for nine days, as well as his arms and the necessary tools and utensils. Whether because of the terrain or lack of discipline, "they took up more space on the march than would a thousand in closer formation."[13] The marchers halted from time to time at the edge of the lagoon that lies between Matagorda Island and the mainland, shown on present-day maps (from historical misidentification) as Espiritu Santo Bay. They bivouacked at night on a small eminence with sentries posted.

About the time the march began, Beaujeu initiated a hurried exchange of letters with La Salle. As d'Esmanville had reported, he informed La Salle that the king's ship could remain no longer in the exposed anchorage. Otherwise, the nature of his remarks may be judged from La Salle's reply; they evidently were short, blunt, and none too polite. Referring to "the way in which you vent your spleen," La Salle replied: "It is not my fault, sir, that you have not already provided for the security of His Majesty's ship. I do not know what justification you have for asking me for pilots to enter that river. . . . You may take [the ship] wherever you see fit."

There was also the lingering matter of provisions due the *Joly* for feeding the soldiers beyond the expected duration of the voyage. La Salle took exception to the captain's complaint "that I wish to make your crew die of starvation," but the foodstuffs could not be transferred until either the sea calmed or the ships were well sheltered: the same as the powder and cannon that Beaujeu was supposed to leave with La Salle. "The discourteous charge you make against me certainly has no foundation . . . I should be much more aggrieved if I had given you occasion for your vexation." Thus La Salle wrote hurriedly while the *Joly*'s clerk, Duval, who had brought Beaujeu's letter, waited for his reply. In sober afterthought, he wrote again the same day in a more conciliatory tone.[14]

Joutel, as he led the march up the island, kept an anxious eye turned seaward, hoping to see the *Belle,* which, according to plan, was to follow close to shore to render aid as needed. No sails appeared. Uneasiness turned to alarm when, at eleven o'clock the evening of February 5, cannonshots were heard in the direction of the anchorage. Joutel's anxiety was heightened by his concern over the uneasy relations between La Salle and Beaujeu. The cannonshots, however, signaled distress of a different sort.

The *Belle* had come close to losing her last good anchor. Only hasty action and a wind change kept her from being swept upon the shore. She spent an uneasy night, secured with only a 150-pound kedge anchor. On the fifth, Minet tells us, heavy seas rolled in, driven by a southeast wind—evidently the cause of the distress. It was on the sixth, with the wind blowing from northeast, that an anchor was taken to the *Belle,* presumably from the *Joly.*[15]

Under Beaujeu's urgency to escape the exposed anchorage, La Salle stood ready to make sail, but the *Belle's* troubles forced postponement: "The *Belle,* which again has lost the fluke from one of her anchors and left her sheet anchor on the bottom needs our shallop to help drag for it, so we cannot sail today. I fear our two shallops may not suffice to recover it. Meanwhile, she is left with only one small kedge anchor, which is not capable of holding her."

The *Aimable's* launch had been sent to the *Belle* the day before to assist her in case the wind blew strong again. La Salle asked the captain to lend the *Joly's* boat also for the dragging operation, and that Beaujeu lend the *Belle* one of his extra anchors, if he could spare it; otherwise, the *Aimable* would have to supply one, which would be a hardship, as one of her anchors had only a single fluke. After the *Belle* was in a safe harbor, *Joly's* anchor would be returned "at the river . . . or at the Baye-du-Saint-Esprit." If Beaujeu could not spare the anchor, La Salle hoped he could at least lend his shallop to take one from the *Aimable.*[16] Whichever ship actually provided the anchor for the *Belle,* it would have to be returned, and the little ship would still be perilously short of ground tackle.

The soldiers with Joutel and Moranget, meanwhile, continued their march in spite of their uneasiness over goings-on at the anchorage and the *Belle's* failure to appear. Joutel quickly discovered the lack of discipline among the troops of which La Salle would complain later. With each man carrying his own provisions, and all of them having been on short rations aboard ship, they lacked the needed self-restraint; they were wont to dip into their food packs during the night. Joutel, on perceiving this, had all the packets gathered each evening and a guard posted over them until morning. Water was available by digging shallow holes near the seashore. Despite their leader's warnings not to eat a certain yellowish-red "fruit or bean," some of the men did so; they became ill and vomited blood. The blind man became lost but was found after spending a miserable night, confused and alone.[17]

Making only short hikes each day, the marchers on February 8 found their way blocked by a body of water they could not cross: Matagorda Bay at Pass Cavallo. As a signal to the ships, fires were built atop dunes "fifteen or twenty feet high." On the promontory that Juan Enríquez Barroto would give the name San Francisco, not far from the latter-day Matagorda lighthouse, the men erected grass-thatched sheds or lean-tos for shelter.

The days that followed were anxious ones. Short of rations, the men shot ducks until the waterfowl were frightened away. *What had happened to the ships?* Faced with this necessity and remembering La Salle's account of how he had crossed rivers, Joutel put the carpenters to work to cut down a large tree and make a dugout canoe. He himself worked at building a raft from driftwood, tied together with vines, an uphill task. With the shortage of food, the large number of men proved to be a handicap. "These were all men who had been taken by force or deception . . . of every nationality . . . ; the soldiers raised by junior naval officers who were paid [an extra sum] for each man, of whatever quality. . . ."[18] Although few of them could do any work, all consumed rations. Joutel allows that 30 good men would have been more useful than the 120 to 130. It would have been a blessing, he reckoned, to have found Indians who could be paid with knives or hatchets to keep some of them for a while.

Where was the Belle?

While others worked at building the raft and canoe, Moranget took several of the do-nothings and went about a league "up the river" seeking a narrower place for crossing to the opposite point. Instead, he saw the wide expanse of Matagorda Bay and an island in the middle of the pass, a changing feature best represented on present-day charts as Pelican Shoal. It had been five days since the band had arrived here; instead of their situation improving, it worsened.

Where were the ships? Had they sailed away, leaving the soldiers to their fate?

Still in the anchorage before Cedar Bayou, the three vessels suffered a continued siege of bad weather that forbade the exchange of goods between the *Joly* and the *Aimable*. With the wind often from northeast, Beaujeu was of a mind to seek shelter in the mouth of a river called the Magdelaine,[19] believed to lie some thirty-five leagues farther south. La Salle, however, must follow his men on shore. With anchor troubles plaguing both the *Belle* and the *Aimable,* the *Joly* was obliged to help them out of their difficulty. Provisions were transferred to the warship to make up for the extra time the soldiers had been on board. The *Joly,* however, still had on board 6,600 of the 10,000 livres of iron for the projected colony; neither it nor the cannon could be removed from the hold without jeopardizing the ship's trim and hence her stability.

At last, after almost three weeks in the exposed anchorage, the ships rigged sail and got underway on February 9. Progress up the coast was slow. Five days were required for the *Joly* and the *Belle* to make good the "ten to twelve leagues" to Pass Cavallo. On the evening of the thirteenth the two ships arrived before the pass that the *Joly* had observed on January 17 and came to anchor off the southernmost point. From the ships was seen "a white tent that the soldiers had pitched." The soldiers on shore, anxious to learn the cause of delay, gave the appropriate signal, but it was next morning before anyone came ashore.[20]

The troop was still expecting to use a boat from one of the ships to cross the bay and proceed toward Galveston Bay, but a change of plans was in the offing; they would dig in where they were, establishing what ultimately came to be called Grand Camp. On the fourteenth, Minet went with Beaujeu and a pilot from the *Joly* to explore and take soundings along the coast. Several stops were made for the engineer to sketch the shoreline. Barbier at last arrived at the soldiers' camp with the *Belle*'s boat. Joutel, fearful at not having seen the *Aimable* or La Salle, received assurance that the ship was on her way with La Salle safe aboard; she soon hove into view and anchored near the *Belle*. Because of a contrary wind, La Salle was not able to send provisions to the soldiers until the fifteenth. He then came himself to inspect the camp, which Joutel now refers to as "the post," and then examined the bay entrance, where pilots from both the *Belle* and the *Joly* had already begun soundings. What happened next is much confused, each account perhaps reflecting things as the writer wished them to be rather than the unvarnished truth. There occurred the first of two shipwrecks on the Texas coast that ordained the expedition's ultimate disaster.

Joutel: "He [La Salle] found [the bay entrance] very good, "and, after considering everything, decided to have the *Belle* and the *Aimable* enter, hoping that this would prove to be a branch of his river, [the one] that he had left on the right when descending [the Mississippi]. The *Belle*'s pilot had reported to him on the soundings he had taken; . . . the anchorage was good and the ships would be well sheltered. He ordered that soundings be made again to see whether the ships could enter that day."[21]

Minet [the same day]: "La Salle sent the pilot of [the *Belle*] to tell Mons. de Beaujeu that he had found a channel for entering the lake, where there were at least sixteen or eighteen feet of water; that the ships could enter easily; and that this was the very place to which the king had sent him. I went with M. de Beaujeu to sound and draw a plan of this channel; we found eight to nine feet on the bar. . . ."[22]

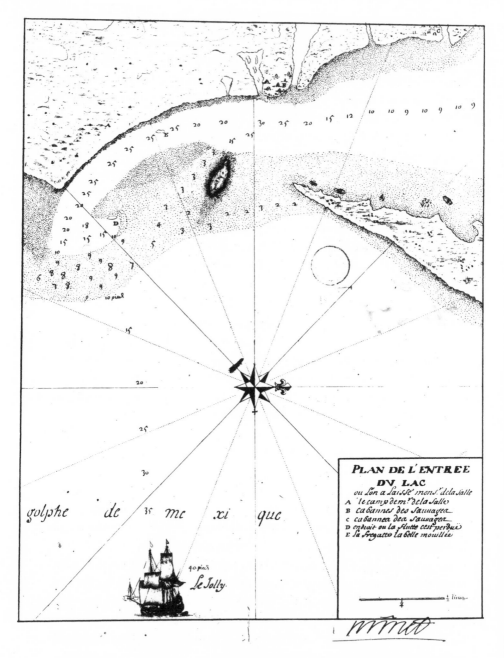

FIGURE 17

Plan de l'entrée du lac *by Minet. Letter designations show: (A) La Salle's camp;
(B and C) Indian huts; (D) site of* l'Aimable *wreck; (E) the* Belle's *anchorage.
The* Joly *(bottom of map) lies offshore in forty-foot water. Courtesy Archives
Nationales, Service Hydrographique, Paris*

This difference in the two accounts seems, implicitly, to underlie the controversy between Beaujeu and La Salle. Beaujeu did all he could to urge caution; La Salle, true to his character, sought to force circumstances rather than face reality. Yet the two leaders, in their extant correspondence, treated each other (at last) with respect and consideration.

Minet, at the same time, found that La Salle had changed his mind since telling him that he was not needed and could hie himself back to France: "That evening M. de La Salle sent [Pierre] Duhaut, who was the sergeant, to say that he was going to have the *Belle* and the *Aimable* enter the lake behind the island that he had sounded, that on the bar there are eleven feet at low tide and it rises five feet. . . . He also gave a summons to Sieur Du Val, the king's notary, to the effect that Monsieur de Beaujeu was to deliver me into his hands."[23]

Beaujeu, far from satisfied with the soundings and in dire need of fresh water, wrote to La Salle: "As there is no harbor for me here, with only eight feet of water on the bar, the depth being so variable and the king's ship in great danger, I shall set sail . . . and seek shelter and fresh water elsewhere." He would proceed to the "river" that La Salle had indicated (Galveston Bay). If he could not enter it, he would go on to the Baye-du-Saint-Esprit, where it was expected that a secure harbor would be found and La Salle could come for his cannon and iron that could not be unloaded in the open sea. Though regretful at leaving, Beaujeu said, he could not afford to let the good sailing weather pass.[24]

La Salle: "After having had the honor of making such a long voyage with you, we cannot part without a sincere feeling of regret. Although we have found a depth of eleven feet where we have sounded and the water has fallen since the wind has come off shore, I do not venture to ask you to take further risk or to stay here longer unless this fine weather would enable you to let us have our powder and iron." Without those things, he claimed, his chances of success would be greatly impaired; he could more easily do without the cannon and cannonballs. Were he not "pressed for time," he would accompany the *Joly* to the river; but he was near the place where he must go. He believed both "rivers"—that is, Matagorda Bay and Galveston Bay—to be branches of the Mississippi. He would send Beaujeu news and provisions (at the mythical Baye-du-Saint-Esprit or Espíritu Santo Bay) "at the time that I have told you."[25]

The *Joly*'s departure, however, was not yet. There was more to-do about the depth of the bar at the bay mouth. At Beaujeu's behest, the pilots of all three ships sounded the pass next day and made this report to La Salle:

On the seventeenth day of February, 1685, M. de La Salle, wishing to take the King's frigate *La Belle* and the flute *l'Aimable* into the River Colbert, which is at about 28°20', and there is a reef or sandbank about half a league from it, a quarter league wide and a league and a half long, we, Zacharie Mengaud, pilot of the flute; François Guitton, chief pilot of the *Joly;* Christophe Gabaret, also a pilot on the *Joly;* and Elie Richaud, pilot of the *Belle,* went to the bank to take soundings. We found there nine feet at low tide and at high tide ten feet, east-northeast and west-southwest with the southern point of the river. . . . [signed by the afore-mentioned pilots and attested by Duval, the king's notary.][26]

Minet, meanwhile, had a second, and a third, notice that La Salle wanted him ashore to build the fortifications for his settlement. Sergeant Duhaut came back aboard the *Joly,* bearing the explorer's letter to Beaujeu, in which he wrote, "I enclose a summons to M. Minet. . . . I beg of you to make him heed it." The captain replied next day: "I am not keeping M. Minet; whether he goes or stays is up to him. The king's letter, which he brought me, indi-cates that I am to receive him on board during the time that I am at sea; I cannot send him away unless you show me contrary orders from the king. It is up to him to carry out the orders that he has and to answer for his own actions."[27]

There were, meanwhile, more pressing matters than Minet. La Salle argued with the sounding report, which, he alleged, the king's notary had drawn up to suit himself. He claimed errors concerning the tides, claiming the high occurred only in the evening and the lagoon was at its lowest ebb because the northern tributaries were still frozen.

La Salle's gunpowder had been sent over from the *Joly.* The explorer ordered some beef prepared on the *Aimable* and sent to the *Joly* to make up for the extra time that Beaujeu had fed the soldiers. There was much ado about La Salle's iron in the *Joly's* hold. Beaujeu, replying to La Salle's plea that he could do nothing toward building his settlement without it, claimed that the iron lay on top of the ballast, "with your cannon, my spare anchors, and all my cargo over it"; three days would be required to move it. La Salle expressed optimism for the success of his undertaking, "except for the post, which I cannot build, as I have no cannon to defend it, no iron to build it, and no engineer to fortify it." Beaujeu at last relented and had the iron brought up and sent to La Salle's encampment with the ex-planation that his reluctance resulted from a lack of ballast to replace it. To maintain trim, he had ordered six of the *Joly's* cannon put into the hold to replace the iron. La Salle would understand that it was impossible for him to give him his four cannon and the cannonballs: ". . . but that cannot prevent you from establishing your post, since you have on the *Aimable* four twelve-pounders and four four-pounders and 1,606 cannon balls. . . . All that is lacking is an engineer, but you . . . know more than M. Minet, whom you have several times told me you could well have done with-out." Beaujeu rejected La Salle's suggestion that the captain take the can-non to the Baye-du-Saint-Esprit (the bay that never actually existed), unload them in the supposed sheltered harbor, and bury them on shore, with markers that could be recognized when the *Belle* was sent to retrieve them after the equinoctial storms were past; such a procedure, Beaujeu feared, might bring him censure for mishandling of the king's property. "Moreover, your cannon could not be taken ashore in my shallop, unless I wanted to sink it."[28]

The two leaders still had a way of getting under each other's skin, but on the whole their attitude toward one another had mellowed. La Salle now seemed genuinely concerned for the safety of the king's ship; Beaujeu, for the plight of La Salle and his colonists. They were much more civil to each other than either Joutel or Minet indicate.

Beaujeu: "I assure you that it is with regret that I must leave you, for I would like to have seen you settled and [to know] that you had found what you are looking for; but the need to provide for the safety of the King's ship compels me to go. If there had been even twelve feet of water over the bar . . . , I would have tried to go in by lightening my ship and to go with you to find your river, which must certainly fall into the lagoon near here. When you begin your search [for it], stand to the west as you leave the lake. I am indeed mistaken if there is not a great river there." Beaujeu also advised against taking the *Belle* into "the lagoon"—probably meaning the body of water now known as Espiritu Santo Bay, between Matagorda Is-land and the mainland—without making a thorough survey. If he himself should find a better port on the "other mouth of the Mississippi" that La Salle had told him about, he would send his launch through the lagoon or come himself with the ship to tell him. If he were unable to enter the river, he would send word from the Baye-du-Saint-Esprit. "Indeed," Beaujeu added—almost pleading for La Salle to have confidence in him—"there is nothing I will not do." The captain further offered to go to Martinique for provisions and reinforcements; the *Aimable* was not suitable for such a voy-age, for she was short of sails, cordage, and anchors. He would ask the in-tendant, in La Salle's name, for the provisions; if the intendant refused, he would receive the provisions on his own account rather than leave without them. "Believe me, I take as much interest in your affair as you yourself. . . . I have resolved to sacrifice my life and my belongings to it. You need only say the word."[29]

How could La Salle have refused such an offer? Whereas he seemingly was genuinely touched by Beaujeu's generous proposals, he kept his guard up and denied his own weakness: "I have never failed to trust you [a bit of forgetfulness here], and it has been *no fault of mine* if harmony has not been complete." But, had it been possible for him to lack confidence in the captain, "such offers would have made me trust you completely." He nevertheless refused them. He was certain of his location; he doubted the intendant of the islands would honor his request; he dared not commit the Marquis de Seignelay to additional expense until he could show substantial progress. He did not wish Beaujeu to pledge himself for the provisions; the king might not accept it; "and, if I should die, you would find it difficult to get back what you had advanced" (as would a number of others who had pledged themselves for La Salle's benefit). But, if Beaujeu would wait at the Baye-du-Saint-Esprit through the month of March, he could send news of substantial progress to the intendant to secure his aid and win the king's approval.[30]

As to Minet, who for a time appeared to be the grand prize in a tug of war, La Salle at last became resigned: "If he has orders different from those that I have seen, he will do well to follow them. I have done my duty by sending him the summons; it is now his affair." Minet had stood fast against the utter foolishness and ineptitude of the enterprise as it was being carried out, justifying himself with what he believed to be a loophole in the king's orders. His assigned role was to oversee the building of fortifications, which in itself looked like an impossibility: "Whom does he [La Salle] want to build these fortifications? Does he have masons . . . laborers? He had about 20 hired men [nearer 40, according to the enrollment contracts], of whom half are dead. Of 100 soldiers there are still 80 ill. . . . What fort does he want us to wall up without bread or water?"[31]

In fact, La Salle, lacking both the engineer and the workmen, never did construct a fort to guard his colony.

Of all those on the expedition whose writings are known, only Minet seems to have concerned himself with the plight of the people on the near-waterless island and those who remained huddled in crowded and miserable quarters aboard ship. No one mentions the women and children who, so far as is known, had not been ashore since leaving Petit Goâve the previous November. For twenty days they had endured the sea's constant pounding while the ships remained anchored off Cedar Bayou; and now, in front of what was supposed to be a branch of La Salle's river, it seemed they were in for another interminable wait. That phase of their trial, however, was about to end.

Beaujeu awaited only La Salle's dispatches for the king before sailing— or so he thought. But again, events conspired to upset plans. On Sunday, February 18, the *Belle* crossed the bar and sailed up the channel, heeding the floating timbers and casks with which the pilots had marked it the day before. She came to anchor about two o'clock in the afternoon in five and a half fathoms according to Joutel; twenty-five feet as shown on Minet's map. She stood half a league southwest of the small island that is identified with today's Pelican Shoal, a considerable distance short of Decros (or Decrow) Point and not actually within the bay.[32] Preparations then began for bringing in the *Aimable.* On the nineteenth, the shallops of the *Joly* and the *Belle* joined in the task of removing the heaviest part of her cargo, that she might more easily clear the bar. They unloaded the eight iron cannon "of about six-pound shot," according to Joutel: the ones that had been registered as part of the *Aimable*'s cargo in La Rochelle the previous July. They were later to be positioned around La Salle's settlement. "Several thousandweight of lead and iron" and some other things were put ashore. Then the captain, Claude Aigron, announced that nothing else need be removed, that he could now take the ship in with ease.[33]

Next day, the twentieth, La Salle sent the pilot Richaud, of the *Belle,* to help bring the *Aimable* into the bay and the shallops of the *Joly* and the *Belle* to tow her over the bar. Aigron, however, spurned all assistance and advice. Contrary to La Salle's orders, he refused the tow and sent Richaud and the boats back to their own ships. At ten that morning, Beaujeu and his second pilot, Gabaret, accompanied by Minet, approached the *Aimable* by canoe and asked how much water she drew, now that part of the cargo had been removed. When told that she still drew eight and one-half feet, they advised him not to try to enter; the bar was scarcely deeper, the swells were high, and the pitching of the ship would surely put her aground or cause her to break a seam. Aigron remained adamant; La Salle had told him to enter, and enter he would.

La Salle, meanwhile, had gone early that morning with Joutel and some laborers to cut a tree for making a canoe. He was to build a fire on the beach when the tide came in, as a signal for the captain to proceed. It was to be a replay of an old story: with a ship in jeopardy, under a captain he did not trust, La Salle found it necessary to be elsewhere. Minet, in his diary entry for January 27, had written curiously that one could not "make over" the captain and the pilot of the flûte (Aigron and Zacharie Mengaud) more than La Salle was doing; in seemingly obsequious manner, the explorer ate and drank with them and, by sharing his wine, kept them in high good humor. Such camaraderie was about to end. The happenings of that day would cause the young engineer to remark that "the wine that M. de La Salle left for the captain and the pilots had rendered them more daring than necessary."[34]

On shore, meanwhile, shortly after the woodcutters had started to work, a band of Indians appeared, the Frenchmen's first contact with the Karankawans of the Matagorda Bay area. "Seven or eight chiefs" were induced to follow to the French camp, but La Salle understood little of what they tried to convey with signs. Some of the workmen, meanwhile, remained with the main native group as hostages. He gave the visitors food and drink and gifts of knives and hatchets.

When the tide was halfway up, the signal fire was lighted for the *Aimable* to enter the channel. The Indians departed, followed by several Frenchmen who expected to find their companions waiting where they had been left with the other natives. The Indians, however, had gone off to their encampment "a league and a half" away, taking the French hostages, among them the Marquis de Sablonnière. La Salle felt obliged to follow, on foot, while casting uneasy glances over his shoulder at the *Aimable*'s progress. He observed that she was steering badly, angling toward the sandbanks to her starboard. There was nothing he could do. Sometime later, a cannonshot signaled the disaster; she began furling her sails. Still, La Salle, hoping that these signs were not what they appeared to be, went on to the native camp — fifty crude huts of pole framework covered with reed mats or bison skins — to rescue his men and partake briefly of the Indians' hospitality. Returning toward the French camp, he saw his worst fears were realized.[35]

From the *Joly,* still anchored in deep water off shore, Minet saw La Salle's signal fire lighted, then the *Aimable* hoisting sail. For a while, she followed the markers and buoys, "but when she came to the bar she grounded. She furled her sails, fired a cannon, and put her flag at half mast."[36]

It was too late to save the ship; the frantic effort must be directed at salvaging as much of the cargo as possible. The wreck lay directly east of the tents and huts of Grand Camp, a mile and a half offshore — quite unlike the oft-published drawing from Hennepin's 1698 *New Discovery,* in which a ship is being unloaded over a gangplank linking it to the bank. If the wind blew ever so slightly from the offing, the shallops could not approach the wreck; valuable time was lost because of the contrary wind and swells.

One of the first needs was to keep the ship from breaking up. The masts, bobbing in the wind, caused the ship to rock, increasing the stress on the hull. The captain made no move or gave any order to cut them down. Father Zénobe Membré, who had been on the ship since leaving Saint-Domingue, observed the hesitancy, seized an axe, and began the work. With all the masts felled, "the people"—including the women and children, although no specific mention is made of them—were put ashore.[37]

Curious mishaps and circumstances attended the wreck and its salvage from the beginning. The channel having been clearly marked and ample warnings given, suspicion that the shipwreck was no accident seemed inescapable. As the ship drifted into the danger zone, even the warnings of the sailor at the masthead to "luff"—steer to windward—were countermanded by the captain, thus directing the ship toward the shoal. If he had let go the anchor the first time the keel scraped bottom, Joutel allows, "he could have got off." Instead, he had taken in his mainsail and set the spritsail, driving the ship still farther into the reef. In response to the cannonshot that signaled the *Aimable*'s disaster, the *Joly*'s launch, in Ensign Du Hamel's charge, came and carried an anchor forward to kedge her afloat again. But the *Aimable*'s first anchor still held, and no axe could be found to cut it loose in time; the moment of opportunity slipped away. The *Joly*'s sailors, instead of completing final arrangements for sailing, worked through the night to salvage what they could from the wreck, carrying goods ashore in both the ship's launch and her canoe. All of them, says Minet, believed that "they [?] wanted to lose the flute."[38]

The *Aimable*'s shallop, which La Salle had taken ashore that morning, also was put to use, as was the *Belle*'s. When Père Zénobe returned to the ship to save the priests' belongings, he narrowly escaped drowning; in going from the heaving boat to the ship, he failed to catch a rope that was thrown him. While the workmen gathered supplies to take ashore, the *Aimable*'s boat, secured to the stern of the ship with a sleeping sailor in it, went adrift, by accident or design. The sailor awoke to find himself ashore on Matagorda Island. By the time he walked the two miles to Grand Camp to tell where the boat was, valuable time had been lost at the salvage.

The greatest handicaps for the salvagers were the ship's distance from shore and the few boats at their disposal. "If we had had several shallops," Joutel avers, "we could have saved even the ship in the beginning." He lamented that a couple of collapsible boats *(brisées)* had not been brought

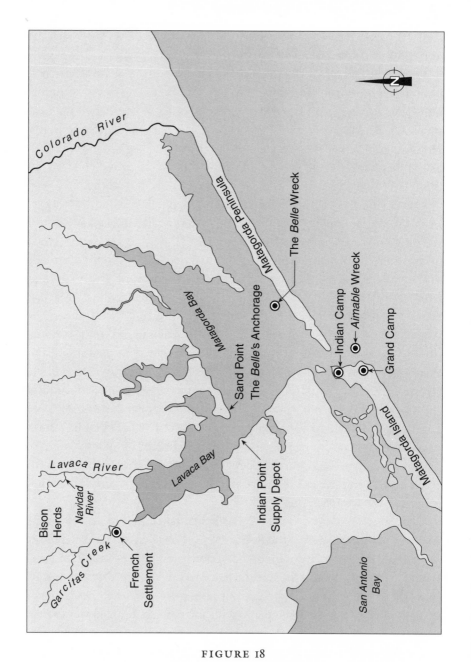

FIGURE 18

Misplaced Landing. Misfortunes multiplied following La Salle's landing on the Texas coast: the wreck of the Aimable, *defection and death of key people, and, ultimately, the wreck of the* Belle, *the colony's last remaining link with civilization.*

from France.[39] The *Aimable*'s boat made only a few trips before she was lost again, two days later. This time the mooring line was cut, and the craft was not recovered till six months afterward, when it was found at the mouth of a creek flowing into the bay. Thus, the work of salvaging the *Aimable*'s cargo fell principally to the *Joly* and her sailors, the *Belle*'s launch being so small.

With the means at hand, the workmen first took from the grounded ship the gunpowder, then the flour. There must surely have been a shortage of labor as well as boats, for Minet relates that all the soldiers were ill with dysentery and other ailments—probably including scurvy, for they had no green vegetables, their rations consisting mainly of a flour gruel made with brackish water, and oysters. The men were dying at the rate of five or six per day, from ingesting brackish water and "wretched food."[40]

By the next day the *Aimable* was sinking noticeably into the sand reef while the launches and canoes worked back and forth, hauling such meager loads as they could carry. While the cargo was being unloaded at Grand Camp, some soldiers out gathering wood sounded the alarm: Indians were coming, as many as four hundred, they said. The number shrank to hardly more than a hundred by actual account. They were armed with bows and arrows and naked except for a bison skin draped around them. About fifty approached the camp in canoes, and twenty came ashore to mingle among the workers, eyeing the goods—guarded by four sentinels—that were being unloaded from the wreck. Barbier, the Canadian *coureur de bois,* employed his knowledge of sign language to barter for some of their dugout canoes. He went with the natives to their camp and returned with two of the crude craft, for which he gave some hatchets. It was not the last time the natives would come around the camp. A few days later, it was visited again by a number, "painted all over and with their arms—that is to say, bows, arrows, tomahawks. . . . They had some evil design." At some point, the native visitors—the posted guard notwithstanding —availed themselves of a bale of Normandy blankets. From this episode came the breakdown of relations between the Frenchmen and the Karankawans, with disastrous consequences of many kinds.[41]

The salvage effort continued, when the wind and sea permitted, for more than a week. On the twenty-second, Captain Beaujeu and his lieutenant, Chevalier d'Hère, went on board the wrecked vessel to keep the sailors working. That night the wind mounted, blowing first from the sea, then shifting to north-northeast with fog and rain. The boats were halted for two days. Then the *Aimable* began to break up. During the night her hull opened and spilled much of the cargo into the gently rolling sea. The tired boatmen awoke to see bundles and boxes of the lighter goods bobbing on the surf. La Salle sent men "in all directions" to gather what they could: some thirty casks of wine and brandy and some barrels of vegetables, flour, and meat. On the twenty-eighth, when Minet went with the *Joly*'s boat crew to see if anything else could be recovered, water stood waist-deep between decks. The salvage effort was virtually at an end. On March 1 the wind blew strong from off shore, driving a heavy sea. The *Joly*'s shallop and canoe were stranded ashore, unable even to return to their own ship until the fourth. The *Aimable* sank deeper every day until finally, on March 7, she was seen no more.[42]

La Salle, meanwhile, had drawn an official report of the loss of the *Aimable.* The document, to be taken to France by Captain Beaujeu, comprises an indictment of Captain Aigron for willfully running the ship aground, then confusing all efforts to float her off and salvage the cargo. Aigron had removed all his own belongings to safety beforehand, but the loss he brought upon La Salle and his colonists was irreparable: 60 casks of wine and brandy, all the beef and bacon but 9 barrels, much of the beans and flour, 4 cannon that fired a 12-pound ball, 1,620 cannonballs, 400 grenades, 4,000 pounds of iron and 5,000 or 6,000 pounds of lead, fittings for the forge, cordage, chests of arms and tools, most of the clothing of soldiers and passengers, and almost all the medicines, as well as Indian trade goods such as axes, tobacco, and knives.[43]

As the *Joly* once more prepared to sail, La Salle wrote also a letter to the foreign minister, resorting again to a litany of excuses and promises. This letter also comprises a sort of self-indictment: "The suspicions I had at Saint-Domingue of this captain's [Aigron's] evil intent, of which I had had several warnings, caused me to embark on that ship [the *Aimable*]." And at Matagorda Bay: "As I thought I had reason to distrust him, I ordered him to have his ship go in under tow. . . ."[44]

If La Salle really had such prescience, what in heaven or earth could have caused him to order the ship to cross that treacherous bar with scarcely an inch under her keel without himself being on board? For the third time, his confusion of priorities had resulted in the loss of a ship at the worst possible time.

Because of the many misfortunes and delays, La Salle informed the minister that he would go to the Illinois country for news from France before proceeding. In an oblique reference to his proposed conquest of Nueva Vizcaya, he pledged "to carry out my enterprise at once," unless peace had been published in Canada, and "proceed as if war were a certainty."[45] For either of his alternate plans, his resources had been vastly diminished. For ascending the real Mississippi (if he could find it), he had only the little frigate *Belle*. For a march overland across Mexico, he had only a sick and inept remnant of his original one hundred soldiers, who—if Minet is to be believed—were still dying at an alarming rate. As for building and fortifying a fort, he had no engineer, and eight of his cannon had either sunk with the *Aimable* or were about to be hauled off in the *Joly*'s hold for want of a safe harbor in which to get them out. And for the cannon taken off the *Aimable* before her disaster, it was claimed, there was not one cannonball. For such reasons, La Salle wrote, "I do not believe Your Highness will disapprove of my going a little farther up this river for this year to be out of reach of Spanish forces while awaiting the relief that I am hoping you will send me." The minister should expect news of his accomplishments toward the end of July.[46]

Still clinging to his geographical misconceptions and confused notions of the coastal hydrography, La Salle wrote:

> I decided to go up the small mouth of the *fleuve* Colbert rather than go back to the larger one, twenty-five to thirty leagues northeast of here, which we saw on January 6 but failed to recognize because we believed . . . that we had not yet passed the Baye-du-Saint-Esprit. . . . If spring had not been so near, I would have gone back there. Dread of spending the winter beating eastward [against contrary wind and current] caused me to ask M. de Beaujeu to examine the other mouth and report to Your Highness concerning it. . . . These two channels issue from a very long and wide bay, salty as the sea, into which the *fleuve* Colbert discharges. There is a tide and, as one cannot see from one side to the other, it was easy for me to make a mistake when I descended into it by taking this expanse of salt water for the sea. Having only birch-bark canoes, I could not cross it.[47]

At this crucial time, the lack of the *Aimable*'s launch would prove in some ways more disastrous than loss of the ship itself. With the *Joly* about to depart, La Salle had only the much smaller boat of the *Belle* in which to navigate the coastal lagoons and estuaries. Early in March he made an oral request of Beaujeu for the use of the *Joly*'s launch for crossing his "people" to the mainland to "escape the flooded area." Whether he had in mind moving his colony to the mainland at once or beginning the exploration that was put off till the following month is not clear. The captain, however, was in haste to make sail for the supposed Espíritu Santo Bay, that his ship might be in a safe harbor before the equinoctial storms set in; the boat was in use, laying in wood and water, which he feared might be even more scarce at his destination; if La Salle would send the *Belle* to the bay in April, he would give him the small boat he carried for emergencies, as well as the four cannon.[48]

At the same time, Beaujeu renewed his offer to go to Martinique and return with provisions for the colony. La Salle again declined, believing the island intendant would not honor the request. Indeed, Beaujeu made known his willingness to do whatever he could to assist La Salle in his plight, which was far more desperate than La Salle seemed willing to acknowledge. Although the captain held out against taking the *Aimable*'s sailors back to France unless La Salle would provide their sustenance, he at last relented; his own crew volunteered to go on short rations to accommodate them.[49]

A day or two after La Salle received Beaujeu's letter denying him the use of his launch, another tragedy occurred that vitally impacted the colony's future. The affair weighed heavily upon him as he penned his reply to the captain. Continually disadvantaged by the lack of boats, he had sent some men to the Indian camp to barter for more of the native canoes. Thus, it came to his attention that the Indians had pilfered goods salvaged or washed ashore from the shipwreck. Besides some iron objects, they had in their camp several bales of Normandy blankets, some of which had been cut in two and were worn as skirts by the women. With such news, La Salle sent his nephew Crevel de Moranget with seven volunteers and hired men to the camp with orders to recover the stolen goods or obtain some of the natives' canoes in exchange. Ensign Du Hamel of the *Joly* agreed to take the men in the ship's launch. Moranget's companions included some of the same young Normans—noted, Joutel says, for having more zeal than prudence—who had accompanied the march up the island from Cedar Bayou.[50]

Their lack of prudence promptly manifested itself, as they barged into the native camp, arms in hand. Many of the Indians fled. Finding some people still in their huts, Du Hamel tried to convey by signs that the Frenchmen wanted the blankets but could not make himself understood. The Indians departed; the rude visitors took the blankets and animal skins left behind, then seized two canoes and started back to their own camp. Unskilled at poling the cumbersome craft and the wind against them, the men could make little progress. As night came on, Du Hamel and his launch crew forged ahead, promising to send help. As soon as the sailors were gone,

Moranget and the seven others secured the canoes, built a fire on shore for warmth, and lay down to sleep. Moranget awoke to a savage cry as an arrow glanced off his chest and another plowed into his arm. Able to seize their weapons, he and some of his companions fired, putting the Karankawans to flight. Moranget then made his way to camp on foot.

Soldiers were dispatched immediately to the scene. By morning light, they found Gayen seriously wounded, Oris and Desloges dead. In flight, the Indians had left a bloody trail. Thenceforth, there would be no peace with the denizens of this savage coast; the French settlers must be ever on their guard.

La Salle's letter to Beaujeu of March 7 reflects his distraction as he tried to deal with the several issues that remained while the *Joly* drew close to her actual sailing time. "Concerning the voyage to Martinique," he wrote, "I have found it impossible to think of the means . . . because of the loss of four of my best men, including my nephew, who through excessive zeal for serving and a great contempt for the *sauvages,* exposed themselves to an ambush. . . . This incident has greatly affected me. I have had so many burdens that it has been impossible for me to think of anything else."[51]

To La Salle, Beaujeu sent his condolences, with best wishes for Moranget's recovery, then reminded him of what he had pointed out previously: that Moranget lacked nothing but experience; the young officer, nevertheless, was receiving good training, "and this affair will make him more cautious."[52] Unfortunately, Crevel de Moranget was heir to one of his uncle's failings: he refused to learn from experience.

This new misfortune, joined to the loss of the *Aimable,* says Joutel, had its effect among the gentlemen who had come with La Salle; it strengthened the design of those who wished to leave him and return to France. These included, he says, the Abbé d'Esmanville, the engineer Minet, and others. (In this Joutel errs, for d'Esmanville and Minet, as already told, had formed their unshakable resolve before leaving Cedar Bayou.) "The talk which the enemies of La Salle indulged in, for the purpose of aspersing his conduct and the alleged rashness of his enterprise, contributed to these desertions to no small degree; but, sustained by his constancy alone, he heard and awaited everything in patience, and still gave his orders entirely unmoved."[53] *Is this the La Salle we have come to know?*

It was a grim scene when the slain men were brought in and buried with solemn ceremony, cannonfire serving in lieu of bells. A few days later the *Joly* unfurled her sails and set course eastward, presumably toward the bay that never was, called by the Spaniards Espíritu Santo and by the French

Saint-Esprit. Francis Parkman, in characteristic eloquence, speaks of "the dejected men and homesick women who were to seize New Biscay and hold for France a region large as half Europe. The Spaniards, whom they were to conquer, were they knew not where. They knew not where they were themselves; and for the fifteen thousand Indian allies who were to have joined them, they found two hundred squalid savages, more like enemies than friends."[54]

Yet, however miserable their plight, it would worsen.

Chapter 10

The Hostile Shore

"A CURSE UPON OUR LABORS"

As the *Joly* prepared to sail, La Salle's people on the beach had little knowledge of what had passed between the two leaders. They may not have known even that the king's ship was about to leave them for good. Or that the colony's fate was firmly bound to the forty-five–tun barque *Belle,* which had a history of near-accidents and whose want of adequate ground tackle kept her perpetually vulnerable. There would be no rendezvous at the Baye-du-Saint-Esprit for the *Joly's* hold to disgorge the colony's four cannon and the cannonballs; La Salle never undertook to go there, and Captain Beaujeu was prevented from seeking the mythical bay by a contrary wind that bore him off toward Cuba. Nor would the warship sail to Martinique to send back relief for the colonists, an idea that La Salle had rejected. In their unknowing state, the people surely reacted to what now passed before their eyes with a mixture of surprise and alarm.

They were accustomed to seeing the tall ship bobbing on the swells three miles offshore,[1] as she had been for almost a month. Only the occasional passage of her launch to and from the beach interrupted the otherwise constant scene. Then, just before nine o'clock the morning of March 12, 1685, they looked up from their work of gathering the *Aimable's* debris to see the *Joly's* sails unfurled and filled with the southerly Gulf breeze. As she tacked east-southeast, gradually sinking below the horizon, each of the onlookers stood silently, lost in private thoughts. The people aboard the *Joly* would see France again, but would *they themselves*? The *Aimable* lay in fragments at their feet. Only the little *Belle,* momentarily safe within the channel, held by her single anchor, offered a link to the civilized world.

If solace is found, as some say, in hard work, the able-bodied and willing among the French settlers had theirs. La Salle employed them for the next twelve days at gathering the *Aimable*'s wreckage that washed up on the beach, loading the *Belle* to her limit, and making a retrenchment; as Joutel describes it, "a sort of fort . . . to defend ourselves against Indian attack" and protect what had been salvaged from the *Aimable.* Among the hired men and soldiers were "men of all nationalities," many of whom did not take well to the discipline of work. Several deserted; by La Salle's prompt action, some were brought back, one to be condemned to death, it is said; others to serve ten years in the colony (should they be so lucky).[2]

Two men made good their escape; one, Joutel says, was "a Spaniard who had enlisted as a soldier and who was said to know how to dress skins and to be a furrier." Actually, the man was Italian, not Spanish; a hired man, not a soldier. He was Pietro Pauollo di Bonardi, age forty, of "Turin, Piémonte [Piedmont]," who on June 12, 1684, had been recruited at La Rochelle by Jean Massiot *le jeune* for three years. Bonardi at that time gave his occupation as *"pelletier et gantier"*—furrier and glover. This "Spaniard" and one of the Frenchmen "fled, and were never more heard of."[3]

Not quite so. The Frenchman was Jean Jarry (often called Géry, or any number of Spanish and English variants), who three years later was found ruling over a tribe of Coahuiltecans far to the west. The Italian, who has long been a mystery, appears again in the Talon brothers' answers to interrogations, where his fate is told.[4]

While dealing with the irritant of desertions, La Salle became increasingly aware of the island camp's exposed position, within easy view of passing ships. He acknowledged his lack of means to fortify it against "the insults of foreigners" and, worse, believed his people incapable of their own defense in any circumstance. Prudence dictated a move inland. On March 24 the leader departed with 51 followers to seek a more suitable site. His band included the Récollet Fathers Membré and Le Clercq and the Sulpician Abbés Cavelier and Chefdeville. Father Anastase Douay, Récollet, remained to minister to the 102 persons left at the island camp under the joint command of Joutel and the wounded Moranget. Le Gros, the commissary, remained; Étienne Liotot, La Salle's surgeon, stayed to attend Moranget's arrow wounds. The rampant illness demanded that the other surgeon (Louis Ruiné) remain also. If, as La Salle maintains, his company had consisted of 200 at the start, death and desertion by this time had claimed 47. His losses continued to mount.[5]

La Salle, after relocating his people, planned to search the bay for its supposed link to the Mississippi. Once that link was found, he would ascend it with the *Belle* to the Mississippi's main channel and establish his fort sixty leagues above its mouth, as he had promised the king and the foreign minister. The plan, as La Salle's plans were wont to do, went awry.

After having the *Belle* moved farther within the bay for security, La Salle and his 51 men made their way northward along the west side of Matagorda Bay in the *Belle*'s small shallop and four canoes. Joutel, who by no means was privy to all La Salle's plans or actions, was puzzled at the course he took. There was "no reason to doubt" that his river lay to the northeast; any stream that might offer access to it would lie in that direction. Yet the explorer chose to follow the western bay shore, probing the bays and inlets that led in the opposite direction.[6]

On April 2 the entourage "arrived on a small river, which empties into the head of the bay from the northwest, eighteen leagues from the [bay] mouth."[7] There, on what is known today as Garcitas Creek, Victoria County, Texas, they found fresh water in nearby springs and deep soil. The site, five miles above the stream's mouth in Lavaca Bay, promised good hunting, with "wild beeves [bison]," turkeys, waterfowl, partridges, turtle doves, rabbits, and hares, as well as good fishing. Lacking, however, was an anchorage for the *Belle*. La Salle, leaving part of his men there, continued his search until April 22, hoping to find a place more accessible to the ship. Finding none, he had to accept the inconvenience of an anchorage "twelve leagues" away, near Indian and Sand Points. Thence, the cargo being sent up from the Matagorda Island camp would have to be unloaded and transported the rest of the way in the four canoes, none of which could carry more than 1,500 pounds.[8]

Back at Grand Camp, Joutel worked to improve the "sort of fort," using the loose boards that had floated ashore from *l'Aimable*'s break-up. The crude redoubt emboldened the colonists to take up the challenge presented by their Indian neighbors, "with whom we carried on a sort of war." The Indians often prowled about the camp at night, howling like wolves, but a few shots would put them to flight.

Beneath the island's sandy surface the Frenchmen found a substratum of clay suitable for making an oven, but other improvements came slowly. "It seemed," says Joutel, "as if there was a curse upon our labors." Badly chosen in the beginning, the men proved incapable of any useful work. Of the "hundred or a hundred twenty of us left at the place"—Joutel was never too precise with numbers—some died every day. Scurvy and *la maladie du païs* ("homesickness") took their toll.[9]

Toward the first of May, La Salle returned to Grand Camp for an overnight visit. He came to report on the site he had found, see how the colony was faring, and learn his nephew's condition, which was satisfactory. (Nowhere is concern expressed, or even mention made, of Gayen's convalescence.) He gave orders for Joutel to begin squaring timbers for the building of the new post on Garcitas Creek. Driftwood was gathered to go with boards and timbers from the *Aimable*. The workmen were sustained by fish, which were easily caught in nets. A momentary pause in their labors was occasioned by the approach of sails from the direction of Pánuco "or the Rivière de la Madeleine." Certain that the small Spanish vessel carried a search party looking for them, Joutel directed the people to lie low behind their flimsy barricade with weapons at the ready. The "trading" galley of Juan Corso and Pedro de Castro passed so near that men could be seen on deck, but—even though Minet had readily spotted the tents from the *Joly*— the men on the galley failed to see the encampment among the dunes. The little ship, whose story has been told elsewhere, sailed on toward its own tragic destiny on the savage coast farther east.[10]

Although the abundance of game and fish relieved the otherwise sparse diet, the quest of fish and fowl occasioned terrible misfortunes. Le Gros, wading into a swamp to retrieve a bird he had shot, was bitten above the ankle by a rattlesnake: his sentence to prolonged suffering and eventual death. Another man, name not told, was swept away in the current and drowned while swimming in the channel attending a fish net. Such ill fortune stalked the little colony.

The threat of Indian attack hung perpetually over the camp. If peace with the neighboring Karankawans was ever a possibility after the rash action of Moranget's company and the Indians' deadly response, it was soon removed by the Frenchmen themselves. When three men from a hunting party came toward the camp, Joutel issued a call to arms and took precautions against flaming arrows being shot into the huts. But, seeing that the approaching Indians were not armed, Joutel and Moranget—contrary to La Salle's standing order—laid down their own weapons and went to meet them outside the encampment. Unable to converse with them by signs, they fired muskets into the air and a cannon in their general direction to put the entire band to flight. "These occurrences," wrote Joutel, "made us redouble our precautions, since we were openly at war with this cunning tribe. . . . Punishment was ordered for those who were found asleep while on guard." A device called "the wooden horse" was used without mercy to castigate offenders. "[Thus] we preserved our lives."[11]

Thus also did Joutel and Le Gros bring upon themselves the hatred of some of their men. Joutel, well schooled in military discipline, expected disciplined performance from those whose lives he was responsible for. From his military perspective, the people of his charge were divided into two groups: those who gave the commands and those who carried them out. Seldom in his account are those in the second group mentioned by name. His military stance became more rigid upon receipt of La Salle's order that the camp was to get ready to move.

Early in June, two boats arrived from the new site. In charge of the boatmen was the sieur de La Villeperdrix, who brought the word from the commander: Moranget—accompanied by the surgeon Liotot, although by now he had largely recovered from his wounds—was to conduct most of the people overland to the new site, leaving thirty at the island camp with Joutel until the *Belle* returned for them.

The barque, meanwhile, had gone on up the bay to discharge her cargo near the place known in the present day as Indian Point, where a supply depot had been set up and manned by sieur de Hurié and a dozen others. Thence, the goods brought up from Grand Camp would be taken in boats "to the place where M. de La Salle was."[12] This was the site where soon would rise the ragged French settlement that chroniclers of the episode since 1713 have mistakenly called "Fort St. Louis." Villeperdrix reported that La Salle was having ground broken for planting the seeds brought from France. Those not employed in this work were a few miles away, where bison were plentiful, killing and smoking a supply of fresh meat.

Moranget, with some seventy persons, left the island camp on "June 10 or 12." Crossing the lagoon shown on present-day maps as Espiritu Santo Bay, the marchers—apparently including Madame Talon and her babe at breast, as well as the other women and children—began what must have been a trek of well over fifty miles. Traveling by foot up the west side of Matagorda Bay, they had to make wide detours around bayous, lakes, and marshes.

Joutel, with thirty of the most robust men, found living easier at the Grand Camp. He was able to reduce the area of "the fort" so as to require fewer sentinels. Food was easier to come by for the lesser number; some of the men had been reduced even to eating rattlesnakes when food was at its scarcest. Now, Joutel says, "Hunting and fishing was our chief occupation." This "greater ease" of living, however, did not please everyone. There were malcontents—"a knot of desperadoes," Parkman calls them—who plotted desertion. When the would-be deserters found themselves unable to obtain guns or ammunition because Joutel and Le Gros kept the weaponry locked up and closely guarded, the desertion plot turned to one of murder. Joutel was to go first, his throat slit while he slept. The plotters then would proceed to the warehouse, where Le Gros slept—still in great pain and unable to defend himself as a result of the snakebite—to finish their bloody work. One of the miscreants, however, had a loose tongue; he confided in a huntsman named Devault, who warned Joutel. The plot frustrated, the man was arrested, he confessed, and he named his accomplice. Joutel identifies one of the plotters as the baker from Saint-Jean-d'Angély, who at Saint-Domingue had baked biscuit to provision the ships for the rest of the voyage. The notarial records at La Rochelle reveal that his name was Jacques Labaussair. At age twenty-two in July, 1684, he had signed on for three years. The reason for his hatred of Joutel and Le Gros may never be known, as Joutel chose not to reveal it. When the *Belle* returned, the two culprits were put on board to be taken to the new settlement. There they were put on trial, as were "some soldiers and hired men," who, having deserted, were tracked down by La Salle's Shawnee hunter, Nika. The punishment meted is not noted: only that they were found guilty of attempted murder.[13]

The *Belle* had brought La Salle's order for Joutel to have the remaining property at the island camp put on board and a raft made of the timbers that had been squared, for towing to the new site. A violent storm intervened; the raft, once begun, had to be dismantled, the timbers buried in the sand.

As the *Belle,* with her passengers and new cargo, weighed anchor near Grand Camp, heavy swells were rolling in from the Gulf, breaking around the headland. The ship took shelter behind the small island, near where she had anchored after first crossing the bar. There the crew made a lucky find: two casks of brandy that had washed up on the tiny island from the wreck of the *Aimable.*

Storm surge, meanwhile, turned Grand Camp itself into an island. The men remaining there set march northward to bivouac near Saluria Bayou, where the Indians who had caused so much trouble had been encamped; the place thenceforth would be known as Le Camp des Sauvages. The next day, Joutel recounts, "we crossed the inlet . . . and went along the shore straight to the Sieur Hurié's camp, where the depot was and all the goods were deposited."[14] The only defensive work here consisted of the barrels and boxes unloaded from the *Belle,* but at this location there was no fear of attack by Europeans. Beyond Sand and Indian Points, access to the settlement was through Lavaca Bay. A shallow bar between the two points prevented the *Belle* from entering. After spending the night at the supply dump, Joutel went on next day by canoe to join La Salle at "the place where he had decided to form his new settlement."[15] This was the location of La Salle's colony, which chroniclers of the episode have since come to call "Fort St. Louis"—an error now fixed in the popular mind.

Joutel, on arriving from Grand Camp in July, 1685, was appalled at the lack of progress. "Surprised to see things so badly started," he saw dry and sterile seed beds, unguarded from the trampling and rooting of swine. The only shelter of any kind was a staked enclosure where the powder was kept. Everything appeared "to be in a miserable state."[16] Illness and death were everywhere.

The task at hand was the building of housing. The nearest suitable timber grew a league away. There were no carts or draft animals to move it to the site. La Salle, nevertheless, sent men to fell the trees and square the logs while others stood guard against Indian attack. Men worked like draft cattle to drag the timbers over the almost three miles of prairie, a back-breaking chore that overcame even the strongest. At last a gun carriage was provided, but to draw it through the tall, matted grass was still a grueling task. The toll of such intense effort moved Joutel, in writing his narrative, to somber reflection: "This excessive toil; the little sustenance that the workers had, and it often reduced for failure in their duty; La Salle's distress that matters did not succeed as he had envisioned, which often caused him to mistreat his people—all this produced a melancholy in many. They declined visibly."[17]

Repeatedly, the veteran soldier advised La Salle that the timber squared at the Matagorda Island camp could be brought by water with greater ease. Each time, the commander replied caustically that he had not intended to bring advisers with him. Joutel said no more at the time. In distant contemplation he wrote, "This work was continued for some time. . . . I can testify that [it] caused the death of more than thirty persons, as much from the punishment they were given as from the affliction."[18]

La Salle himself acknowledges the loss of half his people by the end of July—less than six months after his arrival on the Texas coast. He casts the blame on the men themselves: the soldiers recruited at Rochefort, having begged all their lives and being incapable of discipline, took unto themselves the means of their own destruction by drinking brackish water and eating native fruits.

The toll was especially severe among the *Belle*'s crew, he says, as they were out from under his watchful eye; even the captain (Daniel Moraud) died. The crew diminished to the extent that there were scarcely enough men to work the rigging. The ship itself was afflicted, as worms riddled the lower planking; the bilge pumps had to work continuously. Furthermore, La Salle went on, the workmen engaged by Jean Massiot *le jeune* at La Rochelle were either dead or ill; all of them were incapable of their craft, so that La Salle himself not only had to lay out their work but also to be the carpenter for building the houses. Such was La Salle's litany of complaints and excuses; he had not changed his spots since escaping the hostile and fiercely competitive environs of Canada.[19]

While timber for the building accumulated, the four native canoes and the *Belle*'s shallop—and, presumably, the larger boat mysteriously cut loose from the wrecked *Aimable* but later found—worked back and forth between the settlement and the supply depot, where the *Belle* was still discharging cargo brought from Grand Camp. The eight iron cannon that had been taken off the *Aimable* before her mishap, each weighing from slightly less than 700 pounds to more than 1,100, were carried one or two at a time from the depot to the new site. There were no cannonballs of the proper size, for they had either been lost with the storeship or carried off in the hold of *Le Joly*. The canoes, however, brought a hundred barrels of powder and three thousand pounds of lead bullets, which could be bagged and fired from the cannon with devastating effect upon an attacking force.[20]

As the building got underway, La Salle at last confronted the need for the timbers buried in the sand on Matagorda Island. Joutel took twenty men, including the *Belle*'s second pilot, Sellié, in three canoes and the *Belle*'s shallop. They carried grapnels or small anchors, cordage, and a sail from the *Belle* for making a raft of the timbers and sailing it back to the settlement on Garcitas Creek.

At Grand Camp, Indians had unearthed some of the boards and pulled the nails, which they found useful for tipping arrows. The cordage buried in barrels was untouched and well preserved. To form the base of the raft, the longest timbers were lashed together. Then, secured by a mooring on shore and an anchor in the offing, it was floated. With the smaller boards stacked on top, the raft was completed in four days. A rudder was fashioned on the stern; a mast was rigged to hold a sail, and the strange-looking craft moved up the channel on the incoming tide.[21]

At this point in his chronicle, Joutel digresses to relate that he and Sellié, before launching the raft, took new soundings of "the entrance to the bay" and that they agreed with those taken "the first time," showing a depth of from nine to twelve feet, with five and six fathoms within. The soundings had no pertinence to the launching of the raft, which was built within the channel and did not have to cross the bar. The purpose appears to have been to put a new entry into the record that would counter any future claim against La Salle in connection with the wreck of the *Aimable*. Joutel comments: "The wickedness of the captain of the *flûte* (Aigron) in having purposely run aground was evident, for nothing was easier than entering this bay." The written report on the sounding that he claims to have made to La Salle has not surfaced, but the depths given here contrast markedly with those of Beaujeu and Minet.[22]

The raft, under sail and towing the canoes and shallop, reached the Camp des Sauvages, near Saluria Bayou, to find that the natives had returned since the abandonment of Grand Camp. When the Frenchmen dropped anchor as if to go ashore, the Indians took flight. The raftsmen weighed anchor and made sail again on the favorable wind but, still some distance from shore, ran aground near the promontory where Port O'Connor now stands. After five hours' work with all hands in the water, the rising tide enabled them to float off. That night, with the raft anchored in a creek, the men slept on board. During the night one of the canoes broke its mooring and drifted away, apparently unnoticed by the sentry. Joutel, forgetting one of the first rules of military responsibility, blamed the pilot Sellié, who had tied up the craft, even though he himself rested within a few feet of the boats and could easily have checked the moorings himself. Loss of the canoe, an annoyance at the time, later proved to be a blessing. This, it is reasonable to believe, was the craft that washed up on Matagorda Peninsula some months afterward, opportunely for those marooned by the wreck of the *Belle*.

The rest of the raft voyage went smoothly. The southeast wind carried the unusual craft into the mouth of Garcitas Creek. A day later, it reached the settlement.

The wood that made up the raft, Joutel avers—seemingly indulging himself with an "I-told-you-so"—proved more useful than all that had been taken from the woods at the cost of more than thirty lives. A large house, divided into four rooms, was built first, in the Canadian style; the corners were joined by what is still known in trade circles as a "French dovetail," with a long peg inserted to hold the members in place. The thin planking became roof decking, over which bison hides were tacked to cover the defects and turn the rain. The rawhide covering, however, proved unsatisfactory, as it shrank when dried by the sun, causing it to tear or pull loose from the nails. When finished, one of the four rooms became La Salle's lodging; another, the abode of the Récollet fathers; the third, for some of the gentleman volunteers, others of whom had built their own huts. The fourth room served for storage. The rest of the people were "almost all without shelter." [23]

During this time, Le Gros, still suffering from the snakebite, had remained aboard the *Belle* while she shuttled goods from Grand Camp to the supply depot at Indian Point. His failure to improve caused La Salle to have him brought to the settlement. Gangrene had set in, and the pain and swelling persisted. The surgeon—whether Liotot or Ruiné is not clear—advised him that his only chance was to have the leg amputated. The operation was performed, but Le Gros died two days later, August 29, feast day of the Decollation of Saint John; "to everyone's sorrow," says Joutel. "La Salle, especially, felt the loss keenly, for there was no one else knowledgeable of his affairs. As for myself, I had lost the best friend I had in the country." Joutel and Le Gros, having become acquainted only at the start of the voyage, had since become close.[24]

Encounters with Indians, meanwhile, had become a frequent occurrence. La Salle had instructed his men not to make contact with the natives but to fire at them on sight. Hence, the French were often the aggressors. There may never have been a chance for reconciliation after the bad beginning; yet, the Europeans' truculent stance surely ordained the fate of many who were found defenseless outside the settlement and, ultimately, of the dwindling colony itself. When attacked, the Indians were certain to respond. Joutel should have learned that from an incident that occurred in late August; yet the lesson came to him only in hindsight, after it finally had dawned on La Salle himself.

On one of his several trips to the supply depot, Joutel found a band of natives lingering near a watering place "two musket shots" from Hurié's camp. They had been there the day before, Hurié told him, and had staked the waterhole with arrows. Joutel took the five men he had brought and went toward the Indians, who drew back but gave signs that they wished to speak with the Frenchmen: "Since M. de La Salle's order was to fire on them,[25] there was no reason to speak with them, even though some of our men had motioned for them to approach us." When the natives came within range, Joutel raised his gun and took aim, but his weapon misfired for want of a fresh primer. He reprimed his weapon, aimed again, and fired. The Indians withdrew, leaving Joutel in doubt as to "whether I had been skilful enough to hit any of them." Some of the other men had fired also, although they had been cautioned against discharging their weapons at the same time. Joutel then dropped his guard, believing the Indians had fled. In a thicket, he began leisurely reloading his musket. Suddenly the Indians returned, loosing a shower of "ten or twelve" arrows directly at the French leader. Joutel kept his calm, remembering La Salle's admonition never to run away from the natives, advice that, in this instance, probably saved the Frenchmen's lives. Even with his unloaded gun, Joutel led his men forward, and the Indians retreated. In the open, the six men waited, but the natives would not come out. They picked up the arrows they had shot and again withdrew. During the fracas, Joutel noticed that the Indians had with them a man who, being lighter-skinned than the rest, did not belong to their tribe—likely the Italian Bonardi who, having made good his escape from Grand Camp, lived several years among the Karankawas.[26]

Of the Karankawas, this episode shows three things: first, that the Indians were either not organized against the French or were uncertain of their ability to stand up against European firearms; second, that, when provoked, they were sure to retaliate; and, finally, that they would attack only when they had a clear advantage.

After spending the night at Hurié's camp, Joutel and his companions went on to the *Belle,* anchored a league away. There they learned that the Indians, apparently fearful of being attacked during the night, had moved and were encamped on the farther side of the ship. Their lack of organization seems evident in view of the fact that they had "eighteen or twenty" canoes.[27] They could have destroyed Hurié's meager band at a stroke.

When their advantage became apparent, however, they were quick to act. During the building of the houses at the settlement, La Salle reported, the *sauvages* "made several attempts" but were always put to flight. Three hunters from the settlement were attacked by fourteen Karankawans and might have been overcome but for a lucky shot that killed their chief. Late in September, a soldier who had gone without arms to look for some edible roots a short distance from the settlement was slain by natives, who outdistanced pursuit.[28] It was troubling incidents such as these that first deflected La Salle from his plan to take the *Belle* and go in search of his river.

We have already seen how that plan was deferred by his march against some troublesome natives—four Caucosi (Karankawa) rancherías on the

Guadalupe River, according to Meunier's testimony to his Spanish captors[29]—then frustrated altogether by the loss of the *Belle* and most of her crew. The causes of this tragic event have been seen in the character of La Salle, for whom reality never quite matched the grandeur of his dreams. There is a common denominator in all his four shipwrecks: the barque from Fort Frontenac near the mouth of the Niagara River; the *Griffon,* in a Lake Huron storm; the *Aimable,* whose timbers had been reshaped into the main house of the Garcitas Creek settlement; and now the *Belle.* Each wreck occurred in La Salle's absence at a critical time, when he had knowingly left the ship in the hands of a captain or pilot he did not trust. In each case, he suspected some evil design by the captain or crew as the cause, never his own negligence or confused priorities. In no instance did he pause to reflect that the ship in every instance was more vital to his enterprise than anything he might have accomplished in his absence; he failed to recognize in any of these disasters the lessons that might have prevented the next one.

As for the *Belle,* La Salle left her loaded with the necessities of his colony, in the hands of an unskilled crew commanded by a known drunk, with a single anchor of proven inadequacy. Moreover, she stood in an uncharted bay whose shores were lined with hostile natives, on a seacoast already noted for its gusty winter northers. The risks should have been apparent; so should the magnitude of the disaster that was being invited.

What urgency could have caused La Salle to leave the ship, even for ten days? And what compelling circumstance could have made him stretch his absence from the expected time to more than two months? Perhaps the best answer is given by the Jesuit scholar Jean Delanglez: "A restless urge drove La Salle from one place to another, a peculiar impulse made him think that wherever he was his presence was necessary elsewhere."[30] Yet, surely in this case, something out of the ordinary had triggered the impulse: perhaps the Spanish artifacts he claimed to have seen in the native ranchería. It is reasonable to speculate that he felt the need to learn where the Spaniards really were, for they now appeared to be closer than he had imagined. La Salle's movements, however are shrouded in a vagueness that pervades all the French documents, as well as in the conflicting evidence offered by Spanish and Indian sources.

As for Joutel, he was either not completely informed or else he had reasons for being less than candid. Left in charge of the settlement, he went from early December to mid-February without hearing from La Salle. The first news of the journey, on which La Salle took twenty men, was brought by Pierre Duhaut. Duhaut had started on the march but fell behind and became lost on January 18 after crossing "a very fine river that has since been called the Maline." Returning to the post about the middle of February, after nearly a month on the way, he informed Joutel of the massacre that had occurred more than two months previously of the *Belle*'s six-man sounding crew. Joutel quotes Duhaut as saying that La Salle had sent the *Belle* to "the head of the bay," following the sounding crew. He hoped to find there the branch of the Mississippi that he had seen during his 1682 exploration. La Salle, having assigned the bibulous Tessier to command the little frigate in place of the slain Richaud, sent replacements to make the ship's full complement of twenty-seven (perhaps including the five men he had put on board in irons). His instructions to Tessier called for keeping the ship at the same place until his return, guarding against surprise attack when going ashore for water. La Salle then departed with his twenty men in two canoes to seek "information about the river." Thus they traveled "as far as they could go by water," then sank the craft in the edge of the bay to be retrieved upon their return. Nothing is said of the direction of travel, although Joutel has made it clear that seeking "the river," to him, meant traveling northeast. The mention of the Maline (Maligne) River would seem to support this version.[31]

Pierre Meunier, in his testimony to his Spanish captors, related that "Monsieur de Salas [La Salle] spent all that winter [of 1685–86] in sounding and reconnoitering the entire area around the bay and in taking the eight-gun [actually six-gun] frigate [the *Belle*] farther into the bay. [The ship] had entered the bay as far as the buoys, which this man declares that he saw in the mouth of the Rio de San Marcos."[32] During the time that Meunier describes, however, he was a prisoner aboard the *Belle,* from which he ultimately escaped with the five others.[33]

La Salle, in his official report, relates that he and his company returned to the place where they expected to find the *Belle* on March 15; that thirty-five days of rain had delayed his journey and that they had been forced to cross more than thirty flooded rivers "to reach the Mississippi, where he arrived on February 13."[34] The real purpose of this extended journey, if *not* to find the Mississippi, is not explained. Yet the one point on which all serious-minded interpreters are agreed is that he did not reach the Mississippi, his claim notwithstanding.

Abbé Cavelier, who accompanied his brother on this journey, wrote of it so outlandishly as to make him scarcely worthy of mention. He relates that La Salle with his company of thirty, including the abbé, began the journey on the first of November and "we ran for two months in search of our river, with no hope of finding it." Early in February, he claims, "we came to a pretty large river, which my brother thought might be the Mississipi, although its course was just the opposite. . . . We followed its banks for two days, without seeing man or beast." Cavelier goes on to tell of encountering two Shawnee Indians who had become lost from La Salle's 1682 expedition and had been taken in by a tribe who made war on the Spaniards, of whom all the natives a hundred leagues around lived in fear; and so on into a fanciful tale of finding precious stones, news of the Spanish mines, a river described as he imagined the Río Bravo (Río Grande)—all designed to excite the minister Seignelay's interest rather than to tell the truth. So wonderful was this country, the abbé wrote, that the "honest" Shawnees rejected La Salle's offer to return them to their homeland: "They answered that . . . being in the most fertile, healthy and peaceful country in the world, they would be devoid of sense to leave it and expose themselves to be tomahawked by the Illinois or burnt by the Iroquois . . . where the winter was insufferably cold, the summer without game, and ever at war. . . ." The Frenchmen, the abbé then declares, left the Shawnees' adopted tribe near the end of January and went on to reach the Mississippi—"where we left some men in a little redoubt of pickets"—on March 10 and returned to the Baye-Saint-Louis on March 30 after "passing again through the village of our Shawnees."[35] An impossible itinerary.

As to this journey, neither La Salle nor his brother told the truth. Neither Joutel nor Meunier, in all probability, knew what the truth was. What, indeed, *was* the truth? The answer rests on circumstantial evidence and the reliability of native accounts, as well as the accuracy of Spanish interpreters. But the truth appears to be that La Salle, in the winter months of 1686, traveled west and southwest from the settlement, not east or northeast. Information on the route and manner of travel is scarce, fragmentary, and paradoxical.

The initial clue comes from a Pelón Indian who provided "the first direct news of La Salle's settlement to reach officials of New Spain." The native messenger, having visited near the Río Bravo among the Blanco and Pajarito Indians, reported to the Marqués de San Miguel de Aguayo (Agustín Echeverz y Subiza), new governor of Nuevo Reino de León. His hosts, the Indian related, had told him of strange white people seen on the big river. These strangers, said to resemble Spaniards, came from a settlement ten days' travel farther north. With them was an Indian who wore trousers and a cassock and carried a long knife. The strange native and a companion had been sent as emissaries to an unidentified native village, where the companion was killed. The Indian, though wounded, escaped to the Blancos, among whom he remained until he had recovered, then returned to his masters. Aguayo's letter is dated just a few months after La Salle's expedition of January–March, 1686.[36] The description of the Indian in European dress seems to fit La Salle's Shawnee hunter, Nika.

Still more elaborate evidence of a western trek comes from the Cíbolo and Jumano Indians of Trans-Pecos Texas, led by their famous chief Juan Sabeata. In the 1686 fall, these natives, who annually journeyed to the Hasinai to trade, brought news to the struggling mission settlement at La Junta de los Ríos of strange white men seen among the Tejas. Fray Agustín de Colina paid scant heed until the native traders returned the following year with tales of many kinds: of a "moor" (the Frenchman Jean Jarry), said to have fled other white men near the Tejas to escape a plot against his life (execution for desertion?); of other white men who lived in houses on the water, trading clothing and axes among the Tejas (Cenis, or Hasinai) for food and horses and courting the native women with beads and ribbons. These white men spoke ill of the Spaniards and were seeking native assistance in occupying the region of El Parral. Any doubt that the reference was to La Salle's settlement falls before the detailed nature of the Indians' report. They told of the wreck of one of the "houses on water"; of the strangers' interest in the Nueva Vizcaya mines (an objective of La Salle's expedition while Spain and France were at war); and, finally, of destruction of the settlement by the coastal natives, with no one left alive but "four or five" who remained among the Tejas.

Ultimately, Juan Sabeata and other Cíbolo and Jumano chieftains reached El Parral on April 10, 1689, to testify before the Nueva Vizcaya governor, Juan de Pardiñas Villar de Francos. Through an interpreter the governor heard that some time ago strange white men had come up the Río del Norte on three different occasions, two and three "moons" apart, some by canoe and some on foot. They visited the Cíbolo village north of the Río Grande, an estimated 67 leagues (almost 170 miles) downstream from La Junta de los Ríos. A Christian Indian called don Miguel had conversed extensively with the visitors.

> The Frenchmen, on learning that Miguel . . . knew the Spaniards of El Parral, wanted to know the distance to the settlement, the condition of the road, the number of rivers to cross, and the number of Spaniards in the region where the silver was being mined. Miguel naively answered

all their inquiries. Then the Frenchmen told him and the other natives present that the Spaniards were evil. It would be to the advantage of the Indians, they said, to ally themselves with these visitors, who would treat them as brothers. Instead of going to El Parral to trade, they should deal with the French, who would return with wagons loaded with provisions and would continue on to El Parral to occupy that region.

Such testimony, as Elizabeth A. H. John has noted, was "marked by good will and by a wide margin of misunderstanding."[37] Even though the Indian Miguel conveyed precise information on La Salle's purported intent, several points of the native's report cannot be reconciled. La Salle himself was scarcely ever away from the settlement long enough to make even one such journey, certainly not three. His longest absence from the bay area, excepting only his journey to eastern Texas in the summer and fall of 1686, was from January 3 or 4 to March 20 of that year. The interval is too short, even, for him to have reached the Cíbolo village (above present-day Langtry, Texas, according to the distance estimates) by any but the most direct route. The idea that some of La Salle's men might have stayed behind to pursue their leader's objectives when La Salle himself returned does not seem reasonable; neither he nor Joutel give any indication of that, even though it remains unclear whether all of the twenty men came back with him.

The questions may never be fully answered; yet, certain conclusions seem inescapable: La Salle, after leaving the bay in January, 1686, traveled west or southwest to the Río Grande; he or some of his men made contact with the Cíbolos or other natives who gave the Cíbolos explicit information; his project of conquering Nueva Vizcaya and seizing the mines of El Parral was revealed to the Indians, who relayed it to the Spaniards. The shortest route from the French settlement to the Cíbolo village at its presumed location would be some three hundred miles; if, say, the marchers went first to the lower Río Grande and obtained there a canoe, they would have had to travel well over five hundred miles before reaching the Cíbolos. To have covered this distance and returned by mid-March, they would have had to make good on the average at least eight miles per day during the entire period: a difficult matter, in view of the time that would have been required for hunting for food, treating with the native tribes, and exploring the route. Something in the picture does not fit. The Indians who deposed to Governor Pardiñas in Parral certainly had news of La Salle's colony. When and where they came by it, apart from their visit to the Hasinai, is another question.[38]

The trek westward, in any case, was a hollow exercise; worse, in view of the loss during La Salle's absence of the *Belle,* a death blow to his enterprise. Convinced that a plot was responsible for the little ship's disappearance, the explorer saw "no further hope of undertaking anything; being deprived of all things, even of sending word to France, he was obliged . . . to go by land to New France, for want of people capable of ascending the Mississippi by canoe, and to make a journey of five hundred leagues."[39] Always prone to blame his enemies for adversity and to see treason in every setback, he had not changed. After recovering from one of his periodic illnesses, he made ready to plunge again into an unknown wilderness, this time to seek the Mississippi and the only real Fort-Saint-Louis—on the Illinois River.

Chapter 11

The Fort That Never Was

"SAINT-LOUIS OF TEXAS"

La Salle's Texas colony has the distinction of being the first European settlement on the Gulf Coast between Pensacola, Florida, and Tampico, at the mouth of the Río Pánuco in Mexico. Here arose in 1686 the first Christian house of worship on this stretch of coast and the first for the entire present-day state of Texas except in the Presidio and El Paso areas. In that little chapel of stakes, Texas' first marriage of record was solemnized. The only child born of the colony—the first European birth of record in all of Texas—was surely christened in this "church in the wildwood," although the record does not exist and the name given the child is not known. In that, this infant of unknown gender, whose life was cruelly ended only a few months after its birth, may have common ground with its birthplace, for the colony itself never had an official name.

Popular usage notwithstanding, there never was a Fort-Saint-Louis of Texas. La Salle built no real fort at all, either on Matagorda Island or on Garcitas Creek, where the people moved in the summer of 1685. Joutel, who referred to the beachhead on Matagorda Island as "Grand Camp," derides the notion that anything remotely resembling a fort ever existed on Garcitas Creek (Rivière aux Boeufs). He makes light of the claim by Chrétien Le Clercq that a fort was built and put in a state of defense. This, he says, was purely imaginary, for "there was only the house . . . , having eight cannon at the four corners, unfortunately without cannonballs, and . . . when we left, there was nothing else in the nature of a fort." The bay, he says, "was named baye de Saint-Louis in honor of the King and the country [was] called Louisiana"; he describes the settlement in much the same terms as La Salle: "the habitation on the rivière aux Boeufs, near the baye Saint-Louis."[1]

Spanish sources provide a similar picture. Alonso de León, on discovering the ruined French site in 1689, wrote, "The principal house of this settlement is of ship timbers, built in the manner of a fort [or fortification]," with adjoining chapel. The other five houses, of stakes plastered with mud, were "all quite useless for any defense whatsoever." The Spanish interrogation of a seventeen-year-old accomplice in La Salle's murder (Jean L'Archevêque) in Mexico City brought forth the name "San Luis," which the Spaniards took to be that of the settlement. Despite some ambiguity, however, it seems clear that L'Archevêque, being pressed by his interrogators for names—of the bay, the river, the settlement—came up with the only one he could remember: "not knowing either the bay by which they entered or the land where they settled, they *called it* San Luis."[2] The Spaniards, quite naturally, failed to understand that this was the name that La Salle had given the adjacent bay, not the settlement.

"Fort-Saint-Louis," in fact, does not appear in any of the accounts by participants in the Texas episode during the post's four-year existence. Abbé Jean Cavelier, in his spurious "journal" as it was recast for the Marquis de Seignelay after his return to France, refers once to "the Baye or the fort St. Louis." Jean Michel, in his 1713 abridgment of Joutel, seized upon this verbiage to assert that the "dwelling," like the neighboring bay, was given the name "of St. Lewis [as it appears in English translation]." Interpreters of the episode ever since have perpetuated the error, in both literature and art. La Salle, in fact, never claimed to have built a fort; actually he lacked the means for doing so. He complained to Captain Beaujeu before the *Joly*'s return to France of "the post, which I cannot build, as I have no cannon to defend it, no iron to build it, and no engineer to fortify it."[3]

His engineer, Minet, having become disenchanted with La Salle's scheme and his volatile temperament, returned to France aboard the *Joly;* if any of those who had signed on the voyage as building tradesmen possessed the skills they claimed, they were soon disabled or dead. Furthermore, La Salle at last realized that he had not found the place at which he must build his permanent fort; the settlement on Garcitas Creek was never intended to be more than a temporary landing place while he sought an imagined link to the Mississippi.

Finally, the loss of the *Belle,* while rendering impossible the building of a fort, made it necessary for some of the colonists to remain at the temporary site indefinitely. Plans were made to erect a palisade around the settlement while La Salle went to seek his Illinois post. Those remaining in the settlement, however, found their time consumed by the necessities of daily living. The palisade was never built. The place never had a real name but only a description, given by La Salle in his last report: "the post built in the Baye-Saint-Louis."[4] There were only the main house, constructed mostly of timbers from *l'Aimable;* an enclosure that served as a powder magazine; the chapel; and a few huts to shelter the people, whose number dwindled rapidly.

Our story, then, is not of a military-trading post like Fort Frontenac, or even the real Fort-Saint-Louis in Illinois but rather of a weak and struggling European foothold on a foreign shore and the settlers' desperate attempt to cope with wretched circumstances.

Joutel, left in charge of the settlement during La Salle's first long absence, with sieur Hurié as his second, confronted the environmental strangeness. The thirty-four persons in his charge were without meat, as La Salle had loaded the entire supply on the *Belle* for her expected voyage to the Mississippi. Indians had moved into the vicinity, causing the bison herds to drift away. The colonists' sustenance consisted of a daily ration of bread and an occasional piece of salt pork for making soup, given out individually from the one remaining barrel. When at last the buffalo herds returned, Joutel gathered the most able men but found none who were experienced at hunting buffalo. Ludicrous scenes followed before there was meat for the table. On the first day, Joutel got off a single, ineffective shot before the late Le Gros's bitch and another canine ran at the herd and scattered it. Trying again later, he fired time after time, into one herd after another, breaking the shoulder of several animals without bringing one down. In the midst of "five or six thousand," the huntsmen crawled on hands and knees to get within range, yet the animals would catch their scent and scatter. Going to join the other men at the end of a long and tiring day, his knees raw and aching, Joutel came upon the still-warm carcass of an animal that had fallen out of his line of vision. There would be meat, but the day was extended well into the night by the butchering, a task at which none was experienced. Laden with a portion of the kill, the huntsmen groped their way across the trackless tall-grass prairie late at night, guided by Hurié's beacon fire.

Thereafter, the bison herds ranged within a league and a half of the settlement. The huntsmen developed their skills and knowledge of the animals' habits, and there was always plenty of meat. A smoking place (Le Boucan) was made nearby for preserving the meat and collecting the tallow and marrow. "Thus," says Joutel, "our time was filled with things of this sort." Some of the men grew tired of the work and had to be goaded. A canoe sent back by La Salle before he left the bay in January, 1686, made the transport easier, but it was not the end of difficulties on the hunt. Joutel still had trouble hitting an animal's vital spot. On one occasion it almost cost a life. As his quarry hobbled off on three legs while Joutel was reloading his gun, Father Douay attempted to turn it back by running in front of it. The enraged beast charged. The father's robe and the tall grass impeded his running; the wounded buffalo knocked him to the ground and trampled him while Joutel stood helplessly by, afraid to fire lest he hit the friar. At last getting off a shot, he felled the beast. Père Anastase limped about the settlement from his injury for six weeks.[5]

Somewhat later, Father Membré suffered even graver injury from a similar circumstance. His folly was striking a downed animal with his rifle butt. The beast suddenly arose and charged. Père Zénobe was knocked down and trampled, the skin torn from his face in several places. Barely able to move for weeks, he was months in recovery.

Another of the Récollets, Père Maxime Le Clercq, was attacked by a boar that seemed to bear him a grudge. As he tried to raise his robe while running, the boar overtook him, gnashed his arm with his tusks, and severed tendons, impairing the use of an arm and rendering his fingers useless.

There was always the danger of becoming lost. Before the episode with the boar, Père Maxime had gone out to provide armed escort to those bringing in the meat. He became lost and spent a cold night in the open before finding the river and following it to the settlement. One of the girls who went with the hunters to help dress the kill was left behind and spent two nights alone in the wilderness before finding the river to set her straight.

Anxiety for the lost ones was exacerbated by fear of the natives, for whom the colonists had to be on continuous alert. Sentries posted at each corner of the house stood two-hour watches, subject to Joutel's surveillance. Should one be found asleep, he would be punished "without mercy" by being placed on a version of the whipping post called a "wooden horse [*cheval de bois*]." Joutel seems to blame La Salle's attack on the native ranchería for continued bad relations with the coastal denizens: "It cost us dearly." Indians often stalked about the settlement and staked the nearby spring with arrows, signifying both their claim and a warning. When the colonists made long hunting trips, ascending the Rivière aux Boeufs by boat, they often had to make camp for the night. A brush barricade, or abatis, was thrown up so that no one could approach without detection. Around the settlement itself, trees large enough to obstruct the view of an approaching enemy were cut down.[6]

Lack of familiarity with the flora and fauna, as well as the native peoples, occasioned much difficulty for the colonists. One of the surgeons, while looking for land turtles by probing their dens with his hand, was bitten on the arm by an unseen creature and lost all or part of two fingers from the venom. Joutel questioned whether it was a snake or one of the four-legged toad-like animals he had seen, with a small tail and a knotty back: the harmless horned toad. "We as yet had no experience with this kind of poison."[7] Several animals were bitten by snakes, including the late Le Gros's dog. Recovering, she became the rattlesnakes' fierce enemy. Whenever she found one of the reptiles in the bushes, she would bark continuously until someone came and killed it. The rattlers, slain in considerable numbers, were fed to the hogs. Even the men, in extreme circumstances, had eaten them.

Venturesome eating, however, occasionally had its price. Fruits that looked edible proved deadly. Such was the prickly pear, with its fig-shaped fruit growing around the edges of racket-like pads. A soldier who ate the tunas without removing the almost imperceptible thorns suffered an inflammation of the mouth and throat that eventually choked him to death. According to La Salle, several died in his bay-shore camp of the same cause. Returning from his Indian campaign, he found more than thirty men "ill in the extremity" from eating "this kind of fruit," and some later died.[8]

During La Salle's prolonged absence in the winter of 1685–86, men died in the settlement from various causes. Among them was Thibault, who had come from Rouen with Joutel. He made a will apportioning his possessions among the Récollet friars and others, but La Salle, on his return, "changed matters." The leader, in fact, seemed always to have confiscated anything of value left by those who died. "The married soldier" died about this time; Lucien Talon *père* having previously been "lost in the woods," the colony's families were only two widows and their children: Madame Talon and (presumably) Madame Bréman, whose young son, Eustache, will be mentioned again.[9] Madame Talon's family was reduced further when her older daughter, Marie-Élisabeth, succumbed to an unknown illness.

While the colonists struggled with the harsh and unfamiliar environment, there was one segment that thrived: the swine. Several sows brought from Saint-Domingue farrowed, thus providing the eight pigs put aboard the

Belle with expectations of taking them as seed stock to the colony's intended new site on the Mississippi. By the time Joutel and La Salle left the settlement for the last time, in January, 1687, the swine herd numbered seventy-five, sixty-six of them breeding sows and many of them near farrowing. The original hen and rooster also had increased by that time, as there were "fifteen or twenty" hens. The pigs and chickens, taking readily to eating meat, thrived on refuse from the hunt.[10]

During La Salle's first long absence, lodging was built for the soldiers and workmen. As no suitable timber grew close by, trees were cut farther up the Rivière aux Boeufs and brought in a few at a time when hunting trips were made by boat. Walls were of logs or stakes placed in the ground side by side on end and plastered with a heavy clay mixed with a lighter topsoil to prevent cracking. A similar structure was made for the women and girls. Roofs were thatched with reeds that grew along the streams.

In accord with La Salle's instructions, a trench was begun—perhaps intended as a moat or a root cellar, though the purpose is not explained. The men had to be driven to the task, and the project ended with only an ugly hole in the ground that quickly became a hog wallow.

The settlement, on a small height overlooking the creek, enjoyed a view of level grassland, fringed by wooded stream courses, with grazing for the infinite number of buffalo. The scene evoked memories of the planted fields of Normandy. Whereas the buffalo, or bison, comprised the colonists' "daily bread," other game animals and birds rounded out the fare: deer, turkeys, prairie chickens (by description), waterfowl, and various shore birds. Joutel the gardener's son describes the flora, comparing or contrasting the various trees, plants, and herbs with those of France. The temperate climate with "almost no winter" favored the mulberry trees that grew along the river and produced a fruit that was sweeter, though smaller, than the mulberries of France. In their fine leaves, he—like many another European observer—saw the possibility of silkworm production. The grapes that climbed to the treetops were sharp to the tongue, pulpy, and unsuitable for wine. Yet their verjuice added zest to soups and stews. There were wild blackberries sweeter, though smaller, than those of Normandy.[11]

The first domestic plantings, however, were not successful. Beans planted in February failed to sprout, possibly having been wet with seawater during the crossing. It was the same with wheat. Other vegetable crops, sown in scattered plots to test the soil, fared better: chicory, beets, celery, asparagus, watermelons, and pumpkins came up well, but the lack of fences to protect them from the pigs doomed the plantings to failure.

There seem to have been lessons that Joutel failed to learn from his gardener father. Despite his use of the first person, however, it seems unlikely that he himself performed the daily horticultural tasks while monitoring the watches, directing the personal lives of the colonists, and nurturing the assortment of ne'er-do-wells that comprised his workforce. Joutel has been most widely known from the translated Jean Michel version of his narrative: serious efforts to assess his character and motivation have generally been lacking. Certain facts, however, stand out: he seldom credits the work of others and rarely mentions anyone by name except his superiors, the clerics, or those with whom he had a personal relationship. Guarding jealously his own role as expedition historian, he twice officiated at the burning of other journals. He goes to great lengths—albeit with justification in most instances—to refute statements attributed by Chrétien Le Clercq; indeed, Le Clercq's misstatements moved him to complete his own narrative, much as Bernal Díaz del Castillo wrote his account of the Mexican Conquest to correct the work of Francisco López de Gómara.[12]

Joutel's certainty that Father Douay did not keep a journal may arise from his having personally seen to it that he did not. He had halted such efforts by Fathers Membré and Maxime Le Clercq. Yet he had no control over information that Douay might have imparted after his return to France, or how it might have been embellished. Although Joutel's accuracy and objectivity have seldom been questioned—any more than his omissions or his inconsistencies—it should be remembered that he never strayed far from his allegiance to La Salle and the Cavelier family; what he said or failed to say is known in some instances to have been influenced thereby.[13]

The post, in any case, was a happier place when La Salle was absent and Joutel in charge. The commander's surrogate strove to maintain an orderly, yet relaxed, routine. Probably in mid-February, 1686, the routine was upset by Pierre Duhaut's return without the written authority that La Salle had specified. Joutel found himself on the spot. Duhaut's story—that La Salle's nephew Moranget had refused to wait for him to mend his gear—seemed plausible enough; yet Joutel had his orders, which called for arresting anyone who returned without the stipulated document. Lacking the means to imprison the man, and perhaps moved by Duhaut's tale of hardship, Joutel let the matter drop—much to his later regret. How much better it would have been, he was to reflect, if Duhaut had perished in the wilderness.

Affairs of the settlement went on much as before until La Salle returned a month later with part of his men, the others having gone to look for the *Belle*. His anger at last mollified over the Duhaut affair, he gave Joutel a sketchy description of the country he had traveled through. Yet nowhere—either in Joutel's summary of Duhaut's adventure or in La Salle's account—is there mention of the direction traveled; only, as Joutel says, that "they had not seen the river." The men were in rags, but there appears no certain accounting of how many of the twenty returned. In the group with La Salle were the Abbé Cavelier, Moranget, and "some others." To come later were Captain Bihorel, young Colin Cavelier, Barbier, the surgeon Liotot, "and several others." As was his custom, Joutel mentions by name only those of rank, by family or office.[14]

Next day, the second group returned with the stunning news that the *Belle* was missing. La Salle now saw his error in having placed all his property on the vessel. "It is true," Joutel affirms, "that he was not disposed to take anyone's advice and that he acted only on his own whims. He had always maintained that one of the branches of the river must discharge into that bay, but in this he was deceived."[15]

Loss of the *Belle* closed the options. There could be no voyage to the West Indies for fresh provisions; no search by sea for the mouth of the Mississippi, that the river might be ascended to the Illinois post; no linking of New France and the Gulf with a series of La Salle's trading posts. In fact, the loss of the *Belle* was the ultimate confirmation of failure.

So certain was La Salle that the crew had sailed away in her that he declined Joutel's offer to conduct a search party to the other side of the bay on the chance that the ship might have run aground. He brooded in silence for a time, suffering from one of his periodic illnesses. The anxiety he had felt for the plight of the ship when his recent journey became longer than expected was told to Joutel not by La Salle himself but by his companions on the march. Even the plans the leader intended to put into effect, of sending the ship to the islands with Joutel and Moranget, came to Joutel secondhand. After a period of rest and recuperation, La Salle determined to take the only course left: an overland journey of "five hundred leagues" to New France, that he might send to France for aid. Mexico and the lure of its mines was now forgotten.

After a year in the wilderness, many of the men were without adequate clothing. Linen that had been intended for trade was used for making shirts; garments of the deceased were appropriated to clothe the expeditionists; those who still had serviceable attire shared with those who did not. As La Salle chose his followers, some who had made the previous journey were excluded because they were too debilitated to march with heavy packs. Barbier, lamed by a thorn in the foot, and young Colin Cavelier were among those who stayed behind. Dominique Duhaut replaced his brother, Pierre. The marchers also included Abbé Cavelier, the Récollet father Douay, Moranget, Captain Bihorel, sieur Hurié, sieur Ducler, the surgeon Liotot, and the former pirate called Hiems (James), who had been taken on at Saint-Domingue as a gunner.

Before starting, La Salle composed his official report of the colony since the departure of the *Joly* on March 12, 1685. He wrote what he wanted the king and his foreign minister to believe, much of it false, including a claim that he had reached the Mississippi on the previous march. But he could not dissemble his conviction that the *Belle* had been spirited away by her crew or the fact that his colony was stranded. This official report—La Salle's last known writing—is dated April 18, 1686, from "the post built in the Baye Saint-Louis."[16] Ten days later, he and his nineteen companions crossed the Rivière aux Boeufs and traveled northeast.

Joutel again remained in charge of the settlement. The departing twenty left him short of provisions, and the buffalo herds had withdrawn north. About the same time, Barbier took two boatloads of men far upstream to look for game. The settlement, therefore, was left with few persons to defend it. "Everyone had to take a turn at standing sentry," even the women and girls, who were given training in handling firearms.

A few days after the marchers' departure, a hail from downstream served notice of someone's coming. At last recognizing Abbé Chefdeville's voice, Joutel feared the worst for the *Belle*. After the priest and his five companions had eaten, he poured out details of the ship's misadventure, beginning with La Salle's departure in early January. Joutel expressed his regret for the loss of the ship's cargo; nothing is said of the crew. His greatest concern seems to have been for La Salle's papers and clothing. He attributes to Barbier pleasure at seeing the six survivors but pain for the loss of the ship and the goods. Death of comrades, it seems, had become the accepted norm.

The colonists, meanwhile, continued to confront the strangeness of their existence. The raw buffalo hides used to roof the buildings had shriveled and cracked as they dried. When it rained, the water poured through the ruptures onto the wood decking, which began to rot around knotholes and joints, letting water into the building. La Salle had seen the remedy for this in adding an elm-bark covering. Barbier, on his hunting expedition, was to gather the material. His excursion failed on all counts. He found his way to the hunting ground barred by the flooding Rivière aux Cannes. The bark of the elms, he learned, would strip only when the sap was rising.

The mild winter and long summer, when there was difficulty keeping the meat, inspired an effort to dig a cellar. The heavy soil, likened to potter's clay; the scarcity of workers; and the daily labors necessary for survival stalled the effort. Concerned over the lack of defensive works, Joutel and Barbier decided to erect a palisade. The needed timbers—eight feet long, to be sunk two feet into the ground—would be brought back a few at a time whenever the boat went out. The woods, however, lay well upriver, and the boat did not always go there; little progress was made.

Abbé Chefdeville and the Récollets took it upon themselves to build a chapel, which, like the other huts, was made of vertical stakes and roofed with grass or reeds. A partition in the rear formed a room for Chefdeville, who previously had shared a room with Joutel.

Joutel's garden plantings, on the bank of the river near the spring, somehow escaped the pigs long enough to grow, only to be assaulted by rats and rabbits. Several pumpkins escaped those creatures, but, before they could be harvested, an alligator made a meal of them. Lacking familiarity with the season, Joutel puzzled that his shallops came up well but withered and died in the late spring heat. He planted cottonseed brought from Saint-Domingue, and the stalks grew well; but they, too, were out of their season and were killed by frost before the bolls opened.

Père Zénobe Membré had similar results with his little garden; plants that escaped the rats were consumed by insects. Joutel saw a possible solution to the rat problem in the owls (?) that inhabited the powder magazine, where he found headless rats brought by the raptors to feed their young.[17]

During long periods without extraordinary occurrences, some of the men became restless, doubting that La Salle would ever return. The lack of news from the march added to their despair. Pierre Duhaut, ever the troublemaker, encouraged, and even incited, such discontent. Joutel, learning of his plotting, delivered a reprimand. He was to regret not having put him before a firing squad.

In time, Barbier and his boat crew visited the derelict *Belle* to recover as much as possible of the goods left there. Afterward, he had an encounter near the settlement with Indians carrying firelocks, which he assumed could have come only from Frenchmen whom the Indians had slain. When they signaled their approach by firing two shots with weak charges, Barbier returned the fire, never knowing that his act cost the life of a fellow colonist. The man, sick and lost, had been befriended by the natives, only to be slain when his benefactors viewed Barbier's attack as treachery.

Then there was Barbier's affair with one of the young women who often went with the men on the buffalo hunt to dress and dry the meat. The young officer came to Joutel for permission to marry. Joutel at first refused, urging him to await La Salle's return. Abbé Chefdeville and the Récollet fathers intervened, informing Joutel that the maid was with child; there would be less embarrassment all around if the wedding took place at once. Joutel relented. The banns were published, and Abbé Chefdeville performed the ceremony in the little chapel of stakes that was his pride. Thus, Abbé François Chefdeville of Rouen "gathered the first fruits" of this wild land; he also had baptized the little Indian girl captive who, having been taken aboard the *Belle,* died shortly afterward.[18]

A small hut was built for the newlyweds. Now, when the men gathered in the evenings to amuse themselves and "banish melancholy," Barbier was no longer among them. He was keeping his wife company.

Barbier reveled in his prospective fatherhood. With knowledge that the king offered ennoblement to the first male child born of a French colony, he hoped for a son and sought to claim the prize, even before the birth. He found himself stoutly opposed by Madame Talon, who believed the royal privilege was due her son Robert, born during the passage from France. La Salle, not pleased with Barbier's marriage and not wishing to see the colony begun with a child born before the proper time, would rule against him. Furthermore, Robert Talon was his namesake and godchild. The squabble ended with Madame Barbier's miscarriage. The bitter argument over such a hypothetical matter was perhaps symptomatic of the tension that pervaded the colony.

Not long after Barbier's marriage, the Marquis de Sablonnière, also a lieutenant of infantry, sought permission to marry the young woman called "Mademoiselle Paris." Joutel refused on grounds that the woman was beneath his station. La Salle was to agree. If the marriage ever was performed, it was after Joutel and La Salle left the colony.

Then came the unpleasantness of Père Maxime's journal. Abbé Chefdeville, who seems to have put himself in the role of Joutel's informant, reported that he had seen Le Clercq's narrative and that it was critical of La Salle. Joutel insisted that it be destroyed. Père Zénobe Membré, "who had erred in the same way" in writing of Beaujeu, pleaded with Joutel not to inform La Salle. Joutel refused: "I told him that I could not conceal it, as I was obliged to protect M. de La Salle's interests, that it was not proper for them to write things of this kind."[19]

La Salle returned in October, bringing five horses laden with corn and beans and pumpkin and watermelon seed, a welcome sight for the colonists. Their excitement soon turned to disappointment and grief: disappointment that he had not reached the Illinois and that "his journey had accomplished nothing"; grief that, of the twenty men who had gone out, only eight returned.[20]

Twelve had perished in various ways. Four had deserted. Captain Bihorel had become lost early in the march. Four or five others, including Hurié, Dominique Duhaut, and the soldier named Le Clercq, had become ill two months into the journey and were given leave to return to the settlement. They never arrived. La Salle's servant Dumesnil was pulled down by an alligator while crossing a river.

The only account of this journey comes from the "journal" that Joutel claims was never kept: the narrative attributed to Father Anastase Douay and published by Chrétien Le Clercq. That Douay was not the true author is certain. Like much that had to do with La Salle since his first encounter with the Renaudot group in 1678, facts were twisted beyond recognition; even Le Clercq's own work may have been tampered with. In any case, the disputed editor (Le Clercq) "followed the outline of Cavelier but attributed the work to Father Anastasius." Joutel, never suspecting the true origin of the misinformation, placed the blame on "an indefinite someone who tampered with, arranged, and 'edited' the text. . . ." He failed to realize that in reality he was challenging the Abbé Cavelier, whose veracity he never knowingly questioned.[21]

"That someone other than Le Clercq 'edited' the *First Establishment of the Faith*," Delanglez says, "may be regarded as certain."[22] This "someone" represented the Renaudot "coterie," which had, in effect, manipulated La Salle's career by falsifying accounts of his explorations, altering documents, and pulling strings with persons in high places.[23] The document alterations and outright mutilations extended even to Joutel's own journal, as will be seen.

The "Douay" account, ascribing an erroneous date to the departure from the post in late April, 1686, tells of marching northeast over wide prairies into a forested land of many rivers. On the third day, it is said, the marchers encountered mounted Indians who had both boots and saddles (a figment, according to Joutel, the saddles being nothing more than a piece of animal skin) and claimed to have had contact with Spaniards. Crossing streams on rafts or fallen trees, the Frenchmen traveled among numerous tribes with strange customs, including a nation of weepers like those encountered by Cabeza de Vaca early in the previous century. On one occasion, natives offered gifts of corn and took them across a stream in dugout canoes. Nika, the Shawnee hunter, was bitten by a poisonous snake but recovered after the wound was lanced. In crossing the Trinity River on a raft, La Salle and some others were swept downstream by the current but landed safely on the opposite bank after the raft caught on a fallen tree.

After hacking their way through canebrakes for two days, they found themselves among the friendly people whom they called Cenis (Hasinai, or Tejas, between the Trinity and Neches Rivers). They camped for five days near the native village of houses shaped like beehives, made of long tree trunks set in the ground and bowed and bound together at the tops, the framework thatched with grass. Each house, occupied by two families, had a fireplace in the middle, with beds arranged around the walls and built well off the earthen floor. Here La Salle traded axes for horses and provisions. The Cenis had many objects of Spanish origin, acquired in trade with the Choumans, or Jumanos, from the Big Bend of the Rio Grande, far to the southwest. Some members of this tribe were in the Cenis village at the time. By this account, the Jumanos were perpetually at war with the Spaniards; in fact, they were friendly to the Franciscan friars at La Junta de los Ríos, to whom they took news of the Frenchmen.

After the Cenis had sketched on bark a map showing the location of the Mississippi, they started for the Nasoni, a Caddoan tribe farther north. It was on this trek that four men deserted and La Salle and Moranget became gravely ill of "a fever, which brought them to extremity."[24] This, plus the loss of so many men (according to the Le Clercq account), forced La Salle's decision to return to the coastal settlement.

A different reason for the withdrawal has been alleged: one that had to do with neither the reduction of the force nor La Salle's illness—nor his concern for taking provisions to the settlement. The acquisition of horses, rather than a benefit for the colonists, would prove to be their undoing. In the animals, La Salle and his venal brother apparently saw a different kind of opportunity; by returning to the settlement, they could load the animals with their possessions and remove them to a safer place. Why else would he have returned to the settlement when he was already halfway to the Mississippi? To explain this injudicious about-face, Abbé Cavelier (whose mendacious narrative formed the basis for the account attributed to Douay) "imagined" La Salle's illness.[25]

Certainly, the corn and beans that the horses carried would have been welcome, but this was no more than temporary relief for the colonists. By this time they were doing quite well at feeding themselves. How could the settlement benefit from La Salle's taking from it replacements for the dozen men he had lost, when it was already weakened to the point of being virtually defenseless? Joutel, declaring that the journey had achieved nothing, foresaw that it boded ill for the colony.

La Salle, upon his return, heard for the first time the fate of the *Belle,* which was somewhat different from what he had imagined. He was pleased to see Abbé Chefdeville and to learn that his papers and some of his other possessions had been salvaged from the derelict on Matagorda Peninsula. He was far from pleased with Barbier's marriage. On being told of Father Le Clercq's journal, he became angry and refused to eat with the clerics. Then there was the matter of Duhaut's mutinous scheme and Joutel's leniency. Again, La Salle was not pleased, but such matters were soon forgotten. Or so it seemed.

La Salle began immediately to plan a new attempt to reach the Illinois post but decided to wait until the lingering autumn heat abated. In the interim he talked of planting the seeds that he had brought from the Cenis. From the beginning, plantings had proved useless because of the pigs, which destroyed everything that was not well fenced (and nothing was). Men were detailed to cut stakes for enclosing the garden, and the fence that should have been built in the beginning was begun at last. The project eventually was completed; the Spanish general Alonso de León, on finding the ruined settlement in 1689, noted that a picket fence enclosed a corn patch and an herb garden.[26]

The stockade that Joutel and Barbier had envisioned, however, never came about. La Salle, observing the pile of logs accumulated in his absence, elected to use them in repairing the dilapidated powder magazine.

While the work went on, Barbier's hunting party had a run-in with Indians near the post. The natives, carrying away one dead or wounded from the Frenchmen's fire, quickly withdrew. Not long afterward, they vindicated their loss. Surprising a Frenchman who had gone out to gather firewood scarcely a musketshot from the post, they shot three arrows into his body. Thus, Joutel observes, a bundle of sticks cost a man's life.

The five horses, meanwhile, fed contentedly on the tender grass springing up in the burned area around the settlement. One of the animals grazed too close to a rattlesnake and was bitten on the jaw. It suffered severely but recovered after the wound was lanced and a treacle administered. Joutel nevertheless viewed the region as being ideal livestock country, as there was "almost no winter." Year-round grazing made the feeding of hay unnecessary.

Whereas a new attempt to reach the Illinois post remained uppermost in La Salle's mind, he was mentally dividing his colonists, separating the fit from the unfit. Strangely, he reached an accommodation with Pierre Duhaut, whose mutinous plotting might well have been punished by death. The man posed a serious dilemma. Understandably, La Salle did not want to leave him in the settlement to cause more trouble. On the other hand, his presence on the journey would be awkward, to say the least, for by now the two men surely hated each other. La Salle's decision at last was determined by the same factor that had won leniency for all Duhaut's previous misdeeds: he was a man of substance.

Duhaut, a sergeant, according to Minet, had been accorded special trading privileges at the outset. His merchandise was allowed space on the ships that was needed for effects of the colony. When La Salle found himself without credit in Saint-Domingue, Duhaut lent him money. Although the loan was at least partially repaid before they left the island, bad blood arose between them over Duhaut's unauthorized return from the first long journey; it mounted as he encouraged the malcontents to desert and with the loss of his brother, for which he held La Salle responsible. For practical reasons, however, neither Duhaut nor La Salle at this juncture desired a confrontation. La Salle, having lost much of his own merchandise with the *Belle,* needed what Duhaut still had: "hatchets, knives, and other goods," as Joutel tells it, which would be useful for trading their way through the Indian tribes whose territory they must cross to reach the Mississippi. Although Duhaut thirsted for vengeance, another concern was paramount: to escape this miserable country. For that, he needed La Salle.

Just what La Salle's intentions were as he contemplated the journey is unclear. Abbé Cavelier claimed after the fact that the explorer intended merely to conduct his brother to the Mississippi; thence the abbé would proceed to France while La Salle himself returned to his post on the Baye-Saint-Louis.[27] Joutel implies the same thing: "M. de La Salle asked me one day whether I would be agreeable to undertaking this journey [to the Mississippi], then to Canada and thence to France to bring back a ship. . . ."[28] Yet again, Abbé Cavelier relates that "my brother put before everybody the necessity of making a second attempt to reach Canada by the Illinois country, and thence to France."[29]

Whatever his long-range plan, he was to leave the settlement weakly guarded by "missionaries, women and children, and the disabled." Says Cavelier, in long retrospect, "They all wanted to follow him; nobody wanted to guard the Baye or the fort St. Louis any longer." They agreed to stay, he continues, after the impossibility of providing for so many persons by hunting was pointed out.[30] In fact, La Salle himself decided who would go and who would stay. Whether his choices were made objectively is open to question.

He was upset with Barbier, whom he left in charge of the settlement, because of his marriage and the seduction that had preceded it. Yet Barbier had been lamed on the first long journey and may not have been able to withstand the march. Father Zénobe Membré, who had followed the explorer through the north country and down the Mississippi, had displeased him by keeping the journal that was taken from him at Saint-Domingue. He had scarcely recovered from his bout with a wounded buffalo and may have been unfit for travel. Father Maxime Le Clercq, whose writings critical of La Salle were even more offensive, had lost part of the use of one arm and a hand when attacked by a boar. The young nobleman Sablonnière had long been an irritant to La Salle and had proved his uselessness at every assigned task. Furthermore, he had contracted in Saint-Domingue an ailment that impaired his walking. Whether or not any of these men was in condition to make the journey, La Salle must have been well pleased to be rid of them.

But what of the Abbé François Chefdeville, his cousin from Rouen who had salvaged La Salle's possessions from the wrecked *Belle*? The leader had declined to take him on his first march away from the bay area (intended to last only ten days) because he was not hardy enough to stand the trip. Chefdeville may have been the only one to stay by his own choice. He alone among the five clerics is mentioned as having served a religious function. It was he who baptized the captive Indian girl; he who celebrated mass; he who was responsible for building the chapel and adorning the altar. Having officiated in the colony's only wedding, he would remain to christen the child born of that union and to minister to the colonists.

Also among those remaining were four or five soldiers; a surgeon (Louis Ruiné?); Mesdames Barbier and Talon, and four of the latter's children, the youngest hardly more than two years old; Eustache Bréman, a little boy who had lost both his parents; three young women, each of whom took a turn at the sentry post and was adept with firearms. The total was scarcely two dozen; twenty-three were accounted for in the final tally.

La Salle's choice of those to go was just as curious as of the ones to stay. Besides Duhaut and his youthful cousin and lackey, L'Archevêque, there was Tessier, the drunken mate responsible for the loss of the *Belle;* the erstwhile pirate James ("Hiems"); and the embittered surgeon Liotot. La Salle's personal retinue consisted of his brother the abbé; their two nephews,

Crevel de Moranget and young Colin Cavelier; his servant Saget; and his Shawnee hunter Nika. Rounding out the company of seventeen were the Récollet father Anastase Douay; Joutel; sieur de Marle, one of the volunteers; Pierre Meunier, whom he had once put in irons aboard the *Belle;* Madame Talon's eldest son, ten-year-old Pierre; and a young Parisian, Pierre Barthélemy.

These seventeen, the twenty-odd left at the settlement, and five deserters—three among the Cenis, one among the Karankawas, and one among the Coahuiltecans far to the west—were all who remained alive of almost two hundred left with La Salle when the *Joly* sailed for France. Disease, overwork, the wilderness, and the Indians—and, as Joutel has said, "the punishment they were given"—had claimed well over three-fourths of the colony. The number would dwindle further, as Frenchman turned on Frenchman.

La Salle planned to leave young Pierre Talon among the Cenis to learn the language. The narrative attributed to Père Anastase makes the claim, supported by Joutel, that this Récollet father planned to remain also, to found a mission; Père Zénobe was to join him later (probably after recovering from his injury).

With preparations complete, the Christmas season was observed. It culminated in the Feast of the Kings, celebrated with toasts drunk with water; the wine was gone. On January 12, 1687, the seventeen men took their leave—"from the habitation situated on the rivière aux Boeufs, near the baye Saint-Louis"—with sadness on both sides. The goodbyes were especially sorrowful for Madame Talon, who had lost her husband, then her older daughter, Marie-Élisabeth, and now was being separated from her eldest son, doubtful that she would ever see him again. Père Zénobe "had never before experienced such a regretful parting."[31]

But there was another side to the story. Abbé Cavelier's description of what each man carried, it is said, was designed to convey the idea that they traveled light "for there were things from which he wished to divert the Minister's attention." In fact, says Villiers, the expedition's departure resembled moving day: the explorer carried away what remained of his trade goods as well his money and that which had belonged to the deceased (his papers and clothing saved from the *Belle,* says Joutel); Cavelier, all his luggage, containing a dozen robes or chasubles; Duhaut, eight dozen hatchets and several gross of knives, as well as diverse peddler's packs.[32]

After the leave-taking, the travelers went a league and a half up Garcitas Creek to a point opposite Le Boucan, the smoking place. The horses' packs were taken across in a canoe brought from the settlement by Barbier. The horses were made to swim. Without the canoes thereafter, taking the baggage across streams was to become an onerous chore that slowed the expedition's progress beyond reason.[33]

At the post near the Baye-Saint-Louis, the months dragged by without word from the marchers. A year passed. Then it was two. No ship came, and no messenger arrived from the east to offer the colonists reassurance or hope, or to tell them that there was no hope.

Chapter 12

Fatal Journey

VENGEANCE AND REPRISAL

The expedition moved across Texas as if time were of no importance: as if lives were not at stake in this journey to save the beleaguered colonists huddled in their untenable little post, surrounded by hostiles capable of snuffing them out in an instant. La Salle's parting admonition to Lieutenant Barbier to be constantly on his guard was of little value.

The marchers formed a curious procession: seventeen men walking, each carrying his own pack, even though there were five horses so heavily laden with goods that they could scarcely cross a dry wash without being unburdened. Resentment built among the men, even to Joutel, whose customarily benign countenance turned dour.

The beasts caused repeated delays and created a constant drain on the men, who had to lead them by day and keep watch over them at night. If there was insufficient forage close to camp, the horses had to be taken great distances to graze.

Setting out from the Garcitas Creek crossing, the marchers advanced only a little way before stopping to readjust the loads. Then a buffalo herd blocked their way, and they returned to make camp near the Garcitas crossing. Ensconced in a clump of trees, the men kept careful vigil, respectful of the Indian fires that surrounded them. The second day, January 13, provided a bitter foretaste of difficulties ahead. Recent rains had left the coastal flatlands sodden. Winding among stagnant sloughs, the men often waded water to their knees, then struggled through hip-high grass.

This trek across the marshy plain, "a league and a half or two leagues wide," ended on the wooded banks of the Rivière aux Cannes, or Cane

River, now known as the Lavaca. There La Salle indulged himself in one final act of remembrance of the young lieutenant he had left in charge of the feeble settlement. In satirical commemoration of Barbier's lovemaking on its banks, he renamed the stream la Rivière à la Princesse, "the Princess River," for the pet name that Barbier had given his love. "The proverb is quite true," Joutel was moved to reflect, "that there are no ugly loves. . . . The object [of Barbier's affection] was not too charming."[1]

Five buffalo were killed near the edge of the wood bordering the stream. At the crossing, "five leagues" above the river mouth in Lavaca Bay, the horses were unburdened and the men carried the loads to the other bank. It was a beautiful site, in Joutel's judgment, with fertile soil and abundant timber of various kinds. Had the settlement been placed here, he believed, so many lives would not have been lost in building it.[2] The horses were reloaded to advance to a campsite half a league beyond the river. Thence, some of the men and the horses were sent back across the stream for the buffalo hides and carcasses. The hides served to make shelter for the men and cover for the packs, for rain fell that night. Yet the operation was typical of the daily lost motion. Plentiful game all around rendered needless such a cumbersome operation.

In crossing another plain, three leagues, the men saw more buffalo, most of them on the move as though being chased. While stopped to readjust the load of a stumbling horse, they kept a sharp lookout, suspecting that Indians were near. At last a man was spotted, running after a buffalo herd so intently that he failed to see the Frenchmen. A horse was unloaded, and one of the men, mounted, pursued the Indian and brought him back to camp. Some of the Frenchmen, remembering companions slain by the natives, wanted to kill the man. La Salle, however, counseled peace for the sake of the remaining colonists, who put themselves at risk every time they went out hunting. He at last had seen the folly of his fire-on-sight policy adhered to since the first conflict. The Indians' retaliation, he now realized, had inflicted far heavier losses on the colonists than the Indians had suffered. Joutel, with clear hindsight, reflected that the change came too late; had this been the policy in the beginning, "we would not have had so many men killed."[3]

Many of the colony's problems, Joutel believed, stemmed from the failure to establish friendly relations with the natives; had amity been achieved, the Indians might have guided the Frenchmen to a more advantageous settlement site. They might also have provided "news of the great river, of which the sieur de La Salle had heard nothing even yet." As it was, Joutel lamented, "we were no better off than on the day of the landing; on the contrary, we were worse off . . . in every way: our provisions used up, our goods lost, most of our men dead. We had achieved nothing." La Salle's policy change was long overdue.[4]

The Indian brought before La Salle conveyed by signs that his people had been fired upon some time ago by Frenchmen on the lower Lavaca River. The natives then had laid an ambush in which Meunier received two superficial arrow wounds, and arrows pierced the clothing of Barbier and young Colin Cavelier. Given tobacco to smoke and some "trifles," with assurances of the Frenchmen's peaceful intent, he went on his way. The horses were loaded again and the march resumed. Half a league farther on, the scene was repeated; another buffalo hunter was brought in. Then came groups of Indians, all regarded with caution. La Salle informed them that the Frenchmen were going to the Cenis, "conveying peace everywhere," and thence to their own country to return with things the natives needed, such as knives, axes, and beads, as well as men to join this people in their wars.[5]

Making each night's camp secure consumed time and effort. An abatis was made around the campsite "the distance of an arrow flight." With this continuous ring of brush in place, not even an Indian could approach without making a noise. The tall grass obstructing the view of the prairie was cut down, so that no enemy could conceal himself. Fires were made outside the barricade to illuminate the area around the camp.[6]

On January 15, the travelers began the search for a ford on the flooding Navidad River ("the second Rivière aux Cannes"). Unable to use the crossings that had served the previous year, they ascended the river, traveling "west and northwest" over varied terrain; distance not given. Having slaughtered five buffalo two days previously, they killed several more—well in excess of their need for meat. If they were harvesting hides, they soon had more than the horses could carry. Buffalo and turkeys were killed "from time to time" on the sixteenth. The Indian hunter Nika killed seven or eight more buffalo on the seventeenth, from which "only the best and fattest parts" were taken for food.[7]

Advancing three leagues that day, still traveling up the right (west) bank of the Navidad, the marchers cut their way through dense woods with axes. After passing the bare framework of several hundred recently abandoned Indian huts, they crossed a boggy branch of the Navidad and another small river that was even worse. Deep mud that bogged the horses brought a halt for the night. A cold rain drenched them before dawn and kept them in camp for the day.

On the nineteenth they slogged forward through dense fog, water often up to the thighs, hacking their way through heavy underbrush. Skirting the heads of ravines while axemen went ahead to clear the way, they came at last to a bison trail. Made with animal instinct, it led them on a tortuous route around the worst obstacles to firmer ground, less dense woods and reeds, and easier fords — a welcome alternative but by no means a total solution. Rains turned the paths into running streams; the tracks made in soft mud became immovable stumbling blocks when dry and hard. The marchers' makeshift footwear (rawhide stitched into sock-like moccasins) added to their misery; though pliable and easy to fit when fresh, the crude shoes were hot and uncomfortable. When they dried on the feet, they became so stiff that the wearer had to stand in water to soften them before they could be removed.

At times, travel was through woods so thick that even the buffalo could barely squeeze between the trees. The horses could not pass with their packs until axemen did their work. The travelers, having gone "first in one direction and then another," counted little progress for the day. Finding no suitable campsite, they bivouacked on ground so sodden that every footprint became a puddle. Next day, after a league of hacking through woods and wading a marsh, they reached a plain and a wide buffalo trail leading to the river. Expectations of a ford, however, soon vanished; before reaching the stream, they could hear its roar as it raced among trees that had fallen with caving banks. While waiting for the flood to subside, they made camp and went hunting to kill more buffalo. After another league's travel upstream on the twenty-first, still northwest, the marchers were able to cross the flooding Navidad on trees felled from both banks, their tops meeting in midstream. Over this crude bridge the men passed the horses' packs, piece by piece, from hand to hand. The horses were made to swim.

As confusing as this account of the march is so far, it is more detailed than that of any other part of the journey. The location of the Navidad crossing is crucial to fixing the remainder of the route to the Hasinai, or Cenis; yet the record is insufficient to warrant unequivocal conclusions. Directions given were often askew, and distances (in leagues), were either tentative or lacking. As already mentioned, there is much disagreement among scholars as to the conversion of the French league to English miles. The variation may be crucial. If the league were calculated at 2.76 miles, for example, the crossing would be farther upstream than if it were 2.4 miles. In either case, the number of leagues traveled on a given day could be no more than a rough estimate — especially when the march wound about in every direction to avoid natural barriers or follow meandering buffalo trails. If the larger measurement is applied, it might indicate that the West Navidad River was crossed on January 17, the main branch on January 21; that the Sablonnière River, reached three days later, was the Colorado some distance above present-day Columbus.[8] Actually, any attempt to trace the route and fix precise locations stands on shaky ground. This is reemphasized by the fact that, after February 23, neither distances nor directions are given until after the climactic events surrounding La Salle's murder on March 19.

While camp was being made on the Navidad's left bank, fifteen Indians approached, having heard the gunfire of the Frenchmen's buffalo hunt. They made peace signs and spoke in guttural tones, giving their tribal name as Ebahamo.[9] On learning that the Frenchmen were going to the Cenis, they claimed to be friends of the Cenis and said they were going to war against some tribes to the northwest. They advised the marchers to travel northeast rather than north so as to avoid dense woods and reach the prairies sooner. Thus, the Indians pointed them toward the narrow strip of Blackland Prairie that extends into the Post Oak Belt separating the woods from another finger of blackland farther south. To the west, the Indians indicated the presence of other Europeans, ten days' journey with only four large rivers to cross. Reports of the Spaniards and the presence of Spanish goods and weaponry among the Indians were to keep the Frenchmen apprehensive throughout the journey.

The trek thus far had been stressful for men and beasts. Whereas the men were weary from clearing a path, makeshift gear used in lieu of packsaddles had rubbed raw the horses' backs. A day was lost rearranging the packs and stuffing the saddle pads with dry grass. "Although we had five horses," Joutel says, "we were obliged to carry our own little bundles, for M. de La Salle had brought his whole wardrobe and his papers . . . ; M. Cavelier, a number of church ornaments, even to a dozen vestments, as well as his belongings and food. We had the burden of leading the horses without benefiting from them."[10]

The horses continued to impede the march, now northeast, following the Indians' advice, to avoid the woods. Halted by rain, travel was resumed on January 24 in intermittent showers. After crossing several swollen creeks with difficulty the next two days, the marchers came on the twenty-sixth to the river called the Sablonnière—arguably the Colorado. To reach the other side, Joutel complains, "We had to carry the horses' loads, in several trips, one after the other, which vexed us greatly." Such labor had to be performed

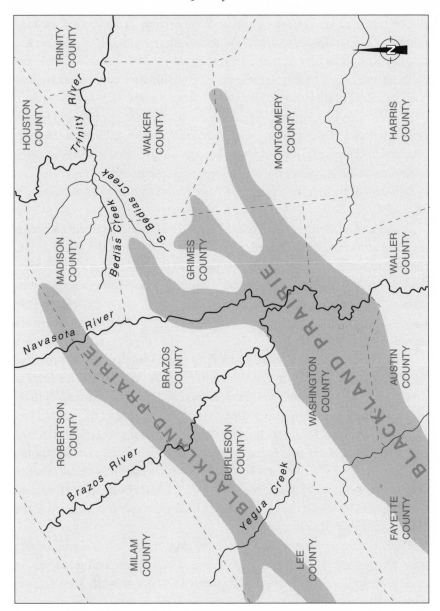

FIGURE 19

*The March across Texas. Descriptions of La Salle's last journey mention features
of the Blackland Prairie: dark soil underlain by limestone. The route appears
to have been along the upper prong delineated at the center of the map.
Thence, the marchers traversed a marsh formed by a maze of creeks
that fed a larger one carrying the runoff of a wide area—perhaps
Bedias Creek, a tributary of the Trinity River.*

not only at the rivers but also at most of the ravines, for La Salle feared the horses would strain their backs. "We found this very tiring, as we also had to carry our packs on our shoulders; the horses were loaded with . . . the clothing and linen of these gentlemen, which could have very well been done without. But, as they did not have the burden, it was nothing to them."[11]

This tedious procedure, bespeaking the leader's lack of concern for the people who had trusted him, carried a terrible price tag. How much more prudent, and humane, it would have been to use the horses as steeds—even without saddles—and send the best men with the singular purpose of carrying news of the colony's plight to Tonti at the Illinois post as quickly as possible?

It was an unfortunate time for such a march. Flooding streams were the norm. Beyond the Sablonnière, a creek overflowed into the camp during the night. Some of the men lost clothing and narrowly escaped with their lives. Withdrawing to higher ground, without wood for a fire, they shivered in the cold rain driven by a chill north wind. On the twenty-eighth they crossed the creek farther up in thigh-deep water, then slogged forward in water up to the knees.

After crossing another river and killing more buffalo, they approached an Indian encampment on the thirtieth. La Salle, taking half his men to investigate, found twenty-five oval-shaped lodges covered with buffalo hides, each inhabited by half a dozen men and a number of women and children. Word of the Frenchmen's coming having preceded them, the natives awaited them at the river crossing. The Frenchmen found trading so brisk—a knife for a dressed buffalo hide—that they had to call it off to keep from overloading the horses. When they asked about horses for trade, the Indians claimed to have but two, which they spirited away after the visitors revealed their interest.

Thence, the march traversed an area of thin, sandy soil and stunted oak trees, then entered a "fine plain a league and a half wide and seemingly of endless length"—actually the flood plain of a "very beautiful river . . . as wide as the Seine at Rouen" and apparently navigable. It was called the Maligne [*malin:* "wicked" or "evil"] because La Salle's servant Dumesnil had been lost here on the previous journey.[12] The Maligne has been identified with both the Brazos River and the Colorado; by whatever name, these two rivers were often confused by travelers in colonial times. For the reasons to follow, the tentative choice here is the Brazos.

The marchers paused on the Maligne's bank for several days to allow the flood to abate and the horses, short of forage for most of the trip, to graze the better grass of the bottomland. Again, the horses and their heavy packs were the cause of most of the delay. Several buffalo, deer, and turkey and other game birds were killed. A cache of glass beads left in a hollow tree on the previous trip was found. Indians of different tribes, having heard of the Frenchmen's coming, came to visit almost daily. Joutel took from them names of tribes living north and west of the river. A few can be linked tentatively to their ethnic group or later tribal identification. Joutel describes the Indians with whom the expedition came in contact from a close vantage point; La Salle, who did not use tobacco, assigned him to smoke with them. All were vagabonds, wandering about where the hunting and fishing were best, with no settled dwelling place. They claimed to be friends of the Cenis and had earthenware pots for cooking and baskets woven from reeds or rushes, but the dearth of Spanish goods indicated that they had little intercourse with New Spain. Only their horses, obtained by either theft or trading with other Indians, were Spanish. Yet they seemed to recognize the Frenchmen's prayer books as objects seen before, pointing westward to indicate the Spaniards as the source. The men went "quite naked," wearing a tanned animal skin only when the cold north wind blew. The women wore a little skirt that covered them from the waist almost to the knees.[13] For all his close contact with them, however, Joutel never really felt at ease among the natives, nor did he trust them.

The Frenchmen worked, meanwhile, at making a rawhide boat for crossing the packs over the river. They sewed four buffalo hides end to end with sinew, fastened them to a framework of poles, and sealed the seams with a mix of charcoal and tallow. The boat completed and the flood abated, the packs were loaded into the flimsy craft and taken to the other side.

As usual, it was the horses that caused the difficulty. Alluvial mud deposited by the recent floods lined the banks and put the beasts at risk of being mired. Time was lost looking for a ford before the horses were taken over one by one, swimming. On the other side, goods and animals went half a league farther for better grazing, but the grass had been cropped close by the buffalo.

February 10—almost a month after leaving the post near the Baye-Saint-Louis. The camp inched forward another half league to a burned area, still smoking, which suggested the presence of Indians and buffalo. Fearing a scarcity of game farther on, La Salle called a halt to kill and smoke meat.

On eight of the thirty days en route, Joutel makes mention of multiple buffalo kills, from "some" or "a few" to "seven or eight" in a single day. The total must have been more than thirty, an average of at least one a day, to feed seventeen men—not to mention the deer, turkeys, ducks, and other game killed. At times the march seems to take on the semblance of a hunting safari, rather than a mission to save the beleaguered colony near the coast. Credit La Salle with an unusual ability to survive in the wilderness, to keep himself and his family members secure against the forces of nature and savage peoples. It was the rest of his followers who paid the toll; within their ranks lurked the direst threat. The buffalo hides from the frequent kills were added to the horses' packs and used as La Salle saw fit. "Some of our men," says Joutel, "had no covering [against the frequent cold rains] except the buffalo hides that they [themselves] had obtained from the Indians."[14] Small wonder that resentment was building among the men as the procession crept along toward its unexpected dénouement.

It was noon on February 12 before they again took up the march, "several" buffalo having been killed in the interim. The march halted at another river two leagues farther on to avoid overworking the horses. A cold front with thunder and rain kept them halted for another day. Then the procession inched forward a league, crossing tributaries of the river just passed and thence over gravelly hills dotted with groves. A dense wood with tangled underbrush, crossed by La Salle the previous autumn, caused a northwesterly detour, facing a chill norther.

Again finding their way along tortuous buffalo trails on the fifteenth, the marchers wielded their axes to clear a path for the horses, which were barely able to churn through the deep mud. Once clear of the wood, the march inclined north-northeast over Blackland Prairie, where springs issued from limestone underlying the deep, dark soil. The prairie having recently been burned off by Indians, the buffalo had gone elsewhere. Deer seen in the distance took flight. With grass starting to grow anew in the burned area, the rolling country reminded Joutel of "the wheat fields of France in April."[15]

Still encountering numerous Indian groups, La Salle made a ritual of telling the natives that he wished to spread peace everywhere; that his band was going to the Cenis and thence to their own country to bring back knives and axes to exchange with the Indians for buffalo hides; that he had been sent by the greatest chieftain in the world with orders to befriend them and join them in war. He handed out presents of knives and glass beads but had to decline the offer of hides in exchange, as the horses were already heavily laden. The Indians understood the gifts, if not the words.

From a tribe calling itself Teao, La Salle heard of the Chouman (Jumano), who had intercourse with the Spaniards. These early-day commercial travelers obtained Spanish horses by raiding the Cannohatino (Kanahotino), who stole them from the Spaniards. Thus is revealed one path by which horses had come to these inland tribes, for the Jumano carried on extensive commerce extending across Texas. La Salle sought to trade axes to the Teao for horses but was told the Indians had but few, and they were needed for transporting the meat taken on the hunt. They did offer one animal that had the skin rubbed off its back from carrying heavy loads without proper rigging; although the natives encountered by the Frenchmen used horses only as beasts of burden, they lacked skill for making saddles, packsaddles, or pads.[16] La Salle bought the horse, hoping to heal its sores so that, with proper rigging, it might carry a load again.

La Salle, still uncertain of the location of his river, gleaned a clue from some Indians calling themselves the Palaquechauré, who were going to war against an eastern tribe with flat heads. Reminded of the "Flat-heads" he had seen on the Mississippi, La Salle concluded that "the River Colbert or Mississippi must lie in that direction."[17] He sent Moranget to trade with the Palaquechauré for horses, but, like the natives met previously, they had only a few and needed them for hauling the kill from their hunts. The chief, however, gave Moranget and his companions some rather startling news. He conveyed by signs that a Frenchman had come to this village months previously and, with promises to bring the French to trade with them, persuaded some of the natives to go with him to the settlement on the Rivière aux Boeufs. As the Indians neared the French post, they were fired upon and one of them was slain. Presumably, they killed the Frenchman, whose identity could be only a guess. Thus was explained Barbier's encounter with Indians with flintlocks.[18] The story must have rekindled Pierre Duhaut's grief for his lost brother and his hatred of La Salle. His concern and anger grew with news from an Indian whom Nika had met on the previous visit to the Cenis. The Indian, having come on a buffalo hunt with several others of his tribe, revealed that one of the men who had deserted La Salle on the first journey was living among the Cenis, two others with the Nasoni. But he had no news of those who had been given permission to return to the settlement; it seemed likely that they had been killed by Indians along the way. Among them was Dominique Duhaut.

The Cenis buffalo hunters, in a temporary encampment a league and a half away, were to furnish guides to direct the Frenchmen toward their village. Still trying to trade for horses, La Salle got the same answer: the Cenis hunters had only two, which they needed to carry their meat from the hunt.

There was yet more trouble with the horses. One got into a bog and was lamed. Half a day was lost seeking an easier crossing. Another league, and the men had to wade a small river, waist deep, with their own baggage and the horses' packs. On February 18, as the march resumed with a fresh norther blowing, one of the horses fell into a flooding stream and sprained a shoulder. The animal stiffened while resting and was scarcely able to walk. To avoid leaving its pack, La Salle decreed a double march: the extra cargo was left under guard while the travelers advanced two leagues, unloaded the other horses, and took them back for the extra load. This cumbersome procedure went on for days, causing further delay; the colonists on the bay seem to have been forgotten in the leader's concern for his goods.

Afterward, on February 22, the marchers traveled through a broken country of fertile bottoms and pleasant uplands cut by small creeks. "We made camp on one of the heights," says Joutel, "which is to say on a rock, at the foot of which passed a small river. The bed was paved with flat rocks good for building and making lime."[19] This mention of a limestone substratum indicates the Blackland Prairie, a segment of which extended along much of the route. This southern strip of blackland, slightly more than thirty miles wide at its base, runs from Gonzales and DeWitt Counties on the southwest to beyond the Brazos and Navasota Rivers on the northeast. In Grimes County, the strip widens and divides into three prongs, all of which end midway between the Navasota River and the Trinity. If the seventeen marchers had failed previously to observe the dark soil underlain by limestone, the signs became inescapable as it traveled along the northern prong. Joutel's several mentions of Blackland Prairie features after crossing the Maligne River, and the absence thereof beyond the Rivière aux Canots, offer possible clues to the route and the identity of these two rivers—judged here to be the Brazos and the Trinity.

On the twenty-third the travelers camped on the bank of a large creek flowing at the foot of one of the highest "mountains" seen on the journey. It was a mountain only by comparison with the flat terrain traversed previously; this high point may have been a limestone bluff that drops off into South Bedias Creek in northeastern Grimes County. The creek, cascading over rocks, was enlarged downstream by several branches and flowed thence through the valley to join a larger stream. Ahead lay a troublesome marsh—perhaps between the two main branches of Bedias Creek—which the marchers reached the next evening. As they made camp beside the marsh, the moon had a reddish ring around it. The Frenchmen believed it an evil omen. When rain came during the night, water gushed down from the hills and washed through the camp, drenching the occupants. The ground became sticky, making walking difficult, as wet blackland soil does; the horses especially had difficulty, as the mud clung to their hooves. The march was halted for two days. La Salle then decided not to wait for the promised Indian guides before trying to cross the swamp, which had been dry when he passed it the previous year. Failing to find a suitable path, the marchers at last went back by a different route to camp near the high point. On March 1 the camp moved forward, overtaking the Indians at the edge of the marsh, where they were halted by rain until the fifth.

In the interim they made a boat of buffalo hides for crossing a large stream into which flowed all the runoff of the extensive valley. This "torrent" joined the great river that La Salle had named Rivière aux Canots (Canoe River) on his previous journey: arguably the Trinity. The description seems to fit spring-fed Bedias Creek, which in its 47-mile course drains most of Madison County, northern Grimes County, and northwestern Walker County.[20] While the Frenchmen constructed a buffalo-hide boat to cross their goods, the Indians watched curiously; because the natives were good swimmers and traveled light, the procedure was strange to them.

After the crossing on March 6, the boat was dismantled and carried on one of the horses for future crossings. It was reassembled four days later to cross a small river, swollen by the previous day's rain, which halted the march. The blacklands were left behind; the soil became thinner, with grazing for the horses more scarce. The number of streams, probably the northern tributaries of Bedias Creek, increased. Many had overflowed, leaving a film of silt that made walking difficult. On March 13, the travelers camped on the bank of the Rivière aux Canots, described as being larger than the Maligne.

Joutel has given no direction of travel since February 23, when the march was northeast. Nor has he offered an estimate of distance covered during that time. At best, his calculations from the beginning are vague and confusing: his directions approximate, his distances gross estimates. Again, any judgment as to specific points on the march should be regarded as hypothetical. Nevertheless, there seem to be indications that travel since February 9 had been between the Brazos River and the Trinity, rather than between the Colorado and the Brazos. The limits of the Blackland Prairie, features of which are not mentioned beyond the Rivière aux Canots, may offer a clue.

Buffalo had been plentiful as far as the Maligne, less so toward the Rivière aux Canots, and almost nonexistent beyond the latter stream. As Joutel recalls after crossing the Canoe River, "The hunting was beginning to fail, because this was the way by which [the Cenis] traveled to and from their village." After the crossing, two of the beasts—wanderers that had transgressed the boundaries of their customary range—were slain. That was the end of the buffalo. The animals, being very wild, as Pierre Talon explains, "habitually avoid the inhabited places so that they are found no nearer the [Cenis] villages than 15 or 20 leagues."[21] This distance, roughly 37 to 48 miles, suggests that the nomadic animals might have appeared east of the Trinity River, even if rarely.

As for the relative size of the rivers, the Brazos is larger than the Colorado and longer than the Trinity. Yet the Trinity, with heavier rainfall in its watershed, carries more water to the Gulf of Mexico. The stage at which the two rivers were observed certainly influenced Joutel's judgment that the Rivière aux Canots was larger than the Maligne, as the Trinity is larger than the Brazos. Nearing the Canoe River, the expeditionists encountered a maze of smaller streams unlike any they had found on the western approach to the Maligne. Such a feature is relatively easy to find along the Trinity River, less so at the Brazos. Beyond the Canoe River, the black soil and limestone substrata are no longer mentioned, having given way to sandy land that Joutel perceived as not being very fertile. Had travel at this time been just east of the Brazos, unmistakable features of the Blackland Prairie would have been observed again before the Trinity was reached.

After the crossing, the expedition approached its climax. The stage was set on the fifteenth, when La Salle sent seven men to look for a cache of corn he had left the year before to lighten the horses' loads. The seven were his servant, Saget, and the Shawnee hunter Nika; the malcontent Duhaut and his adherent, L'Archevêque; the surgeon Liotot; the expirate Hiems; and the incompetent naval officer Tessier, whose conduct was largely responsible for the loss of the *Belle*. Accompanied by several of the Cenis Indians, the men found the cache two to three leagues from the camp, but rain had spoiled the corn. On the way back, Nika killed two buffalo, the only ones the travelers would see beyond the Canoe River. Saget went on to the main camp for horses to transport the meat while the others dressed and smoked the carcasses. On the seventeenth, La Salle sent his nephew Moranget, sieur de Marle, Meunier, and Saget with the horses.

It was a situation ripe for disaster: ten men who had been driven to unreasonable lengths from the start of the journey—among them some of the most desperate and dangerous of the colony—who harbored deep-seated grudges against Moranget. La Salle had always trusted his brash young nephew with important assignments, despite proof of his immaturity and lack of judgment. In this instance Moranget, carrying La Salle's instructions and eager to demonstrate his authority, was not long in showing his stripes.

On arriving at the smoking place the evening of March 17, he took charge of the meat, even to the marrow bones and other parts not usually saved, which the men had cooked for themselves. He then declared that in the future he would have charge of the meat; the men were not to help themselves to it as they had done in the past. Although he may have acted on an order La Salle had issued because of the region's scarcity of game, his officious manner touched the fuse to the flame, which already was burning hot.

Duhaut's resentment of Moranget, having simmered since La Salle's nephew left him in the wilderness during the first long march, grew with the loss of his brother the previous year. Moranget "was indebted to [Liotot], almost for his life," for the care the surgeon had given his arrow wound.[22] The arrogant young lieutenant had repaid the surgeon with abuse, thereby earning his undying hatred. The other plotters were L'Archevêque, who accepted his kinsman's orders; and Hiems and Tessier, a pair of unprincipled louts who in all instances showed poor judgment.

At supper, Moranget fueled the fire by allowing the others little meat, taking the largest share for himself. Then, heedless of the hatred against him and secure in his kinship to La Salle, he lay down to sleep. So did the others not involved in the plot: Nika, Saget, Marle, and Meunier. Meanwhile, the plotters plotted. Liotot, while his cohorts hesitated, seized an axe and began the bloody work. The others stood by with guns at the ready. Moranget was the first victim, then Saget, and finally the faithful Nika, whose hunting skills had kept them all alive. Then Moranget, despite the axe blows to his head, rose to a sitting position without speaking. The murderers compelled sieur de Marle, who evidently had awakened in time to witness part of the spectacle, to finish him.

Perhaps not until it was over did the conspirators realize the position they had put themselves in. They could never excuse themselves to La Salle; he must be disposed of also. This part of their design, however, could not be carried out immediately, for the river that lay between them and the main camp had begun to rise from rains over the watershed. They must make a raft for crossing.

On March 18, La Salle waited anxiously for the men to return. When they had not appeared by evening, he determined to go next day to investigate and arranged for one of the Indians who had been to the smoking place to guide him. He left next morning with the Indian and Père Anastase Douay. As they neared the place of the bison kill, La Salle saw vultures overhead and, thinking he must be near the camp, fired his gun to signal his coming, hoping that the men would reply to give him direction. Instead, the shot alerted the murderers, who quickly laid their ambush. While Duhaut hid in tall grass, L'Archevêque moved into La Salle's view, answering his inquiry in a disrespectful manner. At that moment Duhaut, with a single shot to the forehead, dropped the explorer dead in his tracks.

As Father Douay, uncertain and fearful stood trembling over the corpse, Duhaut showed himself and assured the priest that he had nothing to fear. When the other plotters came up, they stripped their fallen leader of his clothing and all that he carried.[23] Liotot the executioner mocked him as the "great Pasha," now fallen. Then the murderers dragged the naked corpse into a thicket and left it to the wolves. This is as Father Douay told it to Joutel—quite different from the version attributed to him later by Chrétien Le Clercq in his *First Establishment of the Faith.*

"Thus died our wise commander," Douay is quoted as saying in the Le Clercq version, "constant in adversity, intrepid, generous, engaging, dexterous, skillful, capable of everything." The priest gave him absolution, it is further stated, and raised a cross over his grave. Douay did nothing, and said nothing, of the sort. How the distortion came about is a story in itself. Again, the long arm of the "Renaudot coterie and the propensity within that body for juggling texts" had reached out to gloss over the truth. This anti-Jesuit group, having pushed La Salle's career and magnified his accomplishments to bend him to its own purposes, now sought to put its own spin on his death.[24]

At the main camp, Joutel, with four others, anxiously awaited La Salle's return, sending up hourly smoke signals to guide him. With Joutel were Abbé Cavelier and young Colin Cavelier, La Salle's brother and nephew; Pierre Talon, about to mark his eleventh birthday; and the young Parisian Pierre Barthélemy. Toward evening on the nineteenth Joutel was surprised to see L'Archevêque approaching. The young man poured out the stunning news of the four murders, capped by that of La Salle, and warned Joutel that the assassins had intended to kill him also if he offered resistance.

The miscreants had no designs on the rest of the company as long as they remained unopposed. Yet they embarked upon a reign of terror, seizing all La Salle's goods and Joutel's personal belongings. The innocents remained apart, not daring to talk with each other or to address the murderers. Joutel responded to their taunts with silence, while the two clerics stood off to themselves and prayed. At last, when Abbé Cavelier asked for time to prepare himself if they intended to kill him too, the assassins replied that they did not intend to harm him; it was Moranget who had provoked this evil deed, and they were sorry for it. The abbé replied that he forgave them.[25]

On the twenty-first the assassins resolved to continue to the Cenis villages rather than return to the settlement. Joutel estimated the distance at forty leagues; yet he claims that in four and one-half days of actual travel following the tragedy, the marchers came within "ten or twelve leagues" of the Cenis. It seems highly improbable that they covered anything like thirty leagues (seventy-five miles) in that time—an average of almost seventeen miles per day—while still leading the horses that to this point had slowed travel to a crawl.[26]

Most of the Indians deserted them soon after the start, to reappear later. One man, with his wife and two horses of his own, steered the Frenchmen northward onto the path to the Cenis village. As the march progressed, a desire for vengeance seized Joutel and young Colin Cavelier, and there were opportunities. Abbé Cavelier dissuaded them, declaring that vengeance must be left to God.

After reaching the Cenis path on the twenty-third, the travelers came to a river in flood. The baggage was crossed in boats of dried skins made by the Indians, who also conveyed the two boys, Talon and Colin Cavelier, to the opposite bank. The craft, however, was too flimsy to carry the men, and some of them—including Joutel—could not swim. With instruction from the natives, they crossed by holding onto a log with one hand while propelling themselves with the other hand and the feet. The scene became comical when Joutel accidentally kicked Father Douay in the stomach, put him in fear of drowning, and caused him to invoke his patron, Saint Francis.

Thence, they proceeded northeast along the little foot path, so dim at times that they lost it and had to be set straight by the Indians. At the place "ten or twelve leagues from the Cenis," as Joutel says, a swollen stream blocked their path. Whereas La Salle on the previous journey had been able to ford this stream, called the Rivière de Cenis, it was now swollen, and boats had to be made. After the crossing, four men went to the village to obtain provisions and to trade for horses: the pirate Hiems; Liotot the axe-murderer; Tessier, former mate of the *Belle* and coconspirator; and Joutel, who was more than a little uneasy in such company. For trade, Joutel carried knives, axes, and glass beads allowed him by Duhaut, who had seized all the goods. Contributing to Joutel's uneasiness was one of the Indian guides who wore Spanish clothing, including hat, jacket, knee breeches, and white woolen stockings, and who boasted of having visited the Spaniards.

On March 31 the four Frenchmen wound their way among eight scattered hamlets, each comprising twelve to fifteen lodges surrounded by fields. These settlements extended for three miles or more before the visitors reached the chief's lodge. During the next several days, one by one, three of the four men who had deserted La Salle on the previous journey appeared; the fourth had died. All naked like the Indians, they approached with caution, fearing retribution until they learned that La Salle was dead. First came the man known only as "the Provençal"; like the murdering surgeon Liotot, he was from the southeastern French region of Provence. Then Rutre, or Ruter, a Breton sailor, surprised Joutel in the middle of the night at another Hasinai village across the Neches, where the Provençal lived with his Indian wife. These two had taken on Indian ways and were tattooed like the natives. Joutel remained at this village, mistrustful as he was of the Indians, while the Provençal went with the other three Frenchmen to take provisions and a horse they had bought to the nine men and boys they had left behind. On April 6, Rutre brought the other deserter, Jacques Grollet, a sailor from near La Rochelle. Grollet, though dressed in Indian fashion, had not been tattooed as Rutre had. More articulate (and more sensible, in Joutel's opinion) than his companion, he told of having gone to war with the Indians and of winning their confidence by killing one of their enemy with a long-distance musketshot. The Hasinai were now eager to have more of the Frenchmen go with them to make war on their enemies the Cannohatino.

Both Rutre and Grollet had heard of a tribe living on a great river to the northeast, forty leagues away, who were friendly to the Cenis: a likely source, Joutel reasoned, for information on the Mississippi. Grollet also claimed to have heard of a white settlement still farther away in the same direction. Joutel confided to his informants his desire to go there if Abbé Cavelier approved. The two deserters agreed to go with him.

The assassins, meanwhile, espoused a different plan: to return to the French settlement on the bay, build a shallop, and sail it to the French Caribbean islands—a scheme with scant prospects for success, because they had neither tools nor nails, and none of them had the necessary skills. When

Joutel rejoined the others, he discussed with Abbé Cavelier and Father Douay the means of excusing themselves, while concealing their intention of seeking the friendly tribes to the northeast. They found it easy to discuss the matter among themselves, for the five murderers had decided to take their meals together and that "we four," as Joutel says, "should have ours apart from them; namely, M. Cavelier, Father Anastase, the younger sieur Cavelier, and I."[27]

Thus, the abbé told Duhaut, who remained very much in charge, that they wished to remain with the Cenis, being too fatigued from the journey to withstand the rigors of a return trip. Duhaut, though surprised, received the news well, offering to supply them with ammunition and trade goods. The whole plan came unraveled when one of the deserters betrayed Joutel's confidence and revealed that the Cavelier group intended to seek the friendly native village on the route to New France or New England. To their disdain, the assassins changed their own plans: they would join the others. Joutel was "extremely vexed and grieved; for there was nothing that I longed for as much as to be separated from these wretches, whom I could not look at without horror. . . ." His perplexity was shared by the others of the group—the two Caveliers and Père Anastase—for it stood to reason "that the murderers would sooner or later rid themselves of us." There seemed to be no way out but to become murderers themselves; yet Abbé Cavelier remained steadfastly opposed, maintaining "that we must have patience and trust in God to protect us. . . ."[28]

The innocent and the guilty remained encamped at the Cenis village throughout the month of April, making preparations for their journey. The Indian women roasted their accumulated supply of corn and ground it into meal on a mortar made of a log hollowed out by fire. During that time, the Neches River, which ran through the extended Indian village, remained out of its banks, so that some men whom Duhaut had sent to the other side to purchase horses and provisions could not return. On the first of May, Duhaut had the camp moved three leagues to the riverbank to be ready to cross and take up the journey when the waters receded. Then L'Archevêque arrived from the other side to advise Duhaut that Hiems, having succumbed to the Indians' stratagem to get the Frenchmen to stay and go to war with them, opposed the plan to continue eastward.

On Ascension Day, May 8, Hiems arrived with two of the deserters, Rutre and Grollet, and some twenty Indians. After a detached nod of greeting to the others, the expirate went straight to Duhaut, made known his objection to continuing the journey, and demanded his share of La Salle's property and clothing. Duhaut insisted that all of it was his own, as he had made La Salle several loans, and much of the goods had belonged to him in the first place. The wrangle ended when Hiems, saying that he must give Duhaut his due for killing his master, felled his adversary with a pistolshot at such close range that Duhaut's shirt caught fire. Duhaut staggered a few paces and fell dead. If Liotot made a move to Duhaut's defense, it is not revealed; yet, at the same moment, Rutre felled the surgeon with a shotgun blast. As Joutel scrambled to get his weapon and the group of innocents trembled in fright, Hiems assured them that they had nothing to fear. Although he was involved in the original conspiracy, he said, he had not intended that La Salle be killed; if he had been near when Duhaut shot him, he would have prevented it.

Liotot lived several hours and made his confession, while Rutre stood by with pistol in hand, eager to finish him. The surgeon, joined by Abbé Cavelier, pleaded for his life, "hoping that the Indians might be able to heal him." He begged in vain. The confession finished, the savage Rutre carried out his intention.[29] A grave was dug, and the two assassins were buried together, rather than being stripped and left for wild beasts as their victims had been.

With six men already slain, the murderous binge might have gone even further, had not Hiems been dissuaded from his initial intent to kill Duhaut's man L'Archevêque. Joutel returned the favor L'Archevêque had done him following La Salle's death. Going out to meet the young lad as he returned from hunting, he persuaded L'Archevêque to suppress his grievance and make peace with Hiems.

Those intending to continue the journey promised to wait at the Cenis village while Hiems, Rutre, Grollet, and four others joined a Hasinai war party against the Cannohatino. The Provençal, disabled by a splinter in the leg, was forced to remain with Joutel and others: the two clerics, young Cavelier, Pierre Talon, Tessier, and Pierre Barthélemy.[30] The war party returned victorious on May 19. The Frenchmen's firearms had put the enemy to flight; forty-eight men, women, and children were killed or captured. The torture of the captives rivaled in its barbarity that of the Iroquois witnessed by La Salle on his journey with Dollier de Casson and Father Galinée in 1669.[31] Captives were tortured and dismembered while still alive, and a woman was scalped and sent back to her people carrying a lead ball and a powder charge to portend a grim future for the Cannohatino in warfare with the Hasinai.

The innocents, meanwhile, had to wait for the Frenchmen who had gone to war to finish the celebration with the Indians before learning their intentions. The natives had convinced them that the tribes along the proposed route were hostile and cruel, and that they would never be able to pass. Hiems, who had seized all La Salle's clothing and goods, as well as a thousand livres in gold that had belonged to Le Gros,[32] influenced the others. He said that "he was not disposed to go and get his head cut off." He was seconded by the deserters, who, like Duhaut's murderer, "had taken to debauchery with the Indians." Hiems nevertheless shared the axes, knives, and ammunition with the others but kept the best horses. When the departing group asked Hiems for an extra horse, he granted the request. "But," says Joutel, "it grieved me greatly to see that wretch strutting about in La Salle's clothing," flaunting himself in the blue and scarlet coats laced with gold, "the spoils of the man he had betrayed." Hiems asked the abbé to give him a note declaring him innocent of La Salle's murder to win him acceptance by Barbier and the Abbé Chefdeville, should he return to the settlement. Cavelier gave it to him. The abbé was allowed to go through his brother's papers and save "the most important ones." He burned the rest to keep them from falling into the hands of the Spaniards.[33]

The marchers hastened to depart, believing themselves not yet out of danger from the quixotic Hiems. There were nine who had agreed to go, but Meunier and L'Archevêque changed their minds on hearing that the Hasinai's enemies would cut off their heads. Grollet had promised to come also, but, when seven took up the march, he was not among them.[34] Besides the two Caveliers, Douay, and Joutel, the seven marchers included Marle, Barthélemy, and Tessier, whom the abbé had promised help to avoid prosecution. Remaining among the Hasinai with Hiems were Rutre, Grollet, the Provençal, L'Archevêque, Meunier, and eleven-year-old Pierre Talon, who had been assigned to learn the Indian language, that he might help the colonists on the bay.

On May 27, the first seven began their journey eastward, putting their hopes on Providence. "My chief aim," Joutel declares, "was to send some news of us to France, either through Canada or in some other way; I therefore urged that we push on, hoping that help might be sent to those at the settlement. This would have been accomplished had we not met with certain obstacles. . . ."[35] Those "certain obstacles" arose from the Abbé Cavelier's misguided priorities, which were fixed on greed and self-preservation rather than concern for the colonists.

The innocent and the guilty were now intermingled: Tessier, guaranteed immunity by the abbé's pledge, and sieur de Marle, whose defense was that he had been coerced, traveled with the group bound for Canada and France. Marle's fate waited near the Red River. Barthélemy chose to remain at the Arkansas post, rather than continue the tedious journey. Tessier and the other four reached France on October 9, 1688, by way of a path strewn with obstacles—many of them self-imposed—that nullified their mission of mercy. Their objective, as it was pursued from the start, had become self-defeating.

Chapter 13

Legacy of Deceit

THE BITTER FRUIT

La Salle was dead, his colony destroyed. Yet the curtain was not yet rung down on this real-life drama so marked by hardship, tragedy, and deceit. One or more of these elements stalked each of those who sailed away from the anchorage off Matagorda Island or trudged through the wilderness in hope of reaching the Mississippi, Canada, and France.

When the captain of the king's warship *Joly* forsook the crude bivouac on the island promontory, he did so with misgivings. Yet circumstances conspired to prevent his bringing or sending relief to the colonists, who he felt certain were nowhere near the mouth of the Mississippi. Before he could begin his search for the river or the mythical Baye-du-Saint-Esprit, an offshore wind arose. Burdened with extra people and unable to land, the *Joly* ran short of fresh water and wood for cooking. The crew ate raw meat, while the officers took the available wood to boil theirs in seawater or lightly roast it. With the wind adverse for searching the northern shore but favorable for Cuba, Captain Beaujeu set course for Cape San Antonio. There two dozen men went ashore to hunt or take on water. Then, seemingly from out of nowhere, a Spanish galley appeared, firing a cannonshot at some of *Joly*'s crew as they frantically rowed the shallop toward their ship. As the galley came down upon them, two men were killed, others captured and held for ransom. Beaujeu, knowing that "the Spaniards would not dare do anything to a priest for fear of the Inquisition," sent Abbé d'Esmanville to negotiate for the captives' release. The French captain nevertheless paid a heavy ransom to get back his men and his boat.[1]

The *Joly* then fell in with an English merchant ship whose crew assisted the Frenchmen with taking on water and provisions and advised Beaujeu to take his way by Virginia rather than Saint-Domingue. Accordingly, he sailed with the English vessel up the Atlantic coast. "After having been nearly wrecked in the most furious storm ever," *Le Joly,* on May 3, entered Chesapeake Bay, "otherwise called Madre de Dios," where no French vessel had ever been seen before. Thence, Beaujeu sent his lieutenant, Chevalier d'Hère, with Minet and d'Esmanville, to Jamestown, which consisted of fifteen houses of wood and brick fourteen leagues up the James River. The Frenchmen were clearly suspected of being pirates or mutineers, but their request for permission to reprovision the ship was granted after Beaujeu produced for the revenue officer his orders from the king.[2]

While in the port, the Frenchmen heard news from Europe: the English king Charles II had died. They joined in celebrating, with a twenty-one–gun salute, the naming of Charles's brother, James II, as his successor. The change of rulers heralded shifting alliances among Europe's crowned heads, as James, during his short rule, distanced himself from France and showed a new spirit of friendliness toward Spain.[3]

On May 26, the *Joly,* having satisfied her needs, put to sea on a westerly wind that bore her quickly to the offing. She arrived at Rochefort on July 6, 1685, almost a year after her departure. Beaujeu carried a large packet of La Salle's letters and reports addressed to the sieur Morel, chief clerk of the admiralty. Included were La Salle's charge of desertion against Minet; his *procès verbal* on the wreck of the *Aimable;* and his letter to the Marquis de Seignelay, dated March 4, 1685, in which he charged Captain Aigron with purposely wrecking his ship.[4] There was trouble ahead for Minet and Aigron.

From La Rochelle, Minet wrote to Seignelay, sending the extract of his journal and his "most essential [maps] of the coast of Florida where we left M. de La Salle." He had hoped to report to the minister in person, but the intendant, Pierre Arnoul, advised him to await the court's pleasure. In the meantime, Arnoul employed him at drawing a map of Aunis.[5]

The expected word from the Royal Court came on July 28. The order, dated July 22, instructed Arnoul to have Minet and Aigron imprisoned in La Rochelle's Saint-Nicolas Tower. It seemed clear, the king wrote, that the wreck of the *Aimable* "came about through the fault of the captain." With Aigron behind bars, Arnoul was to interrogate him and take depositions from the crew members of both the *Aimable* and the *Joly.* As for Minet, the king wrote, he had erred in returning to France instead of remaining with La Salle as he had been ordered. On the basis of La Salle's report, he judged, Minet had "persisted in interfering and writing impertinent letters to La Salle instead of obeying him." Both Minet and Aigron were arrested and taken to the tower on July 29.[6]

Aigron was held until the king's order to release him, dated October 30, 1685, reached La Rochelle, probably a week later. Not long afterward, in mid-November, his pilot on the *Aimable*, Zacharie Mengaud and the gunner, Pierre Georget, brought charges against him, alleging misappropriation of the colony's goods as well as the intentional wrecking of the ship.[7]

Minet, meanwhile, had been freed from the tower on September 7, 1685, having been incarcerated forty days. He evidently spent his time in prison working on his journal. To his narrative he added a series of sixty-nine questions that he would have liked to ask La Salle. Whereas some of them merely reflect his bitterness at the treatment he had received, others challenge La Salle's decisions or hint at his character flaws: *Why did he so often go back on his word, and why did he tell such an infinite number of lies about his voyage (down the Mississippi)? Why did he forbid his surgeon to help the ill among his own men* [when aboard the *Joly*]? *Why did he order the Aimable to enter the bay when he had business on shore so important that he could not be on board? Was that business of greater importance than saving the ship and those on board?*

From the questions also emerges his accusation that both Aigron and Mengaud, the captain and the pilot of the *Aimable,* got drunk every day on wine made available to them by La Salle. One may infer therefrom that they were drunk at the time of the wreck, which occurred in the afternoon, when they were accustomed to imbibing. Inferences may be drawn also from Minet's questions that soldiers died of starvation while La Salle and the clerics sated themselves with wine and meat; that La Salle was homosexual and enlisted young officers and soldiers for immoral purposes; and that his quarrelsome and officious nature was responsible for trouble with the Indians (and ultimately for the massacre of the few remaining colonists).[8]

Upon his release from Saint-Nicolas Tower, Minet was restored to his rank of *ingénieur du roi* and assigned to work with Louis XIV's commissary-general of fortifications, Sébastien Le Prêtre, Marquis de Vauban. Less than a year later, he was again ordered to map the coast of Spain.[9] This was the project Minet had been forced to abandon in October, 1683, because of the outbreak of war with Spain, resulting in his assignment to the La Salle expedition.[10]

Minet's accusations drew little attention from the king. No more was the monarch swayed by the opinions offered by Captain Beaujeu. Louis le Grand refused to recognize his own misjudgment in trusting La Salle with the command of an enterprise out of all proportions to his capabilities. To Arnoul's reports of July 8 and 10, relating Beaujeu's contrary opinion, the monarch responded with pique: "His Majesty has seen what he [Arnoul] writes as to the Sieur de Beaujeu's opinion that the Sieur de La Salle is not at the mouth of the Mississippi River. It seems that he forms his belief on such feeble conjecture that no great attention is to be given his report, and furthermore that this man has been prejudiced against La Salle's enterprise from the beginning and that he is often too free with his judgment [*abonde beaucoup dans son sens*]. [Arnoul] should . . . tell him that His Majesty will be displeased if he speaks against this enterprise for any reason."[11]

The full text of Minet's writings on the expedition, so far as is known, never came to official attention; in view of the king's attitude, it was just as well. Yet some of the young engineer's written questions that he would have liked to ask La Salle were the very ones that needed to be answered. While Minet whiled away his last few days in Saint-Nicolas Tower, one of his questions hit squarely on a problem that was about to come to a head in the Gulf of Mexico: *Why had La Salle allowed his "good men" to buy their release at Saint-Domingue and sail on a pirate ship?* It was these La Salle expeditionists-turned-pirate who compromised the secret operation. On September 3, 1685, the Spanish Armada de Barlovento, pursuing Laurens de Graff's pirate fleet as it withdrew from the sack of Campeche, set one ship on fire and captured another, taking 120 men prisoner from the two vessels. Among them were 6 men who had quit the La Salle expedition at Saint-Domingue, including the captain of the captured ship. The prisoners were taken to Veracruz and interrogated; at least some of them were hanged. A twenty-two-year-old deck hand named Denis Thomas, by his own testimony, had joined the freebooters believing that they would take him back to France. Thoroughly frightened and disillusioned, Thomas freely disclosed, before hearing his sentence, details of La Salle's voyage and the latter's intention of establishing a colony above the mouth of a river called "Micipipi"—a name that meant nothing to his captors.[12]

Reacting with alarm, the colonial Spaniards launched a search for the intruders that lasted more than three years. In six land expeditions, Spanish troops marched from such diverse points as Saint Augustine, Florida, and Parral, Chihuahua, as well as Nuevo León and Coahuila. In five sea voyages from Havana and Veracruz, the entire Gulf of Mexico was circumnavigated, comprising, in effect, a rebirth of Spanish exploration.

When the Rivas-Iriarte expedition[13] found the wreck of the *Belle* on April 4, 1687, La Salle was already dead, his companions on the march sharply divided. The seven setting out for Canada and eventually France began the northeasterly trek from the Hasinai on May 26, 1687, now with six horses instead of five—each man with the exception of Abbé Cavelier leading one of the animals. Reaching the Lower Nasoni in three days, the travelers waited for others to come and join them. None did. As with other native groups they would meet, they traded knives, hatchets, needles, rings, and beads— some of which had been salvaged from the *Belle*—for provisions. Here as elsewhere the Frenchmen resisted, with a stock answer, the Indians' pleas and ploys to get them to stay and join them in battle: they must go to their own country to bring more people and goods so as to provide the natives with things they needed. Though dreading the road ahead, as Joutel says, "We cast ourselves upon God's mercy" and started for the Kadohadacho on June 13, promising to return "when the leaves fell."[14]

On June 23 they arrived within half a league of a Kadohadacho (Cado-daquiou) village. Here they witnessed the bow-making craft from which a prominent tree in the area derives its French name: the bois d'arc, or bow wood.

The day after the Frenchmen reached the village, between the Sulphur and Red Rivers in present-day Bowie County, Texas, sieur de Marle went to bathe in the stream they had crossed just before arriving. Joutel relates that Marle, who could not swim, stepped off into deep water and drowned; young Colin Cavelier, "who heard that M. de Marle was going bathing, hastened after him" and on reaching the river "saw that he was drowning" and ran back to the camp to tell the others. The chronicler goes on to relate not only the recovery of the body but also the grief over the death, the last rites and prayers, and the burial "in a small field behind the [chief's] hut."[15]

That this account may not be entirely true has been suggested by Kathleen Gilmore in a study of the historical and archeological evidence. Her skepticism has its basis in the 1932 excavation by A. T. Jackson of seven burials in the Eli Moores site in Bowie County. Six of the burials were of Indian children; the seventh, of an adult male with two lead balls just below the rib cage. Skeletal analysis by H. Gill-King shows little likelihood that the remains were Indian. Gilmore lists nine reasons for believing that they "have a high probability" of being those of Marle and suggests several plausible scenarios for his murder.[16]

The most tempting theory is that Marle, having been compelled to fin-ish off the wounded Moranget, was slain out of vengeance. Joutel relates that both himself and "the young Cavelier" had desired retribution against the murderers but were stayed by the appeals of the abbé. Of the two, Colin, lacking Joutel's mature judgment, would seem the most likely suspect. Moranget was his cousin and perhaps his role model. Colin is described by Pierre Talon as "a young boy of ten or twelve years"—about his own age—when La Salle was killed, which would make him an unlikely murder suspect. Parkman, on the other hand, gives his age as fourteen when the expedition left France, seventeen in 1687.[17] Yet, if vengeance was to be taken, why not against Tessier also, who, having participated in the assassination plot, now walked side by side with Father Douay, who had seen La Salle fall?

The travelers, putting this episode behind them, resumed the march on June 30 with native guides. Hearing the name of the Kappa, or Quapaw— one of four groups of the Indians the French called Acancea (Arkansas), whom La Salle had visited—they found guides among the Caddoans' visitors from the east who had actually been to the Acancea villages; they had even seen "people like us" who killed buffalo with guns, lived in a house, and had bark canoes.[18] The travelers thought immediately of Tonti's men; they must indeed be near the Rivière Colbert.

Thence, they followed a winding course "through very bad country," with tangled woods, ravines, and marshes. Joutel was uncertain of the distance covered or the direction. There were delays. One of the horses put out to graze during the night was lost or stolen. Rains flooded the streams. Alligators seen in crossing a river on July 23 brought the realization that they would reach the Mississippi much farther down than they had supposed: near the Arkansas River rather than the Missouri. The Indians they encountered two days later were not the Kappa but another Arkansas group called the Osotouoé, who were eager to extend hospitality and tell the Frenchmen of two white men living among them. Standing at last on the right bank of the Arkansas River near the Osotouoé village, they were amazed to see a large cross on the other side, adjacent to "a house built in the French manner." Two men came out of the house, each firing a shot in greeting. One, after crossing the river in a canoe, announced himself as a Frenchman serving under Henri de Tonti, commandant for La Salle of Fort-Saint-Louis of the Illinois. The two men were Jean Couture, a carpenter, and Delaunay (or Delauné), both of Rouen, sent by Tonti with four others (who already had departed) to establish the Arkansas post. Tonti, they said, had carried out La Salle's orders, brought to him by La Forest, to descend the Mississippi to meet the explorer, taking twenty-five Frenchmen and some

Indians. After reaching the river mouth and exploring the coast in both directions without finding La Salle, he returned to the Illinois fort. Couture and Delaunay were aggrieved to learn of La Salle's death, as Joutel was to tell them: "Had he been with us," says Joutel, "everything might have succeeded."[19]

Thenceforth, the voyagers would have to travel by water; the horses—the cause of so much labor at stream crossings, as well as delays of the march—had to be left with Couture and Delaunay. Left also was some of Abbé Cavelier's clothing and other goods that the men had been forced to carry across torrents on their backs. Ironically, the possessions that La Salle and his brother had prized above a swift journey that might have sent timely relief to the colonists on the bay, and the labor of transporting them, proved utterly useless.

Following the Osotouoé's calumet dance, chiefs or delegates of the other three Arkansas tribes assembled. With Couture as interpreter, the sojourners offered trade goods and promises of a lasting relationship beneficial to the Indians in exchange for four men and a dugout canoe to assist them on their transit to the Illinois. Even with such help, it would be an arduous journey, requiring strong arms for pulling the oars going up the Mississippi. The young Parisian Barthélemy, who was not very strong, did not measure up in Joutel's eyes. He offered no objection to remaining at the Arkansas post, "and we were not sorry for him to remain for several reasons." In the first place, he talked too much. Abbé Cavelier had decided that, upon reaching the Illinois post, he would conceal his brother's death; nor would he reveal it in Canada, or even in France, until he had secured La Salle's possession to preclude seizure. But, if the young weakling "was not good at keeping a secret," neither was Couture, to whom the tragedy had already been confided. Almost a year later, Couture not only revealed to Tonti what he had been told of La Salle's death but also quoted Barthélemy's "ridiculous defamation of La Salle," as Parkman calls it. The young Parisian, Parkman says, was "violently prejudiced against his chief, whom he slanders to the utmost of his skill."[20]

As Barthélemy is quoted by Couture, La Salle, having lost both the *Aimable* and the *Belle* and realizing that he was lost, was so devastated that he recognized no one; he no longer attended the mass or the prayers and went for two years without partaking of the sacraments; he treated his brother with the utmost contempt, having barred him from his table and allowing him nothing to eat but a handful of flour each day, while he himself ate of the best.

Other accusations are so farfetched as to defy credibility: that La Salle himself had killed with his own hands a number of his people and that he struck his carpenters with a crowbar because their work was not to his liking; that he killed the sick in their beds, claiming that they were feigning illness to avoid work. "He had put out the eyes of a young man (still living three years later), not to mention those whom he had hanged; not to mention those he had court-martialed and shot . . . ; in a word, of four hundred persons he had brought from France . . . three years ago, no more than thirty remain."[21]

Barthélemy's charges seem to have been ignored by almost everyone since Parkman, who unhesitatingly brands them the product of the young Parisian's "violent prejudice." The assertions attributed to Barthélemy must surely be exaggerated, although it is impossible to know why, by whom, or to what extent. Couture, who could not sign his name, evidently deposed orally to Tonti in April, 1688. It is surprising that Tonti saw fit to record his remarks.[22]

Barthélemy appears no more in written history. By d'Iberville's time the Arkansas post had been abandoned.[23] We know nothing of the young Parisian except what Joutel tells us, from which it appears he was, at least in Joutel's eyes, a decided misfit. Couture, who reported his remarks, is remembered as a turncoat who served the English of Carolina and led them to the Mississippi for his own selfish reasons.[24] As for Joutel, his relationship with the Cavelier family prevented him in certain instances from telling the whole story. We know that Abbé Cavelier elicited his aid in concealing La Salle's murder. Did he also persuade him to dissemble other matters? What might he have told of the deaths of half La Salle's men in the first five months after the Texas landing?

With the plot well laid to conceal La Salle's murder, the travelers rationalized their deception; they would say that he had brought them to "a certain place" and left them there; that he was alive and well when they last saw him—all true, as far as it went. They hoped to reach France before the year was out and send aid to the colony in the spring. Had La Salle's death been known, Joutel says, "it might have put obstacles in our way."[25] But the real reason had more to do with the abbé's greed, which obscured any thought of timely rescue of the Texas colony. Nothing reflects Joutel's subservience to Cavelier more than his acquiescence to this deception.

Leaving the Osotouoé, they descended the Arkansas River five leagues to the Torimans, then went up the Mississippi two leagues to the Tongengas, on the east bank. They found the Kappa, largest of the four villages, eight leagues farther up, on the west bank. The Kappa had been visited by Jolliet and Marquette in 1673 and La Salle in 1682. Eager to trade, they now displayed their otter and beaver skins. Couture, who had guided the Cavelier party thus far, served as interpreter as the Frenchmen laid foundations for the future. They promised to come via the lower river and purchase all the skins the Acancea could provide.

With a man from each of the four Arkansas villages, in a dugout canoe furnished by the Kappa, the five Frenchmen took their leave of Couture— with one last caution from the abbé to reveal La Salle's death to no one— and embarked for the Illinois.[26]

When the banks were suitable, everyone walked except the Indians paddling the craft and sometimes Abbé Cavelier. The hardest rowing was in crossing from one bank to the other, in the swift current of midstream. They made five or six leagues per day. Joutel excused himself from describing the river's course: "I had no instruments for observing the points of the compass it follows in its meanders."[27] No more had he been able to chart with certainty the course across Texas and Arkansas, especially after he no longer had the benefit of La Salle's knowledge of the route. On September 3 the travelers left the Mississippi and entered the more placid waters of the Illinois River. After meeting several groups of the Illinois Indians, they arrived at Fort-Saint-Louis on Sunday, September 14.

The voyagers were greeted by François de Boisrondet—he who had been given up for dead during the starving retreat from Fort Crèvecoeur with Tonti and Father Membré in 1680 and who had descended the Mississippi with La Salle in 1682.[28] Having been informed by the Indians that it was La Salle who was coming, Boisrondet asked for him at once. Joutel and Cavelier gave their prearranged answer: La Salle had brought them to within forty leagues of the Cenis; "when he left us he was in good health." That was true, Joutel avers, for they had not seen him dead. Father Douay and Tessier, who had, remained silent.[29] The falsehood was repeated—as it would be many times more—to the sieur de Bellefontaine, whom Tonti had left in command of the post while he was away fighting the Iroquois.

Abbé Cavelier asked immediately for the church or chapel, that he might offer thanks to God for having brought them safely thus far—and perhaps to ask forgiveness for his falsity. The Indians gave such demonstrations of joy at hearing news of La Salle that the travelers felt anew their grief over the sorry outcome. The more the sojourners learned of Tonti's post and his success in the Iroquois war—supported by both able Frenchmen and a large Indian force—the more they lamented their own failure. Seeing "the way we could have managed the business of forming a settlement," they mourned in silence the lesson learned too late.[30]

The problem now was how to get to Canada. On September 18 the five travelers set out for Michilimackinac with three French guides and a dozen Indian porters. Delayed by rains, they reached the Chicago portage a week later and descended to Lake Michigan, where they waited a week for contrary winds and high waves to subside. When they had progressed seven or eight leagues up the west side of the lake, an offshore wind forced them to land. Provisions were short, and Cavelier, hearing from the guides the trials of Tonti and Boisrondet in 1680—and no doubt wishing to get what he could from Tonti—determined to return to the Illinois fort. Joutel argued against this further delay to no avail. They returned to Fort-Saint-Louis on October 7 to pass the winter there. "I always thought," Joutel says, "that if we had had the courage to persevere, we could have helped those who remained at the [Texas] settlement and saved the post."[31]

Tonti and his followers returned on October 27 from the Iroquois war. The visitors told him of their adventures and described the country they had passed through but said nothing of La Salle's death. Tonti seemed satisfied, while Joutel continued to suffer from the enforced silence and to grieve that La Salle had not lived to harvest the fruits of his efforts.

As winter waned, the sojourners looked forward to the break-up of the river ice, that they might resume their journey by water. Abbé Cavelier at some point presented to Tonti a note signed "de La Salle, at the camp near the baye Saint-Louis, 9 January, 1687." It read: "Monsieur, I have asked my brother to go to France to make an accounting to the King of the affairs with which he has charged me. I beg you to give him all he asks for the expenses of his voyage, and those four persons I am sending with him."[32]

Tonti, still believing that La Salle was alive, failed to perceive that the note was a forgery. He surrendered to the brother of his partner and benefactor a canoe and beaver skins worth four thousand livres. Making a new start, the travelers were accompanied by Boisrondet, who was going to France. Joutel, his clothing threadbare and having lost everything on La Salle's venture, hired out for a packet of beaver skins to help Boisrondet manage his canoe. Traveling with the group as far as Michilimackinac was Charles Juchereau de Saint-Denis, who held temporary command of the post there. He had spent the winter at the Illinois fort.[33]

The group left Fort-Saint-Louis on March 21. Scarcely five leagues up the Illinois, Joutel began to realize what he was in for. Reaching a rapid, the men were obliged to get into the cold, swift water and drag the canoes upstream. In his apprenticeship as a voyageur, he says, "I went through more hardship and pain than [at any other time] during the entire journey."[34]

The voyagers were held up at the mouth of the Chicago River by foul weather from March 29 till April 8. They reached Michilimackinac on May 10. Abbé Cavelier and Père Anastase were given a room with the Jesuits while they sought for the rest of the voyage companions who dared risk an Iroquois ambush at the portages. In late June they resumed their voyage, the party having expanded to twenty-seven persons in four canoes. Later joined by four canoes of Indians from Sault-Sainte-Marie, the entourage entered the French River in the northeastern sector of Lake Huron's Georgian Bay. To elude the Iroquois, they took an old route seldom used because of its numerous—"as many as forty"— portages. The canoes entered Lake Nipissing on July 5. Finding the outlet at the opposite end, they gained the Ottawa River and followed it to the Saint Lawrence. After pausing at La Salle's old settlement of Lachine, they arrived at Montreal on the seventeenth.

Time after time, along the way to Quebec, Cavelier's deception concerning his brother was repeated: with the Jesuits who lodged him at Michilimackinac; with the governor Jacques René de Brisay, Marquis de Denonville, and the intendant Jean Bochart de Champigny, whom they found at Montreal; with the Sulpicians at the seminary where he lodged; and with Bishop Saint-Vallier in Quebec. Joutel sought solitude as much as possible to avoid questions.

Champigny was left with the impression that La Salle's venture was a success, which he believed might prove disadvantageous for Canada; many, he feared, would move to the supposed new colony, where furs were said to be plentiful and whence shipments could be made in all seasons. The bishop, with whom Abbé Cavelier's stock had taken a sudden though temporary rise, saw the matter in a different light. "Pleasantly surprised" at the arrival of La Salle's brother "from his great discovery," he petitioned for extension of his own episcopal authority over the entire continent. The Sulpicians with La Salle would welcome such a move, although "it would perhaps not be the same with the Récollet Fathers. . . . I think I could not do better than to appoint M. de La Salle's brother as my Vicar-General, since he is a good priest of St. Sulpice and is to rejoin his brother."[35]

At Montreal, the travelers reclothed themselves. Joutel realized that he had indeed been wise to work his way on Boisrondet's canoe, rather than rely on Abbé Cavelier's good graces to provide for him: "If I had had to depend on the promises [he made], I would have been in great difficulty."[36]

Tessier abjured his "reformed faith"—prohibited in France since revocation of the Edict of Nantes on October 18, 1685—before the priests of the seminary; he seems never to have had much difficulty in shifting his allegiance.

At Quebec, Joutel's group went with Father Douay to the Récollet monastery apart from the town, grateful to escape the curious who might inquire after La Salle. Père Anastase, having witnessed the murder, surely was the most embarrassed of all to remain silent while hearing their hosts' expressions of gladness at having "news" of La Salle. The abbé, on the other hand, stayed at the bishop's seminary and dined with His Highness, still unabashedly conveying the false information.

The stay at Quebec ended on August 21, when the sojourners at last boarded a barque that would take them to Île Percée in the mouth of the Saint Lawrence River. There they took passage on a codfish vessel soon to sail for France. They embarked on September 4 and anchored in the Chef-de-bois roadstead at La Rochelle on October 9, 1685.

Abbé Cavelier wrote to the Sulpician superior, Tronson, in Paris, telling him of their arrival and his sacred vow to make a pilgrimage to Saumur and Saint-Michel to thank God for his deliverance. He enclosed a letter to be forwarded to Seignelay, presumably containing the same information. Tronson replied a day after Cavelier and his group had left La Rochelle, urging him to delay the trip to Saint-Michel, on the coast west of Paris and well out of his way, until he had given a full account to the Royal Court: "They are most eager to hear news of that kind. . . . Nothing short of what is binding on your conscience should prevent your coming [to Paris] as soon as possible."[37]

If the letter reached Cavelier along the way, he ignored the advice; he avoided going to Paris until he had made arrangements to secure La Salle's property. Instead, he set out on his walking pilgrimage to Notre-Dame Dardillièrs at Saumur and thence to Mont-Saint-Michel. Father Douay left the group at Saumur to go to Paris; Boisrondet, from Orleans, and his Indian also left the group. The others walked on toward Mont-Saint-Michel, on the Gulf of Saint-Malo: Abbé Cavelier and his nephew; a man named Cellerier; "the natural son of M. Crevel [Nicolas Crevel of Rouen, La Salle's brother-in-law]";[38] two of the Indians Cavelier had brought from the Illinois; and Joutel. (Tessier apparently had remained in La Rochelle.) Thence, they proceeded by Caen and Pont-l'Évêque to arrive at Rouen at six o'clock in the evening of November 7. Much had changed. Friends had died. A war had ended; another waited in the wings. Yet friends, relatives, and creditors were still eager for news of La Salle.

Three days after arriving, Abbé Cavelier, starting for Paris, charged Joutel to keep the secret of La Salle's death until he had informed the Marquis de Seignelay—"which," says Joutel, "obliged me to go into the country to keep from having to account to various persons who had relatives on the expedition." Thus, he was cut off from friends who might have helped him in his destitute state: "Unfortunately, I trusted too much in those people who afterward mocked me; but we must praise God for everything."[39]

Cavelier, in his prompt departure for Paris, was more concerned with securing La Salle's assets before his creditors did than with reporting to Seignelay. He apparently delayed his court visit for some months, still manifesting a callous disregard of the colonists on the Gulf Coast. In the meantime, Cavelier "had been repeatedly called by the Minister, but . . . did not wish to [go] until he had collected all the money lest it escape his grasp as soon as the death of his brother was known. . . . He divorced himself completely from the affairs of his unfortunate companions, stranded on the Gulf of Mexico. Having saved what he could from the wreck of the enterprise, he no longer seriously concerned himself with the plight of the poor people who had believed in his brother."[40]

Officials of church and state had grasped at every available fact and figment concerning La Salle's voyage almost from the day he sailed. It was more so following Beaujeu's return. The king, instead of heeding the captain's news that the colonists had been put ashore at a place other than the mouth of the Mississippi, denounced the messenger and forbade dissemination of his opinions. Yet such an idea soon reached Canada, apparently from information Abbé d'Esmanville had given his superior. Abbé Tronson, writing to a colleague in New France in the spring of 1686, reflected: "If what he [d'Esmanville] tells of this voyage is true, M. de La Salle has made a mistake . . . he has not found his river at the 27th or 28th degree of latitude. . . . He asked that no judgment be made on his discovery until the beginning of 1686. The year is advancing, and no news has been received here."[41]

The Marquis de Seignelay, despite the royal order that Beaujeu's opinions not be circulated, soon found matters beyond his control. During the spring and summer of 1686, Spain's ambassador to England, Pedro de Ronquillo, was in consultation with the new English king regarding French territorial designs in America. James II, in response to Ronquillo's importuning, took up the La Salle expedition with the French ambassador, Barillon. Whatever the sequence, Seignelay, on July 28, 1686, summarized the history of the La Salle expedition for his ambassador and evidently provided him with key documents; amicable relations with England were crucial, as a treaty concerning commerce and territorial boundaries in America was at stake. In the months ahead, the English crown became fully informed on the status of La Salle's colony up to the time that *Le Joly* had left it. The information was quietly passed to Ronquillo, who quietly passed it to his own government. The process continued until officials in New Spain, earnestly searching for the French intruders, had all the available reports, even to copies of Minet's maps of the landing place.[42]

It has been suggested that James II's protest was partially responsible for Louis XIV's failure to send aid to the Texas colonists. In fact, the Sun King, in August, 1687, did order, conditionally, a reconnaissance of the mouth of the Mississippi to seek La Salle's settlement. The frigate *Marin,* later to take part in Iberville's voyages to Louisiana, was fitted out at Rochefort with Captain Beaugé Le Goux in command. The primary objective of the voyage was to resupply Governor Tarin de Cussy at Saint-Domingue. After reaching the island colony, Beaugé, when the weather was favorable, should seek the mouth of the Mississippi, "which is not too far," and obtain news of La Salle's settlement if he could do so without too much loss of time. To that end the king had ordered the intendant Arnoul to provide a pilot and one of the naval officers who had made "the voyage to Mexico" with Beaujeu. Arnoul, in fact, had already assigned to *Le Marin* "le sieur Guesdon" (François Guitron, formerly the *Joly*'s pilot) as lieutenant, and Chevalier d'Hère, of late the *Joly*'s lieutenant, as ensign. Even as the king dispatched Beaugé's orders, excuses were being offered. Arnoul informed the monarch that the eight months' provisions carried by *Le Marin* would be insufficient for a voyage to the Mississippi, since she must lie over at Saint-Domingue until the season of good weather. The *Marin,* on September 2, awaited a fair wind; she sailed some days later. The Mississippi, however, was not to be on her itinerary.[43]

Still, the mystery of what had happened to La Salle remained unsolved, and rumors wafted from sundry sources, most of them bearing scant resemblance to the truth. In March, 1688, His Majesty, uneasy at the lack of news, harkened to reports from Cádiz that a French force, aided by natives of the Baye-du-Saint-Esprit, had defeated eleven hundred Spaniards. The king had before him Henri de Tonti's proposal, which had come via Governor Denonville in Canada, to descend the Mississippi in barques to look for the lost colony. The monarch, fearing rapids might prevent such vessels from reaching the river mouth, thought it a bad idea; furthermore, if La Salle had succeeded, such an effort would create a needless expense.[44]

From Canada to Saint-Domingue, the matter remained under discussion throughout most of 1688. In May, Tarin de Cussy wrote from the islands advice on the possibility of sending "the same frigate [the *Marin*]" to search for the lost colony. By his timetable, the ship would reach Saint-Domingue early in 1689 and spend the ensuing six months on reconnaissance of the "Gulf of New Spain" and the Mississippi. The island governor also offered the foreign minister unconfirmed reports from the buccaneers, the English, and the Spaniards that La Salle's expedition was lost and all his men dead. "What has become of him, or the few people he had with him," he concluded, "is not known." The New Spain viceroy, he reported, had sent as many as three expeditions to the supposed site of the French colony but found only uninhabitable country.[45] Nothing in Cussy's report struck a responsive chord with the court. It was, in fact, valueless, for too much time had already been lost.

Then came Abbé Cavelier and his four companions who, having left the Texas settlement almost two years previously, still held the truth at arm's length. Just how and when La Salle's death became public knowledge in France remains obscure. Cavelier evidently kept the secret, even, from his own family. Abbé Tronson, who seemingly knew as much as anyone, responded in late November to an inquiry from La Salle's sister-in-law, Madame Fauvel-Cavelier: "I have received two letters from M. Cavelier since his arrival in France. He did not stop at La Rochelle, because he was eager to fulfill a vow he had made, then to report to the Court on M. de La Salle's discovery and on every detail of his own journey. He indicated to me that he could not be here before early next month and that he had left M. de La Salle in a very fine country with M. de Chefdeville, in good health. He is waiting to tell you the particulars in person."[46]

After Cavelier finally had revealed to the court his brother's death, a royal order was sent to Canada for the murderers' arrest, should they appear there. The royal establishment must have been as secretive as Cavelier himself. Tronson seems to have had little knowledge of the true state of affairs when he wrote a month later to Bishop Saint-Vallier in Quebec, even though the source was close at hand. "M. Cavelier," he reported, "is stopping here, seeing nothing at present that can be done for the relief of those he left on the Gulf of Mexico. He awaits more favorable circumstances and will take advantage of any opportunity that Providence may offer to sustain them." Tronson, troubled by the outbreak of the War of the League of Augsburg, or King William's War, advised the bishop that the court seemed little disposed "to maintain La Salle's settlement or to send anyone there." Appointment of a vicar-general for the territory, therefore, would be useless. "The present state of public affairs" placed serious obstacles in the way of the good work they could have done in the colony; the people remaining, if abandoned, would suffer severely.[47]

Cavelier, while stalling his court appearance, prepared a special *mémoire* with the dominant theme that the Illinois settlement should be maintained and possession taken of the territory from there to the Gulf of Mexico. There is no mention of the colonists on the Texas coast. The writer's obvious hope was to obtain for himself a trade monopoly in the Illinois and Mississippi valleys.[48] Whether or not the minister Seignelay ever saw this final account by La Salle's brother, it served no purpose for either the Texas colonists or the abbé himself.

Tonti, the first to be deceived by the mendacious priest, learned the truth on April 7, 1689, when Jean Couture arrived at the Illinois post from the Arkansas. He first sent Couture, then went himself toward the Caddoan nations to seek the colony's remnants. Tonti, deserted by most of his followers, neared the Nabedache in eastern Texas in late April or early May, 1690, only to hear that the Spanish mission-founding expedition headed by Alonso de León and Fray Damián Massanet was approaching. He had no choice but to turn back.[49] It is commonly agreed that, had Abbé Cavelier not concealed La Salle's death, Tonti might well have been able to reach the colonists in time to save them.

In Canada, the intendant Champigny responded to news of the explorer's untimely end with just such a thought: "If M. Cavelier had not concealed his death, we would have sent there and would have known the truth by the following spring."[50]

The Sulpician superior Tronson, who had given Cavelier every benefit of the doubt and had welcomed him at the seminary during his stay in Paris, had like everyone else been kept in ignorance by the prevaricating priest. A year after Cavelier had stayed with him, he wrote to Bishop Saint-Vallier in Quebec: "The death of La Salle has nullified the measures that have been taken. M. Cavelier's intention of fitting out a vessel has failed, and he is at Rouen, occupied with picking up the pieces of his affairs which, due to his long absences, are in a sad state. It is distressing to see such a good worker spending a part of his life beset by such difficulties."[51]

Of what went on at the meager French settlement on the Rivière aux Boeufs after La Salle's departure, there is little record. If either Father Membré or Father Le Clercq took up the writing of a journal in the absence of La Salle and Joutel, it is not known. We know only that the picket fence begun before the leader left was finished, enclosing a small garden plot; some of the corn La Salle had brought from the Hasinai was planted; safe from wallowing pigs, it germinated and grew. There were also herbs (endive and asparagus) that Joutel had attempted unsuccessfully to grow when the pigs had free run of the settlement. A sixth house was built.[52]

Madame Barbier conceived again and delivered a healthy child in late summer or early fall, 1688. If anyone died at all, the death rate was much lower than during any like period of Joutel and La Salle's command; whereas the best estimate of the number left in the settlement when La Salle departed is "twenty to twenty-five," twenty-three are accounted for at the end. From all appearances, the little enclave had made the best of its circumstances and was enjoying a more or less stable existence until early 1689. Since La Salle's departure, it is said, peace had been made with the "Clamcoëhs [Karankawas]." The peace, however, was neither real nor lasting.

The only French account of the settlement after La Salle left it comes from Jean-Baptiste Talon, who at age nineteen recalled events that occurred when he was ten. The trouble with the natives, as he understood it, had begun with La Salle's seizure of their canoes. The warfare that went on during the colony's first two years ceased for a time. Barbier and the twenty to twenty-five other persons relaxed their guard. When the Indians learned of La Salle's death and the disunity among his followers, they, "by the worst treachery in the world," launched a surprise attack on the colonists. The massacre was complete except for the four Talon children—Jean-Baptiste, Lucien, Robert, and Marie-Madeleine—and the orphan boy, Eustache Bréman.

Jean-Baptiste, who provides a meager account of the massacre, saw his mother slain, as did his siblings. He and the other four children were carried away on the backs of the Indian women, who saved them out of compassion for their youth. Also spared for a time was Madame Barbier and her babe at breast; but, when the Indian men returned to their huts, they killed the mother, then the infant. Held by a foot, the child died when its head was bashed against a tree.

The Talons and young Bréman "were reared and loved by these same savage women . . . as if they were their own children." They lived as the Indians lived; their faces, arms, hands and bodies were tattooed like the Indians themselves; the younger ones even forgot their native tongue. At last the Spaniards came and took them away to Mexico.[53]

There is no detailed account of the massacre day. Yet, from young Talon's

FIGURE 20
*Lonely Vigil. This red-granite statue of La Salle stands like a silent
sentinel in Indianola State Park, overlooking Matagorda Bay.
Photo by Robert S. Weddle*

few words and the description given by the Spaniards viewing the dreadful site, one may conjure the scene: the chilling Indian yells; the fearful cries of the women and children; the chanted litany of Récollet friar and Sulpician priest; the moans of the dying; then the squealing of pigs as arrows were shot into them too. When no life remained, save the swine that scurried away to the wilds, there was the sound of cracking wood, as the Indians broke off the stocks of the muskets intended to arm La Salle's native allies in the conquest of Nueva Vizcaya. Then, in their frenzy of destruction, they broke up the furniture, tore apart books, and scattered the leaves of manuscripts.[54] Afterward, the rains came, blotting out the words from pages that might have told a more poignant story than we could ever write.

As for La Salle, he has been controversial in death as in life, his life *and* death assessed from various perspectives. "He died on the field of triumph," his countryman Gabriel-Louis Jaray proclaimed on the 250th anniversary of his demise. In sharp contrast, Henry Folmer declares, "La Salle . . . died a tragic failure . . . the victim of his own lies."[55]

Indeed, the celebrated explorer failed on all counts: as fur trader, explorer, military leader, and colonizer. Most of all, in his lack of consideration for those who trusted and followed him, he failed as a human being. Yet he left an indelible mark upon the North American continent and its future; judged on the basis of his lasting influence on America's course, he must be allowed a measure of greatness.

Landmark events often turn on obscure moments; hence the human tendency to ask the question, "What if . . . ?" *What if La Salle's enterprise had succeeded?* Yet his failure had been ordained long before his death and the final collapse of the Texas colony. Failure, in fact, was written into the very concept: in the presumption of unknown geography, in the leader's confused priorities, and in the insatiable thirst of many for glory, wealth, and power; such were the elements that steered La Salle to a destination other than the Mississippi, the vital link between the Gulf of Mexico and New France, the one ingredient essential to his triumph.

The blunder, when at last acknowledged, could not be rectified without the *Belle,* the little ship that had been built specifically for navigating the continent's greatest river. The loss of the *Belle* was the colony's death sentence. The nature and circumstances of that loss, taken in isolation or in full context, cast a dark reflection on the life of La Salle. Yet, while he failed in his own objectives, his life produced a greater result than he could possibly have dreamed of.

Postscript

IN THE BACKWASH OF DREAMS

For the French colonists on the Texas coast, there was no messenger of defeat. Word of the disaster came to France slowly, usually in the form of unverified rumors from foreign sources or pirates. While the foreign minister and the king pondered the proper course, indecision stalled action until it was too late. The War of the League of Augsburg, lasting from 1689 to 1697, closed the options; with French troops on the offensive on the Rhine, in Italy, and in Holland, the time was inopportune for sending a new expedition to the Gulf of Mexico.

It was in this conflict, known as King William's War in the colonies, that Jean-Baptiste Minet was killed in action at age thirty-two. In 1693, he died in the siege of Palamos in the Catalonian region of northeastern Spain. If, following his release from La Rochelle's Saint-Nicolas Tower, he had had more to say about the La Salle expedition, or again complained against another's official conduct, it has not come to light. Indeed, his journal seems to have received little attention until it turned up in the late twentieth century in the hands of a private collector, who then sold it to the Public Archives of Canada.

Spain's search for the French intruders, meanwhile, had at last borne fruit: first with the discovery of the derelict *Belle* and scattered pieces of the *Aimable* in the bay the Spaniards called San Bernardo; then with Alonso de León's arrival on April 22, 1689, at the devastated French colony, where no sign of life remained. General de León buried the eight cannon that had been brought from France on the *Aimable,* then began his search for survivors. Of twenty-three persons at the little settlement when the Indians attacked, no one was left alive but the five children saved by the Karankawa women. Of approximately two hundred persons who had landed on the Texas coast with La Salle, the scattered remnants now numbered no more than twenty.[1]

Besides the five children—four Talons and Eustache Bréman—there were the two men who had made good their escape from the colony during its first few months: Pietro di Bonardi, the Italian from Turin whom Joutel calls a Spaniard, still lived among the Karankawas; and Jean Jarry, a Frenchman, found reigning king-like over a Coahuiltecan group far to the west. Among the Hasinai (Cenis or Tejas) were the expirate James, or Hiems; Jean L'Archevêque of Bayonne; Jacques Grollet of La Rochelle; Pierre Meunier from Paris; Pierre Talon, who had been brought to learn the Hasinai language that he might serve the colony; the man called Ruter, or Rutre; and one from Provence, identified only as "the Provençal."

Additionally, there was Pierre Barthélemy, of whom nothing is known after Abbé Cavelier and Joutel left him among the Arkansas, and the five who returned to France by way of Canada: Joutel, the two Caveliers; the Récollet father Douay, and the ignominious pilot of the *Belle,* Pierre Tessier.

Each of the survivors has his own story. Several were to have a further role in history, in diverse regions of America; some have descendants living in America still. The first to fall into the hands of the Spaniards was Jarry, whom General de León, marching from San Francisco de Coahuila (Monclova), found with a band of Coahuiltecan Indians who venerated him as their chief. Taken into custody on May 31, 1688, in what is today southeastern Kinney County, Texas, Jarry told such widely divergent tales that his Spanish interrogators judged him mentally unbalanced. Yet his services as a guide were utilized by León the following year. León was frank in his appraisal of Jarry's services, declaring that he could not have found La Salle's settlement without his help.[2]

Soon after Jarry was taken from the Coahuiltecans, he was sent to Mexico City for interrogation by a French interpreter. By the following December, he was back at Presidio de Coahuila (Monclova). A month later, on January 11, 1689, he petitioned through the Holy Office of the Inquisition to marry Antonia de Lara, a thirty-five-year-old Spanish woman from San Luis Potosí who was employed as a servant at the military post. Jarry, giving his age as forty, satisfied his interrogators that he was a devout Catholic. Apparently, the ecclesiastic authorities raised no questions as to his mental soundness. His admitted liaison with an Indian woman who had borne him a daughter was disavowed, as she was considered a pagan.[3] Final disposition of the matter, however, has not yet surfaced. The following March 23, León set out to find the French settlement with Jarry as guide. Sometime after their return from this expedition on May 13, 1689, León sent Jarry to the Río Grande to await expected visitors from the Hasinai. At this point the record becomes silent. Jarry does not reappear on León's 1690 mission-founding expedition to eastern Texas. The general afterward reported, "On this journey I sorely missed the old Frenchman, because of his knowledge of all the Indian languages of the region. He was always found faithful."[4] Whether Jarry had returned to his Indian friends or met death in the wilderness remains a matter for conjecture.

On his first march into eastern Texas, General de León found L'Archevêque and Grollet tired of Indian life and ready to give themselves up that they might live again among Christians. After making depositions in the Spanish camp on the Guadalupe River and again at Monclova, they were taken to Mexico City for further interrogation. Later that year they boarded a ship captained by Andrés de Pez y Malzárraga, a principal figure in the maritime search for the French colony, and were taken to Spain. The Spanish War Council, fearful of repatriating them to France lest they spread abroad their knowledge of Spanish territory, acceded to their plea to be sent back to America to serve Spain. Returned to Veracruz on Pez's ship, they were kept in chains until all opportunity for a change of heart had been eliminated. They were then sent to join Diego de Vargas's second expedition in the reconquest of New Mexico. Vargas and company left El Paso del Norte on October 4, 1693.[5]

In the meantime, General de León, accompanied by Fray Damián Massanet, had reentered Texas in 1690 to establish the first Spanish Franciscan mission among the Hasinai of eastern Texas. Stopping by the erstwhile French settlement, they burned the buildings. Thence, they traveled northeast and captured Pierre Talon, age fourteen, and Pierre Meunier, twenty, who had been living with the Hasinai but had fled to escape the Spaniards. When the expedition reached the Hasinai, the two young captives served the Spanish missionaries as interpreters of the native language. The general's troop later found Talon's younger brothers Lucien and Robert and older sister, Marie-Madeleine, among the Karankawas on lower Matagorda Bay. Meunier, after being conducted to Mexico City to give a deposition, returned to San Francisco de Coahuila to accompany the 1691 expedition of Domingo Terán de los Ríos to Texas. Terán brought back two more children, Jean-Baptiste Talon and young Bréman. No known Spanish source mentions the Italian found among the Karankawa and taken to Mexico at the same time. Although the Talons report that he claimed not to have been a part of the colony, there is little room for doubt that he was Pietro Pauollo di Bonardi, who had signed on at La Rochelle and deserted soon after the colonists were put ashore on Matagorda Island. Not knowing that La Salle was dead, he apparently feared punishment should the explorer return and therefore pretended that he had come by way of Canada, rather than with La Salle. His punishment, however, came not from La Salle but the Spaniards, who imprisoned him in the dungeon of San Juan de Ulúa at Veracruz, where he died.[6]

Meunier, upon his return to Mexico from eastern Texas with the Terán expedition, also took the path to New Mexico. He, as well as Grollet and L'Archevêque, were in Santa Fe by 1696—Grollet as a settler, the other two as soldiers. The following year, L'Archevêque took as his first wife Antonia Gutiérrez, a widow. Nothing more is heard of Meunier after he began the legal proceedings to marry Lucía Madrid in 1699. Grollet married Elena Galuegos in 1699 and settled in Bernalillo, New Mexico. The name was corrupted to Gurulé; many present-day residents of the Albuquerque vicinity carry it forth.[7] L'Archevêque's rise to prominence as soldier, trader, and citizen is well known. While serving as interpreter with lieutenant governor Pedro de Villasur on the Platte River in 1719, he died with forty-four other members of the expedition, including Villasur, in a Pawnee massacre. The attack was believed to have been French motivated.

Little is known of the other La Salle survivors left among the Caddoan tribes. Father Massanet tells of being shown "two dead bodies of Frenchmen who had shot each other with carbines."[8] If such were the case, the remains would seem to belong to Hiems and Rutre. Pierre Talon, however, provides a different scenario: "James" (Hiems) killed Duhaut; James was killed by Rutre, "who was subsequently slain by a surgeon; and the surgeon fell while aiding the Toho Indians in a war in which Talon himself was engaged.[9] Talon's "surgeon" may have been the unnamed "Provençal," whom he possibly confused with the other man from Provence, the surgeon Liotot. Pierre's account of the deaths of Hiems and Rutre, however, are more difficult to reconcile with other versions.

It appears that Rutre may have had a longer life than Pierre allows him. Jean-Bernard Bossu, visiting the Mississippi Valley in 1751, "found a halfblood among the Arkansas, . . . the son of Rutel, the Breton sailor who got lost at the time of La Salle's expedition down the Mississippi in 1682."

Although Bossu confuses the expeditions, his report of what the "halfblood" told him is enough to affirm that the reference is to Rutre, who was indeed a Breton sailor: he had been adopted by the Caddo, was made a warrior, and "was given an Indian girl as his wife because he had frightened and routed the enemies of the Caddoes by using his rifle. . . ."[10]

Hiems, too, may have lived on among the natives long enough to take an Indian wife and beget at least one child. There is a persistent legend in a Louisiana family of descendancy from Hiems and an Indian woman named Makaruya. Laura Watanabe (nee Ourso) of Spokane, Washington, tells of a great-great grandmother whose name was Jeanette Hiems. Mrs. Watanabe recalls that she originally gave little credence to the claim, which came to her through her father, that the line extended back to the old buccaneer who figured in the La Salle murders. That changed when she learned that an identical version existed among distant relatives previously unknown to her immediate family.[11]

Whatever the merits of Pierre Talon's account of the murders in Hasinai country, he and his siblings offer perhaps the most intriguing story of all. Taken to Mexico City, they were reared as servants in the household of the viceroy, Conde de Galve, and were witnesses to the unrest among the populace that erupted in the rock-throwing "corn riots" of 1792. A short time before the count ended his term early in 1696 to return to Spain, the three older boys were taken to Veracruz and enrolled as soldiers in the Armada de Barlovento, then commanded by the same Andrés de Pez who had conducted L'Archevêque and Grollet to Spain. They were assigned to the *Santo Cristo de Maracaibo,* flagship of Admiral Guillermo Morfi. Marie-Madeleine and Robert were taken to Spain with the count and countess.

About a year later, Admiral Morfi surrendered the *Santo Cristo* to a French ship, *Le Bon,* in the Caribbean Sea. For Morfi and Pez, the deed resulted in courts-martial. For the three Talons, it meant repatriation to France. Pierre and Jean-Baptiste, ages twenty and seventeen, were enrolled in the French Royal Navy. Lucien, considered too young for service, was employed as a servant at Oléron. The two older boys were interrogated early in 1698 on order of the foreign minister, Louis Pontchartrain, resulting in the revealing document known as the Talon Interrogations. The minister failed in his effort to get the Talon brothers on Pierre Le Moyne d'Iberville's first voyage to Louisiana in pursuit of La Salle's dream. They did, however, sail with Iberville's second voyage, as soldiers in the company of Louis Juchereau de Saint-Denis. They remained in the colony at Fort Maurepas (Ocean Springs, Mississippi) for two years, during which time they probably accompanied Saint-Denis and Jean-Baptiste Le Moyne de Bienville (Iberville's brother) on journeys up the Red River toward the Caddoan confederacies. Returning to France in 1702, they sought a reunion with their sister, Marie-Madeleine, who by that time had returned from Spain and married Pierre Simon of Paris.[12]

Pierre and Jean-Baptiste, for reasons unknown, were imprisoned in Portugal in 1702. In 1714, Pierre and Robert returned to Texas as guides and interpreters for Saint-Denis on his trek across Texas to San Juan Bautista de Río Grande in the interest of trade. While Saint-Denis was escorted to Mexico City to explain his intrusion, the Talons returned to Mobile with his report to the French governor Antoine de La Mothe, sieur de Cadillac.[13]

Further details of the Talons are few: Robert settled in Mobile, married Jeanne Prot, or Praux, who bore him children in 1719 and 1721, and plied his trade as a carpenter or joiner *(menuisier)*. The record is less clear on the other three boys. Jean-Baptiste may have settled in New Orleans. Pierre possibly returned to France, but there is some indication that he settled in Mobile and died at an early age.[14]

As plans for Iberville's Louisiana-founding expedition took shape, Pontchartrain wrote to the intendant at Rouen, asking him to find Joutel, obtain his journal, and forward it to the minister. Joutel, having returned to France destitute, had taken employment at one of the city's gates and was easy to find. His journal was forwarded forthwith to Pontchartrain, who sent it on to Iberville with the expressed hope that he might also "send you the man who wrote it." Joutel, having had all the New World experience he wanted, declined the offer. Iberville took the bulky document on his voyage and kept it more than two years. When he at last parted with it, three of the several large notebooks were missing. The excised portions, comprising crucial phases of the adventure, eventually were recreated by various means, but suspicions have been raised as to their accuracy.[15]

While Joutel resisted Pontchartrain's efforts to enlist him, Father Anastase Douay yielded to the minister's urging. Sailing in 1698 on the frigate *Marin* as expedition chaplain, he participated in Iberville's initial exploration of the Mississippi. On March 3, 1699, Père Anastase celebrated Mass commemorating the discovery of the river mouth. Irritation grew between the Récollet father and Iberville, however, especially from Douay's churlish behavior upon the loss of his breviary and a journal he was keeping. The father at last asked Iberville to return him to France, that he might rejoin his monastery and never leave it again. Thus, he fades from the record.[16]

Pontchartrain, in his effort to inform Iberville as fully as possible prior to his first voyage, sought out all La Salle's former associates whom he considered a likely source. Among them was the explorer's namesake, Nicolas de La Salle, who had made both the 1682 voyage down the Mississippi and the 1684–85 voyage to the Gulf of Mexico as a crewman of *Le Joly*.

There was, however, one obvious omission: Captain Beaujeu. The veteran officer, with his candid assessment of La Salle and his enterprise, had prejudiced himself with the king. Even though it should have been recognized by now that Beaujeu had appraised the explorer and his venture correctly, his advice was not welcome. Possibly because of that, or perhaps out of bitterness that someone else was about to accomplish what he himself might have, he regarded the Iberville expedition negatively. After it had sailed—from Brest on October 24, 1698—he wrote from Le Havre to his friend and confidant of longstanding, Cabart de Villermont, expounding on the hazards the voyage would encounter and forecasting its failure. After Iberville had returned to report the success of his first voyage, Villermont asked his thoughts on the matter. Even if the report were true, Beaujeu replied, he doubted that the Spaniards or the Indians would allow the settlement to remain; he feared that the eighty men whom Iberville had left on the Mississippi were destined for the same fate that La Salle's colonists had suffered, and that no one would be found if he returned there.

Beaujeu was not the only one who tasted sour grapes over Iberville's success. Joutel, as he pondered how those who had laid the groundwork were forgotten in the enthusiasm of the moment, issued a reminder that La Salle was "the originator of the enterprise." He also pointed out that his own journal had provided Iberville with crucial information.[17]

Abbé Cavelier, meanwhile, seems to have taken little immediate notice of Iberville's follow-up to La Salle's attempt to control the Mississippi Valley. Having failed to interest the Royal Court in a new expedition—or in compensating him for his losses—he retired to live with a relative (probably his niece) in Rouen. Perhaps to salve a troubled conscience, he wrote to Iberville after the latter's return from his third voyage, asking news of any of La Salle's colonists who might still be alive in the Texas wilds. Iberville replied on May 4, 1704, enclosing an extract of the Talon Interrogations. The brothers, who had served him two years in Mississippi, had assured him repeatedly "that M. de Chedeville, the Récollet Father[s], and the others have been killed by the savages." Iberville reported that Francisco Martínez, now commanding the Spanish garrison at Pensacola, who on two of the *entradas* from Monclova to eastern Texas had gathered up some of the French survivors, gave similar assurances. From Mississippi, Iberville himself had sent an expedition west along the coast, seeking, without success, news of any Frenchmen still living in the Texas wilderness.[18]

Eventually, Abbé Cavelier acquired considerable means from the inheritance of a large estate. Still not satisfied, he and his nephew unsuccessfully petitioned for possession of La Salle's property in America.

Abbé Cavelier, born at Rouen in 1636, died on November 24, 1722, at age eighty-six. His nephew, Colin Cavelier, who had shared the misery of La Salle's final days, was a regimental officer at the time of his death some years later.[19]

The abbé, unlike his brother, evidently attained his life's ambition: it is said that he died rich. Yet his character comes up short under the scrutiny of his interpreters. "An objective study of the man" claims that he "was and remained all his life a hypocrite, a knave, a liar and a miser." His concealment of his brother's death and the seven months he lost at Fort-Saint-Louis (Illinois) to satisfy his greed, Marc de Villiers points out, prevented Tonti's timely rescue of the Texas colonists.[20]

If Jean Cavelier died rich, it may well have been partly at the expense of his brother's creditors as well as from his inheritance. As he had done in Canada, he had laid hold of La Salle's assets for himself, leaving everyone else holding the bag. Litigation over the slain explorer's defaulted obligations went on well after his death—carried on by François Plet's heirs and others—and probably after the abbé's demise as well.

While Jean Cavelier lay dying, the landscape was being altered at the scene of misery for the long-gone French colonists on the Texas Gulf Coast. Alonso de León and Father Damián Massanet provide the final glimpse of what historians have mistakenly called "Fort St. Louis of Texas"—just as Enríquez Barroto of the Rivas-Iriarte voyage relates the last viewing of the *Belle*. León noted that all the six houses were useless for defense except the largest, which he calls "the fort"; the five smaller ones were "built of poles, plastered with mud and roofed over with buffalo hides." The Spaniards found and buried the remains of three victims of the massacre, one a woman, shot in the back with an arrow.[21] Juan Bautista Chapa, moved by the tragic scene, composed a verse of three stanzas—addressing the site, the piteous French woman victim, and the human remains—viewed as a warning to would-be violators of the 1494 papal bull that granted the territory to Spain.[22]

When León and Massanet returned to the site in 1690, they burned the buildings. Francisco de Llanos and Joseph Manuel de Cárdenas y Magaña, visiting the ruined settlement a few months later, found only wheels of gun carriages, musket breeches, and charred timbers. They uncovered and examined the cannon buried by León in 1689, then restored their covering and left them where they lay.[23] The guns were not to be seen again for three centuries.

In 1721, Domingo Ramón occupied the site for the Marqués de San Miguel de Aguayo, and the Spanish Presidio de Nuestra Señora de Loreto de la Bahía rose there the following year. Thus, remains of the French occupation were scattered and obscured. The picture, however, has now been clarified.

The story of La Salle, his "post in the Baye-Saint-Louis," and the little frigate called *La Belle* could go on and on. The narrative of this first European settlement on the Gulf Coast between Pensacola, Florida, and Tampico, Tamaulipas, Mexico—so far-reaching are its consequences—is never-ending. The next chapter of the saga belongs to the archeologists who found the remains of the little ship—built specifically for sailing on the Mississippi River but never able to fulfill its purpose—and saved it for posterity. As ships go, she was rather small and unimpressive, especially alongside a warship like the *Joly*. Yet, sometimes the little, inconspicuous things—or the lack of them— make the greatest impact.

For want of an anchor the ship was lost; for want of a ship the colony was lost.

> *The stately ship is seen no more,*
> *The fragile skiff attains the shore;*
> *And while the great and wise decay,*
> *And all their trophies pass away,*
> *Some sudden thought, some careless rhyme,*
> *Still floats above the wrecks of Time.*
>
> —*William Lecky*

NOTES

ABBREVIATIONS

ADCM   Archives Départementales de la Charante-Maritime, La Rochelle (France)
AGI   Archivo General de Indias, Seville
AGN   Archivo General de la Nación, Mexico, Mexico City
ALR   Amirauté de La Rochelle [Admiralty]
AN   Archives Nationales, Paris
APR   Archives du Port de Rochefort, Service Historique de la Marine, Rochefort, France
BN   Bibliothèque Naionale, Section des manuscrits, Paris
BHC   Burton Historical Collection, Detroit Public Library, Detroit, Michigan
BTHC   Barker Texas History Center, Center for American History, University of Texas at Austin
NOS   National Ocean Survey, National Oceanic and Atmospheric Administration, United States Department of Commerce
NAF   *Nouvelles acquisitions françaises* (BN)
SwHQ   *Southwesern Historical Quarterly*
THC   Texas Historical Commission

CHAPTER 1. *Navío Quebrado*

1. Juan Enríquez Barroto, "Diary of the voyage and navigation . . . for coasting and reconnoitering all the Mexican Gulf," Biblioteca del Palacio Real, Madrid, ms. 2667; translated by Robert S. Weddle in Robert S. Weddle, ed., *La Salle, the Mississippi, and the Gulf: Three Primary Documents,* pp. 145–205; cited hereafter as Enríquez Barroto Diary.

2. Ibid.

3. Conversations with archeologists engaged in excavation of the *Belle;* personal visit to the site, Sept. 25, 1996, courtesy THC.

4. Enríquez Barroto Diary.

5. "Armemens des Vaisseaux du Roi en 1684," Musée de la Marine, Paris, J 2583 V, 1684, f. 102; construction papers of the *Belle,* and "Liste de Vaisseaux, Frégates, Brulots et autres, batiments du Port de Rochefort," 1688, APR, registers 1 L3 19, ff. 88v-89r, 1 L3 20, f. 25r. Dumont [de Blaignac] to king, Apr. 3, 1684, BN, NAF 21330, f. 78–80v; AN, Marine B2 50:177.

6. "Armemens des Vaisseaux"; *Belle* construction papers; THC archeological data; "Liste des Vaisseaux." The documentary evidence and archeological findings often are at odds with Henri Joutel ("Voyage de M. de La Salle dans l'Amérique septentrionale en l'année 1685, pour y faire un establissement dans la partie qu'il au avoit auparavant descouverte" (in Pierre Margry, ed., *Découvertes et*

établissements des Français dans l'ouest et dans le sud de l'Amérique septentrionale [1614–1754], 3:93–534), cited hereafter as Joutel, "Voyage." Joutel, for example, ascribes to *La Belle* a capacity of sixty *tonneaux* (tuns, or casks). No complete roster of *La Belle*'s crew has been found. Names associated with the ship are drawn from Joutel, La Salle's reports, and various other sources.

7. "Commission pour le sieur de La Salle." This document in Margry, *Découvertes,* 2:382–83, is dated Apr. 14, 1684, as is Seignelay's letter to Dumont, which precedes it, pp. 380–81. The latter document, in AN, Marine B2, 51:171, stating that the king has granted La Salle the *Joly* and 200 men for his forthcoming voyage, is dated March 23, 1684. It is presumed the "Commission" should be also.

8. "Contrat d'affrétement du navire l'*Aimable,*" ADCM, 3 E 1806, La Rochelle, June 5, 1684, 110v–111; "Mémoire de l'équipage de le St. François," ALR, B 5682, f. 178, June 9, 1684; "Liste des Vaisseaux." See also Joutel, "Voyage," p. 93.

9. "Voyage to the Mississippi through the Gulf of Mexico" (hereafter cited as Talon Interrogations), in Weddle, ed., *La Salle,* p. 211; Marc de Villiers, *L'expédition de Cavelier de La Salle, dans le Golfe du Mexique,* p. 164.

10. Jean l'Archevêque in "Declarazión de los franceses en Mexico," AGI, Mexico 616, BTHC; translated in Walter J. O'Donnell, *La Salle's Occupation of Texas,* p. 22. Pierre Meunier, "Declarazion" (AGI, Mexico 617, BTHC), claims four Spanish vessels took part in the seizure. Whether any of them had specific knowledge of the episode is questionable.

11. Joutel, "Voyage," p. 107.

12. [Jean-Baptiste] Minet, "Journal of Our Voyage to the Gulf of Mexico," in Weddle, ed., *La Salle,* p. 92, cited hereafter as Minet, "Journal"; Joutel, "Voyage," p. 114.

13. La Salle to Beaujeu, Petit Goâve, Nov. 23, 1684, in Margry, *Découvertes,* 2:522; Robert S. Weddle, *The French Thorn: Rival Explorers in the Spanish Sea, 1682–1762,* p. 16. "Within soundings" means the point at which bottom can be reached with the lead line. The deep-sea lead line, used to determine the proximity of land before the actual sighting, was 200 fathoms long (six feet per fathom) and weighted with fourteen pounds. In shoal water, as in this case, a shorter line with a seven-pound weight was used. Weddle, *Spanish Sea,* p. 54; J. H. Parry, *The Age of Reconnaissance,* pp. 97–98.

14. Minet, "Journal," p. 94.

15. Joutel, "Voyage," pp. 121–22, 135.

16. The obvious error of these latitude observations is discussed in Weddle, ed., *La Salle,* 99n.34.

17. Joutel, "Voyage," pp. 134–35; Minet, "Journal," pp. 103–104; *Procès verbal de l'entrée du lac où est descendu M. de La Salle,* Feb. 17, 1685, Margry, *Découvertes* 2:239–40. This document is catalogued in AN, Colonies C[13c], as a report "on the soundings made at the entry of Lake Pontchartrain"—a misunderstanding of both time and place.

18. See La Salle's report on the wreck of l'*Aimable,* Margry, *Découvertes* 2:555–58.

19. The supply depot is shown on a map by Manuel Joseph de Cárdenas y Magaña, reproduced in Weddle, *Wilderness Manhunt,* plate 11. Letter designations on the map refer to Cárdenas's diary. At point 8, says Cárdenas, "we found the sites of 48 *barracas* [huts, storage sheds], from which it is inferred that the French ships had not passed this place and that here they disembarked all the supplies and people and took them to the French settlement in launches and canoes." Cárdenas, "Diario De la deRota que han echo para la Bahiya de S. Bernardo," Oct. 12–Nov.

29, 1690, AGI, Mexico 617, BTHC; translated in Kathleen Gilmore, *The Keeran Site: the probable site of La Salle's Fort St. Louis in Texas,* pp. 79–84, appendix 3.

20. La Salle, *"procès verbal,"* Apr. 18, 1685, in Margry, *Découvertes,* pp. 539–40.

21. Ibid., p. 541.

22. Joutel, "Voyage," pp. 185–88. Colin Crevel de Moranget was the son of La Salle's sister, who was married to Nicolas Crevel. Moranget was the Colin Crevel who accompanied La Salle on his descent of the Mississippi.

23. The story of the *Griffon* is in Chapter 3.

24. La Salle, *"procès verbal,"* Apr. 18, 1684, p. 541; Joutel, "Voyage," pp. 189–91.

25. Joutel, "Voyage," p. 198.

26. La Salle, *"procès verbal,"* Apr. 18, pp. 541–42. La Salle evidently had seen such items in Petit Goâve among the pirates who had raided Veracruz in May, 1683. See Robert S. Weddle, *Spanish Sea: The Gulf of Mexico in North American Discovery, 1500–1685,* pp. 399–400.

27. La Salle, *"procès verbal,"* Apr. 18, pp. 542–43; Joutel, "Voyage," pp. 204–205.

28. La Salle, *"procès verbal,"* p. 543.

29. The only man named Ruiné known to have been on the expedition was Louis Ruiné from Vemars, Île-de-France, listed as a surgeon among the hired men who had contracted for the voyage. For this list ("Engagements en 1684 pour la Louisiane avec Cavelier de La Salle—à La Rochelle, Étude Menon [notaires Rivière & Soullard]," ADCM) I am indebted to both Marcel Lussier of Brossard, Que., and Jean de Bry. (See chapter 7, n. 15) There are thirty-seven names, including the surgeon-major from Provence, Étienne Liotot, who marched with La Salle on this journey. A third surgeon remained with Joutel at the post (Joutel, "Voyage," p. 192). Villiers's list of known participants in the Texas colony (*L'expédition,* appendix, pp. 218–20) has Ruiné, Fontaine, Guichard, La Jeunesse, and Turpin (no given names) as soldiers. Meunier, about sixteen at the time, later deposed to his Spanish captors but makes no mention of having been on the *Belle.* See the foregoing note 10. It is not clear whether the six prisoners were in excess of the ship's complement; the number of persons on board, therefore, is uncertain.

30. Joutel, "Voyage," pp. 205, 227 (quote).

31. Ibid., pp. 205–206 (quote, 205); La Salle, *"procès verbal,"* Apr. 18, pp. 543–44.

32. Duhaut evidently *began* his return eighteen days after the start of the march and spent more than a month in reaching the settlement. If La Salle's band left the bay around January 3, Duhaut must have reached the settlement in late February, the *Belle* having been lost prior to that time. Joutel relates only that it was February when some of the *Belle's* crew attempted to go ashore for water after the ship had run aground ("Voyage," p. 229).

33. La Salle, *"procès verbal,"* p. 545.

34. Ibid., pp. 547–48. Joutel ("Voyage," p. 220) tells it differently. While making no mention of La Salle's going to meet the rest of his men, he says the others reached the post one day after their leader.

35. Joutel, "Voyage," p. 221.

36. Ibid., p. 228; BHC.

37. Joutel, "Voyage," pp. 232–33; quote, from BHC, reel 1, does not appear in the Margry version.

38. Chefdeville's account of *La Belle's* end is in Joutel, "Voyage," pp. 227–32. It is summarized in Weddle, *French Thorn,* pp. 32–33.

39. Joutel, "Voyage," pp. 235–36, 253–54.

40. The pages of the *Belle* log have been reproduced by J. F. Jamison as an appendix to Charles Wilson Hackett, ed., *Historical Documents Relating to New Mexico, Nueva Vizcaya, and Approaches Thereto, to 1773,* 2:474–81. See also Weddle, *Wilderness Manhunt,* plate 5 in picture section and chapter 15, and Weddle, *French Thorn,* p. 22. The log entries for October 1 and 2, 1684 (f. 14r); November 25 and 26, 1684 (14v); and January 17 and 18 (f. 33) were contained in a four-page leaf measuring approximately 8 inches by 12 1/4 inches. Photostat copies are in BTHC. The log pages will be discussed in a succeeding chapter.

41. Enríquez Barroto Diary.

42. Fernández Carrasco, "Diario del Viage," Aug. 8–Sept. 30, 1688, AGI, Mexico 616 (BTHC). The direction of "northers" in the Matagorda Bay area varies from northeast to northwest. Archeologists excavating the *Belle* found them to blow most often from the northeast. The bow of the wreck pointed north.

43. Ibid.

44. APR, LS7071.

45. Ibid.

CHAPTER 2. "OUR WISE COMMANDER"

1. La Salle (*procès verbal,* Apr. 18, 1686, p. 540) reported that illness had taken away "more than half the people by the end of July [1685]." By February 20, 1686, anniversary of the wreck of the *Aimable* and the Matagorda Island landing of the colonists, most of the *Belle*'s crew and many of those with La Salle had perished.

2. Attributed falsely to Father Anastase Douay. Quote is found in John Gilmary Shea, ed., *Discovery and Exploration of the Mississippi Valley,* p. 214, and Isaac Joslin Cox, ed., *The Journeys of Réné Robert Cavelier, Sieur de La Salle,* 1:244.

3. Pierre Leprohon, *Cavelier de La Salle: Fondateur de la Louisiane,* p. 20; E. B. Osler, *La Salle,* pp. 1–2; Paul Chesnel, *History of Cavelier de La Salle, 1643–1687: Explorations in the Valleys of the Ohio, Illinois and Mississippi,* p. 3; Frances Gaither, *Fatal River: The Life and Death of La Salle,* p. 10. Pierre Margry, *Découvertes,* 1:346n; Abbé Tronson to Madame Fauvel-Cavelier, Margry, *Découvertes,* 3:182. Margry renders the name of La Salle's mother as "Geest"; Leprohon, "Gest." Although "Gest" is still a common name in Rouen, the name "Geest" is not found. Whereas two of La Salle's nephews went with him on the Texas expedition (as will be seen), Gabriel Gravier (*Cavelier de La Salle de Rouen,* p. 11) mentions another: Jean-Baptiste-François Cavelier, who was ennobled in 1717 and, like his uncle, was styled "sieur de La Salle."

4. Leprohon, *Cavelier de La Salle,* p. 20; W. J. Eccles, *France in America,* p. 27.

5. Jean Delanglez, ed., *The Journal of Jean Cavelier,* p. 4. "Histoire de M. de La Salle," Margry, *Découvertes,* 1:381.

6. See Lewis Thorpe, trans. and ed., *The Bayeux Tapestry and the Norman Invasion,* for an account of the Battle of Hastings and the tapestry that portrays the historical sequence.

7. Miranda Frances Spieler, ed., *Let's Go: The Budget Guide to Paris,* 1995, p. 308.

8. Leprohon, *Cavelier de La Salle,* p. 21. Alfredo Panicucci, *The Life and Times of Louis XIV,* p. 8.

9. Leprohon, *Cavelier de La Salle,* p. 26. French documents of a few years later refer

to La Salle variously as "René de La Salle," "Robert René Cavelier," and "René Cavelier," often followed by "sieur de La Salle." See for example Margry, *Découvertes,* 1:101, 106, 107, 109, 111. One document (p. 111), signed for him by a clerk, gives "Robert René Cavelier." French biographers and historians custom-arily omit "René" from his name, while modern American writers have adopted "René-Robert Cavelier, Sieur de La Salle." An original birth certificate found in a La Rochelle archive gives the name only as Robert Cavelier (Curtis Tunnell, "A Cache of Cannons," *SwHQ* 102, no. 1 [July, 1998]: 19n.). See Fig. 2.

10. Robert's first letter to the superior-general is quoted in Tony Coulter, *La Salle and the Explorers of the Mississippi,* p. 22. He wrote a second letter the following April 5, evidently before he had had a reply to the first. See also Gaither, *Fatal River,* p. 23.

11. This account of La Salle's Jesuit days is drawn principally from Leprohon, *Cavelier de La Salle,* pp. 26–30, which cites Père (Camille) de La Rochemonteix, *Les Jésuites et la Nouvelle-France en XVIIe siècle* (3 vols., Paris, 1895–96), as its principal source. Quotes are on p. 30.

12. Leprohon (*Cavelier de La Salle,* p. 32) assesses La Salle's character differently, as do many other interpreters.

13. Ibid., p. 31. Anka Muhlstein (*La Salle: Explorer of the North American Frontier,* p. 5), states that Robert appealed in 1666 for assignment to missions in China, promising that his father would pay his passage and maintenance. The letter was written in March, 1666; his father had died the previous January.

14. Francis Parkman, *La Salle and the Discovery of the Great West,* in Francis Parkman, *France and England in North America,* 1:797.

15. Chesnel, *Cavelier de La Salle,* p. 5. Parkman (*La Salle,* p. 729): "The capital [of the allowance] was paid over to him, and with this pittance, he sailed for Canada, to seek his fortune, in the spring of 1666 [actually 1667]."

16. Panicucci, *Life and Times,* p. 17.

17. Ibid., pp. 22–23.

18. First quote, Nancy Mitford, *The Sun King,* p. 29; second and third, Judith A. Franke, *French Peoria and the Illinois Country, 1673–1846,* p. 59.

19. Quote from Chesnel, *Cavelier de La Salle,* p. 4.

20. Parkman, *La Salle,* p. 729.

21. Compare ibid., 732n.: Dollier de Casson claimed the Iroquois always called the Mississippi the Ohio, while the Algonquians gave the Mississippi its present name. Osler, *La Salle,* p. 20.

22. Introduction to Margry, *Découvertes,* p. 4, BHC reel 2 (not included in U.S. edition of Margry, published with funding by the Congress.

23. E.g., Osler (*La Salle,* p. 20) portrays his subject as an avaricious trader whose explorations, following Louis Jolliet's vision rather than his own, were directed at grabbing up all the trading rights—an over-simplification.

24. Parkman, *La Salle,* pp. 733–34 (first quote); Sieur Patoulet to Colbert, Quebec, Nov. 22, 1669, in Margry, *Découvertes,* 1:81.

25. The journey up to the parting is told in "Récit de ce qui s'est passé de plus remarquable dans le voyage de MM. Dollier et Gallinée," in Margry, *Découvertes,* 1:112–44. The account continues with the rest of the Sulpicians' travels, pp. 144–66. Gaither, *Fatal River,* pp. 34–49; quote, 47. Adrien Jolliet in this instance is often mistaken for his more famous brother; e.g., Gravier, *Cavelier de La Salle,* p. 20.

26. Concerning the name Lachine (originally La Petite Chine) see Chesnel, *Cavelier de La Salle,* 31–32n.

27. "Mémoire sur le projet du sieur de la Salle pour la descouverte de la partie occidentale de l'Amérique septentrionale entre la Nouvelle-France, la Floride et le Mexique," in Margry, *Découvertes,* 1:330. See Parkman, *La Salle,* pp. 743–45, and Chesnel, *Cavelier de La Salle,* pp. 33–35.

28. Jean Delanglez, *Some La Salle Journeys,* p. 99. See especially Delanglez's chapter "La Salle and the Ohio," pp. 3–39. Renaudot's principal contribution to the early mythical discoveries is "Entretiens de Cavelier de La Salle sur ses onze premières années en Canada," in Margry, *Découvertes,* 1:345–401, which includes (pp. 376–401) the "Histoire de M. de La Salle." Whereas Margry speculates on Renaudot's authorship, Delanglez deals with the matter convincingly in *Some La Salle Journeys,* p. 23.

29. Osler, *La Salle,* pp. 31–34; Talon, "Au Roy: Memoire sur le Canada," Nov. 10, 1670, AN, Colonies, C^{11a} 3, f. 106v.

30. Talon to king, Nov. 2, 1671, ibid., f. 161v (quote), extracted in Margry, *Découvertes,* 1:92. Osler, *La Salle,* pp. 36–37.

31. Delanglez, *Some La Salle Journeys,* pp. 70–71; Osler, *La Salle,* pp. 158–59. The two clerics enjoyed a close relationship with the Royal Court, notably with Esprit Cabart de Villermont, a linguist, geographer, and member of the King's Council; François de Callières, one of the king's private secretaries; and sieur Morel (first name not found), successor to La Salle's extortioner, François Bellinzani. Information on the religious brotherhoods and Bellinzani was graciously provided by Marcel Lussier of Brossard, Que. Chesnel (*Cavelier de La Salle,* p. 85) describes Renaudot as "one of the most distinguished erudites of the Seventeenth Century," a learned orientalist and a profound theologian.

32. "Histoire de M. de La Salle," in Margry *Découvertes,* 1:378–79 (complete in pp. 376–90), following the first part of the document, which begins on p. 345. For a discussion of the "Histoire," see Justin Winsor, ed., *Narrative and Critical History of America* 4:207; Delanglez, *Some La Salle Journeys,* pp. 23–29. Delanglez (idem), noting that the item ascribes neither date nor authorship, postulates that it was written after 1683. Doubtful.

33. Parkman, *La Salle,* pp. 744–45. Heidenreich, "Early French Exploration in the North American Interior," in John L. Allen, ed., *North American Exploration: A Continent Defined,* 2:125.

34. For a characterization of the Jesuit-hating and imperious Frontenac, see Justin Winsor, *From Cartier to Frontenac: Geographical Discovery in the Interior of North America in Its Historical Relations, 1534–1700,* pp. 232–33; also Coulter, *La Salle.* Frontenac (to Colbert, 1677, in Margry, *Découvertes,* 1:300–25) alleges that almost all the internal troubles of New France stemmed from the ambition of the Ecclesiastics (i.e., Jesuits).

35. "Relation de la descouverte de plusieurs pays situez au midi de la Nouvelle-France, faite en 1673," in Margry, *Découvertes,* 1:263. Several adherents of La Salle in his own time questioned or belittled the Jolliet expedition. In the narrative attributed to Father Anastase Douay (in Cox, *Journeys,* 1:257), appears the claim that the expedition descended the Mississippi no farther than 40 leagues below the Illinois—"about midway between the River Ouabache [Ohio] and that of the Massourites River" (to "Cape St. Anthony"). See also José Antonio Pichardo, *Pichardo's Treatise on the Limits of Louisiana and Texas,* ed. Charles Wilson Hackett,

1:234. "Histoire de M. de La Salle" (Margry, *Découvertes,* 1:398, 437) relates that the Jesuits sent Jolliet to France with a "map made from hearsay. This imposture did not redound to [his] honour." An anonymous account titled "Voyage of M. de La Salle à la rivière Mississipi" (idem, 2:102) discounts Jolliet's data, implying that he went no farther than a day and a half's journey from Fort Crèvecoeur). A La Salle letter fragment (idem, 170) faults Jolliet for a "huge mistake" in his map showing the Illinois river flowing west into the Mississippi, when it actually flows south, and the Mississippi flowing from north to south at that point.

36. See Heidenreich, "Early French Exploration," 128–130.

37. Leroy J. Politsch, "The Ellington Stone," unpublished manuscript; "The Ellington Stone," in *Iliniwek* 3, no. 3 (May–June, 1965), 20–21, 24. Daniel Spurr (*River of Forgotten Days: A Journey Down the Mississippi in Search of La Salle,* pp. 110–26, *passim*) discusses Politsch ("The Keeper of the Stone"), his research, and his ideas, which I have discussed with Politsch by telephone on numerous occasions.

38. A letter dated January 21, 1756, by a La Salle kinswoman, with which were sent maps and documents to show that "La Salle had already made two journeys of exploration" by 1675 and may have reached the Mississippi, has failed to settle the question. See Margry, *Découvertes,* 1:379n, and Parkman, *La Salle,* 745n.2. The writer was "Madeleine Cavelier, Dame Leforestier [Le Forestier]," whom both Margry and Parkman refer to as La Salle's niece. Such a relationship is denied by Cyprien Tanguay (*Dictionnaire généalogique des familles Canadiennes depuis la fondation de la colonie jusqu'a nos jours,* 4:108, 235): Marie-Madeleine Cavelier, was born December 18, 1656, to Robert Cavelier, a Montreal gunsmith; she was married in 1670 to Antoine Forestier, a surgeon, and appears to have born him nineteen children. "Aged and illiterate" (says Parkman), she was, as Tanguay shows, ninety-nine years of age when she wrote(?) to her nephew, "M. Le Bailiff," the letter that has been taken both as proof that La Salle reached the Mississippi in the early 1670s and that he did not. Margry (*Découvertes,* Introduction to vol. 1, BHC reel 1, 31–32) claims to have traced the La Salle manuscripts and maps and to have found "what remained of the papers of the discoverer of Louisiana." Presumably, they are among those published in his work. The material sent by Madame Leforestier to her nephew in 1756, however, has not appeared since.

CHAPTER 3. "A STEP FROM MADNESS"

1. Parkman, *La Salle,* p. 778; Heidenreich, "Early French Exploration," p. 131.

2. "Lettres patentes de concession du fort de Frontenac et terres adjacentes au profit du sieur de la Salle," Compiègne, May 13, 1675, in Margry, *Découvertes,* 1:283–86; "Lettres de noblesse pour le sieur Cavelier de la Salle," idem, 286–88. See also Osler, *La Salle,* 62–63. The Prince de Conti married Marie-Anne de Bourbon, daughter of Louis XIV and Louise de La Vallière. Marie-Ann was the sister of Louis de Bourbon, Comte de Vermandois, Grand Admiral of France from 1669 to 1683, when he died at the age of 16. Mitford, *Sun King,* 124–129, 140. Vermandois's name appears with his crest on the three bronze connon retrieved from the wreckage of the *Belle* in 1995. See Fig. 6.

3. At Paris on April 5, 1675, La Salle gave his brother-in-law, Nicolas Crevel, *greffier* ("clerk") of the Ville de Rouen, a note acknowledging receipt of 1,148 livres in

cash and linen cloth "to be spent on goods to be sent to Canada . . . at the profit, risk, and expense of said sieur de Crevel. . . ." Margry, *Découvertes,* 1:280.

4. Parkman, *La Salle,* p. 788.

5. Frontenac to Colbert, 1677, in Margry, *Découvertes,* 1:302; complete document, pp. 300–25.

6. "Histoire de M. de La Salle" (Margry, *Découvertes,* 1:389–90) attributes this deed to "one named Nicolas Perrot, otherwise known as Joly-Coeur." This *dit* name (nickname), however, was widely used among Canadian families of the period. Although a Joly-Coeur appears on the Fort Frontenac roster (idem, pp. 296–98), the would-be assassin certainly was not the famed voyageur Nicolas Perrot, who has been confused also with François-Marie Perrot, the Montreal governor ousted by Frontenac. Compare Parkman, *La Salle,* pp. 755, 798; Osler, *La Salle,* 56–63; John Upton Terrell, *La Salle: The Life and Times of an Explorer,* 57, 66, 93–94.

7. "Memoir sur le projet du sieur de la Salle," in Margry, *Découverte,* 1:330–35. Quote is from Parkman, *La Salle,* 802.

8. *Histoire de M. de La Salle,* 390; Colbert to Duchesneau, Apr. 28, 1677, ibid., 329; La Salle, "A Nos Seigneurs les commissaires deputez par Sa Majesté pour l'instruction du procès du sieur Belizani" [1684?], idem, 338–40; "Extrait des registres de la Cour des aydes," Paris, May 8, 1685, idem, 341. See also Chesnel, *Cavelier de La Salle,* pp. 76–77.

9. "Lettres patentes," Saint-Germain-en-Laye, May 12, 1678, in Margry, *Découvertes,* 1:337 (italics added). Chesnel (*Cavelier de La Salle,* 77) dates the instrument as May 22.

10. "Obligation du sieur de La Salle envers le sieur Plet," Paris, June 28, 1678, Margry, *Découvertes,* 1:425.

11. "Autres emprunts de Cavelier de La Salle pour son enterprise," ibid., pp. 427–32; "Extrait du mémoire au Roy," 1683, idem, pp. 423–24.

12. La Salle, "A Nos Seigneurs les commissaires." ibid., pp. 338–40; [François Plet], "Opposition mise sur les biens de Bellinzani, au nom de M. de La Salle," Paris, May 8, 1685, idem, p. 341.

13. Nicolas de La Salle's account of the Mississippi expedition is in Margry *Découvertes,* 1:545–70, discussed by Patricia Galloway, "Sources of the La Salle Expedition of 1682," in Galloway, ed., *La Salle and His Legacy: Frenchmen and Indians in the Lower Mississippi Valley,* p. 27; see also Jay Higginbotham, *Old Mobile: Fort Louis de la Louisiane, 1702–1711,* p. 35. Jean-Baptiste Minet ("Journal," p. 35, in Weddle, ed., *La Salle*) names Tonti, Le Page, Timbalier, Nicolas de La Salle, La Motte, and Mousignac as being among La Salle's group, plus six other volunteers and hired men and four women, a total of eighteen. La Salle's nephew Colin Crevel (later referred to as sieur de Moranget) may also have been in the group. Henri de Tonti was the son of Lorenzo de Tonti and Isabelle di Lietto, who had sought asylum in France after Lorenzo's involvement in an unsuccessful revolt against the Spanish viceroy in Naples about 1650. In 1653 he presented his "tontine" system of life annuity to Cardinal Mazarin. The failure of this scheme in 1669 is said to have landed him in the Bastille, where he remained eight years. A number of Henri's relatives, including his younger brother, Alphonse, and several cousins and nephews, made names for themselves in New France and French Louisiana. *Dictionary of Canadian Biography,* 3:631–36.

14. [Renaudot], "Entretiens de Cavelier de La Salle sur ses onze premières années en Canada," in Margry, *Découvertes,* 1:345–401, including "Histoire de M. de La

Salle," pp. 376–401; Bernou to Renaudot, Rome, Apr. 11, 1684, idem, 3:82–84.

15. Mitford, *Sun King,* pp. 83–93.

16. La Salle [to Thouret], Sept. 29, 1680, in Margry, *Découvertes,* 2:67.

17. La Salle letter, Aug. 22, [1681], Margry, *Découvertes,* 2:229; BHC reel 1. This letter, written from Fort Frontenac, is misdated 1682, an error made clear by the context. Before writing it, La Salle had learned of the death of Thouret, to whom the letter of September 29, 1680, was written (see preceding note). Thouret and François Plet had consigned merchandise to La Salle that was lost with the *Griffon.* David Levin (ed.), in Parkman, *La Salle,* p. 953n., thinks the present letter was to Bernou. Winsor *(Narrative and Critical History,* 4:225n.4), apparently going only by the erroneous date, describes the August 22 letter as "detailing [La Salle's] experiences" on the Mississippi. Actually, the letter mentions the voyage as forthcoming.

18. La Salle, letter, Aug. 22 [1681], pp. 230–31; La Motte letter, idem, pp. 7–9. The explorer, as time would tell, seems never to have entertained much sympathy for the physically unfit.

19. Louis Hennepin, *A Description of Louisiana,* pp. 86–87. Hennepin, "the most impudent of liars" in Parkman's view (*La Salle,* p. 811), is judged more truthful in this his first work. His self-serving embellishments appear for the most part in his writings after La Salle's death.

20. See Andrew H. Brown, "New St. Lawrence Seaway Opens the Great Lakes to the World," *National Geographic* 115, no. 3 (Mar., 1959): 299–339. The actual difference in the mean level of Lake Erie and Lake Ontario is 324 feet. *The Congressional Digest* 25 (Jan.–Dec., 1946): 227. For a discussion of the navigational impediments confronting La Salle, see "Voyage de M. de La Salle à la rivière Mississippi," in Margry, *Découvertes,* 2:93–95; for his descriptions of the Indians, other Europeans, and the country, idem, pp. 95–102.

21. For the opening of the seaway, see remarks of Senator Kenneth B. Keating of New York in *Congressional Record* (Senate), 86th Congress, first session, vol. 105, part 5: 6768 (Apr. 30, 1959), followed by those of Wisconsin Senator Alexander Wiley, 6768–69; also of Senator Stephen M. Young of Ohio, idem, part 9: 11414 (June 22, 1959). Keating read into the record an editorial of the previous Saturday's New York *Herald Tribune,* which referred to the seaway as "the opening of one of man's greatest triumphs over geography," noting that "the Great Lakes and the St. Lawrence formed one of the great routes into North America from the days of the first explorers—a route that vied with the Mississippi-Missouri-Ohio complex and the Hudson-Mohawk link. . . . The bateaux of the French voyagers and their big bark canoes took adventurers and missionaries, fur-traders and soldiers, on the great looping circuit that once threatened to pin the English colonies to their strip of seacoast behind the Appalachians." La Salle's "triumph over geography" escaped notice.

22. Marion A. Habig, *The Franciscan Père Marquette: A Critical Biography of Father Zénobe Membré, O.F.M., La Salle's Chaplain and Missionary Companion, 1645 (ca.)–1689;* biographical note on Membré in Shea, ed., *Discovery of the Mississippi Valley,* pp. 147–48, accompanying Membré's narrative of Fort Crèvecoeur.

23. Hennepin, *Description of Louisiana,* pp. 87–90; La Salle, letter, Aug. 22, [1681], p. 214; Villiers, *L'expédition,* p. 23; Delanglez, *Journal of Jean Cavelier,* pp. 27–30.

24. Delanglez, *Journal of Jean Cavelier,* pp. 27–30. La Salle's judgment of the man seems to vary. See his letter to Thouret cited in note 15.

25. Hennepin, *Description,* pp. 92–97, 102–104; "Relation des descouvertes et des voyages du sieur de La Salle," 1679–81, in Margry, *Découvertes,* 1:449. This document (complete in pp. 436–544), which Margry calls "Relation officielle," is attributed to Abbé Bernou. It contains almost all the letter to Thouret of September 29, 1680. See notes 15, 16. La Salle enclosed in his letter of August 22 [1681] a copy of the Thouret letter (idem, 2:222), an indication that Bernou was the recipient. See Parkman, *La Salle,* in Levin, ed., *France and England,* 1:953n.

26. Hennepin, *Description,* p. 105.

27. Hennepin (ibid., pp. 131–33), describes the building of the fort and a chapel. Quote is on p. 132.

28. "Relation de Henri de Tonty" in Margry, *Découvertes,* 1:581, 583; Fort Frontenac review, idem, p. 396.

29. Moyse Hillaret, "Declaration faite par devant le sieur Duchesneau," Aug. 17, 1680, in Margry, *Découvertes,* 2:108–109.

30. Fort Crèvecoeur seems to have been named for the Netherlands stronghold that the French had captured in 1672 and recently demolished, not for the "heartbreak"—*crève-coeur*—that had yet to occur. Compare Coulter, *La Salle,* p. 61, and Gravier, *Cavelier de La Salle,* p. 16.

31. See Robert S. Weddle, *Spanish Sea: The Gulf of Mexico in North American History, 1500–1685,* pp. 150–54.

32. Membré, "Narrative of the Adventures of La Salle's Party at Fort Crevecoeur," in Shea, ed., *Discovery and Exploration of the Mississippi Valley,* pp. 148–49. La Salle, in his letter covering the period from August 22, 1680, to autumn of 1681, in Margry, *Découvertes,* 2:125, describes d'Autray as having always been very faithful, saying he was the son of the first *procureur-général* of Quebec (Jean Bourdon). See also Parkman, *La Salle,* p. 855n. "Collin" probably was La Salle's nephew Colin Crevel de Moranget.

33. Hillaret, "Declaration"; "La Salle Arrête Ses Déserteurs," July, 1680, in Margry, *Découvertes,* 2:103–108.

34. Delanglez, *Journal of Jean Cavelier,* pp. 28–30. The letters La Salle received from France are not at hand, but their content is evident from those he wrote in reply. See especially the letter of September 29, 1680, to "one of his associates" (Thouret) and that of August 22, [1681]. See also Membré, "Narrative," p. 161.

35. La Salle [to Thouret], p. 87.

36. "La Salle Arrête Ses Déserteurs." Chesnel, *Cavelier de La Salle,* pp. 120–21; Parkman, *La Salle,* pp. 855–56; Membré, "Narrative," p. 161. Minet ("Voyage," in Weddle, ed., *La Salle,* 35) identifies the slain men as Bois d'Ardenne and "a carpenter," saying that two others were imprisoned for four months. Among those assisting La Salle was Nicolas Crevel, a soldier at Fort Frontenac, probably the natural son of La Salle's brother-in-law of the same name in Rouen and half-brother of Colin Crevel de Moranget. Nicolas Crevel returned to France in 1688 with Joutel ("Voyage," p. 533).

37. La Salle, letter, Aug. 22, [1681], pp. 225–26.

38. La Forest, who had come from France with La Salle in 1675 to command Fort Frontenac, in later years became Tonti's partner in the fur trade at Fort-Saint-Louis-des-Illinois, then governor and proprietor of the post. In 1702 he married Charlotte-Françoise Juchereau, widowed sister of Louis Juchereau de Saint-Denis. He became commandant at Detroit in 1710 and died at Quebec in 1714. René Jetté, *Dictionanaire généalogique des familles du Québec,* p. 310; *Dictionary of Ca-*

nadian Biography 2:169–70. On June 10, 1679, La Salle granted La Forest the island of Belle-Isle, "at the entrance of Lake Frontenac." In the concession document (Margry, *Découvertes*, 2:21), La Salle refers to "the voyage that we are going to make for the discovery of La Louisiane," the first recorded use of that name. La Forest, says Franke (*French Peoria*, pp. 17, 60), was Tonti's cousin—one of several Tonti kin involved in the fur trade.

39. Barbier's name and his *dit* name (Minime) are frequently confused, a common occurrence in this period. Even those who knew him well often referred to him as Gabriel Minime. In the "Relation de descouvertes" he is called Gabriel Minime, le Barbier ("Gabriel Minime, the barber"). Properly, he was Barbier *dit* Minime, Minime being a *nom de guerre* meaning "Tiny." Evidently Barbier was either very small or very large.

40. La Salle [to Thouret], in Margry, *Découvertes,* 2:73–74; letter fragment in ibid (quoted passage, p. 202).

41. Paul Frederic Hundley, "The Construction of the Griffin Cove Wreck" (master's thesis), p. 56.

42. Harrison John MacLean, *The Fate of the* Griffon, pp. 3, 69, 71–72 (quote). MacLean (idem, pp. 13–14) learned that one of his former editors had investigated another reported *Griffon* find, on Manitoulin Island, in 1927, but threaded bolts—anachronistic for La Salle's time—and an abundance of iron, which La Salle did not have—ruled out its identification as the *Griffon*. See also Chesnel, *Cavelier de La Salle,* p. 124 and n.)

43. MacLean, *Fate of the* Griffon, pp. 75–76; Murphy's drawings, pp. 88, 12; Hennepin's, pp. 40–41. See also Gordon Young, "The Great Lakes: Is It Too Late?" *National Geographic* 144, no. 2 (Aug., 1973): 164–65.

44. Hundley, "Construction," pp. 1, 98, 92.

45. "Relation du voyage de Cavelier de La Salle du 22 Aout 1680 a l'automne de 1681," in Margry, *Découvertes,* 2:130, as translated in Parkman, *La Salle,* p. 861. Parkman, (idem, pp. 861–62) refers to La Salle's conjecture as "uncertain." Terrell (*La Salle,* p. 168) relates the episode as though it were a total massacre of the Illinois. See also Muhlstein, *La Salle,* pp. 166–68; Chesnel, *Cavelier de La Salle,* pp. 127–29; Leprohon, *Cavelier de La Salle,* pp. 165–66.

46. "Relation du voyage," p. 133. Various interpretations have been placed on this verbiage. La Salle relates that he recognized the handwriting of "Le Parisien" (Étienne Renault), who remained with Tonti. The explorer surmised that it was intended for the Frenchmen who had gone up the Mississippi, should they return.

47. Muhlstein, *La Salle,* p. 122.

CHAPTER 4. SEEDS OF CONFUSION

1. Membré, Narrative, Feb., 1680, to June, 1681, in Cox, *Journeys,* 1:121–25. See also Tonti, "Relation," in Margry, *Découvertes,* 1:587–92. Hennepin (*Description of Louisiana,* pp. 269–70) gives a different account of La Ribourde's death, attributing his slaying to the "Onnontaguez Iroquois."

2. Parkman, *La Salle,* p. 912.

3. Ibid., p. 913.

4. Letter summary, Duchesneau to the minister, Nov. 13, 1680, and extract of letter

from the king to Frontenac, Versailles, Apr. 30, 1681, in Margry, *Découvertes*, 2:265, 266; Membré, Narrative, p. 130.

5. See preceding chapter, note 9.

6. Order of Duchesneau, Oct. 31, 1680, in Margry, *Découvertes*, 2:110–15 (quote on p. 110).

7. "Testament fait par de La Salle avant de repartir pour achever son entreprise," Aug. 11, 1681, ibid., 2:163–64 (my translation). Compare translation in Thomas Falconer, *On the Discovery of the Mississippi, and on the South-Western, Oregon, and North-Western Boundary of the United States*, pp. 45–46 (second pagination). The preceding quote is from Parkman, *La Salle*, p. 219.

8. Order of Duchesneau, July 14, 1682, in Margry, *Découvertes*, 2:193–96.

9. Ibid., 195.

10. La Salle, letters, autumn, 1681, ibid., p. 158, and Sept. 29, 1679 [to Thouret], ibid., p. 65.

11. Tonti ("Relation," ibid., 1:594) lists the names of participants in the voyage, usually in abbreviated form. Marcel Lussier offers some correction and gives some of the names in more complete form, including the *dit* names (list in author's possession). Lussier confirms my conjecture that Colin Crevel, named by Tonti, was indeed La Salle's nephew, Colin Crevel de Moranget, who was to play an ignominious role in the Texas expedition. Nicolas de La Salle's observations, with Barbier's testimony, are the basis of Minet, "Voyage Made from Canada Inland Going Southward during the Year 1682." This account (in Weddle, ed., *La Salle*, pp. 29–68), is cited hereafter as Minet, "Voyage." It is the first part of Minet's two-part narrative. Written during La Salle's 1684 voyage to the Gulf of Mexico, it is based on interviews with Barbier and Nicolas de La Salle. The second part, cited here as Minet, "Journal," is Minet's own first-hand account. The original manuscript, including both parts, is in the Public Archives of Canada, Manuscript Division, Ottawa, Ontario (microfilm reel H-1022). Nicolas's account in Margry, *Découvertes*, 1:547–70, probably was written soon after the voyage; it is not the one prepared in 1699, at the request of the minister Louis de Pontchatrain, for the benefit of Pierre Le Moyne d'Iberville, then about to sail for Louisiana to begin the colony. For a discussion of Nicolas's writings, see Galloway, "Sources of the La Salle Expedition of 1682," pp. 17–18.

12. Membré, "Narrative," in Cox, ed., *Journeys*, p. 132; Tonti, "Relation," in Margry, *Découvertes*, 1:593. Tonti and Membré seldom agree on the various dates. The frequency of a ten-day difference in dates given in various sources during this period suggests some interpreters' conversion of the Julian Calendar to the Gregorian by which the date is advanced ten days. See also "Avis du succes de la découverte," ibid., 2:203, which dates entry of the Illinois River as January 1, 1682.

13. Color reproduction in Franke, *French Peoria*, plate 8. For the series of Catlin's paintings depicting La Salle's exploits and the story behind them, see "La Salle on the Mississippi," in American Heritage, *A Treasury of American Heritage: A selection from the first five years of the Magazine of History*, pp. 74–87.

14. Membré, "Narrative," p. 133; Tonti, "Relation," p. 595.

15. Minet, "Voyage," pp. 42–43.

16. Membré, "Narrative," p. 134; Minet, "Journal," p. 44; Nicolas de La Salle, "Relation de la descouverte que M. de La Salle a faite de la rivière de Mississipi en 1682, et de son retour jusqu'à Québec," in Margry, *Découvertes*, 1:551; Tonti, "Relation," idem, p. 596.

17. For Vega's single mention of the Chucagua, see John Grier Varner and Jeanette Johnson Varner, trans., *The Florida of the Inca,* p. 423; also Lawrence A. Clayton, et al., eds., *The De Soto Chronicles: The expedition of Hernando de Soto to North America in 1539–43,* 2:385. On Richelet and his two-volume work (*Histoire de la conquéte de la Floride, oú relation de ce qui c'est passé dans la découverte de ce pays par Ferdinand de Soto*), see idem, p. 11; also John R. Swanton, *Final Report of the United States De Soto Expedition Commission,* pp. 6, 8. La Salle's hypothesis concerning the Mississippi based on his canoe voyage comprises the so-called "Chucagua fragment," in Margry, *Découvertes,* 2:196–203.

18. Minet, "Voyage," p. 45. The fact that the two Chickasaws heeded Barbier's pistol suggests that they had had previous contact with Europeans and had learned to respect firearms.

19. Minet ("Voyage," pp. 46–47) describes in rich detail the warm reception by the "Accancea", enlarging upon the accounts of Nicolas, Tonti, and Membré. For the names and the locations of the four Arkansas villages as Joutel found them in 1687, see chapter 13.

20. "Procés-verbal de cette prise de possession au pays des Akansas," Mar. 13 and 14, 1682, in Margry, *Découvertes,* 2:181–185.

21. Minet, "Voyage," p. 49 and nn. 44, 45.

22. Tonti, "Relation," p. 602. See Nicolas Sanson's map *La Floride,* Fig. 10. A similar map from an atlas published by Sanson's nephew Pierre Du Val *(Le Monde ou la Géographie),* in 1663, is reproduced in Peter H. Wood, "La Salle: Discovery of a Lost Explorer," *American Historical Review* 89, no. 2 (Apr., 1984): 300. The statement attributed to Tonti that the identification of the river as the Escondido was later found to be correct is certainly in error.

23. Minet, "Voyage," p. 65.

24. The name Río del Espíritu Santo originated with the map sketch of Alonso Álvarez de Pineda, who approached the Mississippi's mouth on the feast day of the Holy Spirit, or Pentecost, in June, 1519 (AGI, Mapas y Planos, Mexico 5). In all likelihood, the Spanish explorer saw no more than the silt-laden effluent. His depiction of a small bay, therefore, was conjectural. Later mapmakers enlarged the bay, gave it a different configuration, and, in some instances, showed multiple streams flowing into it rather than just one. Robert S. Weddle, "Coastal Exploration and Mapping: A Concomitant of the *Entradas,*" in Dennis Reinhartz and Gerald D. Saxon, eds., *The Mapping of the Entradas into the Greater Southwest,* pp. 108–109, 111, 113–114. Jean Delanglez (*El Rio del Espíritu Santo*) attempts to prove that the river of his title was other than the Mississippi and declares that La Salle's writings "show beyond the shadow of a doubt" that he never identified the river he descended as the Río del Espíritu Santo because he had never heard this name applied to the river discovered by the Soto expedition. For contrary evidence, see Weddle, *Spanish Sea,* p. 229. Maps that La Salle is most likely to have used during his exploration clearly show the Río del Espíritu Santo as the continent's most prominent river.

25. Minet, "Voyage," p. 54.

26. La Salle, "Chucagua fragment," in Margry, *Découvertes,* 2:198.

27. Minet, "Voyage," pp. 55–56; Nicolas de La Salle, "Relation," pp. 561–62; Membré, "Narrative," p. 145. The difference in the water is understandable; the volume of the river's discharge sends a stream of fresh water far out into the Gulf. The Membré letter cited here comes from Chrétien Le Clercq (*Premier établissement*

de la foi dans la Nouvelle France, 1691). Le Clercq is said to have embellished the role of the Récollet friar (as well as others). Compare the authentic Membré letter in Margry, *Découvertes,* 2:206–12. Whereas the Le Clercq version places Membré with Tonti on his exploration of the river mouth, Minet ("Voyage," 55 and n.61) shows that he was not.

28. "Mémoire," Margry, *Découverte*, 3:21. For example, Juan Jordán de Reina, "Diario y derrotero del viaxe," Mar. 16, 1686, AGI, Mexico 616, BTHC. The Spanish diarist, at North Pass, called it Río de la Palizada for the logs that obstructed the mouth and affixed the name Cabo de Lodo (Mud Cape) to the adjacent promontory. See also Carlos de Sigüenza y Góngora in Irving Leonard, ed., *Spanish Approach to Pensacola*, 180; Richebourg Gaillard McWilliams, "Iberville at the Birdfoot Subdelta: Final Discovery of the Mississippi River," in John Francis McDermott, ed., *Frenchmen and French Ways in the Mississippi Valley,* pp. 127–40. None of the La Salle sources mentions having actually sounded any of the Mississippi passes. Richard Condrey of the Louisiana State University Department of Oceanography and Coastal Sciences/Costal Fisheries has prepared from original accounts a map showing the lower Mississippi delta as it might have looked two to three centuries ago: "The Last Natural Delta of the Mississippi River 1687–1785 as Described by [Enríquez] Barroto, Iberville, and [José de] Evia."

29. "Procès-verbal de prise de possession de la Louisiane, à l'embouchure de la mer ou golfe du Mexique," Apr. 9, 1682, in Margry, *Découvertes,* 2:186–93. Translated in Cox, *Journeys,* 1:159–70; B. F. French, *Historical Collections of Louisiana and Florida,* 2nd series, pp. 17–27; Falconer, *Discovery*, pp. 35–44 (second pagination); and elsewhere. The report was transcribed by the notary, Jacques de La Métairie, and signed by La Salle and twelve other members of the expedition. The River of Palms (Río de las Palmas), presently known as the Rio de Soto la Marina, empties into the Gulf of Mexico at La Pesca, Tamaulipas, Mexico; a southern branch still carries the name Río de las Palmas. Jean Delanglez ("A Calendar of La Salle's Travels, 1643–1683," in Mildred Mott Wedel, ed., *A Jean Delanglez, S.J., Anthology: Selections Useful for Mississippi Valley and Trans-Mississippi American Indian Studies*, p. 301) places the act of possession near present-day Venice, Louisiana. A monument to the event stands at historic Fort Jackson on Plaquemine Bend between Buras and Bootheville.

30. Minet, "Voyage," 58 (quote);, Nicolas de La Salle, "Relation," 564. Tonti ("Relation, 607) reveals the role of Crevel [de Moranget], the only mention of La Salle's nephew in any of the accounts, but says nothing of the relationship.

31. La Salle letter to "one of his friends," Michilimackinac, Oct., 1682, in Margry, *Découvertes,* 2:288. Tonti, "Relation, ibid.," 1:611; BHC, reel 1:651.

32. See the preceding note 17. The fragment, in BN, Clairambault 1016, 188–189v, is printed in Margry, *Découvertes,* 2:196–203. Wood ("La Salle," pp. 294–323) analyzes this crucial document and La Salle's geographical concepts, surveys the sources, and offers a critique of published accounts. His analysis and the reasons for La Salle's later passing up the true Mississippi for a landing in Texas are supported by Weddle, *French Thorn,* with additional documentation, including both parts of the Minet treatise. Louis De Vorsey, Jr. ("La Salle's Cartography of the Lower Mississippi: Product of Error or Deception?" pp. 14–18), puts forth a rather specious argument in contravention of Wood's "Lost Explorer" thesis, favoring instead the "geographical hoax hypothesis." Although Bernou's influ-

ence on La Salle's future undertaking does raise the question, De Vorsey's failure to develop this aspect of the matter renders his case less than convincing.

33. Wood, "La Salle," p. 301. Delanglez (*El Rio del Espíritu Santo,* p. 103) declares that La Salle had with him the Sanson-Jaillot map of 1674, a detail of which he reproduces as plate 8. This map does not show the Río Escondido, the central feature of La Salle's hypothesis.

34. [La Salle], "Chucagua fragment," p. 198. The Florida of that period extended to the border of the New Spain province of Pánuco, south of the Río de las Palmas.

35. Weddle, "Coastal Exploration and Mapping;" also Robert S. Weddle, "Exploration of the Texas Coast: Álvarez de Pineda to La Salle," in *Gulf Coast Historical Review* 8, no. 1 (fall, 1992): 31–41. The only known voyage that might have provided the information is that of Álvarez de Pineda of 1519. A stream called Río de Magdalena (or a variant thereof) was sometimes shown in place of the Escondido, sometimes as a separate stream.

36. Delanglez, *Some La Salle Journeys,* pp. 11, 50.

37. Delanglez (ibid., p. 27) failed to understand this point, saying that La Salle, after parting from the Dollier expedition in 1669, could not compute the longitude because Galinée had taken the instruments with him, and "only trained astronomers . . . were able to determine the longitude in those days." See also Gaither, *Fatal River,* p. 288 (referring to a different La Salle journey): "For finding their longitude, they had the old compass and inaccurate tables.") Galinée ("Récit," pp. 125–26) tells of using a Jacob's staff (cross-staff) to take the *latitude* by sighting on the sun on August 26, 1669. With "a very clear horizon," he found the zenith distance to be 33°, which he adjusted for declination to compute 43°12' N. If, as supposed, the sighting was at Irondoquoit Bay on the south shore of Lake Ontario "a hundred leagues southwest of Montreal," the calculation was no more than a few miles off. Gaither (*Fatal River,* p. 43) concludes that the instrument used was the "newer and somewhat improved Davis Back Staff," which enabled the observer to have the sun at his back.

38. La Salle, letter, Fort Frontenac, Aug. 22, [1681], in Margry, *Découvertes,* 2:248. Compare Gaither, *Fatal River,* p. 174. Wood ("La Salle," p. 300) claims that "Longitude played a secondary role in his [La Salle's] calculations throughout his travels." This is not to deny the difference that an accurate longitude computation would have made in La Salle's conclusions, or that an understanding of the lack renders more plausible his subsequent error in seeking his river from the Gulf. For development of the technology for computing longitude from celestial observation, see Derek Howse, *Greenwich time and the discovery of the longitude;* also Dava Sobel, *Longitude: The True Story of a Lone Genius Who Solved the Greatest Scientific Problem of His Time.*

39. Samuel Eliot Morison (*The European Discovery of America: The Northern Voyages,* pp. 151–53) describes the technique for obtaining latitude with the astrolabe.

40. *Procès-verbal,* Apr. 9, 1682, pp. 191–92; Tonti letter quoted in Delanglez, *El Rio del Espíritu Santo,* p. 103 (printed in French and English in Habig, *The Franciscan Père Marquette* (quote on p. 229); Membré, "Narrative," p. 146 (second quote)— perhaps another instance of Bernou's tampering. See Delanglez's treatise on "The Discovery of the Mississippi" in *Some La Salle Journeys,* pp. 42–61.

41. This is the latitude that Minet claims was taken on April 9 at the spot of dry ground three leagues above the forks, to which the explorers had withdrawn to

take formal possession. This information, however, is only Minet's assumption after learning La Salle's intended destination during the 1684 voyage. It conflicts sharply with the *procès-verbal* and the understanding of those present on the Mississippi River exploration.

42. Wood, "La Salle," p. 295.

43. Delanglez, *El Río del Espíritu Santo*, p. 104n; Wood, "La Salle," p. 300n; Jean Delanglez, "La Salle's Expedition of 1682," in *Mid-America* 22, no. 1 (Jan., 1940; new series, vol. 11): 3.

44. Delanglez, *Río del Espíritu Santo*, pp. 105, 108. For proof that Hernando de Soto's *río grande* (i.e., the Mississippi) was understood by his followers to be the Río del Espíritu Santo, see Luis de Moscoso Alvarado to the king (Emperor Charles V), Mexico, Oct. 16 and 17, 1543, AGI, Mexico 95, ramo 3, quoted in Weddle, *Spanish Sea*, p. 229. While interpreters of the Soto *entrada* treat *río grande* as a proper name, Moscoso does not; he writes of "*un río grande . . .* called Río del Espíritu Santo."

45. Wood, "La Salle," pp. 294–95.

CHAPTER 5. THE PAWN GAME

1. Minet, "Voyage," pp. 62–63; Nicolas de La Salle, "Relation," pp. 569–70. The chronology here is obscure. The leader himself (letter, 1682, in Margry, *Découvertes,* 2:288) says his illness lasted forty days from May 10. See Delanglez, "Calendar," p. 303, which tentatively dates Cavelier de La Salle's departure from Fort Prudhomme as June 10–11.

2. Tonti, "Relation," Margry, *Découvertes,* 1:612–13.

3. La Salle to La Barre, Oct. 5, 1682, ibid., 2:310–11.

4. Extract of Meulle's instructions, May 10, 1682, ibid., pp. 309–10.

5. La Barre to Colbert, Nov. 12 and 14, 1682, ibid., pp. 302, 303–304.

6. Diego Dionisio de Peñalosa Briceño y Berdugo, having fled his native Peru to avoid prosecution for official misconduct, had a tumultuous career as governor of New Mexico that put him at cross purposes with the Inquisition. Fined, publicly humiliated, and exiled from New Spain, he went first to England with offers to lead the British conquest of Spanish Santo Domingo or South America. That overture rejected, he went to France, where he ultimately became involved with Abbé Bernou in a scheme to conquer northern Mexico.

7. Tonti, "Relation," Quebec, Nov. 14, 1684, p. 613. For identification and description of this anchor post of La Salle's projected trading empire, see Parkman, *La Salle,* pp. 881–82n.

8. Tonti, "Relation," pp. 613–14; Francis Parkman, *Count Frontenac and New France under Louis XIV* in *France and England,* 2:70–71. Parkman (idem) tells the unhappy result of La Barre's attempts to usurp the Illinois trade.

9. Minet, "Voyage," p. 64. "Mémoire du sieur de La Salle pour rendre compte à Mgr de Seignelay de la descouverte qu'il a faite par l'ordre de Sa Majesté," Margry, *Découvertes,* 3:19. Translation in Falconer, *Discovery,* pp. 21–34 (second pagination), and Cox, *Journeys,* 1:188–204.

10. Jean Delanglez, "Franquelin, Mapmaker," *Mid-America* 25 (1943; new series, vol. 14): 34. La Barre so claims in a letter to Colonel Dongan, Montreal, June 15, 1684, Margry, *Découvertes,* 2:345–46.

11. Delanglez, "Franquelin," pp. 33–34. La Barre's dispatches, carried by the son of La Salle's old rival Charles Le Moyne, would have included the governor's letter to the minister dated November, 1683, in Margry, *Découvertes*, 2:329–36. With this missive, in which La Barre tells of his seizure of La Salle's posts and hints of the explorer's derangement, he enclosed copies of his letters from La Salle. Concerning Radisson's somewhat checkered career, see William Henry Johnson, *French Pathfinders in North America*, pp. 187–221, *passim*. The precise date of the sailing is not known. Delanglez ("Franquelin," p. 33) places it between November 13 and 22.

12. Delanglez, "Franquelin," p. 33.

13. The date is usually given as December 23, 1683. Nicolas de La Salle ("Relation," Margry, *Découvertes*, 1:570) gives January 17, 1683 [1684]. Margry (idem, p. 570n.) believes the correct date to be January 17, 1684. Yet Abbé Bernou, in Rome, seems to have had news of La Salle's arrival (or advance news of his plans) by January 1, 1684. See reference to Bernou's January letters to Renaudot, this chapter.

14. Peñalosa's career is treated in France V. Scholes, *Troublous Times in New Mexico, 1650–1670*. Bernou's involvement in the Spaniard's schemes is revealed by his letters to Renaudot, in Margry, *Découvertes*, 3:73–87. See also the memorials detailing the exiled Spaniard's schemes, idem, pp. 44–70, and the discussion thereof in Henry Folmer, *Franco-Spanish Rivalry in North America, 1524–1763*, pp. 138–54. Three "Mémoires du compte de Pénalossa," dated January, February, and April, 1684, are in AN, Colonies C^{13c} 3, ff. 81, 87, 90., with their resumes, ff. 75–78, 90. The April memorial reveals that the Spanish turncoat was still in the picture—or thought he was—even after orders had been issued to La Salle.

15. See chapter 2, n. 29. Renaudot was publisher of the influential *Gazette de France*, which had been founded by his grandfather (Chesnel, *La Salle*, p. 85). Bernou wrote articles for the *Gazette* and the *Mecure Gallant*. His study of geography having given him expert knowledge of the existing cartography of the Gulf of Mexico, he contributed to the work of well known cartographers, notably Father Vincenzo Coronelli.

16. "Entretiens de Cavelier de La Salle sur ses onze premières années en Canada." See chapter 2, n.26.

17. Bernou to Renaudot, Apr. 11, 1684, Margry, *Découvertes*, 3:82–84. See chapter 3, n.13; BHC reel 1. "Relation des descouvertes" is in Margry, *Découvertes*, 1:435–544. Delanglez ("La Salle's Discovery of the Mississippi in 1682") goes to tedious lengths to prove Bernou's authorship of the official report, from the letters of Tonti and Membré and other sources. The report in French, titled "Relation de la decouverte de l'embouchure de la rivière Mississipi dans le Golfe de Mexique, faite par le sieur de La Salle, l'année passée 1682," is appended (pp. 28–35). By use of different type faces, Delanglez indicates the supposed sources. The report is translated in Habig, *The Franciscan Père Marquette*, pp. 244–56. Delanglez refutes Habig's conclusion that Membré authored the report. See also Winsor, *Cartier to Frontenac*, p. 286.

18. Bernou's letters to Renaudot of Jan. 1 and 25, 1684, are cited in Folmer, *Franco-Spanish Rivalry*, pp. 147, 148.

19. Bernou to Renaudot, Apr. 11; Delanglez, "La Salle's Expedition of 1682," p. 19.

20. La Salle, letter to a friend, Michilimackinac, Oct., 1682, ibid., 2:292–93; BHC reel 1.

21. Folmer, *Franco-Spanish Rivalry*, p. 144.

22. "Relation de la découverte," 1682; translation, Habig, *The Franciscan Père Marquette,* p. 253.

23. "Chucagua fragment," p. 200. Bernou to Renaudot, Rome, Feb. 29, 1684.

24. Idem, Rome, Apr. 11, 1684.

25. "Mémoire sur les affaires de l'Amérique," Margry, *Découvertes,* 3:48–55.

26. Ibid., pp. 55–63; quotes on pp. 55, 58.

27. Minet, "Voyage," p. 65 and n.85; Delanglez, "Franquelin," p. 35.

28. The memorials seeking redress for La Barre's ill treatment are in Margry, *Découvertes,* 3:17–36; those discussing the "discovery" and its follow-up, idem, 2:359–69 and 3:17–29. Both the latter are translated in Falconer, *Discovery,* pp. 3–17 and 21–34 (second pagination). Gaither, *Fatal River,* p. 201 (quote).

29. Falconer, *Discovery,* idem. Quote is on p. 23. How the plan for the new enterprise developed has been little understood, with differing interpretations offered. Timothy Severin (*Explorers of the Mississippi,* p. 148) attributes the "two-pronged plan" to Seignelay, implying that the minister recruited La Salle for the purpose — clearly not the case.

30. Bernou to Renaudot, Feb. 29, 1684, Margry, *Découvertes,* 3:74–75. My italics. Compare BHC reel 1.

31. Ibid., p. 78 (second letter, same date).

32. Ibid. Rome, Mar. 28, 1684, pp. 78–81.

33. Seignelay to Dumont, Versailles, Mar. 23, 1684, AN, Marine B2, 51:171. Margry (*Découvertes,* 2:380) misdates the document April 14, 1684, as indicated in chapter 1, n.7. La Salle's commission, as it appears in Margry, also is dated April 14; it seems unlikely that the *Joly* would be granted La Salle before he was commissioned for the voyage.

34. Bernou to Renaudot, Apr. 11, 1684, idem, pp. 83–84.

35. Idem, Mar. 28. Bernou, in 1682, had lent maps drawn by himself to Father Coronelli for the preparation of his globe (Delanglez, "La Salle's Expedition of 1682," p. 15). Folmer, (*Franco-Spanish Rivalry,* p. 146) makes the ill-considered assertion that La Salle "simply changed his map of Louisiana by redrawing the course of the Mississippi and placing its mouth two hundred leagues westwards."

36. Bernou to Renaudot, Mar. 28, p. 80; italics added.

37. Seignelay to Tarin de Cussy, Mar. 4, 1684, Margry, *Découvertes,* 3:377, and BHC reel 1 (quotes).

38. Louis XIV, "Commission pour le sieur de La Salle," Versailles, Apr. 14 [Mar. 23], 1684, Margry, *Découvertes,* 2:382–83. Margry in sorting the documents, evidently got the instruments issued on March 23 confused with those dated April 14.

39. Falconer, *Discovery,* pp. 16–17; Cox, *Journeys,* 1:186–88; "Mémoire de ce qui aura esté accordé au sieur de La Salle," Versailles, Mar. 23, 1684, Margry, *Découvertes,* 2:378–80. See Seignelay to Dumont, Mar. 23, cited in n.33.

40. Falconer, *Discovery,* p. 16.

41. In 1997, THC archeologists recovered eight iron guns, three- to six-pounders, from the site of La Salle's Texas colony on Garcitas Creek in Victoria County. These guns were among those carried to the Gulf on La Salle's chartered storeship *l'Aimable,* which was wrecked at the mouth of Matagorda Bay on February 20, 1685. (See Curtis Tunnell, "A Cache of Cannons: La Salle's Colony in Texas," p. 20 and n.2.) The four bronze four-pounders were those carried on *La Belle* when she was wrecked early in 1686, three of which have been recovered by THC. Only in the note at the end of La Salle's statement of his needs does he mention

plans for building two fortresses. His intention may have been to guard the Mississippi with fortifications on opposite banks, such as the two Spanish forts (Fort Bourbon and Fort Saint Philip) that stood on either side of the river at Plaquemine Bend after 1795. Compare Margry, *Découvertes,* 3:22; French, *Historical Collections,* p. 9; Cox, *Journeys,* 1:196; Falconer, *Discovery,* p. 27. Plan of the Plaquemine Bend forts is shown in Weddle, *Changing Tides: Twilight and Dawn in the Spanish Sea, 1763–1803,* Fig. 35, p. 226.

42. Falconer, *Discovery,* p. 17.
43. King to Dumont, Versailles, Apr. 14, 1684, AN, Marine B2, 50:177. Margry, *Découvertes,* 2:385.
44. Dumont to Seignelay, Apr. 9, 1684 (with enclosure), Marine B2, 51:210.
45. See Beaujeu to Seignelay, La Rochelle, May 30 and July 10, 1684, Margry, *Découvertes,* pp. 398–99, 304–305.
46. Tronson to [Father Hyacinthe] Lefèbvre, Mar. 12, 1684, and to Abbé Belmont, Apr. 8, 1684, ibid., pp. 353, 354.
47. Tronson to Dollier de Casson, Apr. 10, 1684, ibid., p. 354.
48. Tronson to Belmont, undated, ibid., 2:355. Compare Weddle, *French Thorn,* pp. 12, 13, and BHC reel 1.
49. Seignelay to Dumont, Versailles, Apr. 14, 1684, Margry, *Découvertes,* 2:380–81; king to La Salle, undated, idem, pp. 381–82; king to Beaujeu and king to Dumont, both dated Versailles, Apr. 14, 1684, idem, pp. 384, 385.
50. Beaujeu to Villermont, Rochefort, June 5, 1684, ibid., 428 and n.; Delanglez, *Some La Salle Journeys,* p. 88 (passage translated). Both Margry and Delanglez identify the man referred to as Peñalosa. Two other letters (same to same, June 15 and 18, 1684, in Margry, *Découvertes,* 2:433–436, 436–440) reveal the error.
51. Beaujeu to Villermont, Rochefort, June 5, Margry, *Découvertes,* 2:428; BHC reel 1.
52. Idem, Rochefort, June 15, 1684, p. 435.
53. Idem, June 18, 1684, pp. 436–37.
54. Gaither, *Fatal River,* p. 197.

CHAPTER 6. STORM FLAGS

1. Beaujeu to Cabart de Villermont, Rochefort, June 29, 1684, Margry, *Découvertes,* 2:440.
2. Ibid., pp. 440, 442n. The "affair at Algiers" refers to Beaujeu's capture and imprisonment during the Dutch War, backwash of the War of the League of Augsburg, when hostilities continued between France and Spain after Louis XIV had made peace with the other members of the "Grand Alliance." For the Dutch War in broader context, see Nancy Nichols Barker, *Brother to the Sun King: Philippe, Duke of Orléans,* pp. 144–52.
3. Beaujeu to Cabart de Villermont, Rochefort, May 21, 1684, Margry, *Découvertes,* 2:421. Beaujeu's "certificate of careening" of the *Joly,* dated May 16, 1684, and signed by him and Chevalier d'Hère, is in APR, register 1 L3 19, f. 70. Careening involved laying the ship on its side, cleaning the ballast stones, and recaulking seams.
4. Beaujeu to Cabart de Villermont, La Rochelle, June, 1684 (day not given), Margry, *Découvertes,* 2:423; Seignelay to La Salle, Versailles, June 17, 1684, idem, pp. 389–90 (La Salle's letter of May 30 not found). The minister makes clear the error in

Parkman's statement (*La Salle*, p. 960) that La Salle "had asked for two vessels and four were given to him." The explorer had to obtain the other two ships himself. Beaujeu to Villermont, Rochefort, May 21, 1684, idem, pp. 421–22.

5. See chapter 1.

6. La Salle, "Mémoire," n.p., n.d., Margry, *Découvertes*, 2:370–73; "La Salle . . . cherche a se faire rendre justice," undated, idem, 3:28–30; Parkman, *La Salle*, p. 959 (last quote).

7. "Letter of M. de La Salle," La Rochelle, July 17, 1684, Margry, *Découvertes*, 2:418.

8. "Accounts of La Salle and François Plet," ibid., pp. 414–16; BHC reel 1. Plet, from all appearances, was consolidating La Salle's debts, taking a mortgage on everything he owned or would ever own until the debt was paid.

9. "Plet Grants a Delay," ibid.

10. La Salle to "Our Lords the Commissioners Appointed by His Majesty to Investigate the Case of the sieur Belizani [*sic*]," undated, Margry, *Découvertes* 1:338–40; BHC reel 1.

11. Extract of registers of the Cour des Aides, ibid., 341–42, May 8, 1685; BHC reel 1. I am indebted to Marcel Lussier for information on Bellinzani's arrest and trial. Whereas Chastillon, in his petition for La Salle, mentions houses in the *faubourg* ("suburb") Saint-Germain, the latter plea refers to property in Saint-Cloud. It was at Saint-Cloud, on the River Seine west of Paris, that the late minister Mazarin had purchased a villa for Philippe, Duke of Orleans — definitely an upscale neighborhood. Philippe, who had a passion for building to match his brother's, expanded the villa into a grand chateau. See Barker, *Brother of the Sun King*, 54, 169–71, and illustrations 16–18 in the picture section.

12. Beaujeu to Cabart de Villermont, June, 1684.

13. Commissions in Margry, *Découvertes*, 2:386–87. Sieur d'Autray (Jacques Bourdon), one of La Salle's most trusted associates in Canada who had accompanied him down the Mississippi, was still in Canada. For reasons not apparent, he never joined La Salle's Gulf of Mexico expedition, although he influenced others to do so.

14. Beaujeu to Villermont, Rochefort, June 5 (first quote), June 15 (second quote), and June 29, 1684 (third quote), ibid., pp. 427, 433–34, 446–47.

15. See Beaujeu to Villermont, Rochefort, June 5 and 18, 1684, pp. 427, 437; Delanglez, "Franquelin," pp. 34–35; Osler, *La Salle*, p. 175.

16. Beaujeu to Villermont, La Rochelle, July 10, 1684, Margry, *Découvertes*, 2:450.

17. Beaujeu to Seignelay, Rochefort, June 21, and La Rochelle, July 10, 1684, ibid., pp. 400–402, 404–408; to Cabart de Villermont, Rochefort, June, 1684, and La Rochelle, July 10, 1684, idem, pp. 422–26, 452. See also Minet, "Journal," in Weddle, ed., *La Salle*, pp. 83–126. La Salle had asked that La Forest, upon arriving in Canada, gather his men and property and repair to the Illinois country with orders for Tonti. He then was to return to Fort Frontenac.

18. Beaujeu to Seignelay, La Rochelle, May 30, 1684, Margry, *Découvrtes*, 2:397. The word *fond*, appearing in Margry, is translated in BHC reel 1 as "head," indicating the translator's failure to recognize La Salle's true intentions. The word should be rendered here as "far end," or "farthest part."

19. Beaujeu to Seignelay, La Rochelle, May 30, 1684, Margry, *Découvertes*, 2:397–99. Beaujeu says he had heard that the minister had appointed "the sieur de Tonty" to assume command in event of La Salle's death. His reference to "men who have never made war" indicates Alphonse rather than Henri.

20. Beaujeu to Villermont, June, 1684, and June 5, 1684. (See chapter 5, n.44.)

21. Same to same, June 5, 1684, Margry, *Découvertes,* 2:430. Beaujeu, like La Salle, was a Norman.

22. Beaujeu to Villermont, June 8 and 15, 1684.

23. Same to same, June 15.

24. Beaujeu to Villermont, Rochefort, June 18, 1684, Margry, *Découvertes,* 2:436–40. Margry's note (p. 436) questions whether the date should be June 28. Beaujeu, however, tells his correspondent that "I am writing to you like a journal," which is to say, he related events as they occurred, over a period of several days; hence his telling of occurrences after the date of the letter.

25. Beaujeu to Seignelay, Rochefort, June 21, 1684, idem, pp. 400–402.

26. Seignelay to Beaujeu, Versailles, June 17, 1684, idem, pp. 388–89.

27. See note 4, this chapter.

28. Seignelay to Arnoul, June 17, 23 (first quote), 30, 1684, Margry, *Découvertes,* 2:387–88, 390–91, 391–92.

29. Beaujeu to Seignelay, July 10, 1684, idem, pp. 404–408. Text of the declaration, or memorial, is not at hand.

30. "Au sieur Arnoul," Versailles, July 5, 1684, idem, pp. 392–93.

31. Beaujeu to Villermont, June 29, 1684, idem, pp. 440–48, quotes on pp. 441–42.

32. Villermont to Renaudot, July 7, 1684; Renaudot to Villermont, undated, idem, pp. 461, 460.

33. Beaujeu to Villermont, June 29, 1684, pp. 445–46. No other mention is found of La Salle's confrontation with Saint-Michel.

34. Same to same, La Rochelle, July 10, 1684, idem, 448–52. The capes referred to are the four promontories of northwestern Spain, the most southerly of which is Cape Finistèrre.

35. See Parkman, *La Salle,* pp. 960–66.

36. "Au sieur Arnoul," Versailles, July 24, 1684, Margry, *Découvertes,* 2:394. The memorial referred to here is the "declaration" mentioned by Beaujeu in his July 10 letter; by Seignelay, pp. 405–406; and in the July 5 letter "Au sieur Arnoul." See notes 26 and 27.

CHAPTER 7. THE PARTING GUN

1. Minet, "Journal," p. 84, and "Voyage," p. 29. Minet was born in Paris in 1661. Having attained the rank of *ingeneur du roi,* he was ordered by the king in October, 1683, to undertake the secret mapping of the Spanish coast under cover of a commercial voyage with a ship belonging to Jean Massiot. Before the mission began, Spain declared war on France and the order was canceled. Minet then was assigned as fortification engineer with the La Salle expedition (BN, *NAF* 21329, f. 341). I am indebted to John de Bry (telephone conversation, Apr., 1998), for biographical data on Minet, including his first name.

2. Beaujeu to Seignelay, Rochefort, June 21, 1684. See nn. 26 and 28, the preceding chapter. "Liste des Vaisseaux, Frégattes, Bruslots et autres batiments du Port de Rochefort," 1688, APR, register 1 L3 20, f. 25r. This register entry shows *Le Joly* to be a fourth-class (mediocre) vessel built at Brest in 1671, carrying 34 cannon (rather than 36) and drawing 14 feet when fully loaded. Her capacity was 412 tuns, and, as a warship, she was to be manned by 200 men.

3. Villiers, *L'expédition*, pp. 158–59, 216–220 (Appendix); "Declaracion de Dionicio Thomas," AGI, Mexico 616, cited in Weddle, *Wilderness Manhunt*, pp. 7–14.

4. Habig, *The Franciscan Père Marquette*, p. 132.

5. Osler, *La Salle*, p. 167.

6. Nicolas Colbert, Rouen, May 27, 1684, in Margry, *Découvertes*, 2:475–76; cf. translation from the Latin in BHC, reel 1. Beaujeu (to Seignelay, undated [late 1685]) refers to "one of his [La Salle's] cousins, priests of Saint-Sulpice." Habig (*The Franciscan Père Marquette*, p. 131) identifies Abbé Chefdeville as "a relative of La Salle."

7. The Rouen merchant Chefdeville is mentioned in an entry in "Engagements pour la Louisiana," ADCM, f. 157v; July 16, 1684: "Transport par Robert Cavelier, écuyer, sieur de La Salle, gouverneur pour le roi au pays de la Louisiane, à Estienne Peloquin le jeune, marchand de la Rochelle, de la somme de 1500 livres due par François de Chefdeville, marchand de Rouen." Death of the younger Chefdeville at Petit Goâve is told by Joutel ("Voyage," p. 105), who says that he, like his brother, was a priest. Habig (*The Franciscan Père Marquette*, p. 132n.51) disagreed. Joutel ("Voyage, p. 92) says all the priests began the voyage aboard the *Joly* but for one of the Récollets who boarded the *Aimable*. Habig (p. 133) identifies the latter as Father Le Clercq. There is reason for doubt, as will be seen.

8. "Contrat d'affrétement du navire *l'Aimable*," La Rochelle, June 5, 1684, ADCM, notarial register of Rivière & Soullard, 3 E 1806[2], ff. 110v-111. Quoted portion edited from translation by John de Bry.

9. "Etat du chargement de *l'Aimable*" and "Rolle des officiers, mariniers et matelots qui composent l'equipage du vaisseau *l'Aimable* pour le voyage à la coste de Canada," ALR, B 5682, ff. 374–75. The eight cannon, destined for the Texas settlement on Garcitas Creek, were buried by Spanish General Alonso de León in 1689 and recovered by THC in 1996. See Tunnell, "A Cache of Cannons," p. 21. Almost half the twenty-two men, including Aigron, were from La Rochelle: Pierre Augustin, Debois (first carpenter), Jean Segefardois, Pierre Moreau, Bastien la Pierre, André Prevost, Jacques Bigras, Louis Crûgéon, and Elie d'Alon. From Oléron were Mingaud and Jacques Boutin; from Saint-Gilles, Pierre Georget; Tremblade, Moïse Paugron and Izaac Simonet; Audierne, Clément Normand and Mattieu Normand (possibly brothers) and Yvon Guerigenet; Bénodet, Alain Lemoine; Marennes, Sanceau Perraud; Bordeaux, Pierre Martin; and Meschers-sur-Gironde, Jean Baudry. The register does not altogether agree with La Salle's list of items that were later lost with the ship. See chapter 9.

10. Information on the Talon's marriage and Lucien's relationship with the Bourdons (father and son) has been graciously provided by Marcel Lussier of Brossard, Que., a descendant of the wedding attendant, Jacques Lussier (personal conversation, Oct. 8, 1999). Jetté, *Dictionaire* généalogique, shows all five children born at Neuville and baptized in Quebec except Lucien *fils*, who was baptized at Neuville: Marie-Élisabeth, born Sept. 9, baptized Sept. 10, 1672; Marie-Madeleine, Nov. 2, Nov. 3, 1673; Pierre, Feb. 17, Mar. 20, 1676; Jean-Baptiste, May 25, May 26, 1679; Lucien, Aug. 23, Aug. 24, 1681. The birth dates for the four older children differ from those in Tanguay (*Dictionaire Généalogique*, 1:58), where the baptismal date is given as the birth date. Correction is offered here for misinformation from the latter source in Weddle, "La Salle's Survivors."

11. Minet, "Journal," p. 84; Joutel, "Voyage," p. 92. The Talons (Talon Interrogations, in Weddle, ed., *La Salle*, p. 226) give the number of women and girls as

nine. Joutel ("Voyage," p. 259) says seven remained when he and La Salle left the settlement the last time. Marie-Élisabeth Talon had died, and probably Madame Bréman also, as the Talons had taken her young son into their family. See also Villiers, *L'expédition,* p. 164. Labaussair of Saint-Jean-d'Angély volunteered for three years (ADCM, Étude Sacré, Nicolas & Marchand, notaries, register 3 E 1711).

12. Meunier, "Declaracion," AGI, Mexico 617, BTHC.

13. Minet, "Extrait du journal de nostre voyage fait dans le golfe de Mexique," Margry, *Découvertes,* 2:591, BHC; Villiers, *L'expédition,* 159. Comparison of Minet's "Extract" with the actual journal shows the former to be a separate document with additional information and comments, rather than a mere excerpt of the journal.

14. Villiers (*L'expédition,* 217–220) lists "Liotot or Lanctot," without given name, but shows "Ruiné, soldier." There may have been two men named Ruiné, for La Salle (*procés verbal,* Apr. 18, 1686, Margry, *Découvertes,* 3:543) tells of placing a man by that name in irons aboard the *Belle,* where he presumably died.

15. "Engagements," ADCM, notary files of Rivière & Soullard, 3 E 1806(2); La Salle, *procés verbal,* Apr. 18, 1686, 539. The eleven sailors were Vivien La Treville, twenty-one, of Saujon, Saintonge; Yvon Carlot, nineteen, Audierne, Bretagne; Adrien Crugeon, twenty-four, and Jean Barteau, thirty, La Rochelle; Jean Dubeau, twenty-three, Dieppe, Normandy; Abel Grenot, thirty, d'Esnandes (?); Jean Allais, nineteen, Caen, Normandy; Alain Fougeron, nineteen, Quimper, Bretagne; Jacques Joutard, nineteen, Oléron, Aunis; and Louis Savury, Havre-de-Grâce, Normandy. Carpenters and shipwrights were Jean Morel, thirty-two, Le Havre; Antoine Chappeau, twenty-seven, Brouage, Saintonge; Pierre Couillaud, forty-four, La Rochelle; Pierre Vincent, fifty, Angoulême, Angoumois (master carpenter); François Jean, thirty-six, and Louis Belliard, forty-eight, Matha Saintonge; Claude Marcollay, nineteen, Muron, Aunis; and François Belliard, twenty-two, Rochefort. Coopers, Pierre Chaigneau, twenty-six, La Rochelle, and Pierre La Roche, twenty-two, Saint-Crepin, Saintonge; millers, Jacques Boire, thirty-two, Sables-d'Olonne, Poitou, and Guillaume Vallèe, thirty, Nantes, Bretagne; masons, Noel Lefebvres, twenty-five, Vire, Normandy, and Pierre Varachieux, thirty-five, Tournay, Angoumois; laborers and farm worker, Jean Deveneau, thirty-six, Saint-Crepin, Saintonge, ____ Lebeau, twenty-six, Moeze, Saintonge, and Jean Lespinne, eighteen, Verteuil, Angoumois; gardener, Julien Vigneau, twenty-five, Marans, Aunis; Jacques Haraudi, twenty-two, shoemaker, Thouars, Poitou; blacksmith, Jean Leuraud, thirty, Moeze, Saintonge; cannon-eer (gunner), Jacobus Nicollas, Brandenburg, Germany; ship's pilot, Jean Philix Bouillan, La Rochelle; edge-tool maker, René Pelle, thirty-four, Saumur, Anjou.

16. Gaither, *Fatal River,* p. 248 (first quote); Gabriel-Louis Jaray, "Robert Cavelier, Sieur de La Salle," trans. Marcel Moraud, *Rice Institute Pamphlet* 26, no. 1 (Jan., 1939): 36. Jaray's perspective (as director of the French National Mission Cavelier de La Salle, in 1937) is reflected in his statement (idem, p. 9) that "Cavelier de la Salle is the greatest name in the history of French America."

17. "Engagement pour deux années d'Estienne Liotot," ADCM, Rivière & Soullard, 3 E 1806(2).

18. "Etat des marchandises charées pour les isles de l'Amérique dans le caiche le St. François," La Rochelle, July 8, 1684, ALR, f. 175; "Mémoire de l'équipage le St. François," June 9, 1684, idem, f. 78. Giraud's crew consisted of Jean Lucas, as

pilot, and Abraam Dorneau, both of Avallon; Pierre Ruilia and Pierre Monbeuil of Marennes;, Jean Boutiron of Auvert; Pierre Richard, Jean Cantain, and Helié Dubois of Chaillevette. Joutel ("Voyage," pp. 91–92, 100) mentions thirty casks, or tuns, of wine; meats; and vegetables, which La Salle was sending to Saint-Domingue.

19. La Salle, *procés verbal* on the wreck of the *Aimable*, Mar. 1, 1685, and La Salle to Seignelay, Mar. 4, 1685, Margry, *Découvertes*, 2:555, 561; APR, 1 H3 5. In linking the three bronze cannon recovered from the *Belle* shipwreck in 1995–96 to the Rochefort foundry and the *Faucon*, De Bry consulted hundreds of archival documents. The fourth gun, as evidenced by its imprint in the calcareous bottom, had been removed previously from the *Belle*'s grave by persons unknown. De Bry, having researched APR extensively, concludes that early records were not properly stored and eventually were destroyed; hence the many gaps in the record. Whereas significant information on the *Aimable* and the *Saint-François* are found in ADCM-APR, only commercial vessels are listed in the Admiralty section (ALR). Neither the *Belle* nor the *Joly* is included.

20. Joutel, *Joutel's Journal of La Salle's Last Voyage*, p. 22; "Journal of the Abbé d'Esmanville after the Departure from La Rochelle," Margry, *Découvertes*, 2:510 (quote), BHC reel 1. Concerning the spelling of the abbé's name, see Villiers, *L'expédition*, 60n., and Habig, *The Franciscan Père Marquette*, p. 131 and n. 49.

21. Beaujeu to Villermont, July 10, 1984, f. 53; Machaut-Rougemont to Villermont, Rochefort, July 22, 1684, Margry, *Découvertes*, 2:454; BHC reel 1.

22. Idem. The sixty clauses, or articles, mentioned here refer to the long declaration discussed in the previous chapter, which Beaujeu refused to sign until intendant Arnoul arbitrated points of controversy.

23. Idem.

24. Letter addressed to "Madame Cavelier, widow, rue Sainte-Croix-des-Pelletiers (Rouen)," Margry, *Découvertes*, 2:470. For a translation of the full letter, see Parkman, *La Salle*, pp. 967–68.

25. Joutel, "Voyage" (see n. 6, chapter 1 herein), and *Joutel's Journal of La Salle's Last Voyage*, p. 21. Winsor (*Narrative and Critical History*, 4:240n.7) gives Joutel's age at the time of his enlistment in the army.

26. "Lettre (sans nom d'auteur)," Petit Goâve, Nov. 14, 1684, Margry, *Découvertes*, pp. 492–99; cited hereafter as "Anonymous letter." Habig, *The Franciscan Père Marquette*, p. 135.

27. Joutel, "Voyage;" Minet, "Journal"; d'Esmanville, "Journal," ibid., pp. 510–11; "Journal of the Abbé Jean Cavelier from leaving France," Margry, *Découvertes*, 2:501–509, all translated in BHC reel 1. For a penetrating assessment of Cavelier, his writings, and his motivation, see Delanglez, *Journal of Jean Cavelier*. The Membré incident is told by Habig, *The Franciscan Père Marquette*, pp. 139–40, citing Joutel, "Voyage," pp. 139–40. Joutel ("Voyage," pp. 244–45) also discusses Le Clercq's journal.

28. Beaujeu to Seignelay, Petit Goâve roadstead, Oct. 25, 1684, Margry, *Découvertes*, 2:486; letter to Madame Cavelier. Joutel ("Voyage," p. 92) is in error in placing the number who embarked at 280, which he says included the crews of the *Joly* and the *Aimable* (a total of 92), who were not to remain with the abortive colony. The *Saint François*'s crew of 8 is not mentioned.

29. Joutel ("Voyage," p. 439) says La Forest sailed at the same time as the La Salle expedition on one of the ships for Canada, carrying orders for Henri de Tonti—

not for La Forest himself, as has been indicated previously—to go down the Mississippi to its mouth to join La Salle and carry out the orders that La Salle might give him "in furtherance of his objective."

30. Joutel, "Voyage," p. 93; Cavelier, "Journal," p. 501.

31. Anonymous letter, pp. 492–93; Joutel, "Voyage," p. 93 (quote); La Salle to Seignelay, summary [Rochefort], Aug. [1], 1684, Margry, *Découvertes,* 2:469.

32. Margry, *Découvertes,* pp. 469–70.

33. Beaujeu to Seignelay, on board the *Joly,* Aug. 2 *(sic)*, 1684, ibid., pp. 408–10.

34. Minet, Journal, p. 85.

35. Bernou to Renaudot, Rome, Sept. 9, 1684, Margry, *Découvertes,* 3:85–87.

CHAPTER 8. VOYAGE OF DESTINY

1. *"Les capres Ostendois,"* as they are called in the anonymous letter (p. 493); BHC: "Ostend privateers." The writer associated them with the northwest Belgian seaport of Ostend.

2. Joutel, "Voyage," p. 94 (quote); anonymous letter, p. 494.

3. Idem. The following paragraphs are synthesized from this source and Joutel.

4. Joutel, "Voyage," pp. 95, 96.

5. Anonymous letter, p. 496.

6. Beaujeu to Seignelay, Petit Goâve roadstead, Oct. 25, 1684 (quote), Margry, *Découvertes,* 2:485–86; BHC reel 1. Both September 27 and September 28 are given for the arrival of the *Joly* "before Petit Goâve."

7. Anonymous letter, p. 496.

8. "Journal du premier Octobre 1684" (one of four surviving pages of the *Belle*'s logbook), J. F. Jamison, trans., Appendix, Hackett, *Historical Documents,* pp. 477, 479. [Captain Durand, the anonymous letter writer says (p. 492), was to carry his letter to France, via the Windward Islands.] The *Belle*'s log reveals that Thibault, a volunteer from La Salle's hometown of Rouen who had traveled with Joutel to La Rochelle, sailed on the *Belle*. Imprecise punctuation in Joutel ("Voyage," p. 192) has led to the conclusion here and there that Thibault was a surgeon. No instance of his having served as such is found in any of the documents, although he may have been assigned to the *Belle* to serve in that capacity. His death is told in Joutel, "Voyage," pp. 200–201. The *Belle*'s pilot refers to the *Joly* as the *amiral* ("admiral's flagship") because she was the lead vessel as far as Petit Goâve. There was no designated flagship for the voyage.

9. Cavelier, "Journal," p. 502.

10. Villiers, *L'expédition,* pp. 161, 164; Joutel, "Voyage," p. 191.

11. Joutel, "Voyage," pp. 99–100; Habig, *The Franciscan Père Marquette,* p. 140.

12. Le Clercq, *First Establishment of the Faith in New France,* trans. John Gilmary Shea. Concerning Joutel's criticism of Le Clercq's account, see "Voyage," p. 110 and note (which is incorporated into the text in BHC reel 1); also p. 113 and n., pp. 190–91. Chrétien Le Clercq was a kinsman of Father Maxime Le Clercq.

13. Minet, "Journal," p. 85.

14. Saint-Laurent and Bégon to the king (extract), Jan. 25, 1685, Margry, *Découvertes,* 2:499–501; Joutel, "Voyage," p. 100. Abbé Cavelier ("Journal de l'Abbé Jean Cavelier depuis le depart de France," Margry, *Découvertes,* 2:502) says the ketch was at anchor near Cap François or Port-de-Paix when taken by Spanish free-

booters. Minet ("Journal," p. 87) says she was anchored at Port-de-Paix. The capture is related also in depositions given in Mexico by both Pierre Meunier ("Declaracion," Mexico City, Aug. 19, 1690, AGI, Mexico 617) and Jean L'Archevêque ("Declaracion de los Franceses en Mexico," Mexico City, June 10, 1689, AGI, Mexico 616, BTHC; translated in O'Donnell, *La Salle's Occupation of Texas,* p. 23). Whereas Meunier attributes the deed to four *piraguas,* others claim there were only two.

15. Minet, "Extrait du journal," p. 592 (first quote); Minet, "Journal," p. 86 (second quote).

16. Beaujeu to Seignelay, Oct. 25, pp. 485–92; quotes on pp. 486, 487. Whereas Beaujeu, writing on October 25, says Cussy and Saint-Laurent were expected daily from Port-de-Paix, Joutel (Voyage, p. 100) and Minet ("Journal," p. 87) affirm that the officials had arrived at Petit Goâve on October 20. Minet (idem, p. 88) says that both he himself and Beaujeu became ill on October 24 and ran a fever for four days. Concerning La Salle's asking Beaujeu to return to France, compare Folmer (*Franco-Spanish Rivalry,* pp. 158–59), who is led astray by a mistranslation.

17. Weddle, *French Thorn,* p. 16; Joutel, "Voyage," p. 105.

18. Minet, "Journal," p. 88; Weddle, *French Thorn,* p. 17.

19. Beaujeu to Seignelay, p. 488. Compare Minet, "Journal," p. 89. Sieur d'Iberville found similar depth at Mobile Bay in 1699. Weddle, *French Thorn,* p. 135.

20. Beaujeu to Seignelay, pp. 488–89. See Robert S. Weddle, "Armada de Barlovento," in Ron Tyler, et al., eds., *The New Handbook of Texas,* 1:240–41.

21. Joutel, "Voyage," pp. 102, 105; Cavelier, "Journal," p. 503. Denis Thomas, "Declaracion"; Villiers, *L'expédition,* pp. 160–61; Minet, "Journal," p. 90.

22. Villiers, *L'expédition,* p. 161. "Hiems"—a French corruption of the English "James"—is variously said to have been German or English. Parkman (*La Salle, in France and England,* p. 999) calls him "Hiens, a German of Würtemberg," adding (p. 1005), "He had probably sailed with an English crew, for he was sometimes known as *Gemme Anglais,* or 'English Jem.'" Henri de Tonti refers to him as *un flibustier anglois,* "an English pirate." Joutel ("Voyage," p. 386) says of Hiems, ". . . this man spoke good Latin," spoke English very well, and had a good knowledge of mathematics.

23. Joutel, "Voyage," 103; Meunier, "Declaracion"; Weddle, *French Thorn,* p. 17.

24. Joutel, "Voyage," p. 104; Minet, "Journal," p. 88.

25. Anonymous letter, p. 497; Joutel, "Voyage," p. 103.

26. Joutel, "Voyage," pp. 105–106; Minet, "Journal," p. 89; Cavelier, "Journal," p. 504; La Salle to Beaujeu, Petit Goâve, Nov. 23, 1684, in Margry, *Découvertes,* 2:521–22; BHC reel 1.

27. See chapter 4 herein.

28. Joutel, "Voyage," pp. 105–106; Villiers, *L'expédition,* 27. Compare Beaujeu to Seignelay, undated [late 1685], in Margry, *Découvertes,* 2:583, which says only "others" were carried on the *Joly* after Saint-Domingue, and BHC reel 1, which says "five others."

29. Beaujeu to La Salle, aboard the *Joly,* Nov. 23, 1684, Margry, *Découvertes,* 2:524.

30. Page from the *Belle*'s log for Nov. 25–26, 1684, reproduced in Weddle, *Wilderness Manhunt,* as plate 5; Joutel, "Voyage," pp. 106, 107.

31. Minet, "Journal," p. 90.

32. Ibid., pp. 90–91. (Compare the sequence with Joutel, "Voyage," p. 108.) See

NOS Chart 11013. The Isle of Pines, once the site of a prison that held Fidel Castro, now is called Isla de la Juventud ("Isle of Youth") for the youth-indoctrination facility placed there by the Cuban dictator (Weddle, ed., *La Salle,* 90n.).

33. Joutel, "Voyage," pp. 108–111.
34. Minet, "Journal," p. 92; NOS Chart 11013.
35. Minet, ibid.; Joutel, "Voyage," p. 114.
36. Marcel Moraud, "The Last Expedition and the Death of Cavelier de La Salle, 1684–87," p. 146 (quote). Depredations on the Gulf coast settlements by pirates, privateers, and foreign governments in this period are treated in Weddle, *Spanish Sea,* pp. 378–411.
37. Folmer (*Franco-Spanish Rivalry,* pp. 133–36) summarizes the contest over rights of other nations to free navigation of the Spanish Indies. See also Weddle, *French Thorn,* p. 130; Colbert to Marquis de Villars, Saint-Germain, Aug. 5, 1672; extract of mémoire of Comte d'Estrées, Aug. 21, 1679; king to d'Estrées, May 21, 1680, and to sieur Gabaret, Apr. 13, 1682, Margry, *Découvertes,* 2:4–14. The *Faucon,* one of Gabaret's ships, carried as part of her weaponry the four bronze cannon freighted in the *Belle*'s hold in 1684. On the *Belle,* the cannon were making their second voyage to the Gulf of Mexico.
38. See Weddle, *Spanish Sea,* pp. 398–404. The 1683 Tampico raid was carried out by Du Chesne, the pirate captain with whom Beaujeu had conferred in Saint-Domingue. The pirates' 1684 raid resulted in their capture by the Armada de Barlovento. Fourteen were sentenced to death by the garrote.
39. La Salle to Beaujeu, aboard the *Aimable,* Dec. 18, 1684.
40. Weddle, *French Thorn,* p. 19.
41. Ibid; Minet, "Journal," p. 92. The longitude estimates by the *Aimable*'s pilot, taken singly, are meaningless. Calculated west to east with Paris as the prime meridian, they tended to vary widely and at best were highly error prone. Those given on successive days during the Gulf crossing from Cape San Antonio, however, provide an approximation of the ships' track.
42. Margry, *Découvertes,* pp. 126–27, here borrows two sentences from Jean Michel's *Journal historique d'un Voyage en Amérique par Joutel,* in which it is said that the natives saw on the vessel "sheep, pigs, fowls, and turkeys, and the hide of a cow we had killed [and] made signs that they had all these animals where they lived." Compare Joutel, "Voyage," pp. 190–91, and BHC reel 1:105. Joutel makes no mention elsewhere that the voyagers carried either sheep or turkeys, although the *Joly* had a pair of goats. Nor is there record of cattle except the cow acquired by the *Joly* at Saint-Domingue.
43. Page from the log of the *Belle* for Jan. 17 and 18, 1685, reproduced in Weddle, *French Thorn,* fig. 4, 22. Minet ("Journal," 98) relates that the *Joly* drifted seven leagues overnight from her anchorage near Matagorda Bay. See fig. 16.
44. Joutel, "Voyage," pp. 133–34. Joutel had either become confused in his directions or falsified his account to support La Salle's claim that the separation was Beaujeu's fault.
45. Minet, "Journal," p. 96. Joutel has claimed that two of the three Récollet friars were aboard the *Aimable,* leaving only one (Le Clercq) on the *Joly.*
46. See Weddle, ed., *La Salle,* p. 96n.
47. Minet, "Journal," pp. 97–98.
48. Ibid., p. 99. The map that Minet refers to is not identifiable from the sources at hand. It may have been the 1684 Franquelin map described by Parkman (*La*

Salle, appendix, p. 1048), now known only in facsimile, or one of those in possession of La Salle's niece as late as 1756 (idem, p. 741).

49. Ibid. D'Esmanville ("Journal," p. 514), aboard the same ship, gives the latitude of the reunion as 27°50'.

50. D'Esmanville, "Journal," p. 515; BHC reel 1.

51. La Salle to Beaujeu, Jan. 23, 1685, pp. 526–27.

CHAPTER 9. UNHAPPY LANDING

1. D'Esmanville, "Journal," p. 515.

2. Minet, "Journal," p. 102; Minet, "Extrait du journal," p. 596; d'Esmanville, "Journal," pp. 515–16. BHC has it, "The soldiers of the *Joly* mutinied on account of the provisions." The original context indicates that "the soldiers *from* the *Joly*" is meant; "*se mutinèrent*" does not necessarily mean mutiny in the usual sense. As only d'Esmanville refers to the restless state of the men, it may be assumed in this instance that it does not.

3. Minet, "Journal," p. 102; "Extrait," p. 596. Compare Joutel, "Voyage," pp. 136–39, which scarcely takes note of the weather that put the ships in jeopardy; Joutel is without a clear chronology here, as he had lost his notes and wrote this portion from memory (idem, p. 162).

4. D'Esmanville, "Journal," p. 516.

5. Minet, "Extrait du journal," p. 596.

6. Joutel, "Voyage," pp. 121, 135.

7. Minet, "Journal," pp. 103–104. The anchor recovered from the derelict *Belle* by the Spanish Rivas-Iriarte expedition in 1686, by comparison, was estimated to weigh "up to six quintals"—more than thirteen hundred pounds. (See Enríquez Barroto Diary, p. 172.) No anchor was found by THC archeologists during excavation of the shipwreck.

8. Minet, "Extrait," p. 595; Joutel, "Voyage," pp. 135–36; d'Esmanville, p. 515.

9. Minet, "Journal," p. 102.

10. Minet, "Extrait," pp. 596–97. The "Extrait" differs substantially from the journal itself. Minet, at the later writing, was facing the consequences of having forsaken La Salle to return to France with the *Joly* and was seeking the king's clemency.

11. La Salle to Beaujeu, Aboard the *Aimable*, Feb. 6, 1684, Margry, *Découvertes,* 2:533.

12. Hennepin, *Description*, p. 105; Minet, "Journal," p. 103.

13. Joutel ("Voyage," pp. 139, 143) and Minet ("Extrait," p. 597) differ as to the number, as well as the date of departure. Minet places the number of marchers at 113 and ("Journal," p. 103) mentions the young Normans, probably some of the volunteers named later by Joutel ("Voyage," pp. 140–41: Desloges, Oris, Thibault, La Villeperdrix, Declaire, Arboul, and Gayen. Thibault and Oris, as well as Joutel and Moranget, were from La Salle's hometown of Rouen).

14. La Salle to Beaujeu, "From the mouth of a river that I believe to be one of the mouths of the Mississippi," Feb. 3, 1685, Margry, *Découvertes,* 2:528–31; same to same, Aboard the *Aimable*, same date, idem, pp. 531–32.

15. There is no other direct mention of the cannon shots. The picture becomes clear, however, when accounts of Joutel ("Voyage," pp. 139–40) and Minet ("Journal," pp. 103–104) are compared.

16. La Salle to Beaujeu, Aboard the *Aimable*, Feb. 7, 1684, Margry, *Découvertes,* 2:534–

36. La Salle's date differs from Minet's. Dates often vary among all the accounts: Joutel, Minet, d'Esmanville, and La Salle.

17. Joutel, "Voyage," pp. 140–41. Concerning the fresh water on Matagorda Island, see the 1745 account of castaways from the French ship *Superbe* in Weddle, *French Thorn,* p. 247 (transcript from AN, Marine, B4, BTHC): "Thirty paces back from the beach, the Frenchmen were able to take slightly brackish but potable water from holes dug in the sand."

18. Joutel, "Voyage," p. 143.

19. With several variant spellings, the Magdalaine River has never been definitely linked to a specific Texas stream but was often shown on maps as being the same as the Río Escondido (the Nueces River). It has occasionally been identified with the Guadalupe, sometimes even the Rio Grande. See Weddle, ed., *La Salle,* pp. 99–100n.

20. Minet, "Journal," p. 104. For some reason, Joutel neglects to mention the tent that evidently was erected for the officers, leaving the impression that the only shelter for any of the company was the crude huts he describes. Minet's map "Plan de l'entrée du lac" (fig. 17) shows at least ten tents on the point near the present-day Matagorda lighthouse.

21. Joutel, "Voyage," p. 147.

22. Minet, "Extrait," pp. 597–98; see also Minet, "Journal," pp. 104–105. Minet's map of the coast, "Plan de la Coste de la Floride la plus occidentale," is reproduced with his journal as plate 7, p. 101. It includes soundings in the channel and along the shore from Cedar Bayou to the upper portion of Matagorda Peninsula.

23. Idem, p. 106. Not all the correspondence between La Salle and Beaujeu during this time is found in Margry; nor is it identifiable among the La Salle material listed in the guide to AN, C¹³ 3.

24. Beaujeu to La Salle, the *Joly,* Feb. 16, 1685, Margry, *Découvertes,* 2:537.

25. La Salle to Beaujeu, the *Aimable,* same date, ibid., pp. 537–38.

26. "Procés verbal de l'entrée du lac où est descendu M. de La Salle," Feb. 17, 1685, Margry, *Découvertes,* 2:539.

27. La Salle to Beaujeu, "From the mouth of the rivière Colbert," Feb. 17, 1685, idem, p. 542; Beaujeu to La Salle, Feb. 18, 1685, idem, pp. 544–45.

28. The same two letters, idem, complete in pp. 540–42 and 542–46 (quotes, p. 544); La Salle to Beaujeu, "At the mouth of the rivière Colbert," Feb. 18, 1685, idem, p. 546; Beaujeu, the *Joly,* Feb. 19, 1685, idem, p. 550 (last quote).

29. Idem, p. 548.

30. La Salle to Beaujeu, Feb. 18, ibid.

31. Ibid., p. 548; Minet, "Journal," p. 108.

32. Joutel, "Voyage," p. 148; Minet, "Plan de l'entrée du lac (fig. 17)." The bar at Pass Cavallo, then and now, is off the southeastern point of Matagorda Island, where Grand Camp was situated.

33. Joutel, "Voyage," pp. 148, 175; Tunnell, "A Cache of Cannons," p. 21. The eight cannon, buried by Spanish general Alonso de León in 1689, were recovered in 1996 by THC archeologists under Tunnell's direction. They proved to be two six-pounders, three four-pounders, and three three-pounders.

34. Minet, "Journal," pp. 102, 109.

35. Joutel, "Voyage," pp. 149–54. "Procès verbal du sieur de La Salle sur le naufrage de la flûte l'*Aimable* à l'entrée du fleuve Colbert," Mar. 1, 1685, Margry, *Découvertes,* 2:555–58. The native village as shown on Minet's map, "Plan de l'entrée du lac"

(fig. 17), was more than three miles north of Grand Camp. It stood opposite Decros Point at the mouth of Saluria Bayou, where the town of Saluria stood, 1847–87, and where a United States Coast Guard station was built in later years. See Tyler et al., *New Handbook of Texas,* 5:783–84. Comparison of Minet's maps with present-day charts shows that the eastern end of Matagorda Island has been much eroded. It is cut by a maze of sloughs and channels that are not evident on Minet's 1685 rendering.

36. Minet, "Journal," pp. 108–109. Minet's map (fig. 17) marks the wreck *inside* the bar, indicating that soon after crossing the bar safely, the ship veered to the right of the channel into a cul de sac enclosed by shoal water.

37. Joutel, "Voyage," pp. 154–55. Translation of the portion of Joutel dealing with the salvage, in BHC reel 1, is paginated 132–38. (There are several sets of page numbers in the BHC translations of the Margry papers, assigned to different documents or groups of documents. Joutel's narrative is numbered consecutively 70–425 in reel 1, 426–532 in reel 2.)

38. Ibid., p. 154; Minet, "Journal," p. 109. All the suspicions and allegations against Captain Aigron notwithstanding, none of the witnesses goes as far as Jaray ("Robert Cavelier," p. 37), who says, "We may easily believe that Beaujeu, Aigron, and Minet are the instigators of this plot [to lose the ship]." Minet is so judged because of his refusing to go ashore, Beaujeu for not compelling him to do so.

39. Joutel, "Voyage," p. 155. BHC reel 1:135) renders *brisées* as "folding boats."

40. Minet, "Extrait," pp. 599–600. How long this mortality rate endured, Minet does not say.

41. Ibid., p. 600; Joutel, "Voyage," p. 157; Minet, "Journal," p. 110 (quote).

42. Idem, pp. 110–12.

43. *Procès verbal,* Mar. 1, 1685. Signatories to the document besides La Salle himself include the Duhaut brothers, Pierre and Dominique; Le Carpentier, Thibault, Le Gros, J. Planterose, Huzier, Barbier, Ravenel, and Sablonnière.

44. La Salle to the Marquis de Seignelay, "At the western mouth of the *fleuve* Colbert," Mar. 4, 1685, Margry, *Découvertes,* 2:559–63; quotes on pp. 561, 562.

45. Ibid., p. 563.

46. Ibid., p. 562.

47. Ibid., pp. 559–60. An error in Margry (ibid., p. 559), dating the January 6 sighting of Galveston Bay as January 3, is corrected in BHC reel 1.

48. La Salle to Beaujeu, "On shore," Mar. 7, 1685, ibid., pp. 566–69 (quote on p. 566); Beaujeu to La Salle, Mar. 4, 1685, ibid., pp. 564–565.

49. Minet, "Journal," p. 113.

50. Ibid., p. 112; Joutel, "Voyage," p. 159. See n. 13, this chapter. Whereas Joutel dates the incident March 5, Minet indicates March 6.

51. La Salle to Beaujeu, Mar. 7, 1685, pp. 507–508.

52. Beaujeu to La Salle, Mar. 7, 1685, idem, pp. 569–70. BHC reel 1 corrects Margry's misdating of the letter as March 9.

53. Joutel, "Voyage," BHC, p. 140 (compare Margry, *Découvertes,* 2:161). Joutel remarks a few paragraphs later (idem, p. 161) that he had lost his memoranda written at the time and has drawn this part from memory. That apologia notwithstanding, this passage demonstrates that Joutel did not always know everything that was going on; he could not be everywhere at once.

54. Parkman, *La Salle,* p. 980.

CHAPTER 10. THE HOSTILE SHORE

1. Minet's map (fig. 17) shows the ship in forty-foot water, almost due east of La Salle's camp. The present-day forty-foot depth curve is slightly more than three nautical miles from the southeastern point of Matagorda Island (NOS chart 11316, *Matagorda Bay and Approaches*).

2. La Salle, *procès verbal*, Apr. 18, 1686, Margry, *Découvertes*, 3:537; Joutel, "Voyage," ibid., p. 163. Jean Michel's abridgement of Joutel (*Joutel's Journal of La Salle's Last Voyage*, p. 58) mentions the death sentence; Parkman (*La Salle*, p. 984) says "one man was hung." Joutel, in his own fuller version, makes no mention of the penalty.

3. Joutel, "Voyage," p. 163 (first quote); "Engagements en 1684"; *Joutel's Journal*, p. 58 (second quote). Turin, on the Po River of northwestern Italy, is the capital city of the Piemonte (Piedmont) region, which borders France and Switzerland.

4. Talon Interrogations, pp. 242, 247, 252. It seems certain from Jarry's later emergence in Spanish records that the French deserter was he.

5. La Salle, *procès verbal*, pp. 537–38. Joutel ("Voyage," p. 164) says La Salle "gave me command of the post," making no mention of a shared command with Moranget. The Michel abridgement (*Joutel's Journal*, p. 58) gives the number left at the island camp as 130; those with La Salle, 50. The combined number, 180, has often been taken as the number of colonists landed, exclusive of those who returned with the ships. With many deaths having occurred (as told in the previous chapter), those remaining in the colony at this time were much fewer than the original number.

6. Joutel, "Voyage," p. 164 (quote); La Salle, *procès verbal*, idem.

7. The English equivalent ascribed by present-day interpreters to the French land league in colonial times varies widely, with apparent confusion on several points: the number of leagues to the degree, the length of a degree, and the difference between a nautical mile and a statute mile. Allowing for different values of the league, La Salle's estimate of eighteen leagues suggests a journey of forty-four to fifty miles. Numerous factors enter into the distance calculations of colonial travelers, including natural obstructions, weather conditions, and other occurrences that break the pace. To claim complete accuracy in any case is ludicrous in the extreme. This matter will be discussed further in chapter 12.

8. La Salle, *procès verbal*, p. 538. La Salle represents the site as having wood "here and there," failing to mention that timber suitable for building was some distance away. Nor does he mention the cost of cutting and transporting it in terms of human lives.

9. Joutel, "Voyage," p. 165.

10. See Weddle, *La Salle*, pp. 130–40, *passim*; "The Enríquez Barroto Diary," in ibid., pp. 178–186; also Weddle, *French Thorn*, pp. 42–43, 58–61, 82–83; Diego de Castro, "Testimonio," AGI, Mexico 616, BTHC.

11. Joutel, "Voyage," p. 169; BHC, p. 148.

12. Idem, pp. 169–70, 148–49.

13. Concerning Labaussair, see chapter 7, note 10. Margry omits from Joutel's relation any mention of the deserters' trial. It is found in BHC, pp. 172–73.

14. Joutel, "Voyage," p. 172; BHC, p. 151. This passage is ambiguous, but the context makes it clear that Joutel, as well as Le Gros, his surgeon, and the two prisoners, embarked on the *Belle*.

15. Ibid.

16. Joutel, "Voyage," pp. 172–73; BHC, p. 152.

17. Idem, p. 173; idem. That Joutel wrote this indictment of La Salle later rather than in a daily journal is obvious. The extent to which La Salle mistreated his people cannot be known. The accusations of Pierre Barthélemy (see chapter 12), though ignored by nearly everyone who has written of the episode, surely had some basis in fact. Whether Barthélemy exaggerated the abuse or Joutel minimized it is open to question; perhaps a measure of both.

18. Ibid., pp. 173–74, 179; BHC, pp. 152–53. Compare BHC, p. 158, and Johanna S. Warren's translation (of the first sixteen of Joutel's twenty-three chapters), in William C. Foster, ed., *The La Salle Expedition into Texas: The Journal of Henri Joutel, 1684–1687,* p. 105. The Margry text actually reads: " . . . *tant de la peine qu'ils y avoient eue que de chagrin.*" Neither of these translations captures the meaning here.

19. *Procés verbal,* Apr. 18, 1686.

20. Whereas Alonso de León ("Autos y diligencias," Apr. 22, 1689, AGI, Mexico 616, BTHC) describes the eight cannon as being five- or six-pounders, he tells of finding 32 iron cannon balls, "some of eight and ten pounds, others larger." See Weddle, *Wilderness Manhunt,* p. 185. Musket balls would adhere to a more-or-less uniform caliber, but the lead balls found in great quantities in the *Belle's* wreckage were of many different sizes, suggesting that they were intended for the purpose described here. Two of the cannon were six-pounders, four four-pounders, and four three-pounders. Tunnell, "A Cache of Cannon," pp. 39, 40.

21. Joutel, "Voyage," pp. 175–77.

22. Ibid., p. 177; Minet map (fig. 17).

23. Joutel, "Voyage," pp. 179–80. The French dove-tail was described for me by Larry D. Moss.

24. Ibid., p. 182. Pat Ireland Nixon ("Liotot and Jalot, Two French Surgeons in Early Texas" *SwHQ* 43, no. 1 [July, 1947]: 43–52) claims—probably on the mistaken idea that Liotot was the expedition's only surgeon—that it was he who performed "the first recorded leg amputation in Texas" on Le Gros.

25. *Dessus*: "over" or "(up)on." The context indicates firing *upon*, rather than *above*, the Indians. Idem, p. 180. Compare Foster, ed., *La Salle Expedition*, p. 106. Clearly, Joutel fired *on,* or *at,* them, as per La Salle's orders.

26. Joutel, "Voyage," pp. 180–81. Concerning the Italian, see n.3.

27. Ibid., 181–82.

28. La Salle, *procès verbal,* p. 540.

29. See chapter 1. Meunier, "Declaracion." La Salle (*procès verbal,* p. 541) says the attack was on four *cabanes,* or "huts," rather than four rancherías. It is not at all certain that Meunier was present on the expedition. His testimony should be considered only in the light of all his statements, some of which are confused or false.

30. Delanglez, *The Journal of Jean Cavelier,* p. 145n.71.

31. Joutel, "Voyage," pp. 204–206; BHC, pp. 185–87. The name Maline, or Maligne, as later applied, has been identified as several different streams from the Colorado River eastward.

32. Meunier, "Declaracion." The statement that the *Belle* had "entered the bay as far as the buoys . . . in the mouth of the San Marcos River" is obviously false. Alonso de León, on his first journey to Texas, gave the name San Marcos to the first river east of the Guadalupe: the Lavaca. The *Belle* was unable to get past Sand Point to

enter Lavaca Bay and thus could not have reached the buoys. Concerning the shifting of the name San Marcos as applied to a Texas river, see Weddle, *French Thorn,* p. 232.

33. La Salle, *procès verbal,* Apr. 18, 1686, p. 543. See n. 20, chapter 1.

34. Ibid., p. 545.

35. "Relation of M. Cavelier" in Cox, *Journeys,* 1:175–283. Villiers (*L'expédition,* p. 96) delivers the harshest indictment of this spurious tale: that it contains not a line of truth; that Cavelier purposely mixed up all the dates; and, to confuse Seignelay, "piled up the most impudent lies." Delanglez (*Journal of Jean Cavelier,* pp. 7–8) agrees that this "blanket condemnation has justification, for many of the statements . . . have proved to be inaccurate, misleading, or wholly false."

36. Aguayo to the viceroy, June 15, 1686, AGI, Mexico 616, BTHC; quote in Weddle, *Wilderness Manhunt,* pp. 57–58. Both the Blancos and the Pajaritos lived in the Cerralvo area of Nuevo León. According to Martín Salinas (*Indians of the Rio Grande Delta,* p. 86), Blancos were among the natives missionized at Agualeguas, seventeen miles north of Cerralvo and twenty-five miles from the Rio Grande, as early as 1646. Salinas (p. 102) says the Pajaritos were encountered by Alonso de León (presumably on his march to the mouth of the Rio Grande in 1686) in the San Juan River valley near present-day China, Nuevo León.

37. Quote in Weddle, *Wilderness Manhunt,* pp. 167–68, drawn from Pardiñas, "Declaration of Miguel, captain of the Cíbolos," Apr. 11, 1689, AGI, Guadalajara 186, BTHC; translated in Hackett, *Historical* Documents, 2:269–73. See also Weddle, *French Thorn,* pp. 69–70. John, *Storms Brewed in Other Men's Worlds: The Confrontation of Indians, Spanish, and French in the Southwest, 1540–1795,* pp. 184–85.

38. Proof of at least part of the Indians' tale is the French papers they took to Parral. Included besides pages from the *Belle's* log was the painting of a ship on which L'Archevêque had scrawled his plea for rescue. Comparison of the ship (reproduced in Weddle, *Wilderness Manhunt,* as plate 9) with Minet's drawing (fig. 17 herein) suggests that it may very well have been the *Joly.* As to the timing of the French visits, compare Folmer (*Franco-Spanish Rivalry,* p. 162), who claims that La Salle made two trips to the west, in May and June, 1685, and "continued his search for the Spaniards toward the west . . . during the winter of 1685–86." Not a likely scenario.

39. La Salle, *procès verbal,* Apr. 18, 1686, p. 548.

CHAPTER 11. THE FORT THAT NEVER WAS

1. Joutel, "Voyage," pp. 191, 192, 259; BHC reel 1, pp. 171, 172, 241. The descriptive passage from John Gilmary Shea's translation of Le Clercq (*First Establishment of the Faith in New France,* 2:219) is in Cox, *Journeys,* 1:217. Foster (ed., *La Salle Expedition,* p. 336), in his index to Joutel's narrative, makes forty-seven text references to "Fort Saint Louis." In none of them does the name actually appear.

2. León, "Derrotero y demarcación de la tierra de la jornada," in Canedo, *Primeras exploraciones,* p. 98; see also León, "Auto levantado por Alonso de León acerca del establecimiento francés en la costa de Texas," idem, p. 106. L'Archevêque, "Declaracion," Mexico, June 10, 1689, AGI, Mexico 616, BTHC. O'Donnell (trans., *La Salle's Occupation of Texas*) makes undue assumptions and miscopies L'Archevêque's age as twenty-nine instead of twenty.

3. Cavelier (*The Journal of Jean Cavelier,* trans. and ed. Jean Delanglez, pp. 64, 74) refers to the post as "fort de la Baye" and "fort de la Baye St. Louis." After the post no longer existed (ibid., p. 76), he mentions "the Baye or the fort St. Louis." Hence, the 1714 English translation of Michel's 1713 abridgment of Joutel (*Joutel's Journal of La Salle's Last Voyage,* p. 65 and n.1) declares, ". . . that Dwelling had the Name of St. Lewis given it, as well as the Neighbouring Bay." Cf. La Salle to Beaujeu, Feb. 18, 1685, Margry, *Découvertes,* 2:546 (quote). Artists' concepts of "Fort St. Louis" are examplified by a sketch appearing with Bryan Wooley's article ("Site yields pieces of early settlement") in *The Dallas Morning News* of June 25, 2000. The drawing—signed by Layne Smith but obviously copied with slight modification from Tom Jones's 1975 watercolor "conjectural reconstruction" (*Victoria: A 300 Year Sampler,* plate 6)—shows a well-ordered compound with a palisade enclosing seven buildings that look more like present-day army barracks than the crude huts described by Joutel. See also Tom Minnart's rendition in Carlos E. Castañeda, *Our Catholic Heritage in Texas,* 1: facing p. 282.

4. La Salle, *procès verbal,* Apr. 18, 1686, p. 548.

5. Joutel, "Voyage," pp. 194–200, quote on p. 199. The following account of life at the settlement is summarized from Joutel, chapters 6 and 7, pp. 198–260, except as otherwise indicated.

6. Concerning the *cheval de bois,* see ibid., pp. 169, 193 (quote); second quote, p. 198.

7. Ibid., pp. 216–17.

8. La Salle, *procès verbal,* p. 542.

9. Joutel, "Voyage," pp. 200–201.

10. Ibid., p. 250. The sows seem to have farrowed litters of from four to ten or twelve.

11. Ibid., p. 211. Compare Talon Interrogations, in Weddle, ed., *La Salle,* pp. 232–33; also Del Weniger, "Commentaries on the Interrogations—Natural History," idem, pp. 274–78.

12. Díaz del Castillo, *Historia verdadera de la conquista de la Nueva España;* López de Gómara, *Cortés: The Life of the Conqueror.*

13. Notably missing from Foster, ed., *La Salle Expedition,* is an assessment of Joutel the man. Although he was La Salle's loyal servant, Joutel at times chafed at his leader's actions. His irritation shows in some of his comments written well after La Salle's death. Even then, he shows remarkable restraint.

14. Joutel, "Voyage," pp. 219–20.

15. Ibid., pp. 220–21; compare BHC reel 1, pp. 201–202.

16. La Salle, *procès verbal,* pp. 544–45, 548.

17. Compare Joutel, "Voyage," in Margry, *Découvertes,* p. 238, and two translation of same: BHC, p. 220, and Warren translation in Foster, ed., *La Salle Expedition,* p. 141. BHC, seemingly supplying a phrase from the Margry papers that the published version omits, credits owls with killing the rats in the powder magazine, whereas Warren, like the published Margry, has "cats."

18. Ibid., p. 242.

19. Ibid., p. 245.

20. Ibid., p. 249. Joutel, in relating the 1687 march across Texas, refers to places La Salle had visited on his return from the Hasinai in 1686, "the previous autumn." (E.g., see p. 266.) The confusion seems to arise from the manuscript abbreviation of the month as "8re"—October, rather than August. Compare the Le Clercq-

Douay account in Cox, *Journeys*, 236. The figure 8 as used represents "octo" rather than the eighth month. The date given for the return is October 17.

21. Delanglez, "Jean Cavelier, Chronicler," in Cavelier, *The Journal of Jean Cavelier,* pp. 9, 24, 27.

22. Ibid., pp. 16–17.

23. See chapter 5.

24. "Douay" account in Cox, ed., *Journeys,* p. 235.

25. Villiers, *L'expédition,* pp. 172–73. Delanglez, ed., *Journal of Jean Cavelier,* p. 145n.67.

26. León, "Autos y diligencias," Apr. 22, 1689, AGI, Mexico 616.

27. "Extrait des remarques et réponses de l'abbé Jean Cavelier aux articles du Mémoire de M. de La Forest," Margry, *Découvertes* 3:548–49, n.d.

28. Joutel, "Voyage," p. 253.

29. Cavelier, *Journal,* pp. 76, 77; Delanglez (idem, pp. 145–46n.71) points out that there is no reason to doubt that this was La Salle's plan: "He did not wish to entrust even mere routine business to his lieutenants." While suffering from a hernia, he had refused Joutel's offer to go to the Illinois post for help, claiming his own presence was necessary there. Delanglez: "Was not the most important business of the moment to obtain succor for the poor people who had followed him on this expedtion?"

30. Villiers, *L'expédition,* p. 184; Cavelier, *Journal,* p. 76.

31. Joutel, "Voyage," pp. 259, 260; BHC, reel 1, p. 241.

32. Cavelier, *Journal,* p. 77; Delanglez, ibid., p. 146n.75; Villiers, *L'expédition,* p. 173.

33. Joutel, "Voyage," p. 279.

CHAPTER 12. FATAL JOURNEY

1. Joutel, "Voyage," Margry, *Découvertes,* 3:262.

2. Ibid.

3. Ibid., pp. 263–64.

4. Joutel, "Voyage," p. 265. See information from Jean-Baptiste Talon on the ease of winning the Karankawas' friendship (Talon Interrogations, p. 251).

5. Joutel, "Voyage," pp. 266–67.

6. Ibid., p. 269.

7. Ibid., pp. 269–70. Jean L'Archevêque, ("Deposition," trans. Walter J. O'Donnell, "La Salle's Occupation of Texas," p. 17) later told his Spanish captors that the purpose of the French settlement was "to traffic in buffalo hides, tallow, and lard."

8. See n.7, chapter 10. Foster (ed., *La Salle Expedition,* appendix C, p. 309) ascribes 2.4 miles to Joutel's league and, in his preface, introduction, and notes, tells us repeatedly that Joutel defines the route of the 1687 march with such precision as to warrant "a high degree of confidence" in his accuracy (pp. x, 6, 8, 17, 19n.14, 26, and 43). Not quite so. Mildred Mott Wedel (*La Harpe's 1719 Post on Red River and Nearby Caddo Settlements,* p. 2), on the other hand, notes that the "common league of France" was the equivalent of an hour's travel on foot; in the 1700s the land league was recongnized as 25 leagues to the degree, or 4444.5 meters: "slightly over 2.76 miles per league."

9. See Thomas N. Campbell, "Ebahamo Indians," in Tyler, et al., eds, *New Handbook of Texas,* 2:776, wherein it is suggested that the Ebahamo were one of the several Karankawan groups. This, however, is by no means certain.

10. Joutel, "Voyage," 276–77.

11. Ibid., p. 279. Foster (ed., *La Salle Expedition,* pp. 162n, 165n., 322) identifies the Sablonnière as Sandy Creek or West Sandy Creek, *sablonnière* being a French word meaning "sand pit." Joutel himself ("Voyage," p. 279) says the name was given for the Marquis de Sablonnière "because of an accident that happened to him on the first voyage that he made with La Salle . . . from the bayside." This version is often rejected because Sablonnière did not go with La Salle on his first journey to the Cenis. However, he may have been on La Salle's expedition from the "bayside"—i.e., from Grand Camp at the mouth of Matagorda Bay, as opposed to the Garcitas Creek site—and it is conceivable that they reached the Colorado River and named it for the irresponsible young nobleman, who was judged unfit for any journey thereafter.

12. Joutel, "Voyage," p. 286. See chapter 11.

13. Ibid., pp. 288–89 (list of tribes), pp. 291–92. The list in the 1714 translation of Jean Michel's abridgement of Joutel (*Joutel's Journal of La Salle's Last Voyage,* pp. 94–95, 95n., differs from the one in Margry. Whereas the latter gives Kannehouan, the former includes both Kannehonan and Canohatino, either of which could represent the enemies of the Hasinai living west or northwest of the Hasinai villages.

14. Ibid., p. 281.

15. Ibid., p. 296. R. S. Kier, L. E. Garner, and L. F. Brown, Jr., *Land Resources of Texas* (map series); Texas Department of Transportation, *Texas Natural Regions* and *Bryan Natural Region* (maps delineating the Blackland Prairie). See fig. 19.

16. Joutel, "Voyage," pp. 300–301. Talon Interrogations, pp. 229–30: "The Cenis . . . use [horses] only to transport their kill, since they are obliged to go very far to hunt the buffalo."

17. Joutel, "Voyage," pp. 305–306.

18. Ibid., p. 305; Weddle, *French Thorn,* p. 37.

19. Idem; Joutel, "Voyage," p. 309.

20. Described by Joutel, "Voyage," p. 316. No comparable feature is found along the west side of the Brazos in the area where the expedition seems most likely to have crossed. Compare entries on Bedias Creek vis-à-vis New Year Creek (Washington County) in Tyler, et al., eds., in *New Handbook of Texas,* 1:456, 4:1007. See also Grimes and Madison county maps of the Texas Department of Transportation; southeast and northeast quadrant maps in Kier, et al., *Land Resources of Texas.*

21. Joutel, "Voyage, p. 319. Talon Interrogations, p. 230.

22. Joutel, "Voyage," pp. 327–28.

23. Pierre Talon (Talon Interrogations, pp. 231–32) claims that when he was in the Cenis village, he saw the Indians with fifty or sixty *louis-d'or* that La Salle had on his person when he was killed and that Pierre Meunier traded trifles for the gold coins.

24. Douay, "Narrative," p. 244; Delanglez (ed., *Journal of Jean Cavelier,* pp. 16–17) indicates that the excision of Joutel's manuscript occurred during the time that it was in sieur d'Iberville's care, 1698–1701. "Peculiarities of Le Clerc's text," Delanglez adds, "go far toward identifying" the Renaudot faction as authors of the mutilation of Joutel's journal. "That someone other than Le Clercq 'edited' the *First Establishment of the Faith* may be regarded as certain." The missing parts of Joutel, including accounts of the four murders (Joutel, "Voyage," p. 311), were restored

by Claude Delisle, to whom Iberville returned the mutilated manuscript, and Delisle's son Guillaume (Delanglez, idem, pp. 12–17). See also Weddle, *French Thorn*, pp. 316–17; Jean Delandlez, "Sources of the Delisle Map of North America, 1703," *Mid-America* 25 (new series, vol. 14), no. 4 (Oct., 1943): 276–78.

25. Joutel, "Voyage," pp. 324–25.

26. Joutel records no distance between known points by which the accuracy of this estimate might be judged; it therefore may not be dependable for fixing the location of La Salle's murder in relation to the Hasinai villages. Compare Pierre Talon's statement on the distance of buffalo from the villages. See n.21.

27. Joutel, "Voyage," pp. 360–61. Joutel's exclusion of young Talon, Meunier, and Barthélemy is not explained.

28. Ibid., p. 366.

29. Ibid., pp. 368–71; quote on p. 371. There are, of course, other versions of both La Salle's death and the slaying of Duhaut and Liotot. L'Archevêque ("Deposition," 17), supported by Grollet, tells his Spanish captors that "an English gunner" [Hiems] killed La Salle. Pierre Talon places the blame for the first round of murders, including La Salle's, on the younger Duhaut and "James," while ascribing a different ending for "the surgeon," whom he does not name. (Talon Interrogations,pp. 234–35). Pierre Meunier ("Declaracion," Mexico City, Aug. 19, 1690, AGI, Mexico 617, BTHC) supports Joutel: La Salle was killed by "Monsieur de V." [de U.; i.e., Duhaut] after "a surgeon" had killed the Indian hunter, La Salle's lackey, and "a lieutenant."

30. Barthélemy is not mentioned by name but is described in the same way Joutel has described him previously: "a young lad from Paris." By inference, Pierre Meunier, also from Paris, as was sieur de Marle, went with the war party. See Thomas N. Campbell, "Kanahotino Indians," in Tyler, ed., *New Handbook of Texas*, 3:1029, vis-à-vis W. W. Newcomb, Jr., *The Indians of Texas from Prehistoric to Modern Times,* p. 286. Although the identity of the Hasinai's enemies remains a matter of guesswork, a reasonable conjecture is that they were Waco, a Wichita subtribe living at that time on the headwaters of the Sabine River in Hunt and Rains counties.

31. See chapter 2.

32. Joutel, "Voyage," p. 383. La Salle (*procès verbal*, Apr. 18, 1686) indicates that 2,000 livres of gold, doubtless including what had belonged to Le Gros, was placed aboard the *Belle* in October, 1685. The documents make no mention of its having been recovered. See also n. 23, this chapter.

33. Joutel, "Voyage," pp. 382, 384, 386.

34. Meunier ("Declaracion") claims that he was left because of illness. L'Archevêque ("Deposition," p. 18) makes a similar claim, and Grollet ("Deposition," ibid., p. 19) says he and two others became sick.

35. Joutel, "Voyage," p. 384.

CHAPTER 13. LEGACY OF DECEIT

1. Minet, "Journal," pp. 114–16; d'Esmanville, "Relation," Margry, *Découvertes,* 2:584–88; Beaujeu to Seignelay, undated (Rochefort, July, 1685); idem, pp. 580–82 (quote, p. 581).

2. Beaujeu to Seignelay, 582–83. BHC makes a substition for this portion of Margry,

giving the date of arrival at Chesapeake Bay as May 30, rather than May 3). Minet ("Journal," pp. 120–22) provides an interesting view of Virginia, the bay area, and Jamestown (called "Ville d'Hiems"), including the history, geography, and economy.

3. Idem, pp. 121–22, 122 n.

4. See chapter 9.

5. Minet to Seignelay, July 6, 1685, in Margry, *Découvertes,* 2:602, 604. Whereas Minet, "Journal," p. 122 (manuscript p. 66) gives the date of arrival at Rochefort as July 6, the extract in Margry, p. 604, gives July 5, the same as Beaujeu. Aunis, the region of La Rochelle, was a province in La Salle's time.

6. King to Arnoul, July 22, 1685, AN, Marine B2: Ordres du Roi concernant la Marine, f. 232v.; Minet, "Journal," p. 122.

7. Orders and letters of the king, July 22, Aug. 11, Oct. 30, 1685, AN, Marine B 2–52, ff. 239, 249, 281; Mengaud's complaint, ADCM, 3E-1837, Nov. 16, 1685. The complete record of this trial arrived too late for inclusion in this book. An article or translation treating the wreck and its legal consequences is planned.

8. Minet, "Journal," pp. 123–26.

9. Seignelay to sieur Gennée, Aug. 20, 1686, Dépêches de ministre de la Marine, AN, Marine B2, ff. 620v-621r; Seignelay to sieur Lombard, same date, idem, ff. 624–625; Minet, "Journal," p. 126.

10. King to Minet, Oct., 1683, BN, *NAF* 21329, f. 341; telephone information from John de Bry, Apr., 1998.

11. King to Arnoul, July 22, 1685.

12. Minet, "Journal," p. 124; Denis Thomas, "Declaracion de Dionicio Thomas," AGI, Mexico, 616. Thomas's story is summarized in Weddle, *Wilderness Manhunt,* p. 7–13. Interestingly, the source of his detailed information was La Salle's servant l'Espérance, which name the Spanish scribe entered as "La Esperanza." It was probably a *dit* name, belonging to one of two servants of La Salle, Dumesnil or Saget.

13. This expedition provided the Enríquez Barroto diary, a keystone for THC in locating the 300–year-old shipwreck in 1995. The present author brought the microfilmed document from Spain in 1979 and later translated and published it (Weddle, ed., *La Salle,* pp. 149–205). The original is in Biblioteca del Palacio Real, Madrid, ms. 2667; microfilm copy in author's possession. See J. Barto Arnold III, *A Matagorda Bay Magnetometer Survey & Site Test Excavation Project,* pp. 112–14.

14. Joutel, "Voyage," p. 401.

15. Ibid., p. 407. This account appears in a portion of the narrative that was lost and reconstructed by Margry (idem) from the Michel abridgment and Claude Delisle's notes. The hiatus in the manuscript extends from June 13 to July 9.

16. Kathleen Gilmore, with the collaboration of H. Gill-King, "An Archeological Footnote to History," pp. 303–23. Gilmore (p. 307, after Villiers, *L'expédition,* p. 216.) thinks that the drowning, if such it was, ocurred in an old channel of McKinney Bayou.

17. Talon Interrogations, p. 235; Parkman, *La Salle,* pp. 967, 1005.

18. Joutel, "Voyage," pp. 419–20. See Tonti's *procès verbal,* ibid., pp. 554–58.

19. Joutel, "Voyage," pp. 436–37.

20. "Relation de la mort de M. de La Salle suivant le rapport d'un nommé Couture," Margry, *Découvertes,* 3:601–606; Parkman, *La Salle,* 1013n., 1028n.

21. "Relation de la mort," pp. 605–606.

22. Foster (ed., *La Salle Expedition*, 273n.), shrugs off the allegations as told by Parkman, noting that they "are not supported by any other writer." It should be remembered, however, that Father Maxime Le Clercq wrote such uncomplimentary things of La Salle that Joutel had his journal seized and burned; and Minet asked why La Salle "starved his soldiers to death" while eating sumptuously himself. All the other eyewitness writers had compelling reasons for not discussing such matters. Yet Joutel himself seems to hint at unspeakable brutality on La Salle's part in his claim that the building of the coastal outpost "caused the death of more than thirty persons, as much from the punishment they were given as from the affliction" (see chapter 10 and n. 18). Villiers (*L'expédition de Cavelier de La Salle*, p. 181) says only that Abbé Cavelier fortunately did not have to suffer the embarrassment of Barthélemy's idle talk, by which he gave Couture a highly unflattering picture of La Salle, showing that "the too irascible explorer must have been detested by most of his companions." Tonti reveals Couture's illiteracy in the *procès verbal* of his voyage to the mouth of the Mississippi, p. 558, naming him among those who did not sign the report because they did not know how (to write).

23. Marcel Giraud, *A History of French Louisiana*, 1:8.

24. Weddle, *French Thorn*, p. 177; Patricia Galloway, "Henri de Tonti du village des Chacta, 1702: The Beginning of the French Alliance," in Galloway, ed., *La Salle and His Legacy*, pp. 148–49.

25. Joutel, "Voyage," p. 450; BHC, p. 438.

26. Johanna Warren's translation of Joutel's journal (Foster, ed., *La Salle Expedition*) ends at the Mississippi with the entry for August 2, 1687. Thus, the last seven of the twenty-three chapters are omitted because, as Foster explains (idem, Introduction, p. 29), "Joutel's daily account and richly descriptive narrative is discontinued. . . ." The omission eclipses much, as will be seen.

27. Joutel ("Voyage," 465; BHC, 454) describes the difficulties of ascending the Mississippi by canoe more vividly than the previous explorers.

28. See chapter 4.

29. Joutel, "Voyage," p. 478.

30. Ibid., p. 480.

31. Ibid., p. 490. Compare wording in BHC, pp. 477–78.

32. Printed in Margry, *Découvertes*, 3:549; translated in full in Charles L. Dufour, *Ten Flags in the Wind: The Story of Louisiana*, pp. 27–28. Margry fails to detect the obvious forgery pointed out by Dufour: La Salle, before his death, could not have known that his brother would reach Fort-Saint-Louis with only four other persons.

33. Joutel, "Voyage," pp. 498, 507. Juchereau, a brother of Louis Juchereau de Saint-Denis, later established a tannery for buffalo hides at the mouth of the Ohio River. He and his sister Charlotte-Françoise made a loan of nearly 7,000 livres to La Forest and Tonti, as well as other traders. See John Fortier and Donald Chaput, "A Historical Reexamination of Juchereau's Illinois Tannery," p. 386. Charlotte-Françoise, a widow, married La Forest in 1702 (Patricia R. Lemée, "*Tios* and *Tantes*: Familial and Political Relationships of Natchitoches and the Spanish Colonial Frontier," *SwHQ* 101, no. 3 (Jan., 1998): 346.

34. Joutel, "Voyage," pp. 508–509.

35. Champigny to Seignelay, Aug. 8, 1688, Margry, *Découvertes*, 3:577; Saint-Vallier to (Tronson), idem, pp. 579–80.

36. Joutel, "Voyage," p. 523.
37. Tronson to Cavelier, Oct. 16, 1688, idem, pp. 580–81.
38. Nicolas Crevel (the younger) had been with the explorer in Illinois and taken part in the confrontation with the deserters on Lake Ontario in 1680. See chapter 3.
39. *Mal à propos pour moy, je me suis trop fié à des gens qui se sont moquez dans la suite.* . . . Ibid., p. 534. Compare BHC, p. 522. Joutel thus betrays his true feelings about the shoddy treatment accorded him by Jean Cavelier in recompense for his loyalty. Villiers (*L'expédition,* p. 25) remarks on the abbé's ingratitude toward Joutel, "without whose aid he would never have seen Canada."
40. Delanglez, *Journal of Jean Cavelier,* p. 33.
41. Tronson to Abbé de Belmont, Mar. or Apr., 1686, Margry, *Découvertes,* 3:578.
42. Seignelay to Barillon, July 28, 1687, AN, Marine B2:61; William Edward Dunn, *Spanish and French Rivalry in the Gulf Region of the United States, 1678–1702,* pp. 48–52; Ronquillo, "Copia de la relación" (transmitted to the Spanish king, Charles II, and thence to the New Spain viceroy, Conde de Monclova), AGI, Mexico 616, BTHC.
43. Dunn, *Spanish and French Rivalry,* p. 57; "Liste des officiers choisis par le Roy," Aug. 15, 1687, AN, Marine B2, Ordres du roi concernant la Marine, vol. 60, f. 152; "Instruction pour le sr. Beaugé le Goux," Aug. 17, 1687, idem, ff. 154–60; Arnoul to Seignelay, Aug. 12, 15, 17, and Sept. 2, 4, 1687, BN, *NAF* 21334, vol. 29, ff. 309, 327, 345.
44. "Résponses aux lettres reçues de MM. de Denonville et de Champigny," Versailles, Mar. 8, 1688, Margry, *Découvertes,* 3:575–76. This letter takes note of petitions received by the court from Moïse Hillaret, chief carpenter on La Salle's abortive shipbuilding project on the Illinois river, and various others for payment of what La Salle owed them. They were advised to seek redress from La Salle himself.
45. Cussy to Seignelay, Saint-Domingue, May 3, 1688, ibid., p. 572.
46. Tronson to Madame Fauvel-Cavelier [widow of Nicolas Cavelier and mother of Colin?], "rue de la Chaisne, près Saint-Amand," Nov. 29, 1688, idem, p. 582.
47. Parkman, *La Salle,* pp. 1022–23, quoting a letter from the king to Denonville dated May 1, 1689 (see Minister to Denonville and Champigny, no date, in Margry, *Découvertes,* 3:600); Tronson to the Bishop of Quebec, June 1, 1689, idem, 3:585–86.
48. "Mémoire de l'abbé Jean Cavelier," idem, pp. 586–96. Delanglez (*Journal of Jean Cavelier,* pp. 25–26) traces Cavelier's various writings and evaluates them. They include "Journal de l'abbé Jean Cavelier," Margry, *Découvertes,* 2:501–509; "Relation of M. Jean Cavelier," in Cox, *Journeys,* 1:168–198; and the complete version of his "journal" published by Delanglez himself.
49. Weddle, *French Thorn,* pp. 98–100. León had crossed the Rio Grande on Apr. 2, 1689, with 110 soldiers and 4 priests.
50. Champigny to the minister, Nov. 16, 1689, Margry, *Découvertes,* 3:600–601; BHC reel 2 adds the second sentence, omitted by Margry.
51. Tronson to the Bishop of Quebec, June 1, 1690, Margry, *Découvertes,* 3:596.
52. Alonso de León ("Autos y diligencias," Apr. 22, 1689, BTHC) describes the scene as he observed it some months after the massacre; L'Archevêque, "Deposition," p. 25. See also Damián Massanet to Carlos Sigüenza in H. E. Bolton, *Spanish Exploration in the Southwest,* pp. 361–62.
53. Talon Interrogations, pp. 237–38. The two younger Talon brothers, Robert and

Lucien, and their sister Marie-Madeleine were taken from the Karankawas by Alonso de León in 1690; Jean-Baptiste Talon and Eustache Bréman, by Francisco Martínez, with Terán de los Ríos, in 1691. Martínez had information that a second girl or woman had survived the massacre and remained among the coastal Indians. The natives told him that she had been taken away by another tribe. The female in question was Madame Barbier, who, having been spared from the massacre, later was slain by the Indians in their village—a matter that they obviously did not wish to reveal. Martínez, "Diario del viaje," June 3–17, 1691, AGN, Historia 27, BTHC.

54. León, "Autos y Diligencias."
55. Jaray, "Robert Cavelier," p. 3; Folmer, *Franco-Spanish Rivalry,* p. 164.

POSTSCRIPT

1. See Weddle, "La Salle's Survivors," *SwHQ* 75, no. 4 (Apr., 1972).
2. Conde de Monclova (New Spain viceroy) to the king (Carlos II), Feb. 10, 1687, AGI, Mexico 616, BTHC; Weddle, *Wilderness Manhunt,* pp. 147, 215; León to the viceroy, July 12, 1690, in Canedo, *Primeras exploraciones,* p. 157. In Coahuila, Jarry's information as the Spaniards understood it was rendered graphically. This anonymous sketch map is reproduced in Weddle, *French Thorn,* as Fig. 5, pp. 74–75. Original is in AGN.
3. Prenuptial investigations of "Juan Andrés" (Jean Jarry) and Antonia de Lara, generously shared with me by Patricia Lemée from her research in the Archives of the Guadalajara Diocese.
4. Weddle, *Wilderness Manhunt,* p. 215; León to Viceroy.
5. Weddle, *Wilderness Manhunt,* pp. 235–37, 249–52. Kathleen Gilmore ("Treachery and Tragedy in the Texas Wilderness: The Adventures of Jean L'Archeveque in Texas," p. 65) tells L'Archevêque's "adventures in Texas before he was exiled in New Mexico." Gilmore adduces evidence from parish records in his hometown of Bayonne that he was born on September 30, 1672; he was thirteen years of age when he joined the La Salle expedition in Saint-Domingue. O'Donnell ("La Salle's Occupation of Texas," pp. 18, 26), in his translation of both the deposition taken by Alonso de León on May 1, 1689, on the Guadalupe River in Texas and the one taken in Mexico City the following June 10, has L'Archevêque's age as twenty-nine. The Spanish transcript in BTHC gives his age as twenty in both instances. He actually was seventeen.
6. Talon Interrogations, p. 247.
7. A. F. Bandelier, *The Gilded Man,* pp. 294–302; prenuptial investigations of Pedro Meusnier, Archdiocese of Santa Fe, Hemenway Collection vol. 5, doc. 12, State Records Center and Archives, Santa Fe, N.Mex., for which I am indebted to Kathleen Gilmore; Virginia L. Olmsted, "Grolet-Gurulé: Los Franceses de Nuevo Mexico," *National Genealogical Society Quarterly* 75 (1987): 38–46. By remarkable coincidence, the surnames mentioned in an Associated Press news story of July 3, 1999, concerning troubles in a Texas state prison reads like a roll-call of La Salle survivors. Jarry, a prison guard, was stabbed to death by an inmate. His assailant had been prosecuted by Munier. A death-row inmate who had escaped the same prison only to drown at a creek crossing shortly afterward was (Martin) Gurule.

8. Massanet to Carlos de Sigüenza y Góngora, 1690, in Bolton, ed., *Spanish Exploration, 1542–1706*, p. 379. Parkman (*La Salle,* p. 1039) reports that Hiems "is said to have been killed in a quarrel with his accomplice, Ruter, the white savage. . . ."

9. Talon Interrogations, pp. 235–36.

10. Jean-Bernard Bossu, *Travels in the Interior of North America, 1751–1762,* p. 67.

11. Laura Watanabe to author, telephone conversation, Nov., 1999.

12. Documents relating the capture of Admiral Morfi's ship and the resulting courts martial are in AGI, Santo Domingo 467 and AGI, Escribanía de Cámara 261–A and 261–B (microfilm obtained with the assistance of Donald E. Chipman in the author's possession). Weddle, "La Salle's Survivors," pp. 428–29, 432–33.

13. Weddle, *French Thorn,* pp. 193, 197.

14. Marcel Giraud to author (letter), Paris, Feb. 9, 1972. Paul Newfield III of Metairie, La., claims descendancy from Robert Talon. Roy Tallon of Mobile, Ala., believes one of the Talon brothers, probably Pierre, was his ancestor; the link was broken at some point by a death that left minor children to grow up in an orphanage. (Tallon to author, conversation, 1978).

15. Weddle, *Wilderness Manhunt,* pp. 254–55. Delanglez (*Journal of Jean Cavelier,* pp. 19–20) discusses the vicissitudes of efforts to recreate Joutel's account and discrepancies among the sources.

16. Weddle, *French Thorn,* pp. 127, 148.

17. Margry (Introduction to *Découvertes,* vol. 4 [not included in U.S. edition], BHC reel 2), faults Beaujeu for not heeding La Salle's request in 1685 to return to his position of the previous January 6 (actually Galveston Bay). Had he done so, Margry avers, he "would not have let slip a claim to honor that was almost within his grasp." He did not do so, it is suggested, because he thought to win glory for himself by contriving to be sent back to the Mississippi on a voyage wholly his own.

18. Iberville to Cavelier, La Rochelle, May 3, 1704, Margry *Découvertes,* 3:622. Extract of Talon Interrogations, idem, pp. 610–621 (Feb. 14, 1698, misdated by Margry as Sept. 14).

19. Parkman, *La Salle,* p. 1033n.

20. Delanglez, *Journal of Jean Cavelier,* p. 32; Villiers, *L'expédition,* p. 176.

21. Massanet to Sigüenza, in Bolton, *Spanish Exploration,* p. 362 (quoted in Weddle, *Wilderness Manhunt,* p. 185); León, "Autos y diligencias," Apr. 22, 1689, AGI, Mexico 616, BTHC (translated in O'Donnell, "La Salle's Occupation of Texas").

22. The present author's rhymed translation is in Weddle, *Wilderness Manhunt,* pp. 187–88.

23. Llanos, "Diario y derrota del Viaje que se hecho y Ejecutado a la Bahia de San Bernardo que llaman Bahia del Espiritu Santo," AGI, Mexico 616, BTHC; Cárdenas, "Diario," idem. Cárdenas's map is reproduced in Bolton, "The Location of La Salle's Colony on the Gulf of Mexico," Mississippi Valley Historical Review (Sept., 1915); Gilmore, *The Keeran Site;* Weddle, *Wilderness Manhunt.*

BIBLIOGRAPHY

ARCHIVES

Amirauté de La Rochelle (Admiralty) (ALR)

Archives Départmentales de la Charente-Maritime, La Rochelle (ADCM)
    Notarial Archives: 3 E 1711; 3 E 1806(2)

Archivo General de Indias, Seville (AGI)
    Audiencia de Mexico, legajos 95, 616, 617
    Audiencia de Santo Domingo, legajo 467
    Escribanía de Cámara, legajos 261-A, 261-B

Archivo General de la Nación, Mexico (AGN)
    Historia, vol. 27

Archives of the Diocese of Guadalajara (Prenuptial investigations of Juan Andrés [Jean Jarry])

Archives Nationales, Paris (AN)
    Colonies, C/11a/3
    Marine B-2, B-4, E.

Archives du Port de Rochefort (APR)
    Construction papers of the *Belle*
    Correspondence
    Lists and armaments of ships

Barker Texas History Center, Center for American Studies, University of Texas at Austin (BTHC)
    Transcripts from AGI, AGN, and AN

Bibliothèque Nationale de France, Section des manuscrits (BN)
    Nouvelles acquisitions françaises (NAF), vols. 21306–21444

Biblioteca del Real Palacio (BRP), Madrid. Manuscript 2667

Burton Historical Collection, Detroit Public Library (BHC) Translations of the Margry papers. Microfilm

Musée de la Marine, Paris (Armemens des Vaisseaux du Roi en 1684)

New Mexico State Records Center and Archives, Santa Fe (prenuptial investigations of Pedro Meusnier [Pierre Meunier])

Public Archives of Canada, Manuscript Division, Ottawa (microfilm reel H-1022)

THESIS

Hundley, Paul Fredric. "The Construction of the Griffon Cove Wreck." Master's thesis, Texas A&M University, December, 1980.

UNPUBLISHED MANUSCRIPT

Politsch, Leroy J. "The Ellington Stone." Copy in author's possession.

LETTER

Marcel Giraud to Robert S. Weddle, Paris, February 9, 1972.

PUBLISHED SOURCES

American Heritage. *A Treasury of American Heritage: A selection from the first five years of the Magazine of History.* New York: Simon & Schuster, 1960.

Arnold, J. Barto III. *A Matagorda Bay Magnetometer Survey & Site Test Excavation Project.* Texas Antiquities Committee Publication no. 9. Austin: Texas Antiquities Committee, 1982.

Bandelier, A. F. *The Gilded Man and Other Pictures of the Spanish Occupancy of America.* New York: D. Appleton, 1893.

Barker, Nancy Nichols. *Brother to the Sun King: Philippe, Duke of Orléans.* Baltimore: Johns Hopkins University Press, 1989.

Bolton, Herbert Eugene, ed. *Spanish Explorations in the Southwest, 1542–1706.* Original Narratives of Early American History. General editor, J. Franklin Jameson. New York: Barnes & Noble, 1963. First published, 1908.

Bossu, Jean-Bernard. *Jean Bossu's Travels in the Interior of North America, 1751–52.* Translated and edited by Seymour Feiler. Norman: University of Oklahoma Press, 1962.

Brown, Andrew H. "New St. Lawrence Seaway Opens the Great Lakes to the World." *National Geographic* 115, no. 3 (March, 1959): 299–339.

Canedo, Lino Gómez, ed. *Primeras exploraciones y poblamiento de Texas (1686–1694).* Monterrey: Instituto Tecnológico y de estudios superiores de Monterrey (serie: Historia), 1968.

Chesnel, Paul. *History of Cavelier de La Salle, 1643–1687: Explorations in the Valleys of the Ohio, Illinois and Mississippi.* Translated from the French by Andrée Chesnel Meany. New York and London: Putnam, 1932.

Clayton, Lawrence A., Vernon James Knight, Jr., and Edward C. Moore, eds. *The De Soto Chronicles: The Expedition of Hernando de Soto to North America in 1539–1543.* 2 vols. Tuscaloosa: The University of Alabama Press, 1993.

Congressional Digest 25 (1946).

Congressional Record (Senate), 86th Congress, first session, vol. 105, parts 5, 9.

Coulter, Tony. *La Salle and the Explorers of the Mississippi.* World Explorers series. New York: Chelsea House, 1991.

Cox, Isaac Joslin, ed. *The Journeys of Réné Robert Cavelier, Sieur de La Salle.* 2 vols. Austin, Texas: Pemberton, 1968. First published, 1905.

Delanglez, Jean. *The Discovery of the Mississippi.* Chicago: Loyola University, 1945.

———. "Franquelin, Mapmaker." *Mid-America* 25 (New series, vol. 14), no. 1 (January, 1943): 29–74.

———. *El Rio del Espíritu Santo: An Essay on the Cartography of the Gulf Coast and the Adjacent Territory during the Sixteenth and Seventeenth Centuries.* New York: The United States Catholic Historical Society, 1945.

——. "La Salle's Expedition of 1682." *Mid-America* 22 (New series, vol. 11), no. 1 (January, 1940): 275–98.

——. *Some La Salle Journeys.* Chicago: Institute of Jesuit History, 1938.

——, ed. *The Journal of Jean Cavelier: The Account of a Survivor of La Salle's Texas Expedition, 1684–1688.* Translated and annotated by Jean Delanglez, S.J. Chicago: Institute of Jesuit History, 1938.

De Vorsey, Louis, Jr. "La Salle's Cartography of the Lower Mississippi: Product of Error or Deception?" *The American South.* Vol. 25 in series "Geoscience and Man." Edited by Richard L. Nostrand and Sam B. Hilliard. Baton Rouge: Louisiana State University Press, 1988.

Díaz del Castillo, *Bernal. Historia verdadera de la conquista de la Nueva España.* 2 vols. Mexico City: Porrúa, 1955.

Dictionary of Canadian Biography. Toronto: University of Toronto Press, 1966. 14 vols. of 24 projected.

Dufour, Charles L. *Ten Flags in the Wind: The Story of Louisiana.* New York: Harper & Row, 1967.

Dunn, William Edward. *Spanish and French Rivalry in the Gulf Region of the United State, 1678–1702: The Beginnings of Texas and Pensacola.* Bulletin no. 1705, Studies in History no. 1. Austin: The University of Texas, 1917.

Eccles, W. J. *France in America.* New York: Harper & Row, 1972.

Enríquez Barroto, Juan. "The Enriquez Barroto Diary." Translated by Robert S. Weddle in Robert S. Weddle, ed., *La Salle, the Mississippi, and the Gulf: Three Primary Documents.*

Falconer, Thomas. *On the Discovery of the Mississippi, and on the South-Western, Oregon, and North-Western Boundary of the United States.* Austin, Texas: Shoal Creek, 1975. First published 1844.

Folmer, Henry. *Franco-Spanish Rivalry in North America, 1524–1763.* Glendale: Arthur H. Clark Company, 1953.

Fortier, John, and Donald Chaput. "A Historical Reexamination of Juchereau's Illinois Tannery." *Journal of the Illinois State Historical Society* 62, no. 4 (winter, 1969): 385–496.

Foster, William C., ed. *The La Salle Expedition to Texas: The Journal of Henri Joutel, 1684–1687.* Edited with an introduction by William C. Foster. Translated by Johanna S. Warren. Austin: Texas State Historical Association, 1998.

Franke, Judith A. *French Peoria and the Illinois Country, 1673–1846.* Springfield: Illinois State Museum Society, 1995.

French, Benjamin Franklin. *Historical Collections of Louisiana and Florida: Historical Memoirs and Narratives, 1527–1702.* Second series. Historical and biographical notes by B. F. French. New York: Albert Mason, 1875.

Gaither, Frances. *Fatal River: The Life and Death of La Salle.* New York: Henry Holt, 1931.

Galloway, Patricia K., ed. *La Salle and His Legacy: Frenchmen and Indians in the Lower Mississippi Valley.* Jackson: University Press of Mississippi, 1982.

Gilmore, Kathleen. "An Archeological Footnote to History." With collaboration of H. Gill-King. *Bulletin of the Texas Archeological Society* 60 (1989): 303–24.

——. *The Keeran Site: the probable site of La Salle's Fort St. Louis in Texas.* Office of the State Archeologist Reports no. 24. Austin: Texas Historical Commission, 1973.

——. "Treachery and Tragedy in the Texas Wilderness: The Adventures of Jean L'Archeveque in Texas." *Bulletin of the Texas Archeological Society* 69 (1998): 35–46.

Gravier, Gabriel. *Découvertes et établissements de Cavelier de La Salle de Rouen dans l'Amérique du Nord.* (Paris: Maisonneuve, 1871.

Giraud, Marcel. *A History of French Louisiana.* 3 vols. Vol. 1, "The Reign of Louis XIV, 1698–1715." Translated by Joseph C. Lambert. Revised and corrected by the author. Baton Rouge: Louisiana State University Press, 1974. First published, 1953, in French.

Habig, Marion A. *The Franciscan Père Marquette: A Critical Biography of Father Zénobe Membré, O.F.M., La Salle's Chaplain and Missionary Companion, 1645 (ca.)– 1689.* New York: Joseph F. Wagner, Inc., 1934.

Hackett, Charles Wilson, ed. *Historical Documents Relating to New Mexico, Nueva Vizcaya, and Approaches Thereto, to 1773.* 2 vols. Washington: Carnegie Institution, 1923, 1926.

Heidenreich, Conrad. "Early French Exploration in the North American Interior." In John Logan Allen, ed., *North American Exploration: A Continent Divided,* vol. 2. Lincoln: University of Nebraska Press, 1997.

Hennepin, Louis. *A Description of Louisiana.* Translated by John Gilmary Shea. March of America Facsimile Series. Ann Arbor, Mich.: University Microfilms, 1966.

Higginbotham, Jay. *Old Mobile: Fort Louis de la Louisiane, 1702–1711.* Mobile, Ala.: Museum of the City of Mobile, 1977.

Howse, Derek. *Greenwich Time and the Discovery of Longitude.* New York: Oxford University Press, 1980.

Jaray, Gabriel-Louis. "Cavelier de La Salle, Founder of the French Empire in America." Translated by Marcel Moraud. *Rice Institute Pamphlet* 26, no. 1 (Jan., 1939): 1–42.

Jetté, René (with the collaboration of the Program for Research in Historical Demography of the University of Montreal). *Dictionnaire généalogique des familles du Québec.* Montreal: The Presses of the University of Montreal, 1983.

John, Elizabeth A. H. *Storms Brewed in Other Men's Worlds: The Confrontation of Indians, Spanish, and French in the Southwest, 1510–1795.* College Station: Texas A&M University Press, 1975.

Johnson, William Henry. *French Pathfinders in North America.* Boston: Little, Brown, 1905.

Joutel, Henri. *Joutel's Journal of La Salle's Last Voyage.* Introduction by Darrett B. Rutman. New York: Corinth Books, 1962.

——. *The Last Voyage Perform'd by de la Sale.* Facsimile reprint of 1714 edition; first published in French in 1713. Ann Arbor: University Microfilms, 1966.

——. "Voyage de M. de La Salle dans l'Amérique septentrionale en l'année 1685, pour y faire un establissement dans la partie qu'il au avoit apparavant descouverte," in Pierre Margry, ed., *Découvertes et établissement Français dans l'ouest et dans le sud de l'Amérique septentrionale (1614–1754).*

Kier, R. S., L. E. Garner, and L. F. Brown, Jr. *Land Resources of Texas.* Cartography by James W. Macon, Dan F. Scranton, Barbara M. Hartmann, and David M. Ridner. Austin: Bureau of Economic Geology, The University of Texas.

Le Clercq, Chrétien. *First Establishment of the Faith in New France.* 2 vols. Translated and annotated by John Gilmary Shea. New York: John G. Shea, 1881. First published in French as *Premier établissement de la foi dans la Nouvelle France,* Paris: 1691.

Lemée, Patricia R. "*Tios* and *Tantes:* Familial and Political Relationships of Natchitoches and the Spanish Colonial Frontier." *Southwestern Historical Quarterly* 101, no. 3 (January, 1988): 341–58.

Leonard, Irving. *Spanish Approach to Pensacola*. Translated, with Introduction and Notes, by Irving A. Leonard. New York: Arno Press, 1967. First published, 1939.

Leprohon, Pierre. *Cavelier de La Salle: Fondateur de la Louisiane*. Paris: André Bonne, 1984.

López de Gómara, Francisco. *Cortés: The Life of the Conqueror*. Translated and edited by Lesley Byrd Simpson. Berkeley: University of California Press, 1960.

MacGregor, Mary. *The Story of France*. New York: Frederick A. Stokes, n.d.

MacLean, Harrison John. *The Fate of the* Griffon. Toronto: Griffin House, 1974.

Margry, Pierre, ed. *Découvertes et établissement des Français dans l'ouest et dans le sud de l'Amérique septentrionale (1614–1754)*. 6 vols. Paris: Jouaust, 1876–1886.

McWilliams, Richebourg Gaillard. "Iberville at the Birdfoot Subdelta: Final Discovery of the Mississippi River." In John Francis McDermott, ed., *Frenchmen and French Ways in the Mississippi Valley*. Urbana: University of Illinois Press, 1969.

Minet, [Jean-Baptiste]. "Journal of Our Voyage to the Gulf of Mexico," translated by Ann Linda Bell in Robert S. Weddle, ed., *La Salle, the Mississippi, and the Gulf: Three Primary Documents*.

———. "Voyage Made from Canada Inland Going Southward during the Year 1682." Translated by Ann Linda Belle and annotated by Patricia Galloway in Robert S. Weddle, ed., *La Salle, the Mississippi, and the Gulf: Three Primary Documents*.

Mitford, Nancy. *The Sun King*. New York: Harper & Row, 1966.

Moraud, Marcel. "Last Expedition and the Death of Cavelier de La Salle, 1684–1687." *Rice Institute Pamphlet* 24, no. 3 (July, 1937): 143–67.

Morison, Samuel Eliot. *The European Discovery of America: The Northern Voyages*. New York: Oxford University Press, 1971.

Muhlstein, Anka. *La Salle: Explorer of the North American Frontier*. Translated from the French by Willard Wood. New York: Arcade, 1992.

Newcomb, W. W., Jr. *The Indians of Texas: From Prehistoric to Modern Times*. Austin: University of Texas Press, 1961.

Nixon, Pat Ireland, "Jallot and Liotot: Two French Surgeons of Early Texas." *Southwestern Historical Quarterly* 43, no. 1 (July, 1939): 42–52.

O'Donnell, Walter J., trans. *La Salle's Occupation of Texas*. Preliminary Studies 3, no. 2. Austin: Texas Catholic Historical Society, 1936.

Olmsted, Virginia L. "Grolet-Gurulé: Los Franceses of Nuevo Mexico." *National Genealogical Society Quarterly* 75 (1987): 38–46.

Osler, Edmund Boyd. *La Salle*. Don Mills, Ontario: Longmans Canada, 1967.

Panicucci, Alfredo. *The Life and Times of Louis XIV*. Translated from Italian by C. J. Richards. Philadelphia and New York: Curtis, 1967.

Parkman, Francis. *France and England in North America*. Annotation and text selection by David Levin. 2 vols. Vol. 1: *Pioneers of France in the New World; The Jesuits in North America in the Seventeenth Century; La Salle and the Discovery of the Great West; The Old Regime in Canada*. Vol. 2: *Count Frontenac and New France under Louis XIV; A Half-Century of Conflict; Montcalm and Wolfe*. New York: The Library of America, 1983.

———. *La Salle and the Discovery of the Great West*. Eleventh edition, first published in 1879. Reprinted in Francis Parkman, *France and England in North America,* pp. 713–1054.

Parry, J. H. *The Age of Reconnaissace*. New York: New American Library, 1964. First published, 1963.

Pichardo, José Antonio. *Pichardo's Treatise on the Limits of Louisiana and Texas.* 4 vols. Translated by Charles Wilson Hackett, Charmion Clair Shelby, and Mary Ruth Splawn. Edited and annotated by Charles Wilson Hackett. Austin: The University of Texas Press, 1931–34.

Politsch, Leroy J. "The Ellington Stone." *Iliniwek* 3, no. 3 (May–June, 1965): 20–24.

Salinas, Martín. *Indians of the Rio Grande Delta: Their Role in the History of Southern Texas and Northeastern Mexico.* Austin: University of Texas Press, 1990.

Scholes, France V. *Troublous Times in New Mexico, 1650–1670.* Albuquerque: University of New Mexico Press, 1942.

Severn, Timothy. *Explorers of the Mississippi.* New York: Knopf, 1968.

Shea, John Gilmary, ed. *Discovery and Exploration of the Mississippi Valley.* New York: Redfield, 1853.

Sobel, Dava. *Longitude: The True Story of a Lone Genius Who Solved the Greatest Scientific Problem of His Time.* New York: Walker, 1995.

Spurr, Daniel. *River of Forgotten Days: A Journey down the Mississippi in Search of La Salle.* New York: Henry Holt, 1998.

Swanton, John R. *Final Report of the United States De Soto Expedition Commission.* Washington, D.C.: Smithsonian, 1985. First published, 1939.

Terrell, John Upton. *La Salle: The Life and Times of an Explorer.* New York: Waybright and Talley, 1968.

Thorpe, Lewis, trans. and ed. *The Bayeaux Tapestry and the Norman Invasion.* London: The Folio Society, 1973.

Tunnell, Curtis. "A Cache of Cannons: La Salle's Colony in Texas." *Southwestern Historical Quarterly* 102, no. 1 (July, 1998): 19–43.

Tyler, Ron, et al., eds. *New Handbook of Texas.* 6 vols. Austin: Texas State Historical Association, 1996.

Vega, Garcilaso de la. *The Florida of the Inca: The Fabulous de Soto Story.* Translated by John Grier Varner and Jeanette Johnson Varner. Austin: University of Texas Press, 1953.

Villiers du Terrage, Marc de. *Les dernières années de la Louisiane Française.* Paris: Maisonneuve, 1903.

———. *L'Expédition de Cavelier de La Salle dans le Golfe du Mexique (1684–1687).* Librairie d'Amérique et d'Orient. Paris: Adrien-Maisonneuve, 1934.

"Voyage to the Mississippi through the Gulf of Mexico: Memorial on the questions asked of the two Canadians who are soldiers in Feuguerolle's Company." Translated by Ann Linda Belle in Robert S. Weddle, ed., *La Salle, the Mississippi, and the Gulf: Three Primary Documents.*

Weddle, Robert S. *Changing Tides: Twilight and Dawn in the Spanish Sea, 1763–1803.* College Station: Texas A&M University Press, 1995.

———"Coastal Exploration and Mapping: A Concomitant of the *Entradas.*" In Dennis Reinhartz and Gerald D. Saxon, eds., *The Mapping of the* Entradas *into the Greater Southwest.* Norman: University of Oklahoma Press, 1998.

———. "Exploration of the Texas Coast: Álvarez de Pineda to La Salle." *Gulf Coast Historical Review* 8, no. 1 (fall, 1992): 31–41.

———. *The French Thorn: Rival Explorers in the Spanish Sea, 1682–1762.* College Station: Texas A&M University Press, 1991.

———. "La Salle's Survivors." *Southwestern Historical Quarterly* 75, no. 4 (1972): 413–33.

———. *Spanish Sea: The Gulf of Mexico in North American Discovery, 1500–1685.* College Station: Texas A&M University Press, 1985.

———. *Wilderness Manhunt: The Spanish Search for La Salle.* New edition. College Station: Texas A&M University Press, 1999. First edition, 1973.

———, ed. *La Salle, the Mississippi, and the Gulf: Three Primary Documents.* Mary Christine Morkovsky and Patricia Galloway, associate editors. Translations by Ann Linda Bell (French) and Robert S. Weddle (Spanish). College Station: Texas A&M University Press, 1987.

Wedel, Mildred Mott, ed. *A Jean Delanglez, S.J., Anthology: Selections Useful for Mississippi Valley and Trans-Mississippi American Indian Studies.* Edited with an introduction by Mildred Mott Wedel. New York and London: Garland, 1985.

Winsor, Justin. *Cartier to Frontenac: Geographical Discovery in the Interior of North America in Its Historical Relations, 1534–1700.* New York: Cooper Square, 1970. First published, 1894.

———, ed. *Narrative and Critical History of America.* 8 vols. Boston: Houghton-Mifflin, 1884–89.

Wood, Peter H. "La Salle: Discovery of a Lost Explorer." *American Historical Review* 89, no. 2 (April, 1984): 294–323.

Young, Gordon. "The Great Lakes: Is It too Late?" *National Geographic* 144, no. 2 (August, 1973): 147–85.

INDEX

Abnaki Indians, 69

Acancea (Arkansas) Indians, 72, 240, 241, 275*n* 19

Accault, Michel, 58

Aguayo, San Miguel de, 192–93

Aigron, Captain, 6, 122, 169, 170, 171, 174, 187, 236–37, 284*n* 9

Aimable: cannons, 99, 122, 174, 254–55, 280–81*n* 41, 284*n* 9; capacity, 6; Cedar Bayou anchorage, 153, 161, 162; gulf crossing, 7, 144–47, 148–49; gulf shoreline travels, 7–8, 149–51, 153; La Salle's commission, 6; leasing arrangements, 106, 121–22; Matagorda Bay, 166, 169, 170; ocean voyage, 6, 135–36, 138; Pass Cavallo arrival, 163; personnel, 122–24, 144–45, 284*n* 9; Petit Goâve period, 138, 141, 144, 145; storm damage, 7, 157–58; wreck/salvage, 8, 169–71, 173–74, 180, 190, 236–37, 292*n* 36

Aix (island), 133

Algonquin Indians, 31

Allais, Jean, 285*n* 15

Alon, Elie d', 284*n* 9

Álvarez de Pineda, Alonso, 275*n* 24, 277*n* 35

Aralle, Barthélemy d' (Chevalier de Perinnet), 5

Aransas Pass, 7, 151

Arboul (volunteer), 290*n* 13

Arbouville, Chevalier d' (Alexandre-Adrien Chambon), 5

Arcahay Islands, 138

Ardenne, Bois d', 61

Arguelle, Antoine (Le Picard du Gay), 58

Arkansas (Acancea) Indians, 72, 240, 241, 275*n* 19

Arkansas River, 72, 240–41

Arnoul, Pierre, 105, 106, 111, 114–16, 125, 132, 236, 238, 248

assassination attempts (on La Salle), 44, 56, 60, 228

Atchafalaya River, 158

Augustin, Pierre, 284*n* 9

Autray, sieur d' (Jacques de Bourdon), 58, 69, 109, 272*n* 32, 282*n* 13

baptismal record (La Salle's), 22

Barange, C. (sailor), 15

Barbier, Gabriel (Minime): A. Tonti's complaints, 109, 110; *Belle* salvage, 17; France trip, 86; Garcitas Creek settlement, 203–206, 209, 211; Grand Camp arrival, 163; Great Lakes expedition, 54–55, 61–62; Karankawa Indians, 173, 216; Minet introduction, 119; Mississippi descent, 69, 71, 73; New Biscay commission, 109

Barbier, Madame, 123, 206, 211, 251, 302–303*n* 53

Barillon (French ambassador), 247–48

Barteau, Jean, 285*n* 15

Barthélemy, Pierre, 212, 228, 232–33, 234, 241–42, 255

Baude, Louis de (Comte de Frontenac), 36, 41–42, 66, 83, 85

Baudry, Jean, 284*n* 9

Baugis, Chevalier Louis Henri de, 86

Bautista Chapa, Juan, 261

Baye-Saint-Louis, 196–97. *See also* Garcitas Creek settlement

Bazire, Charles, 41

Beaujeu, Madame de, 105, 112–13, 117

Beaujeu, Taneguy Le Gallois: *Aimable* wreck/salvage, 173; appointment/responsibilities, 6, 100, 102; background, 105, 281*n* 2; conflicts with La Salle in France, 104–106, 108–14, 131; crew members, 120; gulf coast conflicts with La Salle, 153–54, 158–59, 160, 197; *Joly* departure, 126, 133;

Tonti–La Salle reunions, 66, 76, 83; warehouse pillaging, 59

Miguel (Indian), 193–94

military personnel (New Biscay expedition): Beaujeu's opinion, 115; Beaujeu's request, 111–12, 114; Galveston Bay march, 158–60, 161–62, 163, 290*n* 13; gulf coast landing, 154–55, 157; named, 119–20; recruitment, 106; Seignelay's concern, 114–15

Minet, Jean-Baptiste: on *Aimable*'s passengers, 124; *Aimable* wreck/salvage, 170, 171, 173, 174; background, 283*n* 1; *Belle*'s anchor, 8, 158, 161; death, 254; Grand Camp concerns, 168; gulf crossing, 145–46, 149; gulf shoreline travels, 7, 149, 151, 153; illness, 133; *Joly* voyage record, 119, 130, 139; La Salle's land march decision, 158–59; maps, 45, 164; Matagorda Bay entrance, 163–65, 166, 169; Mississippi descent, 70, 73, 76, 79, 87, 274*n* 11, 275*n* 18, 275*n* 19, 277–78*n* 41; New Biscay expedition preparations, 102, 110, 119; Petit Goâve period, 140, 144, 288*n* 16; return to France, 177, 197, 236–37, 238; Vital–La Salle relationship, 86

Mingaud, 284*n* 9

Minime, Gabriel. *See* Barbier, Gabriel (Minime)

Mississippi Indians, 65

Mississippi River (discovery): Ellington Stone, 36–39; European misconceptions, 31; La Salle's journeys, 31–34; Renaudot's document, 34–35; Talon's commission, 35–36

Mississippi River (1681 expedition): assessment of geographical confusions, 77–80, 277*n* 37; Chicago River to Arkansas River section, 70–72, 275*n* 19; creditors, 67–69, 106–107; La Barre's opinion, 84–85; maps, 87, 96, 97, 280*n* 35; personnel, 69–70; return journey, 76, 83; Tronson's opinion, 101; Yazoo River to "mouth" section, 72–73, 75, 275*n* 22, 275*n* 24, 276*n* 28

Mississippi River (gulf voyage searches): Le Sage/Du Chesne information, 142; overland, 174–75, 181,

190–94, 202–203, 204; route from Saint-Domingue, 144, 148, 149, 150, 151; shoreline, 7–8, 9, 149–51, 153. *See also* last expedition

Missouri River, 31, 36, 70

Mobile, Ala., 259, 304*n* 14

Mobile Bay, 142, 288*n* 19

Mohegan (Loup) Indians, 69, 76

Monbeuil, Pierre, 285–86*n* 18

Monclova (Presidio de Coahuila), 255, 256

Monjault, Jacques, 57

Montespan, Madame de, 50

Montreal: arrival of Joutel-Cavelier group, 245–46; described, 30

Moranget, Colin Crevel de (nephew): family relationship, 23; Galveston Bay march, 160, 162; Garcitas Creek return, 203; Grand Camp period, 176–77, 180, 183; gulf crossing, 145; Karankawa Indians, 176–77; last expedition, 204, 208, 211–12, 223, 226–27; Lavaca Bay storm, 10, 11; Mississippi descent, 69, 76, 270*n* 13; New Biscay commission, 109, 119

Moraud, Captain Daniel, 5, 7, 9, 126, 151, 186

Moraud, Marcel, 147

Moreau, Pierre, 284*n* 9

Morel (court official), 102, 108, 134, 236, 268*n* 31

Morel, Jean (shipwright), 285*n* 15

Morfi, Admiral Guillermo, 258

Morguet, Denis, 120, 121

Morice, Marguerite, 22

Mothe, Antoine de La (sieur de Cadillac), 259

Mouret, Père, 25

Mozopelea Indian (slave), 72

Mud Cape, 276*n* 28

murders and murder plots: deception/secrecy about La Salle's, 241–42, 243, 245, 246, 247, 249; Grand Camp period, 184; La Salle's, 228; last expedition personnel, 227

Murphy, Rowley W., 62–63

Nasoni Indians, 223

Natchez Indians, 73

ISBN 1-58544-121-X

90000